49°

VANCOUVER I.

CANADA

115°

Seattle

WASHINGTON

Pend
Oreille Lake

Flathead
Lake

William
Vanderburgh

Ft. Union

MISSOURI

MONTANA

Astoria

Ft.
Vancouver

COLUMBIA

Whitman
Massacre

Flathead
Post

The Dalles

Oregon City

WILLAMETTE

Bannack

Virginia City
Boone Helm
Jack Slade

Hugh Glass

YELLOWSTONE

Glass
mauled by
a bear

Custer
Massacre

OREGON

ROGUE

UMPQUA

SNAKE

Henry
Plummer

IDAHO

Pierre's
Hole

Yellowstone
Lake

POWDER

Bill
Hickok

WYOMING

Jed's × enco

Klamath Lake

41°

Ft. Hall

SNAKE

Pen-Leg's
Horse Camp

Jackson's Hole

WIND

PLATTE

Milton
Sublette

Pyramid Lake

Winnemucca
Lake

California Trail

Great
Salt
Lake

Bear
Lake

SWEETWATER

SOUTH PASS

Ft. Laramie

Henry Fraeb

Danner
Lake

Hastings
Cut-off

Salt Lake City

Ft. Bridger

Julesburg

Carson
Sink

PLATTE

38°

Sutter's
Fort

Virginia City

Lake
Tahoe

SACRAMENTO

AMERICAN

Carson City

PONY EXPRESS

Utah Lake

JORDAN
RIVER

GREEN

GRAND

Denver

San
Francisco
(Yerba Buena)

JED SMITH'S SECOND CALIFORNIA ROUTE

David
Broderick

Walker Lake

John Doyle Lee

Sevier
Lake

SEVIER

UTAH

Bill
Williams

Sand Creek
Massacre

Pike's Peak

Ft. Lyon

Monterey

MERCED

YOSEMITE
REGION

NEVADA

Bent's Fort

35°

JED SMITH'S FIRST CALIFORNIA ROUTE

Tulare Lake

CALIFORNIA

SAN JOAQUIN

Central Location of
Peg-Leg Mine

Mountain
Meadow Massacre

BIG MUDDY

VIRGIN

GRAND
CANYON

COLORADO

Charles
Bent

Taos

McGowan's
Hideout

Santa Barbara

CANYON
DE CHELLY

Aubry's R.R. Route

Santa Fe

Los Angeles

Warner's
Ranch

Herman
Ehrenberg

Mohave
villages

ARIZONA

Albuquerque

Felix Aubry

32°

San Diego

Sylvester Pattie

Ft. Yuma

John Glanton
Jack Swilling

Jake Snively

Phoenix

Tempe Butte

SALT

GILA

NEW MEXICO

Pinos Altos

Mesilla

Santa
Rita

Battle of Bracito

Jed Smith

Yuma
(Colorado City)

Pichaco
Pass

Tucson

Battle
of Bulls

COOKE'S WAGON ROAD

San
Elizario

El Paso del Norte

RIO GRANDE

Tubac

LOWER

Jack Power

Caborca

Henry Crabb

Gulf of California

CALIFORNIA

Continental Divide

Chihuahua City

Capt. John C. Frémont

115°

MEXICO

100°

85°

NORTH DAKOTA

Mandan Villages

GRAND
RED

Arikara Siege

SOUTH DAKOTA

WHITE

Ft.Kiowa

MISSOURI

MINNESOTA

MISSISSIPPI

A SKETCH MAP OF
THE WEST FOR
Bravos of the West

0   50 100   200   300
STATUTE MILES

Sam H.L.Bryant

NEBRASKA

IOWA

Ft.Atkinson   Council Bluffs
PLATTE   Kone

REPUBLICAN   CENTRAL OVERLAND

St.Joseph
(Pony Express Depot)

Kansas City

KANSAS

SMOKY HILL

KANSAS

Santa Fe Trail

Jed Smith

CIMARRON

Independence
Westport
Richard Weightman

MISSOURI

Charlie Harrison

Ben McCulloch

CANADIAN

Adobe Walls

Antelope
Hills Fight

WASHITA

Staked

PEASE

Plains

RED

Ft. Gibson

OKLAHOMA

Drop Line

Ft. Smith

ARKANSAS

Bill Hickok

Butterfield

Paint Rock

Bowie Mine Vicinity

HAYS WAGON ROAD

BRAZOS

Plum Creek Fight

SABINE

Nacogdoches

Natchitoches

Sam Houston

TRINITY

David Long

LOUISIANA

T E X A S

COLORADO

San Jacinto

San Antonio
(Bexhar)
The Alamo

SAN ANTONIO

Ft. Velasco

Anahuac
Las Casas
Campeachy

Goliad
(LaBahia)

NUECES

Laredo

Mier

Camargo

Mustang Gray

Palo Alto

Gulf of Mexico

PECOS

Huamantla   ★ Sam Walker
Mexico City ★ James Long, Ewen Cameron
HONDURAS   ★ William Walker
PANAMA   ★ Joe Stokes

Other books by John Myers Myers
available in Bison Books editions

THE ALAMO

DOC HOLLIDAY

THE SAGA OF HUGH GLASS

TOMBSTONE'S EARLY YEARS

Bravos of the West

JOHN MYERS MYERS

University of Nebraska Press
Lincoln and London

⊖ The paper in this book meets the minimum requirements of
American National Standard for Information Sciences—Permanence of Paper for Printed Library Materials, ANSI z39.48-1984.

First Bison Books printing: 1995

Library of Congress Cataloging-in-Publication Data
Myers, John Myers, 1906–
[Deaths of the bravos]
Bravos of the West / John Myers Myers.
p. cm.
Originally published: The deaths of the bravos. 1st ed. Boston: Little,
Brown, 1962.
Includes bibliographical references.
ISBN 0-8032-8222-2 (pbk.: alk. paper)
1. Pioneers—West (U.S.)   2. West (U.S.)—History.   I. Title.
F591.M94   1995
978'.0099–dc20
[B]
95-16895
CIP

Reprinted from the original 1962 edition, titled *The Deaths of the
Bravos,* by Little, Brown and Company, Boston.

To
Bob Shanahan and Chuck Southern—
one for the literary road.

A Word About Western Lore

BY AND LARGE what went on in the early days of the American West transpired while historians were looking the other way. In other parts of the country, or the world, the principal historical characters were recognized by contemporaries, because they were actors in the main theaters of civilization. They were watched by more or less professional chroniclers who found it easy to identify them. They had large political or military power, or they had mental or mechanical proclivities which changed the way of life for millions in the world's population centers. Or if they were explorers, on the other hand, they returned to the capital cities from which they had set forth, there to post enlightened audiences as to what had been added to the sum of geographical knowledge.

But in general it can be said that what was accomplished by the primary figures of the West was not known about, let alone recognized as important, by the historians or even the journalists of their day. In a majority of cases, it can be added, the West's prime movers had no idea themselves that they were doing more than follow their personal bents.

For most of them recognition of their national importance was postponed until they had been dead for anywhere from fifty to a hundred years. But as they had been remembered as men of mark in their own region, they had by then become citizens of tradition.

The story of the West, indeed, bears about the same relation to formal history as do the Norse sagas, and for the same reason. Oral tradition was the preserving medium, in the cases of episode after episode, for years before they were given written form. What was lost, added or altered, in the course of passing from one memory to another, are questions which it would be easier to ignore, had oral tradition been content to reach print in single versions only. Unfortunately for those engaged in the business of trying to decide what did and did not happen, however, there are multiple rehearsals—as to who did what when, where and why—in an appalling number of instances.

Only occasional hints of that diversity are contained in the following narrative. To have given detailed consideration to all the versions of all the episodes would have resulted in a compendium of quiddities, of interest only to other tracers of the same maze of literary trails.

As for the variations which have been given preference here, they demand stout defense no more than any other matters of strictly personal judgment. *The Deaths of the Bravos*, in short, pretends to be no more than one man's deductions as to what happened in the West during its inchoate, preindustrial period.

But if based on better than a decade and a half of research, the report is an informal one. As the unvarnished lore of the West adds up to the stuff of a rattling good romance, it seemed obligatory to attempt to present it in something of the spirit in which Clio, in a holiday mood, wrought the basic material.

So although the pains as well as pleasures of long study are at the seed of it, this book has been written in the hope that readers will find it—to use Sir Philip Sidney's mellow phrase— "a tale which holdeth children from play and old men from the chimney corner." That being so, it did not seem fitting to freight the work with the scholarly lading of notes and an index.

That leaves acknowledgments yet to be dealt with. I herewith gratefully acknowledge my indebtedness to the dead and living hundreds of other consulted writers about the West, without whose invaluable, if involuntary, aid this work could never have been produced.

J. M. M.

Tempe, Arizona

Contents

A Word About Western Lore   vii

Old Hickory's Horsewhip: A Prologue   3

1   A Pair of Western Mariners   9

2   The Explosion at Natchez   12

3   The Countryless Patriot   20

4   The Camel's Nose in New Mexico's Tent   24

5   The Demise of a Legend   29

6   The Siege That Fizzled   37

7   Hugh Glass's Rifle   41

8   The Character of the Grizzly   48

9   A Buckskin Squire of Dames   57

10   A Tour of a Secret Empire   63

11   Sought and Unsought Meetings   67

12   Westerners on the Warpath   71

13   In Quest of the Santa Buenaventura   76

14   Of Bright and Shaded Red Waters   80

15   Three Legs for Two Men   85

16   The Jostling Beaver Skinners   91

17   Blood in Dusty Country   96

18   The Man of a Knife   102

19	Comanches Met by Water	107
20	An Unlikely Man of Destiny	111
21	From Tom to White Hair	115
22	The End of a Landlocked Pirate	120
23	The Impact of Wyeth's Freaks	125
24	A Pair of Caravanserais	130
25	Colonel Bowie's Bite of Hay	137
26	The Gathering of Blades at the Alamo	142
27	Fighters and a Fainéant	147
28	Gone Beaver	152
29	Old Hickory Has His Way	157
30	A Dreamer Reaches Oregon	163
31	A Wandering Opportunist	169
32	The Fracas in the Council House	172
33	No Pretty Boy for Corpse	179
34	Scalping for a Living	184
35	A Trio of Bad Sendings	190
36	Tom Benton Eyes the Pacific	197
37	The Renegade Missionaries	203
38	Old Hickory's Source of Content	209
39	Looking for a Home	216
40	Incorporated Claret Takes Santa Fe	220
41	A Grizzly on a Flag	226
42	Sam Walker's Dime	230
43	A Dragoon Gets a Baggage Train	236
44	Kirker Gets Even for a Bilking	241
45	Joe Meek Meets a Cousin	248
46	Santa Anna's Wonderful Dress Coat	253
47	Prophets and Profits	258
48	A Mulligan of Disasters	263
49	Good Riding and Bad Planning	268

50	The Golden Catchall	274
51	Saints and Killers	279
52	The City Gold Built	284
53	The Sacking of Fort Bridger	292
54	A Quintet of Hanged Cayuses	299
55	Wild Cat's Confederacy	303
56	Weightman Draws His Bowie Again	311
57	The Great American Desert	316
58	A Pickled Head and a Stovepipe Cannon	320
59	The Stolen City	326
60	The Needle in the Big Haystack	333
61	Jim Bridger Returns a Call	340
62	The Martyrdom of Joe Stokes	346
63	A Beheaded Dead Man	353
64	Sam Houston's Great Scheme	361
65	The Printed Word in the Rockies	366
66	Pistols for the Judge and the Senator	371
67	Slade of the Central Overland	378
68	The Baker from Nevada City	384
69	A Bluff at Pinos Altos	388
70	The Grouse upon the Cadaver	394
71	The Message of the Ditches	403
72	The Tethered Mustang	410
73	Recessional Along the Colorado	416
	The Face Above a Grave: An Epilogue	425
	Bibliography	429
	Tables of Leading Characters and Events	447

Bravos of the West

Old Hickory's Horsewhip: A Prologue

I F   A   B U L L E T   fired at or by Andrew Jackson had killed either him or Thomas Hart Benton, or if it had slain the infant John Charles Frémont, in place of doing no harm except to the walls of the room in which he was quartered, the matter of this chronicle would have taken many other turns. That would have been a pity, for in its achieved form, at once so huge and subtly shaped, it hardly seems that it could have been improved upon. Certainly no author's fancy could have made a whole out of parts so various. The story of the Bravos of the West is history's unicorn, if something outsized and hairy to show the half strain of mammoth.

Much has been written about the many who seized and held the eastern moiety of this country; little enough, and that fragmentary, has been published about the few who turned a large but limited nation into one of continent-spanning dimensions. A glance at comparative figures should suffice to give that tribute legs to stand on.

Of the some 3,026,000 square miles contained in the geographically connected United States of America, roughly 875,000 lie east of the Mississippi River. Approximately 940,000 were included in the Louisiana Purchase, once Napoleon's generosity in throwing in more than he could properly sell had been corrected. The remaining balance of more than 1,200,000 was acquired— the Pacific Northwest having been won by discovery and lost through war—by ways and means which are part and parcel of the Bravos' story.

The characteristics of the adventurers in question were as manifold as their occupations, their goals and their states of grace. What they had in common was a willingness to stake their lives against whatever they wished to achieve, together with a genius for becoming involved in either events of national importance, or ones which have become permanent fixtures in the annals of sundry Western exclaves. Whatever is factual in the heroic or rogue literature which has developed with respect to the region they roamed at large, is the truth about their exploits. Whatever is legendary in the lore of the West is in general no more than a projection or fanciful recasting of their recorded deeds.

They had no idea, it must be owned, that they belonged to the order here postulated; but as they backed or fought each other, or shared the associations which bind the living to the dead, the links leading out from any one of them sooner or later make contact with those of all the others. Their story is thus properly one chronicle.

There were preceding rangers of the West, such as Meriwether Lewis and Philip Nolan, who do not figure in the story, because their activities did not link them directly with those belonging to the great adventurers' guild proper. This was first called into being by the forfeiture of American claims to Texas.

The seed incidents included some with the dignity of high history and others with no claim to dignity at all. The tale could be said to have started when Robert La Salle failed to colonize Texas after claiming it for France, or when Napoleon sold to the United States territory which Spain had long governed as a part of Mexico. Of closer bearing is the fact that William Carroll shot Jesse Benton in the course of their duel, A.D. 1813, the twenty-fourth year since the founding of the nation.

Actually, history being the Swiss watch of delicately adjusted cogs that it is, what mattered was where William shot Jesse. It

4

could have happened to anybody, standing sidewise in order to offer the slimmest target possible, but the wound's location overjoyed the recipient's fellow citizens of Nashville. Their mirth agonized Thomas Benton, who felt that laughter at his brother's expense was a lowering of the clan colors. In the absence of any other outlet for his rage, Tom decided to strike at Andrew Jackson, because the latter had acted as Carroll's second. He therefore said hard things about a man, no less touchy than himself, who had up to that time been his friend.

Perhaps those who reported his words to Jackson undertook to improve their bite. In any case Old Hickory launched a storm of his own upon hearing echoes of Benton's wrath; and by the time he had caught his breath he had a horsewhip in his hand and was being congratulated by those who had heard him swear to use it on a fellow warranted not to submit.

The already battle-scarred Jesse was with Tom when Andrew found him at his place of lodging, while Jackson, on his part, was accompanied by Colonel John Coffee. At the time, as it chanced, the City Hotel also housed the unofficially mated parents of John Charles Frémont, then not two years old. Napping, he was awakened by gunfire, not to mention the sound of a bullet ripping through one wall of his room and thudding to a stop in another.

Though duly flourished, the whip was replaced by the more dangerous weapons with which Jackson was also armed. Since dirks as well as pistols featured what turned into a melee rather than a duel, gore was splattered at large along the hotel's main hall. A great deal of it had belonged to Jackson, though Tom Benton got no good out of falling backwards down a set of rear steps. Both survived, but as no amenities followed the exchange of snap and slash satisfaction, the breach was wider than ever.

They could not entirely ignore each other, though, for they were both officers serving in the War of 1812 with Great Britain. But as the commanding general of the Tennessee-Kentucky area, Jackson did not have to have Benton in the field with him. At once getting an enemy offstage and punishing an ambitious man, Old Hickory forced Tom to serve as a recruiting officer for the duration.

Of Benton's no doubt worthily performed duties it is useless to say more. The actions of his recent opponent, on the other hand, were of importance to the history of the Bravos.

Carrying Benton's bullet in his shoulder, but refusing to worry about it, Jackson followed recovery from the fracas by leading Kentucky and Tennessee frontiersmen against the Creeks during the remainder of 1813 and part of the succeeding year. One he commanded was Lieutenant Sam Houston, who stopped an arrow and two bullets at Horseshoe Bend while showing a valor which led his general to take note of him then and to use him in the West in due course. Another was Joseph Reddeford Walker's brother, Joel. A third was Davy Crockett, not yet a legend on both sides of the Mississippi, but a ranker who conceived a distaste for Jackson which led him to desert him then and oppose him in Congress later.

In 1815 Old Hickory went down the big river and won the Battle of New Orleans with the help of a notable gathering of future Bravos. Sitting in at the officers' mess was Major James Long, the chief surgeon of General William Carroll's brigade. Somewhere down in the ranks were Mike Fink and a man now known only by his surname of Talbott, with whom he was then on comradely terms. Present, but of indeterminate status, was Ben Milam. In service, both on the Mississippi and ashore, was Jean Lafitte.

This pirate had not always been an ally of the United States. From his swamp-protected base at Barataria he had followed his trade with an attention to business which had made many Louisianans anxious to see him hanged. Overtaxed by the War of 1812, the U.S. Navy for long left him in the peace he didn't keep, while Jean was merely amused by the small Army task force which was sent to capture him. After hospitably entertaining the abashed young officer in command, Lafitte had sent him back with the sound military advice that it was futile to advance upon a prepared and better-armed enemy of far superior strength.

Yet for reasons unclear to anybody else, and possibly not fully so to Jean himself, he stepped out of character when the British came to seize New Orleans, an attempt which, if successful, would have throttled the trade of all river-dependent and largely roadless Trans-Appalachia. He not only refused the handsome bribe which England offered, he turned valuable information over to American authorities and wound up by offering to help Old Hickory defend the Crescent City.

Jackson, who had been known to speak savagely of Lafitte, took it all back when he had appraised what the pirate had to put at his disposal. In chief it consisted of the General's most worrisome lacks: artillery and men skilled to operate the big guns. There were also gunboats from which to observe and harry the invaders as they moved amphibiously upstream.

It is typical of the isolation in which the Bravos so generally maneuvered that the battle fought on January 8, 1815, had nothing to do with the outcome of an already ended international conflict. It had much to do with the solidifying of Trans-Appalachian morale and the growth of a regional cockiness, impelling impatience with the theretofore dominant Atlantic Seaboard. What backwoodsman cared about the technicalities of whether the war was over or not? The British had come looking for a fight, and the frontiersmen of the then Southwest had given them a bad beating, which was more than had taken place anywhere else in the country.

As for the details, the troops of Sir Edward Pakenham, who didn't live to see the magnitude of their and his defeat, never had a chance against either the small-arms fire of men who half lived by their rifles, or the cannonading of pirates trained to the precision aiming of big guns fired at sea. Without the roll and pitch of ships afloat to contend with, they were deadly accurate in the primary sense of that phrase. While General Pakenham led some two to three thousand troops into the Great Beyond, American casualties of all types have been variously tallied at but one to two hundred.

After recovering from the gratitude shown by a city famous for high living, the noteworthy victors went their several ways. Because he had met Jane Wilkinson, a niece of the James Wilkinson who had until recently been commanding general of the American army, James Long did not return to Tennessee when Jackson, Carroll and John Coffee did. Ben Milam followed a trail of his own west into wilderness. Mike Fink and Talbott, who was likewise a Mississippi River jack, returned to their old way of life. Finished with his brief tour of duty as a respectable citizen, so did Lafitte.

To the north of New Orleans, meanwhile, Tom Benton glumly heard of the triumph in which he had been allowed to take no part. While all the rest of Tennessee was rejoicing at having produced the newest thing in national heroes, Tom was wishing either that he had never vilified Andy Jackson or had fired at him with more accuracy.

§❦§ I §❦§

A Pair of Western Mariners

A PIRATE FROM no one was sure where, Jean Lafitte was a fellow whose taste, urbanity and good manners, when he chose to display them, suggested a patrician background. When he was not showing his Sunday side, though, he was guilty of all the vicious disregard for the lives and rights of others which the Jolly Roger signifies. He was furthermore a fence on a heroic scale, acting among other things as a middleman in the importation of slaves.

But because of his service during the Battle of New Orleans he left that city swathed in patriotic glory, and he had a presidential pardon in his pocket when he again began plying his spread of malign trades. Included was the kidnaping and forced service of chosen seamen from looted ships. Those not found worthy were pitched overboard—still alive if no one could be bothered to shoot or stab them—while those who refused the chance to be freebooters were also done away with.

One who picked the life of a picaroon in preference to no life at all was a middle-aged sailor called Hugh Glass. Uncertainly he has been ascribed to Pennsylvania; but, granting that as fact, nothing else concerning his early career has been jotted. Probably a shipmaster, as he was both literate and given to solitary action, he had Sinbad's faculty of being forever in peril as well as the latter's granite endurance. So he had doubtless had many other extraordinary adventures before he joined forces with

9

Western history by being offered the buccaneer version of Hobson's choice.

About the time Hugh was drafted, or in any case in the year 1817, Jean established his headquarters on Galveston Island, where he founded a scum port known as Campeachy. From La Maison Rouge, which he furnished lavishly at the expense of unwilling others, Jean ruled his assortment of picaroons and the trulls they consorted with when ashore. In it he often wined and dined many who showed the latitude which the phrase "lawful gain" can enjoy in the minds of otherwise reasonably virtuous citizens.

For in addition to the ships of avowed fences and smugglers, vessels of well-known Philadelphia, New York and Boston mercantile houses came to Campeachy. Their skippers could afford to hobnob with Lafitte by ignoring his piracy and using only the eye which saw in him the defender of New Orleans. The firms they represented favored this procedure because it was clear to men of commerce that a fellow who obtained his goods with Jean's favorable purchasing balance could undersell clearing-houses which procured them at greater expense.

For some years the U.S. Navy gave Lafitte his head, as it was genially understood on both hands that Jean would prey only on the shipping of Spain. That nation he professed to hate on unrecorded and perhaps nonexistent grounds. At all events he was an informer for one or more of the colonial bureaus then trying to hold the collapsing Spanish Empire together, so he maintained liaison with officials of the very country whose Gulf commerce he was effectively crippling.

Not himself a blackbirder, Lafitte captured the cargoes of some that were and disposed of those Negroes as well as the ones voluntarily deposited at Campeachy. In this the laws of the United States were abettive, as a pair of contradictory ones fostered a game by which he richly profited while others took all the risks. For although the Navy and the Marine Revenue Service pounced on craft engaged in the outlawed business of running slaves into the country, the legal code removed the stain of contraband and allowed the sale of imported Negroes once they were on terra firma America.

The dollars realizable from this situation attracted certain Southerners who no more regarded themselves as blackguard than did the captains of Northern merchantmen which sailed from Campeachy laden with pirate loot. One such was James Bowie, then serving his apprenticeship as a legendary figure. Reared in the region, he repeatedly slipped out of southwestern Louisiana by way of Calcasieu Lake and Bayou, beached his pirogues on the rim of the Gulf and fared overland to Point Bolivar. By signaling to lookouts on Galveston Island from there, ferry service to Campeachy was obtainable.

But if others could cheerfully profit from Lafitte's ways of making ends meet, it became increasingly hard for Hugh Glass to keep his gorge in place while assisting. At length he and one other drafted hand refused to go through with some noisome piratical chore. The consequence was that Hugh and his anonymous ally were not given shore leave when their vessel returned to Campeachy. Having reason to know how Lafitte would deal with them, once their mutiny was reported to the master of La Maison Rouge, they slipped overboard that night. Equipped only with knives, a little food, and some articles for trade with the Indians, they made the long swim to the mainland.

The Spanish post of La Bahia was only a few days' march down the Gulf and up the feeding San Antonio River; but as Hugh later confessed, the two mariners had no concept of that part of the world's interior geography. Drifting north, they kept bearing farther west, instead of working east toward the United States, until, deep in Kansas, they were captured by Pawnees.

Probably the band into whose hands they fell belonged to the especially barbarous Loup or Wolf branch of the tribe, notorious for practicing human sacrifice. At any rate Hugh's comrade met such a fate, administered with a readiness which bespoke long use. What Glass was forced to watch was the immolation of his wretched partner, the manner rivaling the ingenuity credited to the stewards of Hell. Stripped, the victim was first made a living pincushion, through the insertion into his flesh of pine slivers rich in resin. These were then lighted while the Pawnees contentedly watched and listened.

Hugh admitted that he himself didn't know what prompted him to make the gesture he did when his turn finally came. He did intimate, though, that he had reached a state of resignation so complete that his mind turned away from himself and focused on an item which he felt should be passed on to somebody as the only legacy he could bequeath. Concealed in the clothes his captors were about to remove, this was that particularly prized Indian trade article, a package of cinnabar, with all its promise of brilliant facial blazoning. Emotionally stunned and talking to a man who didn't understand a syllable he voiced, Glass made a formal presentation of the vermilion to the chief who was acting as master of mortal ceremonies.

The portent of treasure received from such an unexpected source so impressed the unstable mind of savagery that the state of affairs was instantly changed. Deciding that his medicine had sent Glass to him, the chief not only spared him but adopted this man of advanced maturity as his son. Hugh remained with the Pawnees for several years, during which he underwent the transition from master mariner to expert plainsman; and he was still a combination guest and captive of these Indians in 1819.

🙙 2 🙚

The Explosion at Natchez

MEANWHILE JAMES LONG had yet to find out what to do with the fire inside him. Not yet twenty-six, he had been first a merchant and then a doctor before the war with England made him an army surgeon and took him out of Tennessee. Liking being married to Jane, but not enjoying the practice of medicine or being a planter, he moved up the Mississippi from Louisiana for the purpose of returning to trade. At Vicksburg first, he next dropped down to Natchez, where his brother, David, joined him in the commercial firm of J. & D. Long.

By 1819 Natchez had developed lower and upper zones as different as those of a mermaid, which it resembled in being scaly here and sightly there. Down in the mud along the river were the shacks, cabins, huts and lean-tos which served as the offices and homes of gamblers, grifters, roustabouts, assorted cutthroats, and daughters of such joy as they could find. Aloft amid the live oaks and chinaberry trees on the bluff were the homes of planters, professional men, merchants and upper-crust highbinders, as well as the appurtenances of a state capital.

Though at times handsome, the architecture of Natchez-on-the-Bluff was less of moment than the nature of its leading citizens. By kind these tended to belong to a breed of frontiersmen reared in the wilderness by parents who had remained faithful to the teachings of a highly formal Atlantic Seaboard society. The result was a person with a high regard for forms and ceremonies in the same skin with a man who had learned to survive without any aid but that of his wits, muscle and gun. As to attitudes, he had a firm grasp of what was owed to an individual— particularly when that individual was himself—and no reverence to speak of for the government which hadn't been around to help while he was working his way up from a log cabin prowled by Indians.

For sixteen years, in the meantime, the federal administration of the United States had been faced with the problem of what to do about Texas. It had been formally claimed along with the rest of the Louisiana Purchase of 1803, but never occupied by Americans, aside from horse-lifting Philip Nolan and sundry would-be empire builders, of whom all but a few enslaved prisoners were dead. War with Spain was not wanted in Washington, but neither was surrender of a huge province without getting anything in return.

The opening wedge for barter was at last provided by the Seminole Indians, whose raids out of Florida and into American territory Spain proved powerless to stop. Neither could Spain prevent Andrew Jackson from crossing the international boundary and defeating the Seminoles in 1818. Pairing those circumstances, the government found something for which Texas could be used as a swapping horse. Happy to be able to do what other Presidents had failed to accomplish, James Monroe untangled the country from the future Lone Star State by giving five million dollars boot and taking Florida.

This exchange was more applauded east of the Appalachians than west of that range. There it was taken in better part by Northerners, inasmuch as the Louisiana Purchase in their latitudes had not been docked. But residents of the Southwest of that day felt that their natural field for expansion had been jerked from under them by a shameful act of forfeiture. Nor was it overlooked that the Atlantic Seaboard had been lengthened by the same move which had pillaged the frontier.

The historians who refer to James Monroe's tenure of the White House as "the era of good feeling" could not have been in Natchez when its citizens learned of a February transaction in March of 1819. Their western horizon had been curtailed with the abruptness of a shade drawn in the face of a man gazing into a lighted room. Where it had once extended a thousand miles to the Rio Grande's sweep north through New Mexico, it had been narrowed to the ankle width of the Louisiana boot. And an imperial domain which included, by Napoleon's figuring, parts of Oklahoma, Kansas, Colorado and Wyoming, as well as more than half of New Mexico and all of current Texas, had been traded for an infinitely smaller region, a good half of it usable only by alligators at the time.

There were protests from elsewhere in the West; but the men of Natchez did more than condemn the barter at Washington as the act of pusillanimous and probably venal knaves. For the rights of Spain and for the eggshells on which diplomacy forever walks they cared nothing. America had bought Texas; therefore it was as plain as the nose on an anteater that America owned it.

If Washington wasn't willing and ready to stand fast on behalf of the nation, Natchez would not fail.

To all intents and purposes the citizens of this small border city went over the heads of the President and the Congressmen of both houses and declared war on the Spanish Empire. At a mass meeting it was decided that the correct move was to invade Texas and hold it in trust for the United States until such time as an administration with a proper regard for national interests, not to mention the rights of the West, should be voted into office.

To make action possible, a half a million dollars were promptly subscribed by men willing to spend in a patriotic cause. There then arose the question as to who should lead the expeditionary force. General John Adair was offered the post, but he refused, perhaps owing to a professional's unwillingness to engage in unauthorized hostilities, as well as to the fact that he would soon turn sixty. There could have been no want of colonels in a region where impressive military titles were picked off trees and fell with the evening dew, but the will of the move's leading backers was to make Major James Long a general and give him the command.

Much about him can be reckoned from the composite nature of the men who singled him out. He had to be like them to win their regard and excel on lines they admired to be accounted worth following. That is as much as to say that he was doubtless a thoroughbred raised in mustang conditions and showed the effects of heredity and environment to an uncommon degree.

He had to be mentally and physically rugged because of the mixed quality of his following. For many of those who supported the Texas Expedition were men whose affairs and families kept them home. To find the troops to round it out, General Long had to look as much to Natchez Underhill as to Natchez-on-the-Bluff, thus enlisting men who had no legitimate families, and whose affairs were nothing to be discussed with peace officers.

The bait for these volunteers was the usual one of land, of which Texas offered God's plenty, and if one went far enough, the Devil's too; but the anchorless men who trailed with Long had to have more than acreage to hold them in line. Leaders who hold their posts in the absence of official authority have the gift of catching the imaginations of men. In James Long's case the lodestone was a quaint one. He had a personal integrity which hard rascals could good-humoredly contemplate because he was in all else a reckless wolf's head. This he proved to them at the outset when he dodged attempts to arrest him while on his way to take command of the men he meant to lead in defiance of the highest officials of their country and his.

If he held the loyalty of men under circumstances where most could not, he had the allegiance of one who was not a man, and was himself bound in turn. Jane Long was of that desperate order of women doomed to follow mates who keep no common trail, valiant in helping them until the always of danger either fades before triumph or pulls down the curtain as castastrophe.

But there was no thought of that when the Texas Expedition left the American outpost town of Natchitoches and crossed the Sabine, two hundred strong, in June of 1819. By heading it across the international boundary fixed by the solemn pact of sovereign powers only a few months before, Long became an outlaw in two nations.

At that time there were four settlements in Texas, as now realized, three owing to Spanish enterprise in addition to the one founded by Jean Lafitte. To the southwest of Campeachy and some fifty miles in from the coast was La Bahia. Eighty-five miles farther up the San Antonio River was San Fernando de Bexar, the capital. Many leagues to the northeast, or about sixty miles west of Long's crossing of the Sabine, was Nacogdoches.

After extracting it from an outnumbered garrison, the invaders granted prompt amnesty to all who would join them. And overnight Nacogdoches became the capital of the Republic of Texas, with James Long its President and Jane its First Lady. This was rainbow gold for once found, as Alexander never laid claim to more at the end of one battle. Fabled Santa Fe, along with its satellite towns, was in the domain, and the Alamo of

16

what was then called San Fernando, and the mighty southern Rockies that Zebulon Pike had described, and all the land and Spanish silver mines, and Indians and buffalo and wild horses between the great peaks and the Gulf of Mexico.

Nor did Spain see fit to challenge Long for some months, for Governor Antonio Martinez received reports of Texan strength which made him keep what troops he had out of harm's way, and send south of the Rio Grande, begging for many more. So, having got the foothold he wanted, James began the building of a new nation in which the printed word flourished no less than agriculture and other basic crafts. Horatio Bigelow set up the first press to operate west of the Mississippi, publishing Long's roundly phrased declaration of Texas independence and much of interest beside.

But if all went well at first, the might of two large nations was being clamped around the founders of an infant one. Horrified at the smashing of the arrangement to get rid of the Texas sore spot, the United States threw up a blockade for the purpose of cutting off the supplies of all sorts which were being forwarded to Nacogdoches from Natchez. Deep in Mexico alarmed Spanish officials convened with General Joaquin de Arredondo, who had crushed an American-led revolution in Texas half a dozen years earlier. This time he did not go himself, as Spain was having trouble with revolutionists in Mexico proper; but he ordered Colonel Ignacio Pérez to organize a counterinvasion force and move north as soon as he could.

Not known, this or something like it was suspected as the natural response of an attacked empire. James therefore attempted to add to his strength in such ways as he could in the teeth of determined American official hostility. One of them was to try to make an honest man of Jean Lafitte, a task much akin to pinning a live eel on its back.

Lafitte still wore a halo because of the time he had flown the Stars and Stripes above the skull and crossbones at New Orleans. That is how Long, who had been his fellow officer then, remembered him. In the name of the Republic of Texas, therefore, he offered Jean the post of Governor of Galveston, carrying with it the authority to prey on Spanish shipping. When Lafitte accepted permission to do with governmental sanction what he had for years practiced without it, Texas was in some measure provided with a navy.

Meanwhile the squeeze applied to the Texas Republic by the United States had become dangerously effective. Although the country Long was trying to help never fired a gun, it was a more efficient enemy than the one he knew he must sooner or later meet in the field. Not many men, unluckily for him, had James's own genius for going where he wanted to in spite of the U.S. Army, as well as baffled peace officers. The hoped-for recruits rarely got through and the needed food and weapons almost never.

One who was to figure in later Texas wars did arrive, being a fish few nets could hold. Perhaps as a result of one of his expeditions to Campeachy, Jim Bowie arrived to see what could be gained at Nacogdoches. Two years younger than Long, Bowie had reputedly amassed wealth by legitimate commercial means, which bored him. With a definite affinity for riches, he only prized them when they were earned by piercing the dragon ring of deadly peril. Running slaves past patrolling officers and lurking hijackers had appealed, but he had done that. Now he came to see what could be won by fighting Spain.

As yet not in possession of the knife which was to make his name a permanent American noun, Bowie didn't carry the prestige he was to pack. He was a welcome addition to Texas none the less, for he was an educated man as well as a tall frontiersman, and the Republic did not have so many of these. President Long's success would normally have attracted a good few among the Southwest's schooled opportunists, but some were unwilling to challenge the governmental blockade, while most of the rest found it too much for them.

As it also denied a market to those who had grown crops, the end of summer saw bad times at Nacogdoches. Among the crucial needs were meat and leather, and the only way to get them was with rifles. Messages of appeal to Lafitte had gained nothing but courteous evasions, so James took the only steps he could. He divided most of the male citizens into hunting parties, their purpose to bag wild cattle, as well as deer, bear and buffalo. Then he left to confer with Lafitte in person, seeking credit in a pawnshop.

In the meantime Colonel Pérez had organized a force of 350 men, crossed the Rio Grande at the point where there were then no streets of Laredo and marched north to hold council with Governor Martinez at San Fernando. Learning there that the Republic's position was weak, albeit unaware of the extent of its desperation, he promptly struck east and north to Nacogdoches. He was on his way from the Mexican capital of Texas to the American one, as it chanced, at the very time when circumstances forced Long to break down his own fighting forces into the aforementioned hunting detachments.

While en route to Galveston Island, however, James got word that Spanish troops were at hand and rounded up some seventy-five of his scattered men. Putting his brother, David, in command, he then pushed on by land and water to La Maison Rouge. In addition to reinforcements, his asking was ammunition in exchange for a promise of furnishing meat to a town which must import its supply. What neither he nor most others knew until the overthrow of Spanish rule lifted the cap of bureaucratic secrecy, though, was that Jean had sold Long out, being chief among those who had told Governor Martinez of the Republic's forlorn plight.

Accordingly James got nothing but a double-ended smile at Campeachy. Rushing back to the token force under David, he asked them to attempt a holding action on the Trinity River while he rallied the dispersed rest of his troops.

He was not given the time to do so. On October 15 David Long was killed defending the approach to the capital, and those under him who lived to do so went their separate ways. After less than four months of existence the Republic of Texas was a defeated nation. It was not a finished one, however, for

James whisked its records, not to mention Jane, past the United States officials waiting to seize him and them.

❦ 3 ❦

The Countryless Patriot

SURVIVING THE DEBACLE, Jim Bowie joined his brother, Rezin, back in Louisiana. The latter was the designer of the Bowie knife, which he had a local blacksmith fashion about this time. A special feature of it was a guard, to keep a sweaty hand from slipping from haft to blade with unfortunate results—an accident which had recently befallen Rezin. Otherwise it was an eight-and-a-quarter-inch weapon with a single cutting edge. An excellent hunting tool, it could be used on men as well as game. That occurred to Rezin after Jim had emerged from an encounter which had nearly proved disastrous because a pulled trigger had failed to fire his pistol. The older brother turned the knife he'd invented over to the younger, opining that it would never let him down in a pinch.

So armed, Jim stepped from common trails into the shadowy ones of legend, none of them leading to Texas for some years. Being a man of a single destiny, on the other hand, James Long had no sooner fled east of the Sabine than he commenced trying to reconstruct what he had left west of it.

During the next six months he led, in his own native land, the life of a ruler in exile. Rallying veterans of his wrecked expedition, he found many who were ready to go with him again. In clandestine meetings with men of wealth and influence, he built up the capital for a new venture.

Pérez had dealt with Nacogdoches as Scipio had with Carthage, and there was hardly enough left of it for a bug to crawl under. That, however, was not the main reason for choosing a new foothold. Landlocked Nacogdoches had been starved by the blockade, but a seaport capital could be far more readily supplied.

Still unaware of Lafitte's perfidy, James chose to alight on Point Bolivar, directly north of Galveston Island. In April of 1820 he gathered his men there. Then, when a stronghold named Las Casas had been built, he brought Jane thither, and began anew the business of foraging for materiel and recruits.

In a matter of months the second version of the Republic of Texas relinquished claims to naval strength; for Jean Lafitte had attacked an American ship and was called on by the U.S. Brig *Enterprise*, Lieutenant Kearny commanding. Because of what he had done at New Orleans, the pirate chief was allowed to leave unmolested. But as he sailed away in the *Pride*, Jean could see the smoke of La Maison Rouge, among other buildings, for Campeachy was removed from the map as thoroughly as Nacogdoches had been.

Whether James also saw that fire is problematical. He was in and out of the United States again and again, and nobody could put a finger on him, including the federal marshal who toiled after him as doggedly as the Sheriff of Nottingham in pursuit of Robin Hood. New Orleans had become Long's chief port of call, and there rather than in Natchez lived the merchants who abetted his new invasion.

There, too, he found a sailor with the skill to see that supplies, when obtainable, reached Las Casas. This was John Austin, skipper of the *Three Sisters*, a man as hard to pin down at sea as James was on the trails and bayous of southern Louisiana. And another valuable recruit was Benjamin Rush Milam. A couple of years after the Battle of New Orleans had found him trading in Comanche country. He knew more about the interior of Texas than anybody at Point Bolivar and was canny as well as adventurous.

James almost got a man of national standing to take the presidency, for he saw that it could do the Republic much good; and as for him the passion of serving a cause was more important than profiting from it, he stepped down. But he lost his captaincy without scoring a compensating gain. General Eleazar Wheelock Ripley accepted in the theory of word but not in the fact of action; for he stayed in New Orleans, and even from there exercised a caution which was fatal to Long.

For as Spain had drawn Pérez back below the Rio Grande, to help meet the ever-strengthening challenge of Mexicans who wished to imitate Americans in independence, James wanted to advance on San Fernando. With the fortress of the Alamo as a bastion, his grip on Texas would have been much firmer than it was in 1819. Yet General Ripley and the other purse holders kept telling him to wait for men they weren't able to send, and the clock kept running down.

In the summer of 1820 James did lead the men of Las Casas into battle, though not against Spaniards. Much of the territory surrounding Galveston Bay was the hunting ground of the Karankawa Indians, who had a catholic taste in food but a special preference for human flesh. On one occasion they had eaten five of Lafitte's pirates, caught on the mainland, and on June 30 they thought to feast on white humans again.

Asking for trouble, they got it from Long, Milam and company, whose rifles took the appetites of so many that the Karankawas weren't a threat to the new Texas capital again. Yet this solved problem was soon followed by another which was much more complex. South of the Rio Grande the Mexican move to cut ties with Spain had turned from a smoldering revolution into a blaze which was spreading so fast that it was getting out of hand.

One of the revolution's outposts was New Orleans, the gathering place of exiles who couldn't return to their native soil while Spain controlled it. Sitting in with them was a Chilean opportunist with the unrepublican name of Trespalacios, better at talking than doing. Perceiving that the Republic of Texas would offer a safer passage of entry into Mexico than Vera Cruz, he offered Long's backers the bait of claiming he could rally many natives to the cause of taking Texas from Spain. For this the price tag was command at Las Casas.

22

Believing that a Republic of Mexico would honor America's claim to Texas, where imperial Spain had not, Long consented to make way for a man who brought counterfeit currency as garrison pay, and was soon back in conference with General Ripley. Before they had finished talking another year had marked the calendar, and Mexico's colonial government had again sent troops into Texas.

Though starving on unbacked promises, Long didn't give up. For in spite of all delays and disappointments, he never lost hold of the belief that it was up to him to keep the territory of Texas for Americans defrauded by a stupid national government.

Another thing which became clear to James was that Spain defeated could be as much of a threat to his hopes as Spain victorious unless he took some action. Now not strong enough to take reinforced San Fernando, he saw that he had to prove his worth as the ally of the revolutionists, or he would have no voice as to the disposal of Texas, if they carried the day. Leaving Milam in command at Point Bolivar, Long put fifty-two members of his faithful army aboard three ships—one presumably skippered by John Austin—and sailed for the mouth of the San Antonio River.

On September 19, 1821, La Bahia fell to a night attack in which total surprise made resistance minimal. Long didn't have many days to stay in the place now called Goliad, however. His old nemesis, Ignacio Pérez, marched down the San Antonio from San Fernando with a force he couldn't match. Thinking he saw a way out, James offered to settle the matter in a man-to-man duel, of which La Bahia was to be prize. Rejecting an offer which may well have astonished a professional soldier, Pérez offered James terms which would have had the effect of allowing him to back out of Texas on the promise to stay away. This he refused to do and, at the end of fighting which was no more than a gesture of defiance against a foregone conclusion, was taken prisoner.

The months of that fall, and the winter of 1821–1822, he spent moving south prison by prison, closer to the expected firing line at Mexico City with every shift. Yet when he arrived at the capital, he was no longer the enemy of those in power but an associate of triumphant revolutionists which included the cat-balanced Trespalacios.

Things went pleasantly for a little while only, though. When Augustin de Iturbide betrayed the republican revolutionary movement by having himself crowned emperor, Long made his disgust known to that usurper. Iturbide might have swallowed the insult from some, but not from a man he knew to be bent on diminishing the size of the realm over which he had stolen into power. Before James could go forth again to fight for Texas, accordingly, he was shot by one of the nameless agents which tyranny can always find.

So after many months of anguished waiting the news reached Jane Long that the cause of her grief had been murdered on April 22, 1822. The Republic of Texas closed its books promptly and permanently, for not one of its former citizens remained on the same side of the Sabine as abandoned Las Casas.

Jim Bowie, of Long's first invasion, still lived, however, as well as Ben Milam and John Austin of his second. All had filled their eyes with a land which was to their liking, and one who had never seen it thought about it, too. That man was Andrew Jackson, an ascendant political figure who had his own views as to what should be done about America's surrendered claim to Texas.

৪৩ 4 ৪৩
The Camel's Nose in New Mexico's Tent

WHEN THOMAS HART BENTON was released from service following the War of 1812, he was acutely aware that military honors had bestowed civil power on the man he had shot in Nashville. Not thinking to flourish either in Tennessee or in any of the neighboring Southern states, which Old Hickory also held in his hand, Tom crossed the Mississippi in 1815, settling in St. Louis.

In Missouri Territory he strove for authority in many of the ways common to politicians, becoming, for instance, the editorial voice of the St. Louis *Inquirer*. Going beyond the usual, he sought to clear his path of Judge John B. Lucas by firing at him. That in itself might have earned him no criticism, but when he failed to kill the judge in their first meeting, he called him out again and made good the second time.

Notwithstanding this breach of the code duello as well as the peace, he retained the confidence of his fellow citizens, which was a very good thing for the West, because he was precocious in seeing what must be done to advance it. Among other things, he recognized the need of trade with New Mexico, speaking forcefully for it in his newspaper.

The greatest single weakness in Spanish colonial policy, and the prime mover of the rebellions which utterly destroyed Spain's vast western hemisphere empire, was the insistence that the trade of all provinces should be funneled through the mother country. Thus when Spain had owned the Louisiana Purchase no overland links had been established between St. Louis and Santa Fe, which in turn had access to the commerce of Mexico proper through a road running down to the great trading center of Chihuahua City.

Acquiring the Louisiana Purchase territory had made the United States a contiguous neighbor of Spain in America without gaining the benefits of trade ordinarily enjoyed by friendly nations so placed. As Zebulon Pike had found in 1807, Americans were not so much as tolerated in the capacity of visitors by the Spanish officials on guard in New Mexico.

But Benton kept his mind on the possibility of a caravan route to the Upper Rio Grande valley, as he did on the great river which swooped down to Missouri from the Rocky Mountains in an arc that spanned the Great Plains; for he saw that there was more to be made of this stream than federal restrictions allowed. Impatient of Spain's colonial policy, Washington was imitating it, to the detriment of the West's development.

Allied with Tom in decrying this, as well as in politics and personal friendship, was William Henry Ashley, once of Virginia. After the free labor and slave compromise of 1820 conferred statehood on Missouri, Benton became a United States senator. Chosen lieutenant-governor, Ashley listened to the complaints of the traders and trappers who came down the Mississippi's longest arm from points as far away as the west rim of North Dakota. He also took note of the occasional Americans who ignored the risks of being killed or imprisoned and satisfied their curiosity about New Mexico. If it was feasible to reach the southern Rockies without depending on a river, why wouldn't it be possible to do so farther north?

He hadn't tried to answer that question when Tom left to represent Missouri in Washington for the first of many times in 1821. Before doing so, the latter had the satisfaction of learning that one of the things he had long favored was by way of becoming a reality. The success of the Mexican Revolution had operated to sweep away all the obstacles to continental trade which Spain had imposed, and which Mexicans had deplored no less than American frontiersmen. As for citizens of the United States individually, they would be joyously welcomed, so chirruped the happy revolutionists, by people who had newly joined them in the great brotherhood of democracies.

Taking prompt advantage of the new turn of affairs, William Becknell took a mule pack train to Santa Fe, which he reached late in the fall. Joel Walker's younger brother Joe, the ace wanderer of a clan whose graveyard was to stretch from Texas to Oregon, was one who helped pack and herd the animals over a route which had to be decided upon from day to day. What they worked out on that trial run was less specifically the Santa Fe Trail than proof that such a trade thoroughfare could be established without benefit of any road building. For it was found to be country over which quadrupeds could draw wagons as well as tote items lashed to their backs.

26

For all that, a way could have been found only by experienced frontiersmen. For hundreds of miles the country was bare of guiding landmarks except the sandstone upthrust in southwestern Kansas called Pawnee Rock. Water holes had to be smelled out in country whose aridity increased with every day or so of western progress. Then the flatness which made travel easy in mild weather offered no shelter against the zone's sudden blizzards; nor was it possible in this treeless region to escape the notice of its predatory natives.

But the take was good. As the industrial age had not reached Mexico, its citizens were as avid for the common products of American manufacture as were Indians. For mere kitchen tin and similar cheaply produced items the traders of the Santa Fe–Chihuahua axis were willing to give furs, silverware and finely wrought leather.

Finding the profits made the risks worth while, Becknell was back again, in the spring of 1822, this time with Ewing Young in tow. On his second trip—as others followed the path his mules made through the head-high grass—Becknell pioneered the trace which came to be known as the Santa Fe Trail. In place of forging up the Arkansas River to a point above Taos, New Mexico, and dropping south, he crossed it and the Cimarron, cut around a southern spur of the Rockies and approached Santa Fe from the southeast. There was a bad stretch between the two rivers, for water was sometimes unobtainable and migrant buffalo herds occasionally made the trail indistinguishable from the rest of the vast, dusty stretch; but the pack animals could negotiate it with comparative ease.

So the traders used it and brought young men, of whom the most enterprising left them in the lurch. In part they were charmed by high, dry country and a mild climate, where a man could work outdoors without fighting the weather at every turn. More seductive was the way of life in a region so remote from all fountainheads of law and decorum that it had all but lost track of both.

They liked a land where each could make up his own legal

code as he went along. They were at first shocked and then delighted by a country where there were no bars between hot blood and what it desired, and very little to obscure the view. Coming from a land of stays and an era of multiple petticoats, the American frontiersmen found young women who wore a dress next to nothing but themselves, and were more or less indifferent to how much it covered. Far from being indifferent to men, though, they were as lusty as ducks and promiscuous as flies. Exceptions existed among the few who could truly call themselves Spaniards; but most of the rest came of stock that had been native for two hundred years on the one hand and two hundred centuries on the other. From this amalgam sprang dusky girls as far removed from Castilian formality as they were from Spain itself; and youths from the States were pleased to discover that when a man escorted a young woman home from a dance, he needn't shout to make her hear for some while thereafter.

Joe Walker didn't return to Missouri with Becknell, and neither did Ewing Young, even though his plan to start a powder plant fell through because nature had failed to provide New Mexico with the proper minerals. Furs were bringing prime prices, and the Santa Fe trade supplied an insatiable market. Both Americans took to the mountains with traps, and so did William Wolfskill, and George Yount, the Robidoux brothers and sundry more.

At first the unsuspecting New Mexicans were glad to grant them licenses. For many decades the beaver streams of the province had supplied pelts enough to satisfy people who largely depended upon Indians, at once inefficient in their methods and disinclined to make a career of it, to do their trapping. The number of available beaver hadn't sensibly diminished under this dispensation, but when American woodsmen got to work, the story was a different one. When they were through with a stream, it wasn't worth another trapper's visiting. And they were through with one quickly enough in New Mexico, where rain-starved creeks tended to be both narrow and shallow.

Belatedly discovering what was afoot, the native fur traders complained to startled officials. The latter revoked licenses without either reviving gone beaver or removing the peril from surviving ones. The Americans coolly went on trapping, operating farther north and west, as nearer streams were used up.

Liking the country, they had no intention of either leaving or being driven from it. If this was contemptuous defiance, it sprang from the same deep-seated conviction which had urged the men of Natchez to launch Long's Texas Expedition. By their accounting all of New Mexico as far as the Rio Grande was properly United States territory, and the very capital from which Mexicans presumed to issue orders was by rights an American town.

⧼⧽ 5 ⧼⧽
The Demise of a Legend

ALTHOUGH THE United States had technically won the inconclusive War of 1812, it bid fair to emerge as a territorial loser. The discovery of the mouth of the Columbia by shipmaster Robert Gray in 1792 had led to claiming a vast if unmapped stretch of the Pacific Northwest, deep enough to meet the Louisiana Purchase in the Rockies and make the nation continental in breadth. When John Jacob Astor established the trading post of Astoria on the West Coast, American possession had seemed assured. But the war had offered to the North West Company, of Canada, a chance to expand its trapping grounds. Astoria became Fort George, and the American employees of the defunct Pacific Fur Company returned to the States afoot.

The treaty which concluded the war did not return control of the Pacific Northwest to the United States. Instead, joint occupancy by both countries was agreed upon, as of 1818, when three years had failed to produce agreement between America and

Great Britain as to where the international boundary should run. The former held that it should properly be an extension of the 49th parallel, already accepted as the division line in the Louisiana Purchase zone, while the latter held that it should follow the Columbia River.

The stalemate favored British interests, as the North West Company was in position to exploit what had come to be generally known as Oregon, while the nearest American fur trading posts were hundreds of miles to the east of the Rockies. By 1822 the only change that had occurred was that the Hudson's Bay Company had absorbed the rival concern.

The existing American companies could not be reckoned as likely to challenge the British monopoly in Oregon. Ever since France had begun reaching west of the Mississippi for peltries, the regional pattern of the trade had been a fixed one. For nearly a hundred years white barterers and the more or less white voyageurs who propelled their boats had taken cargoes of negotiable goods up the Missouri for the purpose of exchanging what they had brought for whatever skins Indian trappers might have to offer. The system hadn't originated on the Missouri, either. The old Dutch fur companies and the ones in Canada had been built wholly or largely with such a scheme for cornerstone. The only thing peculiar to the Missouri trade was that wide river itself, a water highway of such manifest advantages that it was identified with furs in the minds of men as closely as Wall Street later became with finance.

The well-established Missouri Fur Company clung to the old pattern, and nobody from a director like Mose Carson to an ambitious young employee like Charles Bent thought that it would ever be changed. Like-minded were the members of a competing French syndicate. The only one with different notions was William Ashley.

What he had observed with interest was what the officials of New Mexico had discovered with horror. This was the relative efficiency of the American free trappers who betimes risked arrest, not to mention their lives, on the upper Missouri. By questioning them and comparing notes with fur-company men, he found that the former averaged far bigger hauls than the Indians. Less easygoing than the tribesmen, white trappers had less to divert them from the matter in hand. In addition to having his family to hunt for, the Indian was as involved in clan life as a snail is with its shell.

Ashley was also of the notion that it wasn't necessarily good business to roost forever on the navigable reaches of the Missouri, with all its transportation and communication advantages. He thought it could be profitably followed up to its headwaters in the Rockies, where Lewis and Clark had gone. Ashley had lots of ideas and the gumption to act on them; but he was not a poaching free trapper, and he didn't have a license.

A point that Tom Benton had complained about editorially before being able to do so in Congress was the fact that the power to issue licenses to trade with the Indians acquired along with the Louisiana Purchase was vested in the War Department. That branch of the government had proved niggardly about granting them, preferring to establish trading posts and take in the realizable revenue itself.

This infringement had been generally resented, but prior to Missouri's admission as a state, the objectors hadn't been represented in Washington by a vitally interested spokesman. Benton was such a voice and a vigorously persuasive one. It thus came about that during the opening months of 1822 licenses to enter Indian territory for the purpose of dealing in wild animal pelts were for the first time freely securable.

Among those who at once applied was Tom's colleague Ashley, whose partner, Major Andrew Henry, had been at Astoria. Their plan was to take their own trappers and establish a main post within striking distance of the Rockies. Ultimately their goal was to push on and trap beyond the Great Divide. Their immediate purpose, though, was to put the white-trapper theory to the test.

By advertising for men who were willing to spend up to three years in the far wilderness, they easily raised a brigade of one hundred frontiersmen. Among the names on the roster which came to be notable were those of Jed and Tom Smith, now hardly known by his given name, and Jim Kirker. Steering one of the keelboats, on the other hand, was a man who had already won a wreath of outrageous renown. This was Mike Fink, "the Snag of the Ohio," "the Snapping Turtle of the Mississippi," and now pitting his skill against the longest river of the three. In the boat with him was his protégé, a young roarer whose name has come down merely as Carpenter. Somewhere in the flotilla was Talbott, with whom Fink had fought side by side at the Battle of New Orleans. Now, though, the former kept aloof.

According to one tradition the nose he no longer had was bitten off by Mike himself in the course of the fight which marked the end of their friendship. According to another, the disfigurement and the leather shield with which he protected his exposed nasal passages so disguised him that Fink didn't know he was being dogged by a foe waiting for a chance to get even. According to still a third, he knew, as Mike did not, that Carpenter was Fink's bastard son. Whatever the truth of these matters, they were all headed for the mouth of the Yellowstone together.

The long pull with oars on the lower river, and cordelling, or towing by men ashore against the swifter water farther up, began as soon as the freshet of 1822 had passed its crest. Their first hope was to get above the Great Falls of the Missouri that year, but progress was too slow. Months later they had no more than reached the Mandan villages at the beginning of the huge swing which the Missouri makes before dropping down to more or less the same latitude, at which point the Yellowstone nips across the western border of North Dakota to join it.

To save time Ashley and his partner got horses from the Indians and rode the overland string of that huge bow. By the time the boats carrying the heavier supplies arrived at the junction of the two rivers, the building of Fort Henry was well advanced. Leaving most of the rest to carry on, Ashley sped back with the boats to St. Louis before winter could check him, his purpose being to bring up another brigade the following summer. The veteran Henry stayed to direct operations, which began by looking promising.

As the Indians proffered no trouble at first, the fall hunt was a good one. Winter in those parts is a besieging enemy, though, and in the course of its long grip on the post at least one bad case of cabin fever developed.

Of all the figures who have gained an abiding place in American lore Mike Fink was the most barbarous. He was not a murderer or a thief, or a criminal in any other common sense. But he stood for all that was savage in the at best only half civilized frontier way of life.

Emerging from the Pennsylvania woods not long after the close of the Revolution, he became a marksman whose skill was attested by his ability to shoot the scalp lock off an Indian or small objects from the person of his wife without doing her bodily harm. On one occasion he was said to have shot the heel off a Negro with a proclaimed view of making it easier for him to be fitted with shoes. He became known as the most ferocious rough-and-tumble fighter in the Mississippi Valley's heroic age of mayhem; the deftest eye gouger and masticator of ears, that is to say, as well as a ring bull among butters, a moose among tramplers and a gorilla among twisters and crushers.

By profession he was a keelboat captain, and reckoned the most efficient one from Pittsburgh to New Orleans. Aside from getting drunk to put him in the mood, his hobby was practical jokes like speaking up for the Devil in a camp meeting and beating up objecting worshipers.

As already indicated, his domestic life wasn't domestic. Tradition insists that he defeated Davy Crockett in a shooting match, because Crockett showed more consideration for Mrs. Fink than her husband thought necessary and wouldn't point a gun at her. Mike's method of punishing her for the flirtatiousness of which he held her guilty was to set her bed on fire and restrain her from leaving it until just in time to escape mortal injury. He himself meanwhile was promiscuously in stud and frank as any other brute about it.

There is a pure and convincing lack of sentimentality in the Fink cycle. In all except one respect he was given credit for nothing but the will to exhibit animal prowess and indulge animal appetites. And yet this aurochs had a hurtable spot in his hide.

Having encouraged no lasting marital ties, he formed a friendship in middle life with a stripling in whom he read the ability to rehearse the violent life which was slipping away from him. By example and precept, he taught the youngster all that he had learned about shooting, fighting and whoring. Rejoiced at Carpenter's shown ability to profit by this tutelage, he referred to him as "my boy"; and proud to be the heir of the most illustrious of rivermen, the youngster returned Mike's esteem.

Naturals for Ashley's expedition, the pair did well while there was work to be done afield but became a trouble to Major Henry after winter began confining men to the fort. There'd been a liquor ration imposed. Not believing in sumptuary laws, though, Mike and the man he'd created in his own image would take their full measure of whiskey from the quartermaster at gunpoint. Satisfactorily soused, they would put on a demonstration which amused them and chilled less sturdy stomachs.

This was a voluntary William Tell game, with a tin cupful of spirits taking the place of the apple. At sixty paces they would take turns at shooting the cups off each other's heads, not drilling the vessels, so that they couldn't be reused, but nicking each on the rim.

At some point during the winter, however, these exhibitions of skill and mutual confidence came to an end. The pair quarreled over a woman—improbably Talbott's daughter, though that has been claimed—in all likelihood a squaw, as others have asserted, peddled at the fort by her husband or kinsmen after the manner of Stone Age people. But in any case Mike took his first beating, and from the man who had learned river-boat infighting from him.

Not like King Lear in many respects, Mike resembled him in brooding over the unkindness of the cherished younger generation. Finally he lumbered out of the fort and carried his grief to a cave by the Missouri where he half hibernated, emerging only to shoot food when the weather permitted.

Having a hard enough time with their own tempers while snow made them see too much of each other, the trappers let him alone until spring breezes blew cabin fever out of the air. Then some of them took Carpenter with them and went to Mike's lair to effect a reunion.

As they'd thought to bring whiskey with them, good fellowship was restored, and in the end Fink and his fosterling agreed to prove that all was as it had been by facing each other's loaded rifles. It did not work out as it had in the past. Shooting first, Carpenter drew a dark look from the Snapping Turtle by puncturing the cup and spilling whiskey down his forehead. Taking his turn, Mike shot lower yet.

His claim that it was an accident was accepted by most, for the best of marksmen sometimes miss the bull's-eye, but Talbott did not agree. Whether out of old spite or not, he published Fink as a murderer whom he'd be glad to shoot on sight.

Mike gave him the chance. Either because he had to persuade himself of his innocence, or because he could not bear for anybody to think he had deliberately killed Carpenter, he undertook to try to talk down his accuser, who was the post blacksmith.

Fink was apparently broken by grief to the point of being half out of his mind, but Talbott, who may have been in them before, was not minded to risk the Snapping Turtle's clutches. Catching up two pistols, he warned Mike to come no nearer. Armed with his rifle but not leveling it, the Snag nonetheless did trudge closer.

"I want you to know I never meant to kill my boy," are the words ascribed to him. He tried to say it again after Talbott dropped him with two point-blank shots. "I want you to know I never meant to —"

So the champion alligator horse of them all, the great roaring boy for whom nothing was too rough, while everything was to be laughed at, died in some sort of spirit of grace where the Missouri takes in the Yellowstone, in the spring of 1823. Whether he would have made Talbott eat his words, if he had been allowed to reach him, is something that his slayer did not have long to wonder about. He was drowned while attempting to cross the larger of the freshet-swollen rivers a few weeks later.

As soon as the spring thaw was far enough behind to make swift overland travel feasible, there was more trouble at Fort Henry. The high Missouri country, to which the post was designed to give white trappers access, was owned by the Blackfeet. Matched in numbers only by the Sioux and the Comanches, this powerful tribe was hostile to all others except the allied Gros Ventres. They had not previously had much of a battle record against American palefaces for lack of opportunity. Now they began one of the most unremitting series of attacks in the history of Indian warfare.

Always suspicious of the British, frontiersmen on the upper Missouri blamed the Hudson's Bay Company for the inverterate hostility of the Blackfeet toward Americans. Yet if the Canadian concern may have been guilty, that is not the only story told of the Siksika in this connection. There is also a tradition that their enmity stemmed from a run-in with the Lewis and Clark expedition. Be that as it may, for many years members of this tribe would not so much as fraternize for trading purposes with citizens of the United States.

In May of 1823 the Blackfeet slew four of a field party from Fort Henry and made off with quite a few horses. In the meantime some Missouri Fur Company men had come into the region, for the rival concern had picked up Ashley's idea about using white trappers. They ran afoul of the Siksika, too, losing seven scalps a week or so later.

With months of good warpath weather ahead, Major Henry grew anxious for the reinforcements with which Ashley was due to return. And as the stolen horses had to be replaced, somebody had to apprise Henry's partner of the need before he left the region where they were procurable. With the double mission of speeding Ashley up and urging him to obtain mounts, Jed Smith was sent across country. Due to reach the Missouri again at the completion of its great arc, he was to proceed south along it until he met the upriver party.

৪৩ 6 ৪৩

The Siege That Fizzled

AFTER YEARS as a tribal member, Hugh Glass finally escaped from the Pawnees when the chief of the band which had adopted him chose to make a visit of state to Superintendent of Indian Affairs William Clark. Arriving in St. Louis during the summer of 1822, Glass was too late to join Ashley's first expedition, but in the spring of the following year he was in one of the trader's fleet of boats, heading for the high Missouri along with Tom Fitzpatrick, Bill Sublette, James Clyman and young Jim Bridger, then but seventeen. James Beckwourth was also along, if he can be believed; but the statements he made to his biographer have been proved false at so many points that all unsupported ones are suspect.

Starting earlier than he had the year before and scoring better time, Ashley was well on his way by the end of May, at which time Jed Smith was making all speed to meet him. Not far below the Arikara villages, which in turn were south of those of the Mandans, Smith found the new Ashley brigade pushing up through South Dakota.

Apprised of what the Blackfeet had done, Ashley decided to risk dealing with a tribe given to weather-vane politics and worse. That very spring the Arikaras had had to be beaten back from a Missouri Fur Company post; but as horses were needed, and speed requested, Ashley determined to try to get them at the nearest possible point.

The Pawnees and the Mandans were but two of the Western tribes who did not live in the portable leather homes usually as-

37

sociated with trans-Mississippi Indians. The Arikaras dwelt in huge log-and-earth lodges, each accommodating quite a few families and, in winter, their horses. Like Buda and Pest but without the river between them, there were two Arikara towns, distinct for clan or totemistic reasons, but so close that they made one defensive unit. For added protection against the Sioux and other hostile nomads, the towns were ringed by a 12-foot wooden palisade backed by a dirt ramp on which the warriors could stand to shoot at foes outside.

Situated on the west bank of the Missouri, the twin communities faced a small island where Ashley took the precaution of anchoring his keelboats. From there his men went ashore in smaller vessels, and as the Indians were deceptively hospitable, many bivouacked near the two-in-one town that night. Hugh Glass and Jim Clyman, each with a talent for being where the water was hottest, were among the number.

Their leader, in the meantime, had proceeded to dicker for horses. In this he was successful, for the Arikaras found that he was so anxious for mounts, in addition to the ones which had kept pace with his boats along the shore, that he would even trade guns for them.

Before the trappers who had camped by the town were astir the next morning, however, the weapons Ashley had turned over to the Indians were pointed down from the palisade and fired. Twelve men were killed, and Glass was among the men wounded either then or in the course of the scramble back to the keelboats. Clyman was pursued for miles before he worked his way back to the river and hailed boat-borne comrades, on the lookout for surviving strays.

Although Hugh had managed to hold on to his rifle, most of those who got away either left their gear when surprised by the attack or jettisoned it while swimming. As the Arikaras not only kept their horses but took over the ones Ashley already had, the defeat was a well-rounded one.

The news of it, in combination with the reports of Blackfoot assaults made trappers and traders all along the river bent on joint punitive action, in which they asked federal forces to participate. The Missouri was the sole commercial artery of that section of the country, and bandits along it had to be taught a lesson, or more killings and loss of property would follow.

Without necessarily holding it against them, for a frontiersman was apt to be found on friendly terms with a tribe which he might have found it necessary to fight a season or so back, the veteran traders understood that Indians would be overbearing when they could afford to but would forget it if the price was too high. The only way to keep a primitive people's bent toward viciousness in bounds was to show more power and a willingness to exert it.

In this case they knew that the failure to retort in terms comprehensible to savages would spread the urge for slaying and looting white men along a river patrolled in turn by the Omahas, Sioux, Arikaras, Mandans, Cheyennes, Crows, Assiniboins, Gros Ventres and Blackfeet. Of these only the Rees, as the Arikaras were often called, and the Siksika were then hostile, but the rest were seen as waiting to take their cue from the sequel to the assault on Ashley's men.

In answer to appeal, Colonel Henry Leavenworth, stationed at the U.S. Army post of Fort Atkinson—in the Council Bluffs area—led a force which included Captain Bennet Riley to the chosen assembly point. Joshua Pilcher of the Missouri Fur Company brought Mose Carson and William Vanderburgh to lower South Dakota's Fort Recovery. Ashley was there along with Major Henry and as many men as he felt able to take with him from the post on the Yellowstone. Smaller companies and free trappers, as well as some bands of Sioux who joined in hopes of plunder and Ree scalps, swelled the force that gathered on July 19 to about 1100 men.

They didn't all reach the Arikara villages at the same time, as boats could buck the current of a summer-weakened river faster than the Army's foot troops could pick their way along the bank. While waiting for them, Vanderburgh put his West Point training to the uses of bombarding the towns, behind whose palisade the Indians had fled upon appraising the size of the vanguard. With a small cannon brought by water, the trader from Ohio scored a mortal hit on Chief Grey Eyes, but in the main the besiegers marked time while waiting for Colonel Leavenworth to take the command to which his rank entitled him.

When Leavenworth did arrive, though, the frontiersmen learned that there is betimes a difference between the will of the people and the will of the government of the people. It is true that Captain Riley wanted to storm the offending town. But the way of the Army is to defer to the wishes of those in authority—in this case the Captain's regimental commander. The Colonel had not been robbed, nor had men of his command been slain while lulled by savages professing peaceful intentions. Mindful of Washington's current desire to preserve the Great White Father image, Leavenworth wished to deal gently with the Arikaras in place of driving home the knife of penalty.

Although the traders and trappers stormed, and although Bennet Riley's disgust at being held in check led him to the brink of mutiny, the Colonel had his way. After the beleaguered Rees saw the odds too great and surrendered, everything went wrong for the supposed victors. Their Sioux allies made off with some of their horses while the white men were wrangling with each other, and to cap matters the Arikaras stole away by night without acceding to even the mild terms imposed by Leavenworth. Aside from a few slain by cannon or snipers, the Rees had paid nothing for the massacre and mass robbery of palefaces. It was true that trappers had fired the walled towns, after the Colonel had turned back toward Fort Atkinson, but that was recognized as the spiteful gesture of disappointed men. News of all this, which was cheerfully received by other upper Missouri Indians, passed forthwith from tribe to tribe.

These facts notwithstanding, Major Henry wished to return to the Yellowstone, with a view to pressing on west up the parent stream the ensuing spring. To this move Ashley consented, while having no great hopes of the maneuver, in view of the circumstances.

40

He had reason to be glum. Of the something like one hundred trappers whom he had led upriver five or six months earlier, twelve had been killed and many wounded, while more had been discouraged alike by disaster and the futile attempts to square accounts with its perpetrators. Remaining were the few who elected to join Henry's detachment, and eleven men whom Ashley kept with him when he dropped south to the French syndicate post of Fort Kiowa. From there he himself went back to St. Louis, but before doing so, he made a desperation play which ignored all previous thinking about the fur trade in that vicinity and left the Missouri River out of account.

৪০৪ 7 ৪০৪

Hugh Glass's Rifle

TO GET BACK to the men he had left at the fort bearing his name, Major Henry ordered the supply barges which Ashley had brought to be cordelled up the northwesterly-swinging river and led his men along the overland short cut. Going by way of Grand River, his route lay through territory crisscrossed by the war parties of a number of tribes.

Not otherwise eventful, the trip became a remembered one because a participant was Lafitte's once drafted pirate, Hugh Glass. Wounded by the Arikaras, he had seen too many vicissitudes to be dismayed by another and had volunteered to join the Major.

There are two versions as to how he managed to get in trouble on this occasion. One ascribes to him a hog-on-ice independence, irritating to his companions, which made him refuse to travel with the rest of the party; instead he went poking wherever his curiosity urged him to. When he was occasionally heard or glimpsed, in consequence, men who had lost track of him could not always be sure whether it was he or a scouting Indian.

Other accounts say that Glass was proceeding alone, because he was on special duty. Although carrying some staples, when they could get them, trappers afield expected to live off the country. In transit the custom was for flankers to parallel the main body, thus being able to surprise game which a group of travelers would warn away. Because of the skill at stalking acquired while he was a registered Pawnee, Hugh was one counted on to supply the mess.

Covered by deep grass, in turn dotted by dense clumps of brush, however, the terrain offered spots perfect for animal concealment. As Glass was springing across a small stream a grizzly bear loomed out of one of these, wrathful at what she took to be a menace to her cubs. According to one account Hugh got off a shot which was slow in taking mortal effect, while it is also asserted that in the absence of room to use his rifle, he dropped it and jabbed with a knife. No matter for that; the beast remained active and quarters were too close to make dodging possible.

Grabbing Glass by the throat and so lifting him, she dashed him to the ground, tore a mouthful of flesh from him and fed it to her cubs. When he tried to make off during this respite, she seized him by the shoulder and lacerated a leg and a hand with her talons.

Luckily a fellow hunter, or men drawn because Hugh didn't suffer all this in silence, soon appeared. Charging at one of these, the grizzly was either killed by the newcomers, or collapsed from the effect of her victim's shot, without having quite finished Glass.

Yet those who looked him over were sure that minutes would complete the bear's work. Terribly mangled, crucially scant of blood, and blowing red bubbles with his neck when he breathed, Hugh appeared set to make every gasp his final one. He didn't breathe it, though, and thereby put a burden on men and a leader with serious problems of their own.

In addition to the fact that a party which marked time was inviting encirclement by Indians, Henry was anxious to reach the Blackfoot-plagued men on the Yellowstone, to whom he also had obligations. Trying the experiment of having Hugh carried, the Major succeeded in torturing him without bringing about the death which seemed so imminent. Eventually he offered a reward to any two men—a small enough number to escape the notice, with luck, of wandering tribesmen—who would stay to bury Glass when he quit stalling and died.

Jim Bridger, then no more than nineteen, and an older fellow named John Fitzgerald were the pair who volunteered. They had counted on being able to catch up with their companions in short order, but days passed without bringing either quietus or improvement to their patient. Every day they waited, moreover, increased the odds in favor of discovery by Indians. Fitzgerald pointed this out to a lad whose conscience was struggling with nervousness at their situation. The older man also enlarged upon the folly of remaining. However dilatory about it, Glass was bound to die from his wounds, and there was no sense in two hale men being sacrificed to a soon corpse.

In fairness to them it must be conceded that they had already put their lives in jeopardy, where others had not been willing to. The trouble was, though, they could not admit that they had abandoned a still breathing comrade; accordingly they had to act as they would have, had Glass indeed been dead when they left him. No frontiersman would have left useful accouterments for rust to eat or Indians to find. They therefore took Hugh's rifle, knife and tomahawk, as well as the gear kit containing, among other things, his flint-and-steel fire-making apparatus.

Mentally alert in spite of his general condition, Glass knew what was going on. He tried to dissuade them from walking off with all means of survival, but men convinced that he would never stir from where he lay persisted in doing what they knew they had to in order to avoid embarrassing questions at Fort Henry.

Actually they gave Hugh the best medicine they could have administered. Till then as barren of purpose as most in a critical state of health, he now had a goal and a vitalizing rage to enable

43

him to accomplish it. The great vade mecum of any Western frontiersman of the era was the rifle on which he depended for food and defense against enemies. Chosen with care, it was the one constant companion of men who seldom owned dogs or thought sentimentally of horses. To his rifle the wilderness courser attributed some of the mystical powers which chivalric heroes credited to swords which had served them well; and like the storied knights, he often named his favorite weapon. What Glass called his is not known; but he cherished it, and the kidnaping of it was an enormity which he didn't intend to tolerate. Far from believing he was going to die, he was positive that he would get well, so that he could regain his rifle and have the satisfaction of killing its abductors.

Wolves yanked off his buffalo robe and tore it to pieces, so that exposure to the chill nights of late summer was added to his afflictions. Hugh warmed himself with hate, got the strength to move from berries he was able to reach, and began crawling back to the Missouri.

The distance was about one hundred miles, and the first day he made only a few yards. From having lived with Indians, he knew where to find edible roots, and restored himself to the point where he could make several hundred feet in a day. Following water to the big river, he came across a buffalo which had foundered some while back. The putrid flesh would have killed anybody else, but Glass logged nearly a mile on the strength of it.

His first break came when he caught wolves in the act of pulling down a bison calf which more than sufficed their wants. After the beasts had dined, Hugh did, and the fresh meat put some of the lost blood back in his system. Able to walk then, he finally limped back to Fort Kiowa.

Somebody else might have reasoned that he was due for a respite from hardship, but Glass outfitted himself, on the credit which a trapper could get at a post where he was known, and caught the next upriver barge. What with one thing or another, it was winter by the time this took place. Perhaps it was to get a vacation from boating in cold weather that Glass chose to foot it the short way rather than to ride around a loop in the river which ended near the Mandan villages.

Like the burned ones of the Arikaras, these were composed of log-and-mud lodges. Unlike those of the Arikaras, it was considered safe for a lone white man to approach them. But what Glass didn't know was that hostile as well as friendly Indians were at hand.

Nearing a Mandan village, with the thought of waiting for the barge to catch up with him there, Glass encountered a couple of Arikara squaws belonging to a band camped in the vicinity. The women shrieked the information that a paleface was at hand, and warriors rode toward a still convalescent man who had no horse. Too weak to make a run for it, he braced himself for a last stand. He didn't have to make it, however, for the situation appealed to the sporting instincts of a couple of Mandan braves. Galloping out from their village, they caught Hugh up and raced him away from the baffled Arikaras.

The barge never arrived, for other Rees caught it near shore and killed all those who had stayed with it. Waiting only until these enemies got out of the neighborhood, Glass proceeded to walk to the mouth of the Yellowstone—a distance of two to three hundred miles, depending on how closely he followed the Missouri—in the dead of winter.

Fort Henry was still there, but not the Major or his men. Upon returning to his post, after leaving Hugh in the care of Bridger and Fitzgerald, Henry had found that the Blackfeet had lifted more horses, and were belligerently active in numbers to make trapping operations impossible. He had accordingly shifted his base to a safer position well up the Yellowstone.

Finding a note to that effect on the gate of the deserted fort, Hugh traipsed south himself, arriving in January 1824. This was a searing ordeal for Jim Bridger, whose conscience had been troubling him with respect to collecting a reward for an unfulfilled mission. Now he had the horrifying experience of seeing the embodiment of his sin arise, to all seeming literally from the dead, and confront him.

Fitzgerald was not present, nor was the treasured rifle. The former had taken the latter with him, upon being sent down to Fort Kiowa, passing Hugh, perhaps, while he was with the Mandans.

Unexpectedly unwilling to slay Bridger, Glass let the abject youngster off with a lecture, and concentrated the hatred he thought he had borne two men on the absent Fitzgerald. Winter storms were probably responsible for delaying him a few weeks, but late in February Hugh was on his way again.

Major Henry had meanwhile decided that his original scheme of pushing up the Missouri and over the Rockies would have to be abandoned. His new plan was to look for a better field of operations farther south in the spring. In the meantime he sent a dispatch-bearing trio to Fort Kiowa, whence the information could be relayed to Ashley. Glass, who was no longer an Ashley man but a rifle retriever, accompanied this threesome.

Seeking kinder weather conditions, they went up the Yellowstone instead of faring down it northward. Branching south and east along the Powder, they struck across country from that stream's headwaters to the Platte. As this was navigable by the buffalohide coracles known as bullboats, the trappers made such a craft and began the jaunt from mid-Wyoming on eastward through Nebraska.

In Pawnee territory there, they ran across Indians whom they took to be members of the tribe into which Hugh had been adopted. Upon landing, though, they found that they had walked into a band of Arikaras; and not just any band but the one whose chief had been decapitated by Bill Vanderburgh's cannon shot during the siege of the preceding year.

In Grey Eyes' moccasins, Elk Tongue tried to lull the white men by pretending that he and his were Pawnees, whose speech was closely allied to that of the Arikaras. Knowing better, Hugh gave the alarm and led a break for safety. A man called Dutton, who had stayed with the bullboat, got away by paddling, but Glass and the others were cut off and had to swim for it. Across the Platte, Hugh's woodcraft was equal to outfoxing the pursuing Indians. From where he holed up, however, he saw his two companions slain and scalped.

To a man with a different past, Hugh's plight might have seemed a forlorn one, but he was so much better off than he had been as a deserted and destitute invalid that his mood was chipper. This can be gathered from an attributed quotation: "Although I had lost my rifle and all my plunder, I felt quite rich when I found my knife and steel in my shot pouch. These little fixens make a man feel right peart when he is three or four hundred miles away from anybody or anywhere."

Glass justified his faith in the preserving qualities of "little fixens" by checking in once more at Fort Kiowa, only to be balked again. Having decided to join the Army, Fitzgerald had taken the stolen rifle of rifles downriver to Fort Atkinson.

As this journey was made without delaying calamities, Captain Bennet Riley, who had also been at the Arikara siege, was confronted by a throat-scarred plainsman who explained that he wanted to see a there-stationed soldier for the purpose of killing him. After hearing the story, Riley expressed sympathy for the idea but pointed out that military regulations wouldn't permit his turning Fitzgerald over to Glass for execution. The Captain did volunteer to obtain and return Hugh's rifle, though; and when that was done, its owner found that all his rage and hatred had left him.

Clutching the precious weapon, he dubbed Riley a fine fellow, shook hands and left. After nine months of unparalleled questing, he had found his particular grail, so on June 30, 1824, he contentedly set forth with it, beginning wanderings which took him to New Mexico.

§§ 8 §§

The Character of the Grizzly

WHILE HUGH GLASS was crawling in quest of property and vengeance during the fall of 1823, other survivors of the Arikara attack on Ashley men were on their way off the known map. Making a last effort in a game he had been steadily losing, Ashley had decided to try to put men west of the Rockies by striking away from the Missouri instead of following it to where the Blackfeet implacably straddled the logical gateway to the big mountains.

The dozen men he picked for this undertaking were called upon to upset precedent in divers other ways. They must sever all connections with the posts which, via the Missouri, had been looked to for supplies by other white fur-hunters. Moving west overland, they must depend on Indian nomads to be their professors in the arts of being completely self-sufficient in a routeless wilderness and of keeping their bearings in it.

Most of them had only come to the upper Missouri that season. By right of his year of seniority in the wilds, Jedediah Strong Smith was captain of a crew who had no Western trapping experience, let alone training as plainsmen. Who most of the rest were, only people interested in the crumbs of history know or care. But among them, in addition to Jim Clyman, of Virginia, were Bill Sublette, of Kentucky, not yet known as "Cut Face" or "Fate," and Thomas Fitzpatrick, of Ireland, not yet called "Broken Hand" or "White Hair."

These were all men of unusually sound parts, though something of what their companions were like may be gathered from the jotted observation of Clyman, who had helped Ashley recruit the members of his second expedition. "A description of our crew I can't give, but Falstaff's Battalion was genteel in comparison."

A surveyor with a gift for writing quaint but imaginative phrases, Clyman was ten years older than the cited other three. Scholarly Tom Fitzpatrick, as well as Bill Sublette and Jed Smith, who owed their education to backwoods rearing as well as books, were in their early twenties.

York-Stater Smith, with his passionate desire to add to the known geography of North America, was Ashley's good choice for leader. As guides he had an unnamed but presumably red-skin denizen of the upper Missouri region, useful for only the first stretch of the journey, and Ed Rose. The latter was a mixture of mulatto and Indian, sent along because he had been at Astoria and was one of the rare speakers of some sort of English who had seen the other side of the Rockies.

The party left Fort Kiowa on the 29th of September, which only Fitzpatrick was likely to have thought of as Michaelmas. A few days later, or by early October of 1823, the trappers were learning that there were other Western perils than those represented by Arikaras or Blackfeet.

Unused to thirst, they nearly succumbed to it the first week. The local guide was of no help, as he pressed ahead and was lost to sight, while the trappers lagged back with their suffering pack animals. The crisis was so close to being fatal that Jed conceived the idea of burying two failing men, so that only their heads were above ground, in order to prevent the further evaporation of what little moisture they had left. Clyman finally stumbled across a life-saving pool in one of the up-and-down streams of the West, though, and fired the shots which drew those still with the strength to respond.

After the invalids were exhumed and revived, the party pushed on through country rising toward South Dakota's Black Hills. In that range, so rapidly was experience being thrust upon this detachment of Ashley's men, Jed had an encounter similar to the one which had shattered Hugh Glass a few weeks earlier.

The first of a file leading horses along a brush-choked ravine, Smith all but bumped into a grizzly bear, which promptly reared and seized his head in its capacious jaws.

Jed's companions killed the beast, without being able to do so in time to spare his face from a mutilation which took in one removed ear. The impression made on men new to the Western back country by this startling adventure was later soberly recorded by Clyman, who at times used spelling of his own choosing. "This gave us a lisson on the character of the grizzly bear which we did not forget."

Jed had ten days to reflect on the "lisson" before he was able to go on. Acting on instructions from the patient, Jim Clyman sewed him up, and even tacked the severed ear back on. Amazingly, it remained a healthy part of Smith's anatomy. It was no longer a well-formed one, though, and Jed wore his hair long thereafter.

This was one of the few deviations from former customs made by a man who was remarkable both for his love for the wilderness and his refusal to make concessions to the ways of life it encouraged others to follow. All but solitary in this respect, he kept himself clean-shaven, whenever the availability of water made it possible. In a land of religiously hard drinkers, he dipped into his cups sparingly. It was said of him that a deeply felt but unrequited romantic attachment kept him continent where promiscuity ruled, but there's no recorded detail to support that tradition. In its absence it can only be affirmed that he never chose to bed with any of the squaws that hopes of profit or the laws of hospitality made available in quantity in most Indian villages. He was furthermore a regular consultant of the Bible carried in his possible sack, he never smoked, and even the bear which almost tore his head off didn't draw profanity from Jed.

In the saddle with his wounds yet raw, he ordered a march which completed the crossing of the Black Hills and brought the trappers into villages of a different nature than the ones which the Mandans and the Arikaras had built along the Missouri. The Sioux, Cheyennes and Crows lived as most Americans thought all Plains tribes did, using horses and dogs to take their mobile homes of buffalohide from place to place, as the presence of game, seasonal weather conditions or the hunches of medicine men dictated.

By the time Smith's party was in the area claimed by the Crows, the Rockies were imminent, but the Missouri was hundreds of miles to the west, and also to the north, where it flowed through upper Montana. As winter was at hand, the trappers stayed for months in a tribal encampment along the Wind River, itself tributary to the upper Big Horn. An expected welcome had materialized, because Ed Rose had once functioned as a Crow chief.

Typical of the tent-folding Indians, the Crows lived by hunting and desultory trapping. The avocations of the men were war and thievery. Stealing horses from friends was not thought disgraceful, though being caught at it was. The women, cheerfully and openly wanton, didn't take it in bad part when their husbands lost them at gambling, which was a cold-weather constant. Although Jed went on with his perusal of the Bible, his fellows found other ways of passing their time in a season of poor fishing.

An adage of Jim Clyman's coining averred that although an Indian of that era could never step out of the Stone Age and think and act like the nineteenth century's civilized men, it was no trick at all for a white man to slide down the centuries to the level of primitive conduct. At the posts along the Missouri white men might live barbarously enough, but they were in outposts of civilization and not separate from it. Living with and learning from the Crows, the men under Jed began to accept the wilderness way of life as the normal one. The conversion didn't happen all at once, it can be confidently guessed, but the rubbing off of a degree of savagery on them was preliminary to the change in outlook which made them men of a new order, ranging the wilds not as visitors for one motive or another, but at naturalized citizens.

Ed Rose, to get back to their period of initiation, finally regained his former political power, achieved through giving away the trappers' stock of trade goods at an alarming rate. Glad to be rid of him, they left him as a Crow chief once more, and took the field late in February of 1824. If they watched for horse-hungry prowlers while they were still in the country of their late hosts, they did not fear they would be followed for their scalps, having acquired a knowledge of Crow business philosophy. Tribal spokesmen had explained that they never killed the white men who came among them laden with the useful devices and fascinating trinkets of civilized manufacture, because in that event they could never return to be robbed again.

High Wyoming is not normally warm in February. Trying to pierce Teton Pass in a deceptive break in the weather, the trappers bogged down in drifts such as they had never imagined before. Then the break in the cold which had lured them out of Crow tepees made way for blizzards which rendered hunting, and sometimes even fires, impossible. For some while it was moot whether they were nearer death by starvation or freezing. When they did finally find game—Clyman shot a bighorn sheep and Bill Sublette a buffalo—they learned that flesh can be cut, and liver torn, out of still warm bodies and wolfed raw, if hands are too stiff to start a blaze.

In the course of these experiences they went up the Popo Agie to the lower end of the Wind River Mountains, and then westerly up the Sweetwater to the break in the Rockies known as South Pass. It had been negotiated from the opposite direction by a party returning from Astoria, but the whereabouts of eastern approaches to it had not earlier been understood.

Chroniclers have credited both Fitzpatrick and Sublette with the discovery of the eastern gate to South Pass. While it is highly possible that one or the other may have been scouting ahead of the main party at the crucial moment, neither was the directing mind of that expedition. It can be guessed that one of Balboa's lieutenants might have been leading the van that first descried big water, without seeking to deny Balboa the discovery of the Pacific. Jed Smith was the leader of the men who fared from the source of the eastward-flowing Sweetwater to the headwaters of the westward-running Sandy, and it would seem unreasonable to credit his achievement to anyone else.

Having for days appeased their thirst as best they could by mouthing snow, they hacked at the motionless Sandy but made no headway till Jim Clyman pistoled the ice and drew a gusher. Thereafter, and under increasingly balmy conditions, they rode down along that finger of the Great Basin's drainage system to the northern reach of the Colorado called the Green. Although in western Wyoming by current reckoning, according to that of the spring of 1824 they were in Oregon.

The Astorians had cut through this region. Jed and his mates were the first to pause and examine it. This they did in the course of getting down to original business as employees of Ashley, which was to collect pelts. Otter and marten might be taken incidentally, but the international men's fashion of wearing tall, gray, fur-covered hats made beaver the staple of the trade.

The method of catching these four-footed engineers was to plant, in the water backed by their shallow dams, traps baited with castor. A smear made of beaver genitals, it was redolent enough for smelling under water by the amphibious animals, and fatally attractive to them. A stout stick about six feet long was then driven into the stream bed, serving the double purpose of anchoring the trap, by the means of slipping the terminal ring of a long chain over the pole, and of marking the gin's location. A rawhide thong, stretching from the trap to a tree or shrub ashore, enabled the setter to haul in the works, if he'd caught anything, thus avoiding having to wade about in often freezing water at both ends of the process.

Although designated as trappers, what with their feud with the Arikaras and the months devoted to finding a way through the Rockies which wasn't blocked by Blackfeet, most of Smith's party had been in the West for a year without having had occasion to ply their trade. Now they made up for lost time in a region where the Indians had no interest in competing with them, because the trading companies which alone made it worth while for the natives to collect peltries had yet to appear.

Not preyed upon before, the beaver were as unwary as they were numerous. High-country swimmers, they had thicker fur than ordinary; the plews, or superior skins, swiftly added up to bales which were put in caches, so burdened animals wouldn't slow the business of pressing on in quest of more and yet more.

The underground safety deposit vault known as a cache was lined with branches and other vegetable insulation, to prevent soil-contact rot, and thatched against rainfall seepage. Its roof had to be far enough down so that keen-scented prowlers would not smell the contents and be tempted to dig. Lastly, it had to be covered so cunningly that Indians wouldn't suspect its presence and investigate.

Pelts were by no means all that was so stored. A cache might contain a supply of preservable food against the time it was wanted; or powder, shot and an emergency arsenal of extra rifles; or robes and heavy clothes not needed in a year's milder months; or the medicinal brandy supply; or the knives, tinware, gimcracks and items of adornment lumped as "Indian trade goods."

After making safety deposit vaults for supplies and skins as described above, Jed split his party. He himself led one detachment down the Green. Tom Fitzpatrick and three others, of whom one was Clyman, went in the other direction.

Up to that point Ashley's dozen had not been troubled by Indians, but now Fitzpatrick's party became acquainted with the Shoshones. An encountered band of the latter, after making themselves agreeable in return for being fed by the white men, honored tribal tradition by stealing their hosts' horses.

The still-learning frontiersmen continued trapping until it was time to meet Jed, whom they expected to find at the far side of South Pass on the upper Sweetwater. Perforce they cached all their furs and traipsed east, not glad about the treachery which had left them afoot. Their luck turning, though, they stumbled on the same Shoshones, three of whom were mounted on purloined nags. After they had stopped the Indians at gun-point, they got the other mount back. It took a while for the savages to remember where it was, but they did when the classically trained

Fitzpatrick tied one brave up in the presence of his fellows and threatened to shoot him.

Smith didn't show up on schedule, and those at the tryst on time were in a region where a failure to keep an appointment could reasonably be read as disaster. Beginning to figure that he and his three men were the lone survivors, Fitzpatrick, in company with Clyman, investigated the navigability of the Sweetwater. As without the horses of Jed's party they couldn't hope to pack all their furs back to the Missouri, their thought was to bring them up from the Green in relays and float the lot down the river in bullboats of their making.

After reaching what they decided was the head of Sweetwater navigation, the two trappers parted, Fitzpatrick going back for the pair waiting upstream. Clyman went farther downriver, his missions to pick out a good base of operation and to bag the buffalo out of whose hides the coracles would be fashioned.

Finding a satisfactory campsite, Jim had luckily not yet made a betraying fire when a band of twenty-two male Indians rode up and bivouacked directly across the stream from where he had taken to cover. His own later comment on the situation is above challenge: "I did not feel myself perfectly safe with so large a war party in my near vicinity."

Creeping clear of that neighborhood after nightfall, he reached a rocky ridge which wouldn't publish his tracks. A rabbit's foot was watching out for him, as he had hardly got clear of his original hiding place when some of the war party's horses strayed to his side of the Sweetwater, with Indians in pursuit. They didn't see Jim but, still not feeling perfectly safe, he chose to give the warriors time to go elsewhere. Although he let only a day or so pass before returning to the river, his precaution caused his friends to strike him from the roster. For Jed was at the upriver camp when Fitzpatrick returned to it, and with a change of plans which he wished to discuss with all hands. Going to look for Clyman, Smith found Indian tracks but not Jim. Regretfully adding up these clues, he subtracted a comrade.

The decision Jed had reached was to explore the Great Basin

farther instead of returning to report to Ashley. That duty he delegated to Fitzpatrick, who was to bring their employer to a rendezvous on the Green the following spring.

Jed, Bill Sublette and company then recrossed the Great Divide, leaving Fitzpatrick and his two remaining men to pack furs down along the Sweetwater to where they might be floated to whatever major, and eastward-flowing, stream it might eventually join. Meanwhile Clyman was watching time pass with increasing dismay. After waiting eleven days without hearing anything from his companions he at length, as he admitted, "began to get lonesome."

Concluding that the Indians had left him the solitary white man within a couple of hundred thousand square miles or more, he decided to strike for the posts on the Missouri, some 235 leagues away as a crow flies, and he didn't even have a horse, let alone wings. He was almost as short of bullets, having less than a dozen with which to supply himself with food on a march which was a continued story from late June to the latter part of August.

Following down the Sweetwater, he inevitably came to the North Fork of the Platte, but he had no means of knowing this. Disturbingly, it arched north and dipped south before it got down to the business of running in the general direction of the rising sun. He was offered proofs that he was bordering a stream which white men had at least visited, though. It cheered him to find the wreck of the bullboat which Hugh Glass's associate, Dutton, had abandoned some weeks earlier, pursued by Arikaras. Less cheering was the nearby discovery of the bodies of two of Hugh's companions.

Clyman himself fell afoul of Pawnees, who robbed and would have killed him but for the brainstorm which struck one among the braves. His medicine or some other still, small voice prompted him to save Jim, feed him and smuggle him out of camp, complete with his rifle. This last may not have interested the Indians much in any case, because by then Clyman had only a bullet or so left.

56

Living by such means as killing badgers with the leg bones of a wild horse skeleton, Jim finally brought what was all but his own skeleton into Fort Atkinson, nearly two months after beginning his trek. He had passed by the Council Bluffs post some fifteen months earlier as a Western tyro. He returned as that masterpiece of endurance and the ability to cope with all wilderness conditions and weathers, the mountain man.

Tom Fitzpatrick was meanwhile having some experiences of his own. Floating the pelts entrusted to him down the Sweetwater, he and the pair with him were bullboat-wrecked. Diving for the furs, they dried and cached them, but most of their supplies were either carried away by the swift current or were damaged past salvaging. They, too, made it to Fort Atkinson, however, reaching it while Jim Clyman was still getting back in shape through the hospitality of Captain Bennet Riley.

⚜ 9 ⚜

A Buckskin Squire of Dames

WHEN JEAN LAFITTE sailed from Galveston Island in the *Pride* he set his course out of history and into the mists of legend. He was said to have died about 1825, but there were multiple rumors as to the manner of his death. The last of the famous Spanish Main pirates was reaped by plague in Yucatan, or a hurricane capsized the *Pride*, or a British man-of-war scuttled it. The only certainty is that some fatality overtook him more or less within the indicated twelvemonth, for he was neither seen nor heard of thereafter.

A year earlier a fugitive from his service took his rifle west along the Santa Fe Trail, which now was beginning to be traversed by caravans of wagons in place of freighted mules. This was possible because Tom Benton had at last driven a nail he had been hammering at and secured from Congress an appropriation large enough to cover improvement of some of the worst stretches. It had also covered the erection of markers, in order to make the trail traceable in spots where sandstorms at times buried all wheel tracks.

Helping Benton had been a man who still carried Tom's lead around. A freshman senator from Tennessee, Andrew Jackson likewise had his eye on the West. Upon reaching Washington, Old Hickory had fallen into conversation with a political colleague who didn't mention Nashville's City Hotel either; and from then on they resumed their friendship as though there had never been a rift.

The improved Santa Fe Trail, which was one of the results of their renewed amity, was still nothing which would have been considered a highway by automobilists of the next century. Negotiating its eight hundred miles and coping with the problems posed by drought and chancy weather demanded fortitude in depth.

Man was as much of a hazard as nature. Moving west from Independence, on the Missouri border, the traders first met the Osages. These Indians weren't emotionally at odds with white men, but they had beliefs which made it mandatory to kill them, if no actual enemy was handy. This was the case when Mad Buffalo slew a couple of trappers in 1824. Defeated by the Pawnees, he was obliged by his religion to slay somebody in recompense for warriors he had lost. The Pawnees being out of reach, he perforce killed men who were available. He had nothing against the murdered men, as he frankly avowed to puzzled American officials; but his duty was clear, and he did it.

So the Osages were a friendly nation, but no less dangerous on that account, while others were open enemies, who would steal weapons or leave men afoot in the prairies, even if they forbore to lift scalps. After Osage territory was left behind, the trail entered that of the Republican Pawnees, who owed their name to a river rather than to being political disciples of Alexander Hamilton. Beyond them were the Pawnee Loups, addicted to the type of human sacrifice which Hugh Glass had barely escaped, as well as to other customs which might make encounters with them unlucky. Hardest to get along with, as well as most numerous, were the Comanches, while tribes from the north which theoretically had no business in the area rode down to hunt men or buffalo.

Hugh Glass was not the only former Ashley man to go west along the Santa Fe Trail in 1824. Tom Smith did it, and so did James Kirker. As for Milton Sublette, if not an Ashley man himself, he was a younger brother of Bill, then west of the Rockies with Jed Smith.

The men referred to left no record of their experiences, but what it was like to cross the Great Plains at that time can be found by following the path of James Ohio Pattie. Not a modest man, he bequeathed to irritated historians a report of his adventures which they have vainly tried to impugn. While he did not take the Santa Fe Trail, Pattie met all its hazards during his journey from the lower Missouri to Santa Fe in 1824.

James and his father, Sylvester Pattie, had originally meant to ascend the big river to trap, but as they did not know that a license was requisite, they had failed to apply for one at St. Louis. Snubbed short at Fort Atkinson, they crossed the Missouri and joined forces with Sylvestre Pratte. A son of one of the founders of the French syndicate, the latter was leading a large brigade across country for the purpose of investigating reports about the Santa Fe trade.

These were favorable, while news along the Missouri was nowhere good. Ashley's last-ditch effort, in sending out the Jed Smith party, seemed to have led to nothing but the death of more white trappers. Backed by the Hudson's Bay Company, or so Americans believed, the Blackfeet were more aggressive than ever. The day of the river trader seemed at an end in view of the general Indian hostility which had followed the abortive Arikara siege. Something had to be done, and Pratte was trying to do it.

In moving south and west from the Council Bluffs area, he and the Patties entered Pawnee country, yet Pawnees were not the first Indians they encountered. Another afterclap of the

Arikara siege was the uprooting of the Rees, who had not tried to rebuild their burned towns. Instead they had reverted to nomadism, their hands against everybody and their hunting grounds wherever they chose to be.

A band of them raided the French-American party while it was still in the valley of the Platte. That was a small affray, in which the frontiersmen suffered no serious casualties. A few days later, though, they were attacked by the Crows, who scalped and otherwise mutilated two men before their bodies could be recovered. Still a third trapper was lost in a counterassault, but that time the Crows more than paid the man price.

Although the Republican Pawnees received the white men well, there was a near miss of trouble with the Pawnee Loups over a captive Indian boy whom the Wolf Pawnees wanted to burn as a climax to a scalp dance. These were but some of the experiences which made a veteran plainsman out of the twenty-year-old Kentuckian by the time he reached New Mexico.

Once James Ohio and his companions were besieged by a large band of Comanches; and, meeting the Crows yet again, they killed thirty in the brisk engagement which followed. Yet grizzly bears were a more frequent and bolder menace than the Indians. Drawn by their craving for horseflesh, they would attack any guards who tried to come between them and their prey. Standing watch over the mounts on one occasion, young Pattie was the death of a comrade in a case of mistaken identity. For although James had wounded the beast, the bear ascribed its pain to a man he charged and grounded. Reloading, Pattie made sure of the kill by jamming his gun against the silvertip's head; but the man thus succored, not having Hugh Glass's constitution, was too mangled to be salvaged.

Bison were a menace, too, but in their case not a deliberate one. Hurrying for any reason, a herd would turn aside for nothing; for even when the leaders saw cause to wish to, they were unable to withstand the pressure from behind. Or even if they were not running, a vast number of buffalo might simply envelop all the unmounted horses of an encampment and walk off with them. Sometimes the animals so abducted could be recovered by men with the patience to follow for twenty miles or so; at other times night came too soon, and the equines were never viewed again.

In a word James Ohio had seen much of the Western elephant by the time he reached Taos. That deep in the settled portion of New Mexico, he and those with him congratulated themselves that they were safe from the hostile Indian threat. Yet at Santa Fe itself, while they were waiting for the trapping license which they had been told they must have, they found that there was no sanctuary in the entire province. In November 1824 a large war party of Comanches raided ranches suburban to the capital and carried off everything movable which took their fancy, young women included.

Asked to help, the frontiersmen took the field. Inasmuch as the raiders were slowed by the stock they were driving off, the Americans were able to swing around them and wait at a pass suitable for ambuscade. The agreement was for Mexican allies to box the Comanches by closing in from behind, but this the former proved uneager to perform.

From his place in the thicket where the frontiersmen awaited the senior Pattie's signal to fire, James Ohio saw what the climax of a Comanche raid was like, in all the ruthless triumph of the reavers and all the sorrow of the surviving victims. Behind the hundreds of lance-bearing warriors the sky was black with the smoke of ranch houses and outbuildings. In front of them walked five women, stripped to punish them with the frostiness of that hour and season in high country, and to make them ready of access when the customary relay rapes should take place, as soon as the Indians were clear of the settlements. Forced to act as herders of the stolen sheep and horses now, they would be allotted to various warriors, or sold as slaves to another tribe, pursuant to reaching Comanche land.

Although Pratte was commonly in charge of a party largely composed of his French followers, Sylvester Pattie, who had captained a company in the War of 1812, was its war chief. When

61

he judged the Comanches to be within range, he gave the word which sent bullets over the heads of the trudging señoras and señoritas and at the mounted warriors to their rear.

At this sign of a rescue attempt, the young women commenced running toward the black powder smoke drifting above the thicket which had made the surprise attack possible. Yet even as they broke their dense formation and deployed away from their dead, some Indians tried to make sure that their captives could not be saved. Three of these fell with arrows or lance wounds in their backs. Yet the fleetest two escaped because James Ohio and another trapper of his years dashed forward and used their guns to discourage pursuing lancers, who else would have headed their quarry off.

Each hand in hand with an Eve wildly babbling Spanish, the youthful Americans rushed back to the thicket under the protecting fire of their comrades. Showing more compassion than Rogero evinced for Angelica under like circumstances, James Ohio ripped off his buckskin hunting shirt and gave it to the young woman in his care, who took it all the more thankfully because December was at hand.

After two Comanche charges had been broken, and before the Mexicans arrived to lance the wounded and the dead with equal enthusiasm, Pattie found that the señorita he had rescued was Jacova Melagres. A sightly girl some years his junior, she was the daughter of the last governor of New Mexico to serve while it was a Spanish colony. Throwing in with the Mexican republicans, however, he had stayed in office after the revolution, only to lose his position, as James Long had his life, when Iturbide took over as emperor in 1822.

Don Facundo Melagres had continued to thrive, nevertheless, as he had vast property holdings and continuing influence in New Mexico. On that account James Ohio and his companions were granted the trapping licenses which Americans in general were finding it difficult to get. Through Melagres, too, Sylvester Pattie secured permission to conduct copper-mining operations in southwestern New Mexico.

Too restless to wish to join his father, young Pattie drifted back to Taos, which was by way of becoming the favorite gathering place of American trappers, with or without portfolio. In part they preferred it to Santa Fe because it was closer to good beaver country. A greater advantage, in their eyes, was the distance that separated Taos from the stronghold of Mexican officialdom.

Joe Walker had returned to Missouri, where he became sheriff of the county whose seat was Independence. But Ewing Young, Tom Smith, George Yount, David Waldo, several of the Robidoux brethren and Milton Sublette were among those whom James Ohio met at Taos from time to time, when the place served as a resting point between their respective far-rangings. After a while Hugh Glass was of their number. Either not prospering as a trader, or not enjoying anything so comparatively confining, Hugh had contracted, in the capacity of free-lance trapper, to turn all his furs over to one Etienne Provost. Possibly not the Ashley man some have styled him, but certainly once of the upper Missouri, Provost was one of the growing number of former operators in that region who had gone to the Southwest because of reasoning that the fur trade had been killed farther north.

⸙ 10 ⸙

A Tour of a Secret Empire

TOM FITZPATRICK HAD no more than eaten his first real meal after weeks of privation than he followed Jed's instructions by commissioning a trapper to speed downriver to St. Louis. There this dispatch bearer delivered to a man who had resigned himself to forgetting his hope of making a fortune out of furs news of a huge and yet barely tapped supply west of the Rockies. Not one to dawdle when there was profit in the wind, William

Ashley promptly began organizing an expedition designed to tryst with Smith's veterans of Great Basin trapping at Jed's Green River depot of cached pelts and supplies.

Smith himself was meanwhile far to the north of that stipulated meeting place. After parting from Fitzpatrick, he, Bill Sublette and the six with them had wandered north into a different natural subdivision of Oregon.

Throughout most of its length the Great Basin is drained by the Colorado River system, discharging into the Gulf of California. At its upper extremity, though, streams run north out of it toward the Columbia. Leaving the headwaters of the Green behind, Jed soon found himself following currents which took an opposite course. By continuing along them he left a largely unexploited region and reached one where the trapping of fur was being systematically advanced.

Six years after the agreement calling for the joint occupancy of Oregon, pending settlement of the international boundary dispute, Canadians were occupying the territory in question and Americans were not. By politely insisting on the Columbia River line to which United States diplomats would not agree, the British government created a stalemate which granted it control of territory it didn't claim as well as the region which it did.

The difference between the powers of the two countries, in the matter of taking advantage of the joint occupancy agreement, was the Hudson's Bay Company. In addition to its wealth, it enjoyed the position of being an unofficial arm of the British government and a century and a half of experience in directing a wilderness empire. The struggling fur-trading companies along the Missouri could offer no competition; and whether put up to it by Canadians or not, the Blackfeet had effectively obstructed the one more or less charted approach to the region west of the Missouri's headwaters.

Wishing nothing better than license to proceed unwatched, the Hudson's Bay Company had worked out a scheme to loot the regions south and east of the elbow bent by the Columbia of their fur-bearing animals—or those whose pelts were negotiable rather. In 1823, or the year in which Jed had set out to look for a pass west of the Rockies, a Hudson's Bay brigade leader named Finan McDonald had gone east of the range, trapping in what was undisputed American territory as far as the Missouri's Great Falls. To the south the company was trapping on the fringes of the Great Basin, a region in which it counted on carrying out the fur-stripping policy it did not practice north of the Columbia.

The purpose of this plan was to prolong a monopoly which might well turn into something more advantageous to the British Empire as a whole. Seeing fur as the only means of attracting Americans to the region, the scheme's sponsors reasoned that they might gain all Oregon by default. If Americans didn't find it worth while to exploit the area during a prolonged period of theoretical joint occupancy, Britain seemed sure of gaining its point about the Columbia River line, and in train to wind up in outright possession of the Columbia estuary's port facilities, as well as with unchallenged ownership of Puget Sound.

Most American political leaders were but little concerned with a region to which none of their citizens now ever went. It is doubtful if even Tom Benton and Andrew Jackson gave much thought to a portion of the continent which seemed as far away as central Asia and was certainly almost as little known. Nothing, in short, appeared likely to interfere with the orderly confiscation of the Pacific Northwest until Jed Smith and his companions met some Iroquois Indians along the Snake River in September of 1824.

Far from their native stamping grounds in the Great Lakes region, these strays from the Five Nations had been brought in by the Hudson's Bay Company. Operating under a chief with the unlikely name of Pierre, they had not only trapped beaver, as per instructions, but got themselves in a brawl with the indigenous Shoshones. As the Snakes had robbed the Iroquois of both their food and their guns, the eastern Indians were starving and helpless to better their condition.

It was the bad luck of the Hudson's Bay Company that the

American party which encountered these redskin waifs was led by a man with a quick mind and the brass of a counterfeit gold piece. No citizen of the United States had previously had any means of guessing what the Canadians had been up to; but what Jed learned by pumping Pierre gave him an inkling, and he promptly maneuvered to get behind the enemy lines.

What he offered the Iroquois was food, as well as escort to the Hudson's Bay brigade leader under whom they served. What he asked in return was the Indians' entire take of furs. If this was more akin to hijacking and extortion than Christian charity, Jed was thinking as an American trapper rather than as a Bible student. Taken along the Snake River, south of the Columbia and hundreds of miles west of the Pacific, the pelts in question had been removed from what he regarded as United States beaver.

Mountain men had, of course, as little feeling for the checks and balances of international diplomacy as did the men of Natchez. Whatever officials at Washington might be willing to sacrifice to political expediency, the trappers knew that the land west of the American Rockies had for long been part of their country, and they held that it still was. So Jed not only confiscated the furs skinned by the Iroquois but proceeded to inform officers of the Hudson's Bay Company what he had done.

Pierre's commander in the field, Alexander Ross, wasn't happy about the loss of the pelts, but he was less happy to see Americans on the Pacific side of the Rockies. Yet he was the servant of an institution, and, as such, he was handicapped when dealing with a free agent. If he doubtless didn't like Jed's cool proposal to accompany him to Flat Head Post, neither did he want to lose sight of the mountain men until he got instructions from higher up. He therefore perforce acceded.

For the next few months Smith and Bill Sublette observed the workings of the company, beginning with the Indians who did the trapping. Ill paid and always in debt to the organization, these were a weakness. Although the brigades or large groups in which they traveled were a plus factor, when it came to facing down local tribes, they made for a high overhead and slack efficiency as compared with the risky American method of dispersing small parties which could cover a large area with a tenth of the personnel.

Most interesting to Jed and Bill, though, was Flat Head Post, where the plans and effectiveness of the company were most in evidence. In the first place, the fort stood beside the Clark Fork of the Columbia, east of the latter river and far outside the territory Britain was publicly claiming. With this commercial instrument the Hudson's Bay Company had established a peaceful dominion over an area which stretched deep into Montana. Tribe after tribe showed up by a prearranged schedule, bringing in furs which they exchanged for goods stocked by the post.

A few days after the mountain men got there, or in November of 1824, Peter Skene Ogden arrived. The man in charge of the company's drive to pillage as much as possible of Oregon, Ogden was stocky and dogged, where Jed was a lanky, outwardly mild shark. Even less pleased to find Americans in his bailiwick than Ross had been, Peter sized Smith up, nevertheless, and saw that the critical moment in a hitherto softly played game had arrived.

Watching each other, Jed's small party and Skene's brigade began moving south just before the turn of 1824–1825. After they finally went separate ways, Ogden pushed south through the Great Basin, where he hoped to reap at large. Bearing more to the east, Smith led his men to where he expected to find Ashley.

§♦§ II §♦§

Sought and Unsought Meetings

THE NEWS OF waiting fur fortunes west of the Rockies which Clyman and Fitzpatrick had brought to Fort Atkinson was passed up the Missouri as well as down it to St. Louis. Interested parties much nearer the Rockies than the city in question, and needing no preparations for wilderness journey other than catching up their rifle and possible sack and mounting a horse, were west of South Pass before the snows of late 1824 could block it.

Among them were Ashley men who had been cast adrift after luckless Andrew Henry had despaired of profiting from peltries a few months too soon. Some of the men who had wintered on the Yellowstone shared a disgust with the Far West which had led to Henry's severing his partnership with Ashley, but others had adopted the country and its way of life as their own.

Included was Jim Bridger, so determined to live down his misstep in deserting Hugh Glass that earnestness perched on the shoulder of a formerly lighthearted youngster and invested him with a precocious maturity. Another was Johnson Gardner, tough but loyal to such lights as he had.

These and others had fared west of the Green and were trapping the Bear River when Peter Skene Ogden optimistically led his brigade down it. He promptly ran into trouble, for if he was disappointed at finding American trappers ahead of him, they were outraged at encountering what they considered Canadian poachers.

Actually Bridger, Gardner and the rest were themselves trespassing on Mexican territory, as the Oregon line ran something to the north. What they believed, though, was that they had met British invaders of United States territory. Under Gardner's leadership, the mountain men gave the Hudson's Bay Company officer a rifle-backed ultimatum. Ogden stood firm, however, until he was routed by other factors.

Carefully briefed by Jed, the Canadian's Indian trappers verified Smith's pointer that Americans would pay them eight times as much for furs as the company did. Chief Pierre not only deserted Ogden but encouraged others to do so. And when they went, they took horses, guns, traps and food supplies with them. The company drew nothing but red ink from what had seemed a promising expedition, and its raging leader retreated north without then seeing the site of the Utah city which was later named for him.

Ashley, in the meantime, had assembled a brigade of his own, upon receiving Fitzpatrick's heartening message, together with the pack animals needed to bear supplies west of the Rockies and furs back east again. Disdainful of the imminence of winter, he had left St. Louis in mid-fall, picked Clyman and Fitzpatrick up at Fort Atkinson and set out along the Platte. Frosty weather at its fiercest battled them much of the way, but the promise of rich rewards kept morale high. If they missed South Pass because of the conditions, they found a negotiable one not far below it. Penetrating the mountains, they reached the Green, and under the guidance of Tom and Jim reached the spot where Jed was due to meet them.

When that tryst materialized, Smith and Sublette learned, after having counted him dead friend for many months, that Clyman was very much alive. Following that reunion, Ashley's third expedition began operations under the guidance of Jed and the other pioneers who had made up his party. Before breaking into small groups in that spring of 1825, though, the trappers agreed to bring their furs to a specified but now not plainly identifiable point on the Green River late in June. By that time Ashley was confident that the ordered mule train, bearing the wherewithal for gaiety as well as trade goods, would have arrived from Missouri.

Defeated on two other occasions, Ashley's men trapped at large and harvested prodigiously. Jim Clyman had another close call when attacking Shoshones put a bullet through the hat he was using as a pillow; but after shooting his way out of that corner, he was present when William Ashley held the first of the great mountain-men festivals known as rendezvous.

A sort of outdoor Valhalla, the occasion likewise combined some of the properties of a bazaar, an alumni reunion, a liar's contest, a board of directors' meeting, the Olympic Games, a geographical discussion group, Monte Carlo, a newspaper exchange and, of course, a saloon. If this was a wild gathering by some standards, it was closer to metropolitan life than many in attendance had been for two and three years. It was such a complete success that it became an institution on the strength of but one trial. A rendezvous, scheduled to be held in Cache Valley on the Bear River in the spring of 1826, was announced before the meeting broke up.

Ashley returned by way of the Missouri, down which barges would float faster than pack animals could shamble. In spite of having trouble with both Blackfeet and Crows on the way to the big river, his party brought their beaver bonanza safely to St. Louis. Yet the mountain men were by then as married to the wilderness as Venetian doges to the sea, and even those who made the trip to the Mississippi shortly wested again. Of these Jed Smith was one. A partner of Ashley now, he returned in the fall of 1825, having capped three and a half years of trapping and exploring with only four weeks in town.

Charmed by an apparently limitless region, which was opening out before them and offering new discoveries with the regularity of the turned pages of a fascinating book, many felt they could not spare the time to visit the States and partake of a way of life in which they'd lost interest. In their new one, conducted in a region so different from the terrains in which they had been reared that it seemed part of a different planet, they had learned to be astonished at nothing.

Traipsing down along the Bear, prior to attending the rendezvous of 1825, young Bridger was drawn by the sight of sea birds to discover Great Salt Lake. Gratified, if not too certain of his geography, Jim thought he had reached an arm of the Pacific.

He marked the area as good trapping country, though, so Peter Skene Ogden had another disappointment. Having returned to his headquarters for the purpose of assembling and outfitting a second brigade, Ogden set out to prove that the Great Basin was a region from which his concern could not be permanently ousted.

Probably with a clearer idea as to where the Mexican boundary ran than most mountain men had, the Hudson's Bay Company officer was as indifferent as they to the rights embodied in Mexico's sovereignty over the area into which he advanced. What the corporation wanted, he was prepared to take and hold.

Given the time to expand and consolidate, ambitious and capable Hudson's Bay Company servants like Ogden would have capitalized on Mexico's failure of occupancy by greatly adding to the territory they were engaged in taking from the United States. As in the case of purloined American territory, they were counting on turning squatters' enterprise into freehold. Yet when Ogden arrived at Great Salt Lake, deeper south than any company brigade leader had ever marched, Bridger had preceded him by a few weeks. So it was not long before other mountain men were in the vicinity, taking pelts with a rapidity unknown to the company's poorly paid, halfhearted Indians.

ঞ্জ 12 ঞ্জ

Westerners on the Warpath

THE MISSOURI RIVER traders who had participated in the abortive Arikara siege had depended on military intervention, in order to make the Indians behave. A little earlier Major Henry had thought one hundred men inadequate to hold the fort on the Yellowstone against the Blackfeet and had sent Jed to speed the coming of Ashley's reinforcements. Up until the emergence of the mountain men the frontiersmen of the Far West had not been confident of their ability to hold their own against the warrior tribes which so greatly outnumbered them.

This was not for lack of courage but for lack of competence. Being rivermen, they had not known what to do about hit-and-run raiders who disappeared in vast mountain ranges or vaster plains.

But the mountain man was at home in both, and what he had learned about Indians from living among them made him sure that he could beat the savages at any game they proposed. To him the hostile Indian represented no more than the chanciest of many occupational hazards. Like the moss-trooper of the Scotch-English border, the new type of Western trapper had come to take sneak attack, thievery and bloody reprisal as a normal part of existence.

The Bannocks learned that American frontiersmen could not be raided with impunity as early as the fall of 1825. When these Indians drove off eighty horses belonging to mountain men camped in the Great Basin, the latter were divided into pursuing parties, led respectively by Tom Fitzpatrick and Jim Bridger. Surprising the Bannock encampment, Fitzpatrick led a charge which stampeded the several hundred still able to run. Bridger meanwhile was shooing off nearly as many mounts. Of these not all were captured, but the net of 120 in exchange for the 80 stolen meant a nice 50 per cent profit.

But there were trapper defeats to go with trapper successes. Working as they did in small parties or alone, the mountain men were often beset by war parties which diminished their numbers and left their unburied bodies who knew where. How many were so slain nobody could guess; for only the ones who lasted long enough to establish reputations are remembered. All that was ever known about the passing of many was that they vanished into the wilderness after leaving one rendezvous and were not seen at the next.

They could have perished of thirst or hunger, to be sure. Or they might have ridden in the path of a landslide or avalanche, been caught out in a blizzard, or drowned like Mike Fink's nemesis while trying to cross a freshet-swollen stream. They could have been attacked by a grizzly, stranded afoot in front of a buffalo stampede, poisoned by a rattlesnake, or contracted rabies from a prowling mad wolf or skunk. But when a mountain man wasn't seen again, his associates took it for granted that his scalp was hanging in some Indian buck's tepee.

Even when the signs all pointed to peace the Indian was an omnipresent menace, as Hugh Glass found while in the Great

Basin a short year after the avenged Bannock raid. And though a man who would never forget him emerged in triumph from that episode, Hugh's luck was out again.

Engaged to trap for Etienne Provost, Glass and a small number of companions struck northwest from Taos into Utah, where they reached the Green and in due course streams to north of it. In the end they must have been on the Snake or one of its sizable tributaries, for it was estimated that they were seven hundred miles from their starting point and traveling by canoe when they met redskin disaster.

Gliding alone in the silent native craft, they saw a solitary squaw seated with her back to them. As has not always been true of men where unescorted women are concerned, their intentions toward this one were benevolent. They had been skinning newly trapped beaver while in transit, and it occurred to one of them, as they themselves were not short of meat, that it would be the kindly thing to see if the woman would like to have the carcasses.

Indians of that day were credited with sharp hearing, but perhaps this squaw was partially deaf. In any case she didn't hear the trappers land or approach in their moccasined feet until one of them spoke to her. Not the nerve-controlled stoic of tradition, either, she imitated startled female palefaces by shrieking.

From where they had been taking their ease in deep grass nearby, Shoshone braves erupted and commenced slinging arrows. Hugh could have made it back to the canoe in safety, but the groans of a downed trapper drew him to the latter's assistance. It was useless, though, as the man himself pointed out. All he asked of Glass was to reload the gun with which he had just killed one of the oncoming warriors, so he could shoot another before the rest finished what they had begun.

Delaying to accommodate the dying man, Hugh himself was hit by an arrow as he dashed for the canoe again. Its point lodged in a spinal bone, from which none of his comrades felt equal to extracting it. As the wound festered, it doubtless would have been fatal to most other men. But the constitution which had sustained Glass during his crawl to the Missouri carried him through the agonizing trip to Taos, where another mountain man dexterously removed the arrowhead with a razor.

One of the few Americans who trapped with the blessing of the Mexican government, James Pattie may not have been at Taos when Hugh rode in to be operated upon. Late in 1826 he had received permission to trap the Gila River, and before doing so he had reported to his father. Sylvester at the time was west of the Rio Grande, still operating the mining concession he owed both to his own willingness to fight Comanches and his son's eagerness to rescue distressed beauty.

Joining a party of French trappers led by Michel Robidoux next, the younger Pattie began riding down the Gila toward Arizona in January of 1827. The preceding fall Ewing Young had scouted the region, only to be beaten back by unidentified hostiles, in all likelihood Apaches. Not taking to that, Young had returned to organize a larger party, of which such redoubtables as Milton Sublette, George Yount and Tom Smith were members. But because he had left Taos quite a bit earlier, in order to visit Sylvester at the Santa Rita mines, James Ohio probably knew little or nothing of Ewing's plans.

Somewhat ahead of Young's party, in any case, that of Michel Robidoux proceeded through cactus-studded Arizona to where the Gila is joined by its largest tributary, the Salt. Electing to investigate, the trappers rode east past ranges of treeless hills to a point occupied by the wattle-and-mud huts of an Indian village.

The inhabiting Papagos were unctuously friendly, offering not only women but a beverage akin to the Apache corn beer called *tiswin* as reasons why the trappers should spend the night with them. Most of the other members of the Robidoux party were overjoyed at the proffered hospitality, but something in the manner of the Indians bothered James Ohio, who said he would remain outside the town and cook his own food. He and Michel quarreled over the point, or rather the Frenchman expressed his outrage at the idea of turning down both drink and a bed companion for the night, while Pattie's hunch strengthened the more the other tried to shame him out of it.

74

Impressed by Pattie's suspicions, one of the Frenchmen agreed with him, after sampling the atmosphere of the town, and snaked back out. The some dozen and a half who didn't were slaughtered by the Papagos while the former were enjoying post-dissipation slumber. Only their leader got away, but James and his companion did not then know there had been any survivors.

The site of the massacre appears to have been approximately that of Phoenix. Fleeing farther up the Salt, the two trappers forded it and took refuge in a clump of brush on Tempe Butte. Watching anxiously from there, they saw what they at first thought was a Papago pursuer but which turned out to be the badly wounded and crestfallen Michel Robidoux.

This dark fortune was followed by an almost incredible turn of luck in their favor. Seeing fires while traveling by night in order to escape further notice by the Indians, the three destitute survivors found Ewing Young's party camped on the Gila. The meeting took place within twenty-four hours of the massacre and changed their minds about returning to New Mexico proper.

One thing which trappers had learned, and which had become a byword among them ever since the Arikara punitive fiasco, was that an unpunished Indian aggression was a guarantee of trouble to come for every still-living white man in the area. Young, Yount and the rest therefore dropped all other business and told Pattie and his companions to show them where the malignantly hospitable Papagos lived.

Numbering thirty-two only, the frontiersmen were divided into two parties by Ewing. Of these one had the duty of sucking the Indians into ambush where waiting riflemen picked them off. One hundred and ten Papago bucks didn't answer roll call ever again, nor did any of the tribe remain in the village, whose charred ruins smoked near the graves dug for the butchered Frenchmen.

After trapping all of the streams tributary to the Gila, Young's party followed the main river down to the Colorado and bore north toward the Grand Canyon, which they were the first Americans to see. Before reaching it, though, they encountered the Mojave Indians, predatory, bloodthirsty—and previously unacquainted with trappers from the States.

When they sought to rob a party which included Kentuckians Pattie, M. Sublette and Tom Smith, these Indians were met with rifle fire which left many squaws in mourning, and which inspired in the Mojaves a subtler method of dealing with any party of white men they might plan to pillage in the future. As it chanced, they were soon to meet such a one, angling southwest through the Great Basin rather than westward from the valley of the upper Rio Grande.

৪৩ 13 ৪৩

In Quest of the Santa Buenaventura

IN FEBRUARY OF 1826 Jim Clyman and a Pennsylvania Dutchman called Henry Fraeb determined that the Great Salt Lake was not connected with the Pacific by cruising all around it in a bullboat. Their feat left untouched a rumor that there was a water link between the Great Basin and the western ocean in the form of a river.

Meanwhile Bill Sublette and a fellow Kentuckian, by turns known as Black Harris because of his exceptionally heavy growth of dark whiskers, or Major Harris because he had held that militia title, snowshoed out of the Rockies to guide Ashley to the early Bear River rendezvous scheduled for that year. It was the last expedition headed by the man whose boldness and sound thinking had led to the opening of the transmontane West.

After the Cache Valley foregathering, beaver-enriched Ashley sold his trading company to one headed by Jed Smith. Allied with the latter were Bill Sublette and David Jackson, a faceless man in spite of having immortalized himself by his discovery of the admired spot, east of Wyoming's Teton Range, known as

Jackson's Hole. This was trapper talk; meaning not a spring or a natural orifice but a break in rugged country, equipped with all the appurtenances of good camping for many.

Now able to dictate in such matters, Jed stipulated that the two ensuing rendezvous would be on Bear Lake, partly in the Idaho sector of old-style Oregon and the rest below the Utah-topping Mexican line. Smith then told his partners that circumstances would determine whether they might expect him at the 1827 meeting or the one after that. He then pushed south and west in a region whose geography was legendary, where it was not so unknown as to be out of reach of speculation.

Pioneer though the Spanish had been from Texas to California, they had not applied curiosity to the Great Basin, witness the fact that they had not heard of its inland sea. From Indian traditions or their own imaginings, nonetheless, they had evolved theories as to the existence there of other bodies of water. The most interesting of these myths was the Rio Santa Buenaventura, a stream which accomplished what neither Spaniards nor Mexicans had done by piercing the Sierra Nevada mountains.

There was a difference of opinion as to where it disembogued, some holding that it poured into the Pacific at a point near Monterey, others that it first merged with San Francisco Bay. Jed could have picked up this bit of Hispanic lore from Etienne Provost, for whom Hugh Glass trapped, or Joseph Robidoux, brother of the man with whom James Pattie had trapped the Gila and the Salt, as both had found their way to the rendezvous on the Green in 1825. Or Smith may not have heard of it until, after leaving Cache Valley, he explored the vicinity of Great Salt Lake. For by that time this novel body of water was frequented by trappers pushing up from Taos as well as by those who had crossed the Rockies.

However that may be, Jed decided to add definite knowledge of the Santa Buenaventura to the facts about the West which he was collecting and recording in journals he hoped to build into a complete general guide to the region. Nor was the notion of a mountain-piercing stream fantastic, inasmuch as he knew that the Columbia cut through the Cascades.

Among several Great Basin possibilities, his first candidate was the Sevier River. This, however, persisted in heading more south than west. The Virgin and its master stream, the Colorado, for a time seemed Pacific-bound, but when the larger river began flowing at right angles to the setting sun, Jed got some sort of bearings from Indians and struck west through the Mojave Desert. Crossing the San Bernadino Range, he and those with him became the first Americans to reach the West Coast overland, and no thanks at all to navigable waterways en route.

Others were not as pleased with their feat as they were. Mexican officials were not in train to raise cheers for a Western exploring feat which ranked second only to the initial one of Lewis and Clark. The commercial enterprise and the refusal to be schooled which American frontiersmen had shown in New Mexico had been bruited to all parts of the nation to which it belonged. The appearance from nowhere of a well-armed party of men from the States disturbed the governor of California, who summoned Jed to Monterey, his capital, in December of 1826.

His Excellency had a right to be worried, if he prized the *status quo ante* as highly as entrenched politicians customarily do; for wild as the mountain men looked and were, they represented the vanguard of modern civilization crowding in on the rear guard of something far older. In California, as in some other parts of what had been New Spain, the Renaissance drive which had sparked discovery and settlement had retreated into static medievalism.

This had been simplified by the peaceful nature of the southern coastal tribes, who took to subservience in a manner foreign to the assertive mountain and plains Indians. So they had become a peasantry, supporting by their unpaid efforts the hidalgo owners of vast estates on the one hand and mission fathers on the other.

Having exactly the odds in their favor they wanted, the two ruling classes wished no upsetting representatives from a differ-

78

ent way of life. Smith was accordingly told by Governor Echeandia that he must go back the way he came.

But Jed, who had bearded the Hudson's Bay Company, was not the man to be overawed by the head of a drowsing, backward province. Once east of California's coastal mountains anew, he cut north in search of the river he had come to locate. Although it failed to materialize, he did find beaver in quantity along the Stanislaus.

The trappers were in the midst of harvesting when word reached Monterey that the Americans had not gone back to United States territory. Echeandia sent troops to arrest Captain Smith; but, suspecting that such an effort would be made, Jed had flown in a direction which the Mexicans hadn't thought possible.

In the some sixty years since California had been settled, none of its residents had seen the east side of the Sierras. This Smith now undertook to do with but two companions. The rest he left in camp, in charge of more skins than they had the wherewithal to carry away.

Having ample other sources of prosperity, the Californios had not taken up the fur trade; in fact they seemed to have regarded rumors that men caught wild animals for the purpose of skinning them as an absurd legend. The peltries which Mexican officers found amassed by the Stanislaus, though, convinced them that the frontiersmen were indeed the trappers they claimed to be and not the spies of Governor Echeandia's suspicions. The Americans were therefore allowed to stay where Jed had promised to return for them.

Smith meanwhile had managed to leave the Sierras to westward, his purpose to secure the pack horses needed to retrieve his rich California haul. It nearly cost him his life to do so, for in arid Nevada he and his companions nearly shriveled for lack of moisture. Yet they reached the Bear Lake rendezvous with tales of a new beaver field, and of a mountain range—its peaks soaring above forests of unmatched grandeur—as tall and rugged as even the Rocky Mountains.

❦ 14 ❦

Of Bright and Shaded Red Waters

JED SMITH WAS not the only one at the second Bear Lake
rendezvous with interesting news. Moving toward the gathering
place after having wintered east of the Rockies, Bill Sublette had
found at least some of the marvels for which Yellowstone Park is
now famous. Not the first American to see a region where water
emerged from the ground with a roar and soared into the air like
an inverted waterfall, he was the first to gain some degree of
credence. John Colter, a former Lewis and Clark man who had
been caught by Blackfeet, stripped and given a start, to make
sport for a host of pursuing warriors, had reached this haunt of
wonders seventeen years earlier.

After outrunning most of his pursuers over prickly-pear country in his bare feet, and killing two who still dogged him with
their own weapons, Colter had found sanctuary up the Yellowstone, as nature's display of virtuosity about that river's headwaters had so awed the Indians that they had marked the vicinity taboo. Apparently it wasn't even supposed to be mentioned,
for white men hadn't heard of it until Colter reported back to
St. Louis—where he was laughed at as an American Münchau-
sen. Since the verified discovery of Great Salt Lake, though,
men were not so inclined to doubt improbability; and unlike his
predecessor, Sublette had supporting witnesses.

After the trading had been done, the whiskey drunk, the tales
of Indian assaults and counterattacks told, and information
about their astonishing world exchanged, the mountain men
again separated into small parties. Bill undertook the risky business of trapping in Blackfoot country, where he was especially
unwelcome, after just having helped a combined force of Snakes

and Utes crack back at the Siksikas. The latter had assaulted bands of the other two tribes while they were on their way to Bear Lake to trade. But Bill had met this threat to the success of his company's first rendezvous in a manner which had left six Blackfeet dead and the rest headed elsewhere.

Jed also went where he knew he wasn't wanted. Heading west with eighteen men and plenty of pack horses, he counted on bringing out the men and beaver pelts he'd left on the Stanislaus before the onset of cold weather made the passage through the high mountains difficult. As he had had enough of Nevada, he followed his former route as far as the lower Colorado, from which point he meant to strike northwest to the pass across the Sierras which he had recently negotiated.

By the river in question he met a band of Mojave Indians; the very ones in fact who had mistakenly tried to strong-arm and rob Ewing Young's party only a few months earlier. Having learned some caution from that experience, the Indians here began by offering smiles and hospitality.

Not mindful of their feud with the men of Taos, Jed took these overtures at their pleasant apparent value, and went ahead with preparations to raft men and mounts across a stream too deep for fording. He was thus vulnerably engaged when the Mojaves made a mass assault with bows, arrows and clubs.

Of Jed's following only eight survived this treachery, and of these only five were able to retain their rifles. The rest might have been massacred to a man when they were attacked the next day, but Smith led a charge which broke through the ringing Indians and called for a stand in a brush clump. To make up for the shortage of firearms, spears were improvised out of hunting knives lashed to sticks. By these, as well as by bullets, enough Indians were killed to make the remaining Mojaves lose heart.

Yet they had amply accomplished their purpose where thieving was concerned. The plight of the trappers was that of being afoot, in addition to being short of weapons and supplies, in a desert. So situated, Jed decided that the best of two bad courses was to cut across the Mojave to coastal California again, in hopes of obtaining supplies and permission to rejoin his other party from Mexican officials.

While he did succeed in obtaining some horses from Indians met along the way, fortune didn't otherwise smile on Smith. Having been bamboozled once by Jed, who had next flitted out of reach of the men sent to corral him, Governor Echeandia was wrathful at the return of a man now more than ever suspected of being an American spy. Only the absence of a government vessel, indeed, saved Jed deportation to Mexico City.

After he had been detained for months, though, he was allowed to leave Mexico via Oregon. Echeandia didn't want him to head east, and thus possibly establish a trail from New Mexico which other Americans might follow. And the winter season kept the trappers from attempting to cross the mountains, when north of where they were under Mexican surveillance.

Perforce, accordingly, Jed led his party up toward a region dominated, if not owned, by the powerful organization he had challenged a couple of years earlier, and which by no means had forgotten a man whom one of its officials had observed to be "a damned, scheming Yankee." Smith probably wasn't concerned by what Hudson's Bay Company men thought of him when he began leading the way north, in the early months of 1828, however. The joint occupancy agreement gave him the right to take such furs as the brigades of the company didn't find first, and perhaps he thought to get clear of the country without encountering servants of the rival organization.

So he and his men went ahead in the roundabout fashion of men pausing to trap all likely streams en route. In the process, though, they picked a way linking hitherto unconnected regions, for no white men had earlier fared overland either from California to Oregon or the other way about.

Men and beasts gave Jed a hard time while he was the prime mover in thus breaking trail. Already scarred by the grizzly which had taken his head in its teeth in the Black Hills, he was forced to move fast in order to escape being maimed or slain by two more. On one occasion he escaped only by taking to water, just as Meriwether Lewis had done when jumped by a silvertip along the Missouri. Later a pursuing bear caught Smith's horse by the tail and was dragged for about fifty yards before it could be persuaded to let go. As for the Indians, they turned out to be as rampageous as the ones in southern California were docile.

The mountain men first gained this knowledge in the Sacramento Valley, where redskins spent all of one April day in shooting arrows at men and steeds from hiding. A plague in California, the Indians were worse in Oregon, where they were at once more numerous, more persistent and safer from counterattack because of woods so luxurious as to undergrowth that horses were a handicap instead of an aid to pursuit.

Sometimes able to make only a few miles a day, Jed led the expedition in the physical sense of starting out before the rest each morning and finding where it was possible for peltry-laden animals to cross or avoid streams, swamps and the often as treacherous humus of a virgin forest in country with a very heavy rainfall. For many weeks the fogs of a seaboard region and the dense foliage of a country without lookout points made it hard to keep bearings. So Jed was still floundering in this tanglewood months after the rendezvous he had so confidently expected to attend was a bygone of 1828.

Certain tribes, as it happened, were more of a nuisance when they sought to be friendly than they were when hostile, because when paying visits they tried to sneak off with whatever caught their fancy and would put up an argument if detected. In part this tendency was a normal phase of people who saw no wrong in thievery; in part it defined the inevitable relationship between savages and those more industrially advanced.

To Stone Age humans the superior weapons, tools and articles of adornment owned by white men were marvels, because they had no inkling of how they were made. They craved them with the desperate craving of small children for shiny toys, and they had to get them from white men, for they had no other source of supply. So they would take, and were genuinely indignant if that was objected to, for they felt the white man could get more from the mysterious cornucopia whence he had whisked his array of wonders.

As for the white traipsers of the wilderness, it didn't matter whether they were philosophers enough to sympathize with the Indian point of view, which some of them were. They had to discourage theft or be left destitute, and they sometimes had to be rough in order to put their point across.

It was this complex of viewpoints that Jed's party stumbled over when visited by a branch of the Kelawatset Indians along the Umpqua River. One of their chiefs had tried to steal an ax, and was denied this ambition in a way which injured his patrician pride. Yearning to get his lost face restored, he persuaded some one hundred warriors of his tribe to approach the trappers' camp wearing the mask of amity.

Jed was not with his men at the time, as he had found a guide who had promised to show him a way out of the soggy forest in which he had so long been bogged down. Having learned about smiling Indians from the Mojaves, though, Smith had given strict orders to let no savages loiter in camp, but they disobeyed.

While in a canoe on the Willamette River, Jed learned that he, too, had been taken in by Kelatwatset wiles, for his guide steered him to where fellows of his tribe were in ambush. Smith's first warning of betrayal was when his cicerone seized his rifle and dived overboard with it. Fortunately the Indians lurking ashore were poor shots, so Smith and the two trappers with him were able to paddle to the other bank unscathed. But they were cut off from the rest of their party; at least they would have been, had there been any rest of their party to speak of.

Of the seventeen men Jed had left, twelve were rewarded for fraternizing by being slashed or clubbed to death on the spot; at least the Kelawatsets later said they thought they'd killed twelve along the Umpqua, though only eleven corpses were found. What happened to four or five others isn't known, for no trace or word concerning them was ever turned up. The only sure survivor had been out hunting when he was jumped by Indians, who robbed him of even his clothes, though sparing their owner. By following running water, this trapper reached the ocean and thence made his way along the shore to the Columbia.

Having guessed that the Indians had moved against his men as well as himself, Jed also made his way north. In due course, therefore, he was ferried across the upper estuary of the Columbia to Fort Vancouver, the key post in the Hudson's Bay Company's plan to confiscate the American Northwest.

𝄢 15 𝄢

Three Legs for Two Men

ONE OF THE consequences of Tom Benton's interest in developing the Santa Fe Trail was the arrival in the Southwest of William Sherley Williams. Old Bill, as he was universally known, reached New Mexico in the capacity of interpreter for a federal trail-surveying party in 1825. Not altogether to the satisfaction of Mexican authorities, he did not return to his native Missouri. Yet he didn't stay in New Mexico either, for none among the wilderness vagabonds of the West ranged it more widely than he.

Like Hugh Glass, he became a mountain man late in life, having first become a Methodist minister. In due course, though, he had aspired to convert the Osage Indians to his faith, an experiment which had earned Christianity no converts. But the Osages had made a pagan out of Old Bill, who also developed a non-ministerial ability to take in fabulous quantities of hard liquor.

Of no historical character, perhaps, have more contradictory things been asserted. He was said by some to be so untrustworthy that it wasn't safe to let him get behind one if provisions were short and quadrupeds weren't available. He was said by this school to have been cantankerous to the point of being unbearable, eccentric to the point of madness, and ungrammatical to the point of speaking a dialect of his own invention. Yet to be set against this evidence is the testimony of those who reported him as a thoroughly dependable, agreeable gentleman whose conversation mirrored his cultivated mind.

The poet Albert Pike, who traveled with Bill in New Mexico and Texas after the mountain man had achieved eminence among his kind, described him as a "man about six feet, one inch in height, gaunt, red haired, with a hard, weather beaten face, marked deeply with small pox," in addition to being "all muscle and sinew and the most indefatigable hunter in the world," having "no glory except in the woods." Even among wilderness razorbacks, Bill was noted for being dirty and greasy, and a voice once mellowed by training as a deliverer of sermons had become high-pitched from speaking Indian dialects, with a range of tonal qualities similar to those employed by speakers of Chinese. Still Pike went on to say of a man who had tried to translate the Bible into Osage that he was "a shrewd, cute, original man and far from illiterate."

Williams seems to have been original in whatever he undertook. Although he could walk mighty distances, he couldn't cover any two yards in a straight line. His rifle, Old Fetchem, was the deadliest in the West, but it wobbled so when Bill raised it that nobody else could understand how he could come near any target. He rode with his knees high, in a manner impossible to anybody else. And as he so fared he kept up a running monologue, addressed rather to his rifle and the raw-boned mule which bore him than to any human companion.

Although he had more fetishes than a cannibal witch doctor, he hadn't entirely forgotten his early evangelical bent; for now and again when a burial service was called for, Williams would come forward in his phenomenally filthy buckskins and perform the rite with dignity and eloquence. Yet this was the man who told the following story about himself, preserved by a nephew who heard it while Bill was on a rare visit to the settlements. Something that might have happened to any mountain man, it is superbly illustrative of the utterly self-dependent life which trappers led in the face of competing predators.

In Blackfoot country—for where in the West was he not?—Bill was setting traps alone when arrows zipped from a nearby clump of brush. Although two scored hits, Williams scrambled out of the creek where he was at work, dodged the three braves who wanted hair that nobody but a scalper would willingly touch, and lost pursuit as only he could do. For his ability to disappear approached so near the miraculous that he could vanish, together with his mount, and leave no tracks which a scouring war party could find.

But Bill had naturally had to leave his rifle ashore while engaged in the damp business of sinking a beaver trap, so the Blackfeet had captured Old Fetchem and, of course, all his lesser equipment except the knife hanging from his belt, plus whatever may have been in his pockets.

One of the arrowheads lodged in him was removed without difficulty, but Old Bill had to cut the other one out of his leg. That done, and finding that the Indians were no longer searching for him, the mountain man went looking for them.

He survived as Hugh Glass had survived—another mystery. But apparently he thrived on whatever diet he contrived, for he was able to keep pace with three active savages for the several days he dogged them. For three nights the Blackfeet, living on the sun-dried strips of preserved meat known as jerky, were light sleepers; but on the fourth day they shot a buffalo, and Old Bill grinned. He knew Indians and knew they'd gorge on meat and entrails. They did, and thereafter they slept as though they'd smoked opium.

They were lying with their feet to the fire, from which they fanned out in three directions, when the ex-minister of the Gospel stole among them. The first buck he slew by slitting his throat, clamping a hand over the Indian's mouth at the same time, so that his last breath hissed softly out instead of forming a cry. That scalp taken, Bill stabbed a man lying on his stomach, pushing his face into the ground to exact silence. The third brave, though, he waked by scalping him alive and kicking him in his bloated stomach.

Asked why he let this fellow escape as soon as he could pull himself together enough to make off, Williams gave an answer which spoke both for practicality and warrior pride. He wanted, on the first count, to have someone warn the other Blackfeet that he was a trapper whom they'd best let alone. There spoke the white man. But he made it clear that he also wanted to have his fame spread among Indians who'd appreciate the magnitude of his coup, and would tell the story of how he'd regained Old Fetchem around many campfires. And there spoke the Indian he'd half become by habit if not by blood.

If that exploit is undated, an accident which befell a companion of his, who was by way of being the bird of the next oddest feather among the mountain men, took place in 1828. By that time Tom Smith had completed the great sweep through the Great Basin and the Rockies executed by the Ewing Young party (after having lessoned the Papagos), and was far to the north of Taos once more.

Milton Sublette was again a companion; and Old Bill Williams had also enlisted with the group's leader, a French trader of note called Ceran St. Vrain. But trying to lead mountain men was often something akin to attempting to put a bridle on running water. Like Old Glass, as many of his juniors referred to Hugh, young Tom Smith had a penchant for ignoring the demands of teamwork. Built like a two-year-old bull, and tough and cocky as one, Tom thought wilderness watchfulness was for ninnies. He preferred to act as though there were no Indians anxious for scalps and attendant loot within miles of the North Platte, along which Clyman had nearly lost his life to Pawnees a few years earlier.

Seeing Tom lolling in the open in spite of several recent brushes with war parties of one tribe or another, St. Vrain was undertaking to remonstrate with him when rifles cracked from ambush. The trader was lucky, but the trapper wasn't. A bullet had broken both bones of Smith's lower left leg, which collapsed and splintered under his weight.

As it couldn't be set, gangrene was just around the corner. Facing that fact, Tom ordered men who were already figuratively perching on the mourners' bench to quit moping and cut his leg off. When his companions blenched at the thought, Tom began hacking away at himself with his hunting knife. Then Milton Sublette, who was to remember the event when his own time came, finished the gruesome job.

Perhaps it was too cold for germs to be about. Or perhaps microbes balked at the thought of invading a carcass as tough, and neighboring a spirit as ornery, as that of Tom Smith. An unlaundered hunting shirt was wrapped around the raw stump; yet no harm came of it.

Instead of dying during the night, as everybody had expected him to, Tom was strong as to pulse and language when his friends took a look at him in the morning. As he refused to perish, they had to carry him—carry him over the Rockies to the valley of the Green, and so south to winter quarters among the Utes. There Tom used the knife which had cut off his real leg to carve a wooden substitute. When he began trying it out, "Peg-leg" Smith had come into being.

Where Old Bill Williams went when the spring of 1828 made going elsewhere feasible is a matter of guesswork. Milton Sublette, though, returned to St. Louis that year, there to encounter his brother Bill. Peg-leg Smith in all likelihood required some months in order to get used to his timber limb, but by 1829 he was back in the Great Basin with Ewing Young.

Near where the Virgin joins the Colorado a member of the party called Dutch George found a mint of tawny pellets which he thought might be gold. Young decided it was copper, however, and was anxious to locate the free metal, as they were short of lead, and experiment showed that the soft mass could be molded into spherical form. But George could not find his way to what have since been called, by those who are convinced that treasure was missed, the Lost Dutch George Placers—or gold which can be picked up instead of hewn from close-fisted rock.

As the trappers were nearer to the Pacific Coast than to the upper Rio Grande, Young decided to try to market his furs in California instead of New Mexico. Undertaking this chore, Peg-leg and a Frenchman named Maurice Le Duke set forth with the necessary pack animals.

They did not head directly west across Nevada. For Peg-leg had been at the 1827 rendezvous on Bear Lake when Jed Smith reported the harsh desert experiences which had nearly finished him, following his eastward crossing of the Sierras. They accordingly chose to drop down the Colorado to the vicinity of Yuma, turning west on the occasionally used caravan route to the Coast from Tucson and Mexican points south.

But he had avoided one desert stretch only to brave another; the water problem became acute. Casting about for a spring, Peg-leg used one of a trio of buttes for a lookout spot. It turned out to be covered with what appeared to be sizable black stones. Upon moving some of these, the better to seat himself with comfort, Smith found they were exceptionally heavy. The cause, as investigation showed, was that these were big lumps of pure metal, blackened, as it probably did not occur to Peg-leg to say, by the process of oxidization. In color it resembled the metal chunk found by Dutch George a few weeks earlier, so Smith did not pay too much attention to the bearings which could have helped him to find the place again.

It is now assumed that what has taken its place in legend as the Lost Peg-leg Smith Mine was discovered in the rugged country east of the famous but then nonexistent Warner's Ranch. This was located only some forty or fifty miles northeast of San Diego. But as, from where he stood among spurned treasure, he espied terrain promising water to the northwest, Peg-leg and his companion struck out in that direction and in time arrived in Los Angeles.

Although he there learned that all that glitters isn't copper, Peg-leg was disinclined to retrace his steps, as he was in pocket from selling furs and a spree claimed him. Of all the whingdings in a region renowned for them, the wildest were said to have been thrown by the Smith who needed only one moccasin. In the course of this one Tom found that wooden shanks have uses beyond the reach of real ones, for he settled the first of many fights so won by unlimbering his timber peg and bashing his enemy over the head with it.

Shocked by a rambunctiousness so foreign to the mores of a normally drowsy community, the alcalde of Los Angeles asked Smith to leave. Unwontedly obliging, Peg-leg did so but took three hundred head of unpurchased horses with him. As early as 1829, that is to say, he pioneered a field of Western endeavor in which, as in the matter of tossing sprees, his only rival for primacy was Old Bill Williams.

⧬ 16 ⧬

The Jostling Beaver Skinners

OUT OF HISTORY'S sight for some while, Hugh Glass wandered north of Great Salt Lake in 1828 and joined the second of the two rendezvous at Bear Lake set by Jed Smith. The latter was not himself in attendance, although it was thought that his relation to earth was known, when he failed to put in appearance a year after departing on a trip not reckoned as requiring more than a couple of months.

But if regretful at the supposed death of one of the first mountain men, spirits were high at the annual gathering, among the trappers at least. Some traders, like Charles Bent and William Vanderburgh, who had gone west of South Pass to see if they could find any nourishment for their firm in the open-air fur market, forlornly decided that the company of Smith, Jackson and Sublette had a monopoly they couldn't hope to break.

Small outfits like that of Bent and Vanderburgh, meanwhile,

had been driven from the upper Missouri, where another monopoly was in the ascendant. With a ruthless dynamo named Kenneth McKenzie at the helm, and with large Eastern capital for backing, the American Fur Company was building posts and adopting policies aimed at complete dominance of the trade and the stamping out of competition by means which didn't stop short of inciting Indians to attack white rivals.

The trappers were happy about this new development, because McKenzie had announced that he would pay premium rates for pelts brought into his posts. What they didn't see was that this was but one more step in carrying out the plan to grab everything, and that when the scheme was consummated, the mountain men would be paid no better than the Hudson's Bay Company had paid Indians until American competition had forced them to be more generous.

Wishing a firsthand report on the intentions of the American Fur Company, the free trappers in attendance at the rendezvous chose Hugh Glass as their investigator. So at the close of the gathering Hugh went east of the mountains and bullboated down the Yellowstone to the Missouri. Ascending that stream, he arrived at Fort Union, the huge post which was being built on the edge of Blackfoot Country.

Although a cold-blooded thief, McKenzie knew how to get on well with those he had to, and just now he needed the mountain men. Presumably Glass sent back a favorable report, for he was satisfied enough with conditions at Fort Union to agree to trap for the American Fur Company himself. So, too, did Johnson Gardner and others who thought they knew a good thing when they saw it.

Among those who as yet took no interest in the power which McKenzie was readying himself to exert were the owners of his local rival—the firm without trading posts or indeed so much as any fixed spot in which to operate. Carrying on as usual, in the absence of a vanished senior partner, the two remaining split up, some months after the 1828 rendezvous. Staying in the field, Jackson rode north to Montana, while Sublette went to St.

Louis to attend to business matters, which included arranging for trade at the next great meeting of mountain men.

West of the Cascade Mountains, in the meantime, the head of their firm was dealing, as well as he could with a poor hand, with the giant trading concern which had yet not greatly felt the impact of either of the other two. Arrived at Fort Vancouver, following the Umpqua massacre, Jed Smith was forced to ask help of men who were prompt to identify him as the one who had hijacked Hudson's Bay Company furs from Chief Pierre of the Iroquois.

In particular he found himself confronted with Dr. John McLoughlin, a huge Scot who dressed as though he had gone to seed but had the bearing and notions of the emperor he more or less was. His ambitions were personal to only a minor degree, though. Devoutly dedicated to the interest of the company, he dedicated a strong intellect and powerful will to furthering the expansion of its holdings in what is now the United States; and his thoughts reached as far south as San Francisco Bay.

The only weak spot in his make-up, considering him as a corporation's agent, was that he was a man of principle. Had Jed applied to one of lesser stature, he might have been fobbed off or frankly told that accidents befalling Americans in a joint-occupancy zone were not a British concern. McLoughlin, however, accepted the consequences raised by the logic of his position. Confident that the Hudson's Bay Company, operating for the Crown, would be recognized as the owner of Oregon, he had ruled it as a political as well as a commercial viceroy. But if glad of his powers, he was willing to assume a ruler's responsibilities.

Relieved that Jed didn't expect the exaction of blood vengeance, the Doctor detailed one Alexander McLeod, at the head of a strong brigade, to accompany Smith back to the realm of the Kelawatsets. As their sneak victory over white men had bolstered these Indians, they at first hinted a willingness to try conclusions in the open with McLeod. But as the company's prestige induced buckling in favor of peace, interment of the mangled and rotting bodies of the slain mountain men was followed by

93

powwows in which the Kelawatsets confessed their error and agreed to make such restitution as they could.

This was limited by their customs. For by that time their loot —consisting of horses, weapons, trade goods, supplies and personal effects as well as peltries—had been given or traded to fellow tribesmen, or swapped to other Indian groups, living all over Western Oregon. Then items not found usable had been thrown away.

It took months to assemble what could still be located, and to pry some sort of indemnity for what was lost out of the culprit savages. But that done, a basic problem remained as tanglefoot. No pathway through the Cascades had yet been found, and a party of four men was unequal to the task of barging a pack train through the great gorge of the Dalles to where land travel was again possible on the east side of the mountains.

What Jed then proposed was that the Hudson's Bay Company should buy his pelts and spare equipment in return for credit redeemable at posts on the upper Missouri. This was finally arranged, albeit to the tune of caustic comments from no less a personage than the head of the company, who wasn't above rubbing in the difference between the treatment accorded Smith as compared with the latter's un-Samaritan conduct with regard to Pierre.

Sir George Simpson had arrived to see for himself the progress being made by his firm in Oregon; and Jed took an interest in this matter, too, drawing conclusions which might not have occurred to a less thoughtful trapper. Among other things, he observed that a larger fort was being built at a point where its 12-pounder cannon, hardly necessary in order to fend off Indian war canoes, could sweep the fine harbor made by the confluence of the Willamette River and the Columbia estuary. He also saw the company's trading vessels bringing in goods from London. Paying no duties for the privilege, company servants would distribute trade items to posts in United States territory. These could thus draw Indians away from American traders by underselling the latter in their own country.

94

He took note of the company's regional policy of not trapping north of the 49th parallel but only in such territory as might revert to the United States should the company's plan to acquire the Pacific Northwest and adjacent areas fall through. He also took note of the fact that Fort Vancouver was concerned with other occupations than the garnering of beaver skins.

Inside its walls the post employed blacksmiths, gunsmiths, carpenters and a tinner. Nearby were a sawmill and a gristmill, while in the surrounding area French Canadian farmers were raising wheat, barley, corn and garden truck, as well as horses, cattle, hogs, goats and a range of domestic fowl.

When the spring of 1829 brought prospects of being able to negotiate the Rockies, Jed made a second visit to Flat Head Post. Learning there that Americans were trapping Flathead River, he and the one man who had elected to stay with him encountered the first good luck of a disastrous trip. The mountain men found in Montana were headed by Jed's partner, David Jackson.

The rendezvous which they jointly attended was held at Pierre's Hole, west across the Tetons from the one named for Jed's business associate. The Iroquois chief wasn't taking pleasure in the honor of having his name thus perpetuated, though; for he had been killed by the Blackfeet in 1827.

Milton as well as Bill Sublette was at that rendezvous. So was Joe Meek, of Virginia, one of many youngsters who were being lured into the Far West by the fame of a profession which now seemed as assured of permanence as law or medicine.

With good money to be made at the price of adventure; with good companionship enjoyed in complete independence of all the legal and social trammels which hobbled the movements of those who stayed where they had come from, the mountain trappers seemed to themselves, as well as to youthful admirers, to be favored beyond all others. And yet there were men too restless for even space and freedom to hold to any one way of life. Jim Clyman had already gone east to try to settle down; and in 1830 one more of the original dozen mountain men left the Rockies.

After the rendezvous of the year before, Jed had sent a report, signed also by his partners, to John H. Eaton, Secretary of War under President Andrew Jackson. In addition to covering the activities of the Hudson's Bay Company which Jed had discovered, this communication pressed the feasibility of bringing wagons over South Pass—wagons, in short, which could serve as the supply train of a military force faring overland to the Pacific.

But after spending the winter of 1829–1830 on the Wind and Powder rivers Jed came to a decision which made the ensuing rendezvous his last. At it, the firm of Smith, Jackson and Sublette sold its interest to a new concern called the Rocky Mountain Fur Company, whose chief directors were Tom Fitzpatrick, Jim Bridger, Milton Sublette and Henry Fraeb. Subsequent to that transaction, Jed turned his back on the mountains, with the intention of visiting his New York kindred.

⧉ 17 ⧉
Blood in Dusty Country

BY THE YEAR 1828 the Americans who put goods on sale in New Mexico were having trouble doing business there, as angry officials tried to help native traders by taxing the foreigners who were peddling local beaver or bringing in merchandise. Some deftly met this emergency by taking out Mexican citizenship and ceasing to be foreigners. Others defied the tariff laws outright. An example of this contempt for local authority was Milton Sublette, who before going to St. Louis had seized impounded pelts and made off with them, the governor of New Mexico being among the spectators.

The Indians were not to be circumvented or shouldered aside, however. American caravans, running as deep into Mexico as Chihuahua City, had to reckon with Apaches, who now and again wiped out whole parties. Then the Indians along the Santa Fe Trail were becoming steadily more numerous, as reports of the plunder to be reaped from wagon trains drew raiding parties from supposedly distant tribes as well as the ones which normally ranged the trace's vicinity. Cheyennes, Arapahoes and even Gros Ventres were thus added to the Pawnee, Kiowa and Comanche brigands who were hourly apt to sweep into view.

Slow-moving, the trains of freight wagons couldn't outrun attack, nor were they in any way protected targets, as were the trading barges of the upper Missouri, whose watchful boatmen could maneuver away from archers ashore on the waters of that wide river. Raided, the traders could form their wagons into a makeshift fort, if they had time. If they didn't they were vulnerable from all sides, with their draft animals making especially fine targets.

While the mountain men took their chances with hostile redskins and never thought of asking anybody to make things easier for them, the men of commerce held a different view of matters. Just as merchantmen on the high seas felt that it was the business of the government to shield them from pirates, so these Santa Fe traders felt that they should have protection while coursing what was recognized as an international highway.

Although Tom Benton was sympathetic, they got no results from clamoring to him until Old Hickory became President of the United States in March 1829. Then a military detachment was assigned to Santa Fe Trail escort duty. In charge of it was Major Bennet Riley, who had been restrained from attacking Arikaras by Colonel Leavenworth. And in his command was Lieutenant Philip St. George Cooke, another officer who believed that fighting was among a military man's duties.

These and others along were able soldiers, but they were not able to outmaneuver the swift-wheeling horsemen of the plains on shanks' mare. There was at that time, so little had the War Department reckoned with conditions west of the Mississippi Valley, not a cavalry unit in the U.S. Army.

Unhappy about looking to infantrymen for protection against

centaurs, many merchants were furthermore glum upon learning that their escort would not be allowed to follow them across the Mexican border into the territory where most of the scalps lost by traders in 1828 had been ripped off. Only some three dozen wagons set out under Major Riley's protection the following June, where several times that number had opened the trail the preceding year.

Owner of at least one of the vehicles was Charles Bent, former partner of William Vanderburgh, whom he'd left still trying to find a footing in the northern fur trade. Through with the Missouri and not liking the looks of the situation beyond the Rockies, Bent was new to the Santa Fe Trail. Nevertheless, he was chosen train captain, in spite of the fact that veterans like David Waldo were members.

Already at a disadvantage because of being infantry, Riley's men showed up with a supply train which some military procurer had frugally equipped with ox power. The bovines couldn't possibly keep up with vehicles drawn by mules, putting the Major in the position of lagging behind himself in order not to run away from his commissary.

The Arkansas River was the boundary beyond which the troops were not allowed to go, though they would wait on the United States side, with a view to convoying the merchants back to Missouri when these recrossed the stream, perhaps three months later. Apparently tribal scouts had been keeping close tabs on developments. At all events the no longer guarded caravan was but a few miles south of the river when Indians struck in force.

Bent's younger brother, William, was among a flanking party attacked from one direction, while Charles himself was under arrow fire from the wagon train's other side a moment later. Rallying together, these broke the charge launched by allied Comanches and Kiowas, although one white man was caught in the open and scalped.

A shot from a trader's dwarf cannon went awry but so startled the savages with its roar that they scampered for shelter. They came on again as soon as they were sure that the big gun's bite didn't match its bark, but by that time the caravan had been drawn into a circle, with the stock herded inside. From their positions in protecting pits, riflemen then covered the messengers sent to Riley, who had gone on toward wooded Chouteau Island, where he meant to bivouac his men.

The siege maintained by the Indians was broken when dawn revealed that they were sandwiched between the advance column which the Major had swung beyond the raiders and the oncoming main body of his forces; but most of the traders were low as to morale after their experience with the realities of the Wild West. One even went so far as to try to join the Army, in order to have the protection of other soldiers. After Riley had expressed his view on this proposal, however, the battalion proceeded back to the Arkansas without the anxious recruit.

The merchants were not nervous without cause, as it turned out. After they were too far from the troops to make sending for help thinkable, they were harried by Indians for six consecutive weeks. At the end of this time a prayer carried by courier to Santa Fe was answered. Ewing Young led a rescue effort, only to find the savages in such strength that he was beaten back. Gathering more men, Young tried again and this time drove the marauders off.

Major Riley's four waiting companies didn't have a peaceful time of it either. Some soldiers whose enlistment period expired while they were on Chouteau Island insisted on their right to return to Missouri. One never did, because he was slain by Indians almost within sight of camp. Usually red raiders left a body where they scalped it, after following their other custom of making off with all clothing and other belongings. For some reason, though, these warriors carried the corpse away, necessitating the sending out of squads detailed to find the remains and bring them in for burial.

Seeing much of Riley's battalion thus dispersed, the Comanches then charged the camp. Hit by grape canister and caught in the rear by returning troops led by Cooke and others, the

Indians fled and, after but one other assault, left the soldiers alone.

Yet if the wild riders of the plains couldn't beat the infantrymen, neither could they be pursued by them. Foot troops were not an effective Western police force, as Bennet made strenuously clear in a report which in time got senatorial attention.

Charles Bent, meanwhile, had been unexpectedly able to arrange for an escort of Mexican troops for the return trip to the Arkansas, there to pick up their American guard again. Before they got that far, however, it developed that it was the soldiery from Santa Fe who needed, and got, protective action.

Along the Cimarron Colonel Viscarra's men were parleying with some Gros Ventres—who had signified peaceful intentions —when the Indians suddenly went into deadly action, killing officers, among others. Leading to the rescue men who had become seasoned since their first timorous days under fire, Bent drove off the Indians who did not quietly remain. Several of the once squeamish merchants, furthermore, showed their acquired Western sophistication by skinning the dead braves and nailing red pelts to the sides of their wagons as a challenge and a warning to any others who might be tempted to molest them.

In the saddle again, at this time, the man who had pulled the caravan through on the New Mexico leg of its westward journey was moving toward the Pacific, whither he had sent Peg-leg Smith earlier in the year. And among those with Ewing Young on this occasion was one who had helped him rescue the Bent caravan. This was Christopher Carson, whose older brother, Mose, had been Bent's superior in his upper Missouri trading days.

At the age of seventeen Kit had left Kentucky in 1826 and gone to New Mexico in the capacity of caravan cook. Later he had worked in the Santa Rita de Cobra mines, leased out to Sylvester Pattie, until a desire for more varied action had induced him to seek employment with Ewing.

He had come to the right man, for nobody in the Southwest combined daring with more imagination or enterprise than this ex-cabinetmaker from Tennessee. After Bent's party had been pulled out of the fire, Kit found himself a part of a plan which had been inspired by reports of Jed Smith's trips to northern California.

In Arizona Ewing was called upon to repeat the military ruse he had used against Papagos a couple of years earlier, although this time its victims were hovering Apaches. Concealing most of his men, Young advanced with about a third of his party, which faked panic upon coming under fire. When they gleefully pursued the runaways, the Apaches ran into the range of rifles which picked off fifteen, ending the engagement.

Harried, in revenge, all the way to the Colorado, the trappers crossed the Mojave Desert to San Gabriel Mission, as Jed had done. Unconcerned with California authorities, they spent the winter of 1829–1830 trapping the Sacramento and its tributaries. They were not alone there, nevertheless, for Dr. John McLoughlin wanted to bring at least all northern California into the Hudson's Bay Company orbit; and Peter Skene Ogden was on hand with a band of French *engagés* and Indians.

Young had been one of the Americans who had availed themselves of the temporary convenience of Mexican citizenship. Doubtless this had saved him from the harrying with which California authorities had visited Jed; but when some of his men let off rough steam in Los Angeles, after months of being dry stags, an attempt to arrest the whole party was made.

Getting his party out of town at rifle point, Ewing managed the retreat without bloodshed, until one of his uncurried followers cured another of his hangover by shooting a comrade who had annoyed him. This demonstration of savagery so impressed the Mexican posse that it left off pursuit then and there.

In the meantime two Americans who left New Mexico with Young had proved his wisdom in refusing to accept Mexican incarceration. At the Colorado, Sylvester and James Ohio Pattie had elected to drop down to where a Spanish trace, spanning the river near its junction with the Gila, led them to San Diego. There Jed's old antagonist, Governor Echeandia, clapped men he took for spies into jail, pending the arrival of a ship in which to deport them to Mexico City. Sylvester Pattie died while still in San Diego bondage. James Ohio survived to return to Kentucky, though, and was not again in the West for nearly two decades.

❧ 18 ❧

The Man of a Knife

DUE TO THE national fame acquired by the wielder of the prototype, the Westerners of whatever section had begun at some uncertain point to refer to the large knives they all carried as bowies. By the onset of the 1830's, the term had gained a safe footing in the English language, where it stood for a particular use for border cutlery. Although originally designed for hunting purposes, "bowie knife" suggested a weapon to let human blood with. In cities or in other well-settled portions of the country, men might fire at each other from prescribed distances with single-shot pistols; but on the frontier, before the development of the revolver, the favorite dueling tool was the blade designed by Rezin Bowie, who gave it to Jim.

Upon leaving Texas, following the breakup of James Long's first expedition, Jim had a series of adventures which became fixtures in tradition without being nailed down to any spot on the calendar. Once he killed John Lafitte, a son of Jean, in a pistol duel fought aboard a Mississippi River packet; but on all other occasions he was armed with his always triumphant knife. With it he and a New Orleans swashbuckler entered a night-darkened house, from which only Jim emerged. He fought a man while both straddled a log across a bayou, the loser to feed waiting alligators. He fought with his left wrist tied to that of his opponent, or while both gripped with their teeth corners of the same bandanna.

Where most of these encounters took place nobody thought it worth while to record. Some of them could have occurred in Texas, though, for Jim was in and out of it, from 1824 on, in his restless pursuit of trouble and wealth.

By then Americans were again in residence west of the Sabine River, for Stephen Austin had followed up negotiations which his father had commenced with Spain, their purpose the establishment of colonies of settlers from the States. The younger Austin had his troubles, for when Spain was overthrown, he had to apply to the Mexican Empire, and when that collapsed, to the Republic of Mexico. But he was a patient man, and one in whom Mexicans were glad to read none of Long's leanings. Stephen Austin, once of Virginia, did not share the frontier point of view that Texas was properly a part of the United States.

So he became an impresario, or sort of baron, granted large land holdings by Mexico City which he was empowered to parcel out to immigrants of his selection. The profit to the Mexican government was the development of a so far unexploited territory, as well as a buffer of settlements inserted between northern Mexico proper and the ranges of several aggressive tribes. The Americans saw the advantage of larger property grants than they could hope for in their own country, together with climate and soil conditions favorable to realizing the then general ambition of achieving prosperity through big-scale farming.

There can be no doubt that most of these original Texas pioneers were industrious folk who asked nothing better than to be allowed to go their ways as law-abiding Mexicans. They might have done so, and Mexico might still stretch into Wyoming and as far up the Pacific Coast as Oregon, if all had been of the ordinary stamp of frontier freeholders. Yet there were men of unquiet dispositions among the colonists, too, and thus the elements of foment and change.

In addition to Austin, who screened his settlers, precisely with a view to eliminating the frontier wild streak, Mexico licensed less discreet impresarios. One of these was Long's friend and quondam second-in-command of his second expedition, Ben Milam. A hearty man himself, he did not pick men solely because they seemed disposed to get along with the powers that be; nor did some others.

Another returner was the wily Downeast skipper John Austin. Akin to Stephen no more by disposition than blood, he was, by the mid-1820's, sailing legally in waters where he had once done so in defiance of Spain and the United States, in order to keep Long supplied with food and equipment.

The presence of such men notwithstanding, the experiment of strengthening Mexico's grip on Texas by the importation of American settlers appeared to be working out well for some years. During that period Mexico City let the immigrants alone, and they did what they were supposed to. That is to say, they cleared land, caught up wild cattle and horses, and pushed the Indians back from the Gulf toward the still-expanding Comanche empire.

Active from the plains of eastern Colorado to the northeastern Mexican province of Coahuila, these Indians were themselves as yet no threat to the American colonists of the Gulf coastal plains. But after invading the hunting grounds of the Lipan Apaches—dominant in central Texas when the Spanish first colonized the area—the Comanches had pressed so near the Mexican metropolis of San Fernando de Bexar that their warriors sometimes swarmed through the town in disturbingly large numbers.

Aware of the nervousness they evoked, the savages displayed a truculence which once prompted Bowie to knife down one of their chiefs. Not geared to strive for the slowly amassed profits of farming, Jim was first drawn to that part of Mexico by the profits to be realized on Spanish land-grant speculation.

Permanently in Texas by 1828, Bowie embraced Catholicism, a prerequisite for doing the same to Ursula Veramendi, whose preserved portrait shows why he wanted to. Marrying this daughter of the lieutenant-governor of the Rio Grande-straddling state of Coahuila-Texas, he settled down across the San Antonio

River from the Alamo. Not for very long, however. The honeymoon was not remarkably far back in time when Jim got on the trail of the first and most famous of all the lost Spanish mines which mistily dot the map of the American West.

Among the missions which the Spanish had established in Texas was that of San Saba, 150 miles northwest of the town whose name was usually shortened to Bexar. Built in 1757, the mission set up to give spiritual comfort to the Lipans was sacked by the Comanches, yet not before it had become associated in tradition with a silver mine of wondrous richness.

What gave the color of truth to this story was the fact that Comanches and Apaches kept riding into Bexar, wearing large ornaments of undoubtedly high-grade silver. As the Lipans were more commonly in the San Saba area than the Indians who eventually drove them from Texas, Bowie went to live with them. Winning the good will of the Apaches by going on the warpath with them, he got himself adopted into the tribe with a view to finding out what he wanted to know.

The whereabouts of their natural hoard, however, was something the Apaches weren't ready to reveal to a new recruit. Made suspicious by his searchings, the Indians told him to leave their hunting grounds and stay gone. But Jim Bowie had reportedly seen a shaft walled with solid silver, and the Apache threat only served to add the fillip of excitement he prized. Knowing another who wouldn't shy away if the purse was big enough, he sent for his brother, Rezin. When the latter arrived, in November of 1831, they enlisted nine other men and went forth.

Expecting opposition from Lipan Apaches, they got it from another tribe. The American settlers of Texas were not the only displacers of Western Indians at that period. Savages from east of the Mississippi, moving west of it under the relentless pressure of an expanding white population, were in turn squeezing the tribes which had been nearest the States. The federal policy, strengthened after Andrew Jackson became President, of moving most of the Eastern tribes to as yet unsettled portions of the

Louisiana Purchase, increased the gravity of a situation not at all understood by its aggravators.

Among the displaced peoples were bands of Cherokees from the Southeast, Shawnees from Ohio, and Delawares, indigenous to the vicinity of the so-named Eastern river. Warriors all, they seized new hunting grounds, from which they ousted the smaller tribes found in possession.

The situation affected Texas in two ways. In the first place, the immigrant Indians neither knew nor cared where American territory left off and that of Mexico began. Thus Cherokees settled in force between the Red River and the American colonies established by Austin, Milam and the rest. Neither did the Western tribes which had to move over care about the international boundaries of organized nations. Thus bands of Kickapoos, once of Kansas, pushed south in hopes of finding an area where game was so plentiful that the larger tribes could afford to tolerate the presence of small ones.

Once a forest people, settled in and about Louisiana, the Caddos had become a plains tribe, larger than the Tonkawas and others moving westward from the Gulf of Mexico but not of numbers to rival the Lipans and Comanches. Yet it was with these Indians, rather than the ones they had looked to for trouble, that the Bowies and their associates had to contend.

The Caddos had no stake in the mine the Americans counted on looting, nor were they taking up any tribal quarrel. They were just male Indians whose occupations, aside from hunting, were war and theft; and almost any group they much outnumbered, or could catch unawares, was a potential target.

Apparently the war party in question had hoped to take the Bowies by surprise; for the white men didn't know what was afoot until a Comanche caught up with them. Either because he wished to spoil the Caddos' game or because he wanted to speed up the fight he foresaw, this warrior warned the treasure seekers that a large band of scalp hunters was stalking them.

Still short of the ruins of San Saba Mission and a crumbled Spanish fortress nearby, the Bowie party made for an oak grove which they fortified with a breastwork made of piled rocks. Shooting from behind this makeshift wall, they held 164 Indians off for 14 hours. At least there were 164 to begin with. The Bowies and their companions killed 50 and wounded many more, while sustaining a loss of but one man and three lesser casualties.

Having had enough, the Caddos withdrew. So, when their wounded were able to travel, did the Bowies. With their effective strength reduced to seven, it didn't seem feasible to proceed farther into a region where news of their exploit was being spread from tribe to tribe. For Jim, at least, knew savages well enough to understand that while they had won the admiration of all the area's Indians, they had created an excitement which might spur other war parties to try to see if they could do what the Caddos had failed to and lift hair which had become doubly coveted.

That of Jim Bowie was reddish, and by the time he rode back toward Bexar late in 1831, Texas had gained another red poll. Now among the settlers along the Gulf was the personification of the kind of American whom Stephen Austin was anxious to exclude from the colonies. Christened William, he was generally called "Buck" Travis.

⣷⣿⣷ 19 ⣷⣿⣷

Comanches Met by Water

AFTER ESCAPING THE fate of the Patties by force of arms, Ewing Young's party withdrew through the desert eastward of Los Angeles and thence back toward the upper Rio Grande along the Gila. Unforgiving Apaches were willing but not able to stop the trappers, and ended by presenting them with an unexpected bonus. Attacking a band which came down the tributary San Pedro, after having made a raid into Sonora, the Americans emerged from the engagement with the two hundred horses which the Indians had lifted in Mexico proper.

Charles Bent's brother William and the small party with him were not so lucky later in 1830, in the same general vicinity. Apaches not only drove off most of their pack horses but picked half their traps out of the Gila. A jockeying for position then ensued, as the frontiersmen tried to ease out of a country in which they found themselves surrounded by Indians who attempted to close in without drawing fire.

The white men on their part would shoot but one or two of their half-dozen guns at a time, holding the rest in reserve, for they knew that except when told to do so by their medicine, or on other rare occasions, Indians wouldn't use superior numbers to overpower men sure of killing some of them. Extremely daring though he might be when in pursuit of glory, the Indian warrior was a self-centered calculator, much more interested in living for his country than in dying for it. As each savage realist asked himself, "But what if I should happen to be one of those shot?" the urge to take advantage of group odds seldom overcame the individual's healthy ambition to survive. In consequence two white men, standing back to back and holding their fire, could sometimes hold off a sizable war party until its members got bored with inaction and trotted away.

On this occasion, after failing to outmaneuver the trappers or to lull them by peaceful overtures, 183 Apaches ringed them and began creeping near the hastily assembled circle of rocks in which the frontiersmen made their stand. But after eleven braves had been picked off, young Bent and his companions were able to slip up the San Pedro into Sonora, there swinging east to Chihuahua and thence north to Taos.

Charles Bent was also in old Mexico, on a trading trip which took him as far south as Durango, in the winter of 1830–1831. Yet by the spring of the latter year he was once more in Missouri, which he left as the leader of a large caravan. This time, however, he wasn't first off the mark. Of two that were ahead of him, one wagon train belonged to the firm of Smith, Jackson and Sublette.

Changing his mind about going east, Jed had decided to enter the Santa Fe trade. Probably his motive was to visit one of the two sections of the West, Texas being the other, which he had not yet examined. But at all events he and his partners took a trail which must have seemed like a city street in comparison with so many which they had pioneered as mountain men.

With them, as it chanced, was Tom Fitzpatrick, head of the concern to which they had sold their fur-trading interests. Coming out of the mountains a little earlier, Tom had decided to try the experiment of securing the goods with which to do business at the next rendezvous in Santa Fe. His reasoning was that from there it might prove easier to pack items up the Great Basin than to repeat the process of taking them over a pass in the Rockies.

In the past the four mountain men had survived under such seemingly impossible conditions that they may well have been contemptuous of the bruited perils of a commonly traveled thoroughfare. It appears, in consequence, that they did not take the recommended precaution of loading up with water at the Arkansas before crossing the stretch—grimly named the Pathway of the Dead—which lay between it and the next sure watering at the Cimarron River.

The trail in this arid region was not visible whenever huge herds of buffalo made all the area a dusty flatland printed by hoofs, piled with chips and pocked with wallows at all points alike. There were no landmarks as aids for unraveling confusion, while mirages addled the direction sense of men who were drying to death.

They did find several spots which had been water holes and would be again. But the year had been particularly rainless, and digging failed to turn up moisture.

When only Jed and Fitzpatrick were still capable of action, these two left the trains, scouting amidst the clear shimmers of false water for the muddy reality which could save the lives of themselves and their companions. After some hours they found a moist depression which looked as though it might yield water if delved in. Tom's horse here collapsed from thirst, so the two men agreed that Fitzpatrick should see if any trickles could be squeezed out of the sponge in hand, while Smith went on in search of a more promising supply.

Watching from time to time through a telescope, Tom at length saw Jed dip from sight, not to reappear. What became of him was not known until a Comanchero, or merchant that specialized in trading with the tribe incorporated in the term, reported. In the course of his profession he had met the Comanche band which Smith had encountered just after leaving Fitzpatrick's ken.

For Jed did find open water, but converging toward it were warriors whom it was useless to try to avoid on his weakened horse. Accordingly he rode straight toward savages who made no response to signs that his mission was a peaceful one. By swinging his rifle, though, Smith kept any of the Indians from carrying out attempts to get behind him until they succeeded in making his horse nervous. Suddenly swinging about, it exposed his back.

There were arrows in it by the time Jed again faced men who were surging to surround him. He had time to fire only one shot, but with it he killed the war party's chief before the long lances of a dozen braves went in and through his body.

Thus in June of 1831, after having survived as many marvelous vicissitudes as Gulliver, Jed Smith died. Whether he had plans for other explorations, after reaching Santa Fe, is not known. The journal he kept, and in which he may have jotted schemes for the future, perhaps ended in the medicine bag of a Comanche buck, there keeping company with such items as animal teeth, curiously shaped stones or twigs and the shriveled head of a rattlesnake.

As Fitzpatrick found water, too, the men who had left Missouri with Smith were able to go on west. This they did, knowing that it would be useless to try to follow Jed, while he could cut the trail of the wagon train, if he were still alive to do so.

After the news reached Santa Fe that Smith had been killed, Bill Sublette completed the round trip to Independence. Fitzpatrick, on his part, went to Taos, where in due course he carried out his plan to assemble a Rocky Mountain Fur Company caravan.

Although Ewing Young had returned to California in 1831, Kit Carson had not gone with him. Having celebrated his return from the West Coast with a drunk featured by a brawl with Mexicans, young Carson had killed one of them and fled Santa Fe to avoid the consequences. He was thus in Taos when Tom Fitzpatrick was looking for men to guard his trading expedition. Wintering in the north under the tutelage of one of the great masters of wilderness lore, Kit had achieved a well-rounded Western education by the time of the 1832 rendezvous.

৪৩ 20 ৪৩

An Unlikely Man of Destiny

AFTER CARRYING IT for nineteen years Andrew Jackson had finally had removed from his shoulder the lead slug which Tom Benton had put there in the course of the melee at the City Hotel in Nashville. He did another thing later in 1832. Having just been elected to his second term in the White House, he felt powerful enough to stir up a fire which many would prefer not to have stoked, and he knew just the man he meant to use as a poker.

Put out of mind as a burned-out meteor by everybody else, Sam Houston had had a strange career. The young hero of the Battle of Horseshoe Bend in the Creek War had gone on to become Jackson's successor as governor of Tennessee, with the possibility of following him into the presidency a promising one. Then, because of finding that an adored bride had married him to please ambitious parents rather than on account of any enthusiasm of her own, he had resigned the governorship. More than that, he had reverted to a boyhood bent which had once before induced him to cut himself off from his people's way of life and live among the Cherokees.

Upon his return to these Indians, it is true, he had risen to enough political power among them to have become a chief known as the Raven. In less poetical moments, though, the Cherokees called him Big Drunk.

A souse gone native would not seem a usable diplomatic tool, but Old Hickory was seldom orthodox in his thinking. He had been delighted when Sam had enlivened Washington by caning a pistol-armed member of the House of Representatives who had relied too heavily upon Congressional immunity when passing personal remarks. Now he asked a man whose basic strength and ambition he understood to step back into civilization and become the personal emissary of the President of his country. In a word, Andrew asked Sam to further the American interests in Texas which the federal government had officially renounced in 1819.

There had, in the meantime, been developments which had convinced Old Hickory that intervention was timely. Brewing for several years, trouble had erupted, in 1832, in peaceful colonies of Stephen Austin's dreaming.

With neither Mexicans nor Americans essentially guilty of anything worse than following their traditional bents, the struggle could be said to have had a background of all the centuries during which the political thinking of their ancestral races advanced along divergent paths. The colonists were impatient of government by fiat. The Mexican authorities had come to regret a colonization policy which was flooding Texas with men whose tradition of independence drove them to quarrel with the political practices of their adopted country.

In the first instance the men from over the Sabine had begun objecting to the fact that Texas was not a separate state but one in combination with Coahuila. There, south of the Rio Grande, the capital, as well as courts with alien principles of jurisprudence, were located. Dissatisfaction with such matters had inspired one 'rebellion as early as 1829, taking the form of setting up the fleeting Republic of Fredonia by Ben Edwards. Stephen Austin and others who were trying to be faithful to their pledges of loyalty had marched on rebuilt Nacogdoches, the capital of sovereign Fredonia, just as it had been that of Long's Republic of Texas at the outset. Mexican political leaders caught a scare from the incident, however, and agreed upon a measure tantamount to shutting the door on American immigration.

From that point on the Texas colonials were a divided people. The majority, composed of those anxious to avoid trouble, wished to let problems iron themselves out, which they were sure would happen, after the Mexican government had been given time to ascertain that their citizens from the States were peaceful, diligent and faithful. A minority, not anxious to avoid trouble, scorned to be long-suffering.

In addition to John Austin and Ben Milam, this group included Deaf Smith and William Travis, who entered Mexico illegally and perhaps was drawn to Texas because there was a fence for him to jump. These and their ilk had more to say in 1832.

The political bomb of that year was that Negro slavery was abolished in Mexico, leaving only Indians still in a state of bondage. In effect this limited emancipation act deprived the few Texas colonists of their bought servants and left the numberless native Mexican slaveowners undisturbed. Americans who didn't mind having chips on their shoulders had reason to raise the war cry of discrimination. In reaction the government clamped the screws down by ordering the military control of garrisoned towns.

Always a poor way to get along with Americans, this did not suppress steam but strengthened its intensity, as General Juan Bradburn, himself from Virginia, should have known. He gave his troops license to be rough and overbearing in Anahuac, though, and thus fell afoul of Buck Travis.

A South Carolinian, Buck had practiced law in the frontier

courts of Alabama before the breaking up of his marriage moved him to seek even more remote parts. Texas was his chosen zone, as of 1831; and there he had already achieved standing as a man opposed to tyranny when Bradburn's uncurbed soldiery raped a settler's wife in the spring of the following year. Organizing a group of militia, Travis grabbed a Mexican regular. The latter was being coated with tar and feathers in downtown Anahuac when Bradburn arrived with overpowering guns.

Incarcerated in Anahuac Fortress, Buck was denied recourse to civil law. The cause of local rebellion wasn't lost, though, for John Austin was present, and knew of a fellow skipper who had two cannons. In Brazoria, sixty miles away, Austin took charge of this ordnance as well as the ship in which he dropped down the Brazos River toward where it flowed into the Gulf near Galveston Bay.

Just above this point it was necessary to run past the guns of Fort Velasco. John first suggested to its commander that he should look the other way; but when the latter refused, Austin made an amphibious assault, sending a detachment ashore to snipe at the post's cannoneers, while he dueled with the fort's guns from the river.

The strategy was effective, because the post's architect had visualized it as a defense against sea attack only. Insufficiently protected on the landward side, the garrison were under fire from sharpshooters whenever they tried to service their artillery. Relative to the number of defenders, casualties were heavy and at length crippling. Colonel Dominago Urgatechea surrendered and Austin sailed on, his purpose to slug down the walls of Anahuac Fortress and free Travis and his companions.

This turned out to be unnecessary, because Jim Bowie had been diverted from a second attempt to get at San Saba's silver by the news of what was going on in eastern Texas. Never having associated with the colonists when they were at peace, Bowie hastened to take their part in a quarrel in which he had no stake.

Temporarily the uprising of the colonials was general. It did

114

not take the form of rebellion against Mexican rule, though. The Americans rather declared themselves opposed to the incumbent national administration, and in favor of its replacement by a man whose Mexican followers had sung them a song. Ironically, in view of what was to come, the aroused colonists had declared themselves adherents of Antonio López de Santa Anna Pérez de Lebron, then rising to power in the guise of a liberal. And they were avowedly in his service when they advanced on that cockpit of Texas, Nacogdoches.

Trying to withdraw from a territory he was unable to control, Colonel José de la Piedras found himself cut off by Bowie. Although Jim had a following of only twenty men, the point he'd picked to defend was a ford commanding the exit to a defile. With colonists pressing toward him from the rear, Piedras was boxed and surrendered. John Austin was thus possessed of prisoners to bargain with; and Travis and company were freed from Anahuac Fortress without bloodshed.

With Santa Anna continuing to gain ground in Mexico City, it looked to the hopeful proponents of peace as if stormy days had been left behind. But as that was not the view of the President of their former country, Houston the Raven entered Texas in December of 1832.

🙴 21 🙴

From Tom to White Hair

BY RENDEZVOUS time in 1832, the surviving original mountain men had had that status for eight years, while many others were scarcely junior to them in wilderness experience. Probably most of them had set out with the ambition of making a stake which they could bring back to some starting point in order to invest their profits and settle down. That hadn't been done, though, even by the ones who had prospered handsomely. The mountains themselves had come to matter more than the wealth which could be taken out of them.

Yet if they hadn't gone back to the girls they had expected to marry, they were males of mating age in a country where females were available. At first only the objects of transient lechery, squaws had begun to be women to share tepees with, and literally in the plural. Romans in Rome, some mountain men had learned to ignore the principle of monogamy. After having helped the Utes fight the Snakes in 1830, Peg-leg Smith was offered as many wives as he wanted by the grateful Chief Wakara. "As I was a modest man," Smith later recalled, "I only took three." And former Methodist minister Williams also had at times as many as three Indian women to make his moccasins, cook his food and spend a conjugal session with every third week, when in camp.

Others were monogamous and took a decent interest in the children produced. But even the most harum-scarum of them seldom had difficulty in finding squaws eager to mate with them. Better shots and better trappers than the Indians, the mountain men were kinder and more indulgent husbands than were Stone Age males. These were in general licensed by tribal custom to ignore feminine prerogatives to a degree unthinkable to all but degenerates of the civilized world; and whatever else the mountain men might be, they were not that.

But the wives they bought with horses were strong links with savage ideas about art, nature, cosmogony and human conduct. Looking to animals for their clothes and to Indians for sartorial models, the mountain men came to enjoy the swank of beaded moccasins, whangs fluttering from buckskin sleeves and an eagle plume in the cap. Their tastes had been changed in other ways as well. Once regarding dogs with fondness in a more spiritual sense, they joined the tribesmen in prizing them as a delicacy for the pot. When it was available, fresh meat made up almost their entire diet, which did not include unavailable salt.

If they didn't wear bonnets garnished with feathers bespeaking individual battle and hunting achievements, they talked of counting coups with the matter-of-factness of an Indian, and lifted scalps with the regularity of one. Some of them, besides, bore *noms de guerre* by which Indians on both sides of the Rockies distinguished them.

In the course of one of his numberless Western adventures, Bill Sublette had collected a prominent chin scar which led tribesmen to refer to him as Cut Face. For more obscure reasons—and it is anybody's guess as to what the word meant to savages—they betimes called him Fate. As for Tom Fitzpatrick, he was given a war-won name in 1832.

As senior partner of the Rocky Mountain Fur Company, Fitzpatrick had named early July at Pierre's Hole as the time and site for that rendezvous. As the date of the meeting neared, Bill Sublette was known to be on his way through the mountains in charge of laden mules. His coming was eagerly awaited by Fitzpatrick, because the former's trading firm of Sublette and Campbell was now affiliated with the latter's fur company. Robert Campbell had replaced Bill's surviving partner, David Jackson, who had gone to California with Ewing Young the previous fall.

As Fitzpatrick knew, Fate Sublette was engaged in a caravan race with Lucien Fontenelle, a lieutenant of the American Fur Company. The one who reached the rendezvous first could line up the waiting free trappers first and freeze out the other. It was a race, that is to say, in which the loser would have done better not to have started at all.

The contest was conditioned by the grazing en route. It wasn't enough for the snow to be out of the way; the new grass had to attain a certain height before it could keep hard-working draft animals fit. Fontenelle had the advantage of having his trade goods brought upriver by steamboat to comparatively near Fort Union, but he had to wait longer for feasible conditions than did his rival from Missouri.

Making far the longer overland journey of the two, Cut Face followed the old route along the Platte to South Pass. Along the way he picked up Nathaniel Wyeth of Cambridge, Massachusetts. One of the few Easterners to give Oregon a thought, he had been tempted to try to reach the region by the favorable reports of certain sea captains, as well as that of Lewis and Clark.

Fontenelle had company, too, before he reached the western side of South Pass, because he met the expedition of Benjamin Louis Eulalie de Bonneville. In his presence both the dead hand of Jed Smith and the live one of President Andrew Jackson can be seen. For this enterprising captain had secured the unusual privilege of two years' relief from active duty in the U.S. Army in which to explore the possibility, urged by Jed, of marching military units and the needed supplies cross-country to Oregon.

Earlier Bill Sublette had been the first to take wagons as far as the eastern end of South Pass. Guided by Joe Walker, formerly of Taos, Bonneville made history by rolling wheels across the Great Divide.

Meanwhile Sublette, who had gone through the pass ahead of Bonneville and Fontenelle, had been met by the anxious Fitzpatrick. Sure that his man was in the lead, Tom raced back to the rendezvous in order to spread the word that trade goods were on the way, and to begin making deals with the various assembled free trappers and Indians.

Milton Sublette was on deck at Pierre's Hole, in spite of having been knifed in a fight over a Bannock girl during the past winter, not to mention having escaped death at the hands of Snakes. In company with Joe Meek, he had been saved through the secret intervention of a Shoshone chief and a daughter of his named Mountain Lamb.

Another partner cheered by Fitzpatrick's message was Jim Bridger. Uncheered by the news was William Vanderburgh, the cannoneer of the Arikara siege. Having failed to make good in an effort to work the high Missouri independently, he had become a brigade leader of the ever-expanding American Fur Company. Vanderburgh's presence, though, was a sufficient warning that Kenneth McKenzie's traders were imminently expected. Therefore Tom galloped back to urge Bill to lose no time; but in cutting across Blackfoot country as the shortest route, Fitzpatrick was sighted not by actual Blackfeet but Gros Ventres, often called by the name of the larger tribe because of their alliance with it.

Promiscuously on the warpath from Montana to New Mexico, the Gros Ventres promptly gave chase to a man who was boxed between them and the mountains, to which Fitzpatrick perforce turned. Unable to compete with fresh ones, his horse foundered on a steep, rocky slope, so Tom had to push on afoot while a couple of hundred warriors closed in.

All that saved him was a crevice between rocks, whose entrance he was able to block from the inside with a natural-seeming accretion of dirt and brush. Hunched behind this fragile protection, he heard the Indians going through the ceremonials and boasts of individual prowess with which they prepared themselves for the man hunt which followed.

Thorough as it was, and conducted over a period of three days by Indians who knew he must be in the area, it was fruitless. But living so long in the expectation of fatal discovery silvered Fitzpatrick's pow.

When he did finally sneak past the camp of the Gros Ventres at night, his troubles took a new turn. In default of a horse, he had to raft himself across the Snake River, whose strong current took his makeshift craft apart. When he reached the other side of the stream, therefore, he was without his small supply of food or a rifle with which to replace it. The one thing he did have was his bearings, which enabled him to cut his traveling time to the minimum while making a crow line for Pierre's Hole through country which shredded his moccasins and offered his energies nothing but sparse vegetable fuel for five days.

Tom arrived again at the rendezvous on July 8—not long after Bill Sublette, who didn't recognize a man he had seen only ten days before. Taking a look at Fitzpatrick as he then stood, the assembled Nez Percés and Flathead Indians dubbed him White Hair.

After the rendezvous Milton and Fate Sublette and Henry Fraeb led a mixed crew of mountain men and Indians against the Gros Ventre band which had nearly put an end to his friend. Wounded in the arm before the so-called Blackfeet managed to withdraw by night, Bill then went east of the Rockies again.

In Sublette's company for part of the journey, Nathaniel Wyeth made his way to the Hudson's Bay Company fort on Clark's Fork of the Columbia, which Bill and Jed Smith had once visited. At Flat Head Post, however, Wyeth found no disposition to encourage an American man of commerce; nor did he fare any better at Fort Vancouver.

But in the meantime the great Canadian company had a challenger in the West whom it knew nothing about. Wintering in the northern reaches of the American Rockies in 1832–1833, Captain Bonneville was not only ostensibly engaged in the fur trade, he was most anxious to profit from it. But the man whom the Indians called Bald Head had other items on his mind as well; and from time to time he jotted down the things he had learned about the operations of the Hudson's Bay Company, among other facts, in preparation for a report he meant to make to the U.S. War Department.

৪৩ 22 ৪৩

The End of a Landlocked Pirate

AFTER THE RENDEZVOUS of 1832 the four principal partners of the Rocky Mountain Fur Company agreed to trap in widely separated territories. Remaining west of the Great Divide, Milton Sublette and Henry Fraeb were on their way to try their luck along the Ogden in Nevada when the Pierre's Hole fight temporarily interrupted them. White Hair Fitzpatrick and Jim Bridger, though, rode north and east into the Missouri headwaters country.

To their annoyance they found themselves shadowed by an

American Fur Company party led by Vanderburgh and a trader whose family pride or thick skin enabled him to cling to the name Andy Drips. Veterans at dealing in beaver, these had not built up mileage enough as mountain men to know where to find the best trapping areas deep in the wilderness. They were therefore playing tag-along to a pair renowned for their knowledge.

Having vainly tried to shake their rivals while trapping, Tom and Jim decided to drop work for a spell. Lightened of other duties, they were able to lose the American Fur Company men, after first leading them deep into Blackfoot Country. Not long thereafter, a Siksika war party surprised the would-be claim jumpers. His horse shot out from under him, Vanderburgh tried to rally his men, but was soon drilled by lead himself.

So ended, in the fall of 1832, the career of the man who had stuck to the wilderness after losing every trick since his one coup, scored on the Arikaras. Why it amused his slayers is a mystery with no clue outside the quirks of Stone Age mentality, but they found it worth their while to strip the flesh from his bones before dumping them in the high Missouri.

While trying to make up for the time lent to losing the rivals they hadn't meant to lead into a death trap, Fitzpatrick and Bridger had a run-in with the Blackfeet themselves which came near being fatal to the one who had come to be known as Old Gabe before he was much past twenty-five. Conferred on Bridger by trappers rather than Indians, this nickname was owing to the paternalistic seriousness with which he carried out his duties as a brigade leader.

Meeting Blackfeet whose peaceful overtures they didn't trust, Jim and Tom parleyed with some of the Siksika spokesmen. Then one who approached Bridger made a gesture which Old Gabe interpreted as a hostile move. He tried to answer it, but nothing went right. The rifle he brought hastily into action fired prematurely. The explosion frightened his horse into swinging about, whereupon the Blackfoot chief plunked three arrows into Jim's back. Next afoot and wrestling for control of the rifle whose barrel the Indian had grabbed, the wounded man lost and was hit in the neck with the stock of his own weapon.

It would have killed most men, but a peculiarity of Bridger's build was that his neck was exceedingly powerful, being of about the same circumference as his head. He was thus alive when Fitzpatrick checked on him, after having led an attack which drove the Blackfeet off, minus the nine who couldn't budge. A pair of the arrowheads stayed in Old Gabe's pelt, though, being too near the spine for safe removal by hunting-knife surgery.

While Jim was recuperating, the man who had prematurely aged him by failing to die as expected was still trapping for the American Fur Company. For years working out of Fort Union, Hugh Glass went up the Yellowstone he had once ascended in search of Bridger, with the intention of wintering at the new post, with the rhyming name of Cass, of the company now known as Amfurco.

Among those there at the time was Edward Rose, the guide who had led Jed Smith's original party of mountain men as far as Crow country in 1823. In his company, as has been said and denied, Hugh went out hunting at some point in the cold season of 1832–1833. But whether he was alone or accompanied, Hugh's destination was a wooded island in the Yellowstone, reckoned as a likely haunt of game.

Out on the snow-covered ice, he made a good target for Indians trespassing on the territory of the Crows, themselves feed for letting Amfurco men trap the vicinity and unhostile. Not expecting trouble, the man who had once swum from Lafitte's Campeachy may never have seen the lurking enemies whose missiles slew him. But whether he lived long enough to identify them or not, Hugh Glass fell and Arikara warriors accomplished what members of their tribe had several times failed to do by bearing off his scalp.

He was not long unavenged. In April of 1833 some Arikaras who tried to palm themselves off as friendly Minitaris visited a party of Amfurco trappers working out of Fort Cass or Fort Union. The Indians had a plan which called for half of them holding the attention of the white men while the remainder ran off the horses browsing nearby. Unfortunately for them as well as their scheme, however, one they found about the campfire was Johnson Gardner.

Peter Skene Ogden remembered him, for Gardner had been the man chiefly responsible for making the Hudson's Bay Company officer's trip to the Great Basin an abortive one in the spring of 1825. An old-timer, Johnson now recognized the rifle carried by one of the self-styled Minitaris as the one which Hugh had long ago made an epic journey to recover.

Although not caught in the act, the murderers of Glass had been identified as Arikaras by one or more of the many ways by which such things were learned there and at that time. The arrows which killed a man could name the tribe of those who had shot them. So could the size and shape of the wound created by scalping, for some tribes prized only a small patch of hair, while warriors belonging to others were covetous of larger trophies. Or the killers themselves might boast of having made way with such and such a warrior or mountain man, thus putting the news on the extensive wilderness grapevine.

So in addition to telling Johnson Gardner that he was beholding Hugh's slayers, the rifle warned him that they were Arikaras, and by that token in camp for no good. At his signal the Indians in hand were seized by some trappers while others began scouting for prowlers. With the executions that followed, the story which began with Hugh's impressment as a pirate was ended.

The preserver of much of that story was George Yount, of Taos among many other places, with whom Kit Carson had trapped the headwaters of the Arkansas in 1832 before returning north to winter on the Snake. Little-known in the spring, Kit had achieved by fall warrior feats which had marked him as a comer among the younger generation of mountain men.

At some point between Glass's death and the atonement exacted by Gardner, Kit's camp was raided by a band of forty Blackfeet, who made off with eighteen horses. Taking their trail with twenty men, Carson engaged the Indians in a fight in which both sides dismounted in order to have the cover of trees.

Seeing a friend menaced, when he leaned aside to fire, Kit killed the Blackfoot who was looking down his companion's throat, but in so doing, he exposed himself to the fire of a ready Indian. The bullet he caught nearly did for Carson, whose discouraged men thought he was dead when he dropped. The Siksika got away, complete with every one of the lifted horses, and had such a head start that even Jim Bridger couldn't track them, when he tried to finish what Kit had unluckily begun.

Amfurco and the baseless Rocky Mountain Fur Company were meanwhile girding themselves for another race to control the rendezvous, which in 1833 was set for the Green near Horse Creek. This time Bob Campbell was in charge of the pack train from Missouri, while Fontenelle was again the caravan leader for the rival outfit. After Henry Fraeb had first established the whereabouts of Campbell, Fitzpatrick met him and marked the easiest path through country he knew better than any, for Horse Creek was named for the theft of mounts committed against Tom and Jim Clyman nearly a decade earlier.

As a result of expert guidance, Campbell was at the rendezvous while Fontenelle was still three days short of it. If that was victory, the partners of the Rocky Mountain Fur Company learned, when the rival train did arrive, that they couldn't dominate an open market again. Having big capital behind it, the American Fur Company was prepared to absorb great losses in order to drive opposition from the field. So although the smaller concern got the trade of all the early arrivers, the latecomers to the rendezvous did business with a trader who had been authorized to pay trappers more than twice as much as their peltries would bring, wholesale, in St. Louis.

While ways to meet this new situation were being mulled over, Milton Sublette agreed to help Nathaniel Wyeth, eastward bound after being frozen out by the Hudson's Bay Company, to float his gear downriver beyond South Pass to the easy sailing on the Missouri. The craft Milton put together, once they had reached the Big Horn, seems to have been a cross between a bullboat and a canoe, as it was made of buffalo hides, but was eighteen feet long by nearly six wide, as opposed to the usual circular skin vessel.

With two French half-breeds and a couple of Indian youths, the mountain man and the Cambridge merchant paddled, in August of 1833, down a stream which ran through Crow country. That proved costly, for the Crows had been bought by the American Fur Company and instructed to make it tough for all other traders. They were thus stopped by a succession of bands which they were powerless to dodge, and Wyeth lost trade goods at every halt for blackmail.

Skimming next by Glass's Bluffs, which overlooked the stretch of the Yellowstone where Hugh had been slain, they reached the Missouri and ascended it six miles to Fort Union. They were then in the den of the American Fur Company's head hatchet man, Kenneth McKenzie.

The King by the Missouri, as he rejoiced to be known, had acquired justifying power by selling rifles and liquor to Indians who were only too glad to follow his orders and be truculent toward other white men. He shared Lafitte's liking for swank and for impressing others with his lavish hospitality, however. Sublette and Wyeth were welcome, and the latter was enabled to buy a log canoe with which to continue his journey at better than bullboat speed.

⸙ 23 ⸙

The Impact of Wyeth's Freaks

IN HOPES OF recouping his steady losses, Captain Bonneville sent Joe Walker to look for beaver in California after the rendezvous of 1833. Joe Meek was of Walker's party from the outset, and in the vicinity of Great Salt Lake, Old Bill Williams joined.

As Milton Sublette and Fraeb had learned a year earlier the river still called the Ogden rather than the Humboldt led through bad country, while the stream itself, which disappeared in a marshy area in place of joining a large body of water, grew progressively alkaline. The Digger Indians were an aggravation, too. A debased, insect-eating people, they didn't make raids in the ordinary sense, but trailed the trappers like a pack of hungry dogs, ready to snatch anything not momentarily watched.

Increasing in numbers and sullenness, they tried to block a stream crossing. It was too much; and many died there before the frontiersmen proceeded.

At the western side of the Nevada desert stood the great rampart of the Sierras, which only Jed Smith had pierced. Gaunt horses were eaten, by men who found nothing else digestible, before they had reached the bleak eastern slopes of the range and skirted them until a penetrable point known as Walker's Pass was found. But their reward was waiting for them, for they were the first white men to gaze upon what seemed the supernatural wonders of the Yosemite area.

They were in big-game country then, and were restored to the vigor which made their advance into ever new and strange parts a joyous one. Perhaps it was because they had just been through barren country that some swore they had never seen better land than they found beyond the Sierras. But they had other reasons, notably the elsewhere unduplicated sight of sleek longhorn cattle and horses in amazing abundance.

They saw the great Bay of San Francisco and the Pacific itself before reaching the pastoral richness of which the San Juan Bautista Mission was the heart. This was pastoral California, remote from suspicious government officials; and a happy-go-lucky, isolated people were glad of something new in their lives. The brandy and wine cellars of the mission fathers were open to the mountain men, and the doors of prosperous ranchers, and the arms of señoritas.

Then there were horse races and shooting contests, together with the local sports of lassoing grizzly bears and pitting them

126

against bulls. There were fandangos by the score, and no work at all. This was Fiddlers' Green. It had everything that a trapper could ask for. Everything except beaver, that is.

In the meantime the man who had sent them was more prosaically engaged. Bonneville's leave of absence from the Army, issued in 1831, allowed him only two years of absence from duty. He was thus overstaying his leave by failing to return to his military station by the end of 1833.

Well after that he rode farther west than he had yet strayed, determined to see at first hand the operations of the Hudson's Bay Company along the lower Columbia which Jed Smith had reported. Dropping down by boat from Fort Walla Walla, Bonneville found the new and greatly enlarged Fort Vancouver, just begun when Jed had left the vicinity five years earlier. And in addition to having an imposing headquarters, Dr. John McLoughlin had a stronger-than-ever general grip on the country. Not wanting Americans in his domain, he refused to deal with Bonneville, just as he had done in the instance of Wyeth.

The latter had by then created a furor which was no part of his planning. After parting from Milton Sublette, Nathaniel had returned to Massachusetts, determined to win a place in the Western fur trade despite all the competition. How he came into bodily possession of the two Indian youths he brought with him is unimportant. He had picked them with care, though, one being a Nez Percé and the other a Flathead.

As Wyeth's interest in the West was purely commercial, his attitude toward these Indian props was utilitarian. In order to persuade people to invest money in his next venture, he planned to give lectures for which the nose-pierced and flat-pated lads would serve as good publicity in advance, and good scenery during the performance.

What Nathaniel probably didn't know was that at some time in the past a Catholic missionary from Canada had briefly visited the Flatheads and had stirred a longing for more knowledge of Christianity before going elsewhere. Through Hudson's Bay Company channels, apparently, a request for a special mission-

127

ary had been sent east. Knowledge of the plea seems to have been relayed to several sects of American Protestants; certainly Methodist leaders in New England and New York knew about it. No action had been taken, however, until Wyeth started touring with his two-freak sideshow.

When a hard-drinking opportunist began exhibiting his star attractions, he did so at a time when evangelical fervor was raking the United States from Maine to Florida. Boston had its share of those religiously on the peck; and the sight of a youngster with a warped cranium, and of another with a drilled nose, aroused a missionary zeal which had not been stirred by tales of the sadistic cruelty and rapine practiced by Indians who did not alter their features in the name of beauty. The Nez Percés in particular were a relatively enlightened tribe which dodged trouble when possible. Yet the harmless aesthetic ideals of these Indians were much more horrible to those who saw them as taking liberties with God's image than were the ferocious activities of savages who didn't change their physical appearance.

It was then that the petition of the Flatheads was acted upon, a Methodist minister named Jason Lee being appointed joint missionary to them and their neighboring mountain tribe. While this was being arranged, the man who had unwittingly brought it about went on with his preparations to bring trade goods to the next rendezvous.

He had arranged with Milton Sublette for the Rocky Mountain Fur Company to take over what he brought to the mountains. The former, though, was not at the great gathering of 1834, as earlier in the year his horse had rolled on his leg when falling. The resulting compound fracture had bred an infection which did not respond to treatment.

Learning of his brother's commitment, though, Bill Sublette had sent to Fitzpatrick asking him not to honor it. Perhaps it contradicted an agreement which other partners of the Rocky Mountain Fur Company had made with Cut Face. But in any case Wyeth was out of pocket. And then the concern he accused of bilking him went out of business.

Except for Fate Sublette, who had become primarily a trader, the mountain men were essentially fur hunters; and as in the instance of many another business, the profits went to the marketer, not the producer. The American Fur Company was founded on this realistic principle; that of its rival was not. For years the partners of the Rocky Mountain Fur Company had managed to disregard the actualities of commerce through more knowledge of the country than others had and the prestige they had earned as seniors of their craft. They had in fact lived as virtuosos of barter rather than businessmen, but the professionals of trade caught up with them and forced them to choose between art and Mammon.

Their choice was art: to continue to live in the wilderness they loved and to roam it as free agents. Yet in order to do that, they sacrificed their commercial independence to the great concern they had fought and beaten so often while operating out of nothing but their saddles and the winds which blew past them. So at the rendezvous of 1834 the Rocky Mountain outfit, no address but the West, dissolved itself. In its place there emerged the firm of Fitzpatrick, Milton Sublette (though absent at the time) and Bridger. Their market was McKenzie's Amfurco monopoly, to which they were pledged to turn over all their beaver.

Enraged but undaunted by his bad fortune this while, Wyeth packed his trade goods to Idaho's Portneuf River and built a post not far above where it joins the Snake. Called Fort Hall, the trading station was named for the most enthusiastic of his Eastern backers.

During that same period Missionary Jason Lee took a look at the members of his two prospective flocks and threw up his hands. The Flatheads, a kindly tribe, were especially profuse in their welcome, but Jason wanted no part of them. The rugged mountain country in which they lived also appalled the minister. But from Wyeth the Reverend Lee had learned that the country around the Columbia estuary more nearly resembled the Atlantic Seaboard. Ignoring the wishes of the people who had commissioned him, he passed up the tribes he was supposed to convert and went on to establish a mission in coastal Oregon.

৪৩ 24 ৪৩

A Pair of Caravanserais

HAVING FOR SOME years been out of the West, Jim Clyman enlisted for Black Hawk's War in 1832, serving in the same company with another long drink of water called Abe Lincoln. Although on good terms with his fellow volunteer, Jim later noted that there was little talk around the campfire concerning the former's chances of being President.

More to the Western point, Clyman also served at this time with a man called James Reed. In after years, Jim was to meet this fellow in the company of some California-bound pilgrims called the Donner Party.

Another Westerner who was active in the campaign against the Sac and Fox chief was Lieutenant Philip St. George Cooke. After its conclusion he was detailed as a recruiting officer for the Army's first dragoon, or mounted rifleman, regiment. This in turn had been an outgrowth of Bennet Riley's rage at having to police the Santa Fe Trail with foot soldiers helpless to pursue the horseback predators they were supposed to overawe.

A Virginian of the clan which produced the novelist John Esten Cooke and the poet Philip Cooke, their uncle had himself the gift for expressing himself on paper which Riley had utilized after his first exasperating tour of escort duty. But as Stephen Watts Kearny, executive officer of the new regiment, had also found the lieutenant verbally persuasive, he was sent into the Volunteer State, in hopes that it would live up to its reputation.

Stiff-necked where his sense of duty was involved, and not at all afraid to challenge superior rank, Cooke was a promising junior officer whom Kearny had to rescue from court-martial more than once. But he had a likable way with those not crowding him; and on this occasion it led him, among other things, to join the celebration with which Jackson, Tennessee, signified its approval of Congressional candidate Davy Crockett. It was a lively expression of the will of the people, and one whose flavor Cooke exquisitely preserved by quoting one West Tennessean's advice with respect to whiskey: "Good God, stranger! don't drink *that; this* is three weeks old."

How many recruits Philip St. George Cooke got while thus being regaled, he didn't record; but he must have been somewhat successful, for in 1833 the First Dragoons began training at Fort Leavenworth, built by and named for the now wiser pamperer of the Arikaras. While still in the boot-camp stage, though, the regiment was ordered to proceed south to Fort Gibson, in Oklahoma. Riddled by diseases there which included cholera, it didn't get around to performing the service for which it was created until 1834. In that year General Leavenworth led the three hundred well enough to keep their saddles into Pawnee and Comanche country—not on battle bent, but to show the harriers of Santa Fe Trail commerce that the Army now had horsemen as well as what the Indians had dubbed "walk-a-heaps."

That military gesture killed Leavenworth, while about one hundred and fifty more died or were unable to complete the trip. But the Indians were impressed, and the U.S. Cavalry had begun its long series of Western police actions.

Where the Santa Fe Trail crossed the Arkansas was by then no longer the terminal point for escort troops, for wagon tracks went on up the river to where Charles Bent had at last found a trading zone which he didn't reach too late. Frozen out on the upper Missouri and unprepared to compete in the Rockies, Bent had for years been looking for an unexploited area where he could be the dominant commercial power. Now he was building a huge headquarters post in the high plains along the upper Arkansas.

131

On the north bank of the river, it stood on American territory, as it had to; for the exorbitant Mexican system of duties would have ruined his venture in no time. As for competition, it didn't exist. There were large tribes—the Comanches, the Kiowas, the Arapahoes and the Pawnees—which would find his fort the most convenient to deal with. The post stood in good buffalo country, meaning that the Indians would feel confident of being self-sustaining while on the way to and fro. It was furthermore so situated that it would invite merchants plying either the Santa Fe Trail or another, somewhat to the west of the station, which ran directly to Taos.

In partnership with Bent was Ceran St. Vrain, who had been leader of the trapping expedition in which Tom Smith had become Peg-leg Smith. The adobe stronghold they built was 180 feet long by 140 wide, the walls being 14 feet high and a yard thick. Kittycorner from each other were a brace of towers, defended by small cannon and pitted with loopholes from which riflemen could control the interior of the fort, as well as approaches to it, in the event of rioting by Indian guests.

Without rioting, some guests misbehaved before the fort was completed in the summer of 1834. Southward-straying Shoshones conducted themselves with decorum while at the post but took a bunch of horses when they departed. Running across them, or at any rate some Shoshones, not much later, William Bent and certain companions killed three in order to make the point that the stock was not to be lifted from the Bent and St. Vrain post, commonly known as Bent's Fort.

The Bents weren't so hidebound where stock belonging to other people was concerned, a fact made apparent when Old Bill turned up during the post's first season. Williams had been with Joe Walker in California, but he had not returned with him.

Others had been fascinated by the way of life in California, or by the region's farming possibilities. What had taken Old Bill's eye, though, was the abundance of unwatched horses.

As Peg-leg Smith had done a few years before, he somehow

132

herded the animals across the deserts of Southern California and Arizona to New Mexico. While disposing of some at Taos, he had heard of the new fort on the Arkansas and had gone north to do business.

"Roll out a barrel," Williams was quoted as demanding, upon meeting Charles Bent at the fort's gate. And, after looking the mounts over, Charles did produce liquor as well as whatever else was asked for. Although the horses were gaunt, they were prime stock and would bring good prices when fattened in a region where buyers didn't require bills of sale.

Well east of South Pass, as it chanced, another post was being built at the same time. For Bill Sublette had decided to supply his company with the trading station it had never had, although the very prosperous firm of Sublette and Campbell had office premises and warehouses in St. Louis. The location chosen was a point near the confluence of Laramie Creek with the North Platte. When the wooden bastions of this post were completed, Cut Face christened it Fort William; but as the mountain men decided to call it Fort Laramie, that, for all practical purposes, was its name.

The site was remarkable on the score of not being located on a regularly navigable stream, as were all its predecessors except Bent's Fort. Fort Laramie was a post designed for overland commerce in a region where caravans were yet scarce, however numerous along the Santa Fe Trail.

Another unusual thing about this Western post was that it had not been built with the fur trade primarily in mind. What both Bill Sublette and the American Fur Company moguls knew ahead of the mountain men was that a sudden shift in European fashion trends had lessened the hatters' demand for beaver, long thought of as permanent. Ascendant, meanwhile, was a demand for buffalo hides, for use as sleigh and wagon robes, as well as for meeting the increased calls for leather by the expanding industrial age. Fort Laramie stood in the heart of buffalo country and was surrounded by tribes adept at hunting the animals now prized.

In order to increase the number of hide suppliers, Sublette invited the Sioux to move from their usual haunts farther to the north and look over the advantages of his post and its vicinity. The Dakotas did, and liked the area so much that they shifted the focal point of their activities to one which wedged them between the Crows and Pawnees, already their dearest enemies.

Yet the Sioux were not given much time to deal with the man at whose invitation they had moved. Within a few weeks after its completion Fort Laramie was sold by Bill Sublette and Campbell to the Rocky Mountain Fur Company, which soon became the firm of Fitzpatrick, Milton Sublette and Bridger.

As of 1835 it was a partnership of ailing men. Married to the pretty Shoshone girl who had helped him escape from her own people, Milton spent more time with Missouri doctors in 1834 and '35 than he did with Mountain Lamb. Even when the man who had operated on Tom Smith became single-legged himself, his troubles weren't over. A bone infection developed which was not cured by several shortenings of the original stump. He came back to the mountains with the latest thing in the way of artificial limbs, a rubber shank; but he never got the satisfaction out of it that Peg-leg did of the one he whittled for himself with his bowie.

In 1835 Tom Fitzpatrick earned another *nom de guerre*, and one more commonly applied to him than White Hair, the hard way. For in a brush with the Blackfeet a gun he was firing exploded. Because of the three fingers of which the accident robbed his right fist, the Indians called him by a name variously translated as Broken Hand and Bad Hand.

The arrowheads which a Blackfoot had put in his back three years earlier had continued to torture Jim Bridger, furthermore. But in his case relief was at hand in 1835.

The story of why it was available is one with enough curious leads and coincidences to furnish a dozen mystery novels. Abbreviated, it can be approached by the problem with which the Hudson's Bay Company found itself faced, as of the year before.

The chain of events leading up to the arrival of Jason Lee in western Oregon has already been dealt with here. Up to that time the company had stood firm on its policy of discouraging Americans showing a disposition to linger about the Columbia estuary. And because the company controlled the region's Indians as well as all its trading facilities and sources of supply, disapproval by the Canadian concern was equivalent to canceling the joint occupancy which England and the United States had agreed upon; for it made any enterprise desired by a citizen of the latter country impossible of realization. Any enterprise but one involving religion, that is.

The Reverend Jason Lee had double-crossed the Methodists and the Flatheads alike; but he was a man of God and presumably up to something worthy of applause. Dr. John McLoughlin decided that he should be made welcome, so the worm stayed in the Hudson's Bay Company's apple.

It was a capable worm, if not along religious lines. Jason hated the Indians of Oregon as much as he had the Nez Percés. His missionary efforts were never more than halfhearted, but he talked a good game of Indian conversion for two reasons. The first was his need of funds from the East and the general co-operation of the Methodist Church. The other was his shrewdness in seeing that McLoughlin would tolerate him as a missionary, but would force him out of the country, if he found out what the minister really had on his mind.

This was the establishment of a colony of white Americans, of whom he expected to be the temporal as well as spiritual chief. For he promptly grasped the possibilities of coastal Oregon, with its mild climate, rich soil, abundant rainfall, as well as forests to supply building material and fuel. He mentioned these things, too, while stressing the need of people to help him save the Indians of the vicinity, painted as being in need of such rescue above all others.

Brought to the Atlantic Seaboard, his letters were published, in some instances, as well as passed around. They made their point, too, for their readers included people anxious to earn heavenly crowns at the cost of converting savages, while having a chance to prosper amid pleasant earthly surroundings in the meantime.

Thoroughly subdued by the company, the Indians in the shadow of Fort Vancouver were a sad lot rather than an especially savage one. Compared with any of the fierce tribes of the Great Plains, they were gentle; but Jason Lee's propaganda convinced Easterners that it was the unspectacular natives of western Oregon—not the rampant Blackfeet, Sioux or Comanches—who most needed to be taught to mend their ways.

Methodists were not alone in this point of faith. It thus came about that among those in attendance at the rendezvous on the Green in 1835 were two Oregon-bound Presbyterian missionaries. Of these one was Dr. Marcus Whitman, a New York minister who doubled as a physician and surgeon. While studying medicine, he probably never dreamed that he was destined to win a high place in mountain-man lore by removing Indian arrowheads from the muscular back of Old Gabe Bridger.

Perhaps the most bizarre surgical operation in American medical annals, it was attended by hundreds of trappers and double that number of Indian warriors, perched on any eminence which gave them a view of the proceedings. Working to the tune of cheers and excited comments in sundry languages, Whitman cut through the gristle which had grown around the most deeply imbedded of the iron gaffs, and unhitched it from the bone in which a shoulder of it was hooked. He could have been the head medicine man of any tribe in the mountains after accomplishing that feat.

Bonneville was not among the awed onlookers, as he had finally left the West some months earlier. More than a year late in reporting back for duty in the Army, he had taken the precaution of writing to request an extension of his leave; but his petition had got lost in some crack in the floor of the War Department. A trip which had drained his pocketbook and gained him no profit therefore almost wound up by ruining his career as well. All that saved him was the interest in the West owned by the man in the White House.

Actually Bonneville was court-martialed and dismissed from the service, although not for very long. After ascertaining that the cashiered officer had brought back information which confirmed and enlarged upon Jed Smith's report, Old Hickory Jackson ignored his generals and had the Captain reinstated.

‣ 25 ‣

Colonel Bowie's Bite of Hay

IN TEXAS, HOUSTON the Raven ceased to be Big Drunk. Pulling himself together as none besides Andrew Jackson thought he could, he kept his own counsel while seeming to go along with the prevailing will of the American colonists.

Separation from Coahuila and Mexican statehood for Texas were the things they wanted, and they held a convention in 1833 at which a formal petition was drawn up. Stephen Austin then took it in person to the supposedly liberal administration which had been fostered at Mexico City by General Santa Anna.

Bowie had represented Bexar at the colonial congress, but in that same year an event occurred which killed his interest in all things Texan for the time being. Cholera took Ursula Bowie and their two children out of Jim's life. Turning his back on even the San Saba mine, he rode east of the Sabine and was not seen west of it for another year.

The plague of that season snuffed out John Austin's spark, too, denying the services of this skeely skipper and resourceful partisan to men who were soon to feel the need of them. For the news from the nation's capital was all bad for men of democratic principles, as Santa Anna worked steadily at forging a dictatorship for himself.

As months slipped by, leaving grievances unredressed, the colonists again became divided. A minority belonged to the War Party, anxious to take the field with Patrick Henry's words in their mouths. Most were of the Peace Party, whose members felt that only ruin could come of defiance.

Some of their confidence in the uses of arbitration went from the pacifists, though, when emissary Stephen Austin was at length imprisoned in Mexico City, where he languished for eighteen months. Ben Milam was also incarcerated, though not at the capital. Asserting the rights of Texians, as the colonists called themselves, in Coahuila, Ben was first put behind bars there and then shifted to Monterey in Nuevo León. Here he ate prison fare in the same calaboose which had once held his friend James Long.

Bowie hopefully returned to Texas, upon learning of the possibility of another colonial uprising, but the Peace Party discouraged girding for storm. This in turn was a cause of concern to men anxious for the thunderheads in which they best operated. As Buck Travis wrote to Jim, the chances of a revolt against Mexican oppression didn't glitter with promise. Noting that many were for submission, in spite of a steadily worsening situation, he went on, "I don't know the minds of the people upon the subject, but had they a bold and determined leader, I am inclined to think they would kick against it."

That leader was making his way with a persistence and patience not to be expected of a man who'd thrown away one career because of disappointment in love. Yet it was not strange that Travis hadn't marked Houston down as the man he was hoping for. In addition to the fact that Sam had had no military experience worth noting since he had served as a subaltern more than twenty years earlier, he was not doing anything which would lose him the confidence of the still dominant Peace Party. He was, in fact, not ambitious of being the fiery John Hancock of the revolution he was working for, but its deliberate Washington.

Meanwhile the first to kick against Mexican tyranny again was Travis himself. Soldiers had once more been moved into Anahuac, this time for the purpose of exacting outrageously high customs duties. Having viewed their activities for just so long,

Buck drummed together a volunteer company which ambushed the Mexicans and gave them marching orders.

As Travis learned then, if he hadn't known it before, pacifists would much rather kill countrymen who disagree with them than foreigners engaged in doing them an injury. Members of the Peace Party were all for turning Buck over to the Mexican authorities, who no doubt would have shot him. But the return of Stephen Austin, his notions about the possibility of solving problems by arbitration changed by what he had seen and suffered in Mexico, robbed the faction he had once led of its talking points.

In that same month of September 1835, another Mexican military move caused an explosion elsewhere than at Anahuac. Commanding at the key fortress of the Alamo by then was the Colonel Urgatechea from whom John Austin had once taken the stronghold at Velasco. Uneasy about the presence of a cannon which had been given to the frontier town of Gonzales, for defense against Indian attacks, the Colonel sent troops to commandeer it. Rallying settlers, the War Party gentry of Gonzales spread a banner which read, "Come and take it." The Mexican captain did what he could, but it wasn't enough. Rebellion had flared not only in the coastal colonies but within seventy miles of what was then being called San Antonio as well as San Fernando de Bexar.

Due to Bowie's reconnoitering of the Mexican port of Matamoros, it was learned that five hundred additional troops were on their way to the Alamo, where General Martin de Perfecto Cos was due to replace Urgatechea as commander. That plain threat of military rule won more recruits from the Peace Party. The decision that the Mexican State of Texas was in revolt against the federal government, moreover, was formally made at a convention at which Sam Houston was chosen commander in chief of the Texian Army.

Somewhat prior to that appointment, or early in October of 1835, volunteer troops who had chosen Stephen Austin as general had already taken the field. Not wanting to deal with men who had only pledged themselves to serve for a couple of months, Houston busied himself at forming a cadre of a regular army and let the pick-up one do its best.

Although Austin's generalship had little bearing on what occurred, his volunteers did very well for a while. When the garrisons at Goliad (known to James Long as La Bahia) and Lipantitlan fell to them, only the Alamo stood for Mexican military power in Texas. Determining to take this fort, then commanded by Santa Anna's brother-in-law, General Cos, the Texians advanced on Bexar.

In command of the vanguard was Colonel Jim Bowie, assisted by a Captain James Fannin. The latter was a Georgian, ambitious of military laurels, who had recently come from the United States. The plight of the Texian colonists had called to many Americans, who had come to help individually, or in such units as the New Orleans Grays.

At Concepción Mission an intercepting force sent out by Cos was met by the men under Bowie and Fannin late in October. What took place was competently described by Colonel Jim in a report to Austin.

The engagement commenced at about the hour of eight o'clock A.M., on Wednesday, 28th of October, by the deadly crack of a rifle on the extreme right. The engagement was immediately general. The discharge from the enemy was one continuous blaze of fire, whilst that from our lines was more slowly delivered but with good aim and deadly effect, each man retired under cover of the hill and timber, to give place to others while he reloaded. The battle had not lasted ten minutes, before a brass double fortified four pounder was opened on our lines with a heavy discharge of grape and canister, at the distance of about eighty yards from the right flank of the first division, and a charge sounded. But the cannon was cleared as if by magic, and check put to the charge.

What was not in Jim's report was the testimony of others to the effect that he led a charge of his own and captured the cannon, ruining the enemy's strategy and morale. In consequence, as he went on to write, "A small detachment of ninety-two men gained a most decisive victory over the main army of the central government, being at least four to one, with the loss of only one brave soldier, and none wounded; whilst the enemy suffered in killed and wounded near 100, from the best information we can gather."

Retreating to Bexar, the Mexicans held the town and its fortress. Advancing, the Texians commenced a siege which was memorable for one break in the routine of watching for a bear which wouldn't come out of its cave.

Among the notable frontiersmen present was Deaf Smith. A New Yorker raised in Mississippi, Smith had moved farther west, perhaps to be free of a place where it was known that his name was Erastus. He had come to Texas, perhaps in 1817 as a hunter, perhaps in 1821 to join Long, or perhaps in 1824 as a colonist; authorities differ here. But when he emerged from a misty past and took a certain place in history, he was both hard of hearing and recognized as about the most able plainsman in a province where maneuvering in the outdoors was every man's profession.

Possibly the Mexican señorita he married in 1826 called him Erastus, but to all others he was Deaf Smith, and thus is called the Texas county now named for him. But if he couldn't hear, his vision was phenomenal, by night or day. It was popularly believed that he could see around a corner; and this man was one of the operatives of Captain William Travis, chief of scouts for the Texians at Bexar.

Colonel Urgatechea, as Deaf had found out before the siege began, had gone south for the purpose of getting pay for the garrison. So when the condor-eyed plainsman saw a train of loaded mules approaching Bexar as dawn was whitening one day, he had no doubt that he beheld the approach of thousands of pesos.

Silver and a risk to run for it? Bowie was in the saddle before Deaf had finished reporting. Rounding up sixty other prompt riders, they dashed forth to make new and different history in an engagement known as the Grass Fight.

In the rolling country south of San Antonio, the Texians in-

tercepted the pack animals and an outnumbering force of protecting cavalry. This unit lost its advantage, though, as soon as
Jim grounded his men and deployed them as snipers. Forced to
dismount in turn, the Mexicans began firing away, too, while
support for both sides streamed out of the Alamo and the Texian
camp respectively.

When the struggle was finally decided in favor of the frontiersmen, they were free to seize the prize for which they had put
their lives in jeopardy. It consisted of bundles of wild hay, reaped
to feed the hungry animals of the surrounded San Fernando
garrison.

Despairing of being able to keep all the mounts of his cavalry
alive after losing the Grass Fight, General Cos decided to send
one hundred of them down to the Rio Grande, there to fatten
on pasturage in safety. A sensible move, it failed of paying off,
because Buck Travis was on the alert and captured their guards
as well as the horses.

🙐 26 🙐

The Gathering of Blades at the Alamo

BEFORE THE ASSAULT which climaxed the siege of Bexar,
Bowie seems to have been busy elsewhere on a mission assigned
by Houston, while Captain Travis did not have the rank to lead
an army where colonels were as numerous as kings in the one
which hammered at Troy. The man who finally got tired of trying to starve the Mexicans out was Long's former chief lieutenant, then known as Colonel Milam.

At length escaping from prison at Monterey, Ben had made his
way back into Texas just in time to participate in the attack on
the Mexican garrison at Goliad. Now, or in December of 1835,
he by-passed the caution of Austin's replacement, General Burle-
son, and called for volunteers to join him in a storming party.

Bexar was taken as the result of Milam's daring and capacity to inspire others with it, but Ben was not among those who celebrated the victory. While shooting at troops in the Alamo from his position on a rooftop of the taken town, he received the bullet which ended all gunning on his part.

It could almost be said that when Bexar's fortress fell, so also did the army which took it. Effective in action, the volunteer corps came apart after achieving its goal of freeing Texas of Mexican garrisons. A small force, largely composed of outsiders who had rushed to get in on the excitement, stayed on at the Alamo. Most of the Texians proper went on home as coolly as though they had never defied the authority of a government with the power to put many more soldiers in the field than they had yet dealt with.

Meanwhile Sam Houston was finding his efforts to put together a body of regulars who'd stay on the job hampered by a controlling council, itself in rebellion against Governor Henry Smith. Reserving the right to appoint all Sam's subordinates, the council wound up with two other outright commanders in chief and one plain commander in chief of volunteers. These were all for attacking the Mexican depot port of Matamoros first and organizing militarily later.

In the Raven's army, but not at his command, were troops jointly being jockeyed by a Colonel Johnson and a Dr. Grant. At Goliad there was another commander in chief in the person of Fannin, upped from captain to colonel. This was a rank in the regular army which Houston had been unable to obtain for Bowie, notwithstanding the latter's record of distinguished service. The chief reason seems to have been that Jim was remembered for land speculations of which members of the council disapproved on nonmilitary grounds.

The moves Sam was free to make were few, but he retained the loyalty of at least this man, whose good sense and soldierly willingness weren't blanketed by personal ambition. In January of 1836 Houston sent Jim Bowie to Bexar to determine whether the Alamo was worth defending, in view of its condition and the military wherewithal needed to repulse a soon-expected Mexican assault.

At the time Colonel Bowie had been engaged in trying to raise a regiment of volunteers. With the few he had so far enlisted, he rode up the San Antonio from Goliad, arriving at Bexar on January 19. He had been the Alamo's near neighbor during the years of his residence in the town across the river. Now he was called upon to assess the familiar.

Although ranked as a fort and scarred by mementos of numerous bloody struggles for its possession, the Alamo had been built as a mission for the conversion of Indians. Its disadvantages as a military stronghold were implicit in the alien nature of the purpose for which it was designed. The walls adjacent to the chapel were not built to sustain cannon fire, nor did they offer adequate protection to defending riflemen.

Appraising the premises, Bowie found that it would have required something like a thousand men to garrison it properly, whereas Colonel Joseph C. Neill had 104. Not all of these were armed, because in default of promised pay some had exchanged their rifles for walking-around money. As to larger guns, there were fourteen, where forty would have been preferable. Covering the approach from the east there was but one cannon, mounted in the apse of the chapel.

Yet if Jim perceived that the Alamo was poor stuff as defense bastions go, he realized that it was still the best which Texas had to offer. If invading Mexicans could not be stopped here, where there was something to work with, where was the next line on which a stand could be made? Both on the San Antonio, Bexar and Goliad formed a natural defense axis which the abandonment of either would invalidate.

With these points in mind Bowie informed Houston and Governor Smith that he was not only of the belief that the Alamo should be held but that he himself would remain to bear the gaff of his decision. "Colonel Neill and myself," he wrote, "have come to the solemn resolution that we will rather died in these ditches than give them up to the enemy."

144

Houston at the time was occupied in trying to convince the council-appointed commanders in chief that he had been elected by the citizenry of Texas, not they. Hearing from Jim, the Governor did what he could to strengthen the Alamo's garrison. As in Sam's case, there were not many upon whom Henry Smith could call with the assurance that he would be obeyed; but Buck Travis had not joined the chickenheads then engaged in trying to split one very small army into four pieces.

Being a colonist and strong politically, now that the War Party had triumphed, Buck had been accepted as a regular and promoted, where Bowie had been spurned. Colonel Travis was not happy about leaving the business of building up his cavalry regiment, in order to go to an ill-garrisoned fort where somebody else was in command; but he was a soldier and acted like one. On February 3, accordingly, he and the thirty men he'd so far recruited checked in at the Alamo.

Something over a week later Colonel Neill chose to take a vacation before dying in the trench outerworks which Jim had referred to as ditches. In so doing he left two officers who had been friends and allies in a state of disgruntlement shared by factions in the garrison. When absenting himself Neill had passed command on to Colonel Travis as the next of rank in the regular army. Following frontier tradition, however, the non-Texian volunteers who predominated had held an election at which they chose the famous Bowie, known to them by reputation as Buck was not.

The latter, hot at having to share command with a militia colonel, accused Bowie of slackness, because little was being done to strengthen the fort. Irked at having been denied a commission, Bowie refused to yield voted honors. As for Buck's complaints, Jim knew the futility, furthermore, of trying to drive men who would demand their back pay before they consented to do any hard labor.

In the meantime the garrison grew as small groups of volunteers, riding or walking from the United States, were sent to Bexar by Governor Smith. Already cheered by the presence of the renowned Jim Bowie, the men of the Alamo got another boost in morale when Davy Crockett eased his long frame and rifle into the fortress.

The young woodsman who had served under Jackson against the Creeks had grown into a figure whose name was almost as much of a national byword as Old Hickory himself. His skill with the rifle was such that it was popularly believed that only Mike Fink had ever bested him, and then only because Davy had scrupled to shoot an object from Mrs. Fink's noggin. Crockett's rough-and-tumble fights, his mighty bear hunts, and his position as the arch nemesis of raccoons had given him epic stature among a race of foresters who also reveled in his skill as a raconteur unharnessed to fact. He had conquered the Atlantic Seaboard, too, for his deliberately picturesque dress and speech had at first scandalized and then entertained the gentry of Washington and other Eastern cities.

In Congress Davy had opposed Jackson, their one point of agreement being that Texas was properly a part of the United States by virtue of the Louisiana Purchase. He was no longer in Congress because of Old Hickory, who was also indirectly responsible for Crockett's arrival at Bexar. Davy had sworn that if he wasn't re-elected, he'd go to help fellow Tennesseans gain their liberty in Texas. Making good, after Jackson purged the House of Representatives of a troublemaker, Colonel Crockett led twelve followers to the fort on the San Antonio.

There were some others, worthy of personal note, present. According to the belief of the family to which Joe Walker belonged, his brother John helped garrison the Alamo. James Bonham, of South Carolina, did that, and so did young William Oury, of Virginia.

Crockett reached Bexar on February 11, 1836. He and his comrades in arms had just a week and a half in which to enjoy the señoritas and cantinas of San Antonio before the punitive expedition which the federal government launched against the rebels of Texas put in its appearance. Anticipated, it had not been expected so soon. Only a cloudburst which bogged down

146

the mounted Mexican vanguard, indeed, saved most of the garrison from being caught *hors de combat* at a fandango.

But the men who had taken things so easily when no emergency was in sight were as ready for war as for play. Back in the Alamo, they accepted the determination of their leaders to hold the fort, in spite of their weakness in numbers and weapons, until reinforcements could be sent.

Sure that they would be, once it was learned in eastern Texas that invaders were north of the Rio Grande, Travis drew up dispatches for couriers, while Bowie led a furious drive to make up for lost time in the matter of defense preparations. They had one more day of grace. On February 23 Santa Anna, ranking general of Mexico as well as its president, arrived in Bexar, learned the scantiness of the opposition and demanded the surrender of the Alamo.

Hardly pausing in their preparations for defense, Jim and Buck sent the flag-of-truce bearers back with the same message which the men of Gonzales had sent when asked to give up their cannon. The attackers then proceeded to establish siege headquarters in Bexar, although they learned that they must stay farther away from small-arms fire than Mexican military experts thought necessary. Strolling into view, after the bearers of rejected surrender terms had withdrawn across the river, one of Santa Anna's men astonished his comrades by dropping before the crack of a rifle reached their ears. Davy Crockett had drawn bead and pulled trigger for first blood of the siege.

❦ 27 ❦

Fighters and a Fainéant

I T W A S N O T until several days after the arrival of Santa Anna at Bexar that all of his troops, complete with supporting artillery, were on the scene. Assembled, the besiegers of the Alamo numbered better than 6000.

Mustered within the fortress were something over 150 men, not all fit for duty. Jim Bowie joined these as the result of a heavy fall while he was trying to help mount a disabled cannon. Pneumonia seized him before he could throw off the shock to his system. Hardly able to stir, he passed word to the volunteers that Buck Travis would be sole commander, pending his own recovery.

Sure of himself and the mettle of his men, Travis also felt certain that he could give the rest of the Texian army time to heal its fractures and rally to his aid. By then, though, the men upon whom he had been counting had almost entirely left the field. Commanders in Chief Johnson and Grant, having been forced to give up their projected Matamoros expedition because they couldn't enlist enough followers, had retired from the war entirely. The only effective force left, aside from the Alamo garrison, consisted of about four hundred men under Fannin, almost all of them volunteers from the States.

Mutinous to Houston, Fannin ignored the call for help brought to him by Colonel Bonham and subsequent couriers from Bexar. Their hands tied, Houston and Smith could do nothing in answer to the appeals for reinforcements they received.

While the messengers from the Alamo were galloping fruitlessly hither and yon, Santa Anna was methodically placing batteries for an artillery envelopment of the fort. Travis balked it with cannon as well as he could, but the strength of the garrison lay in the fire of skilled riflemen. From redoubts and other outposts they bit at the enclosure and made the operation an expensive one; but the time came when encirclement by the big guns was complete.

Although the sniping of squirrel hunters continued, the outposts were steadily pushed back, while news from the outside was negative or none. Bonham's first report of failure to secure aid was matched by another he brought later on. A series of

148

more men—William Oury was one who did so on February 29—
slipped through the Mexican lines by night; but they were still
looking for somebody to guide back days after they reached the
Texian settlements.

The solitaire who succeeded in bringing any reinforcements
was one John W. Smith, who had been sent to the "come and
take it" town of Gonzales. En route he met Captain George Kimball and thirty-two gallant followers, riding to join men whose
situation they knew to be desperate past the ability of any small
detachment to help.

Under Smith's guidance they won through to the Alamo the
night after the one during which Oury had stolen out of it. And
behind them sped Bonham, back again from Goliad.

A schoolmate of Buck's in South Carolina, James Butler Bonham had come to Texas only the year before. Possibly through
the influence of Travis, this newcomer had been given the colonelcy denied to Bowie; but no matter for that. Dispatched to
Fannin a second time, and once more refused by that fainéant,
Colonel Bonham rode back to the Alamo alone, to stand with its
defenders when the inevitable took place.

It began to do so a few days later. During the intervening
period the besieging batteries had moved ever closer, some providing covering fire as the others advanced. On March 5 a wall
of the fortress was breached, and Santa Anna was ready to make
his final play.

Against the advice of his commanders, who had already lost
more men to frontier marksmanship than they liked to think
about, the President of Mexico decided on an attack by successive waves of infantry equipped with scaling ladders. Some
four thousand men were detailed for this action, while another
thousand made up a reserve column. To the tune of "Degüello,"
a wild trumpet and drum call whose meaning was "assassin," the
Mexicans advanced in the night, scaling ladders to the fore,
bayonet-lengthened guns behind.

The worn men of the Alamo had largely fallen asleep during
the respite from cannon fire which Santa Anna had ordered with

just such a possibility in mind. Instantly alert, though, Buck Travis gave the rallying cry and leaped to command the battery which had been moved to guard the fort's shattered sector. Stationing themselves at this and other threatened points, the American riflemen waited until their foes were near enough to offer individual targets in the dark. There then began an apocalyptic reaping of troops attacking shoulder to shoulder.

The first assault never reached the fort from any side. In the course of the second, ladders were planted, but the men who swarmed up them were crumpled by rifle butts, shot by pistols and slashed by imitations of Bowie's famous blade. The "Degüello" went on howling for slaughter, though, and eventually the men it maddened broke over the north wall of the fortress, the men behind pushing the doomed front-rankers, whose bodies yet shielded their upsurging comrades.

It cost the Mexicans 1600 men, in slain alone, to enter the Alamo, but they were eventually pouring into its plaza over all the environing walls; next they were in the court before the chapel, and lastly inside that citadel. There the killing went on until it had to stop unless the Mexicans turned on each other in their frenzy to do as the "Degüello" bade.

Just how Bonham and Kimball died there is now no record to show, but die they did, for all the men of the Alamo fell there and then. Travis was slain near the battery whose slaughterous grape fire he had directed. Crockett died in the court, a tangle of seventeen battered Mexican corpses showing how effectively he and two of his Tennesseans had swung their bulletless rifles. Bowie, in sick bay, was one of the last to go; but he took enemies with him, too. All but dead from pneumonia and focusing with difficulty because of the fever consuming him, he pistoled two of his assailants before bayonets dug in and lifted him. A Mrs. Dickenson, a feminine inmate of the fortress who survived through the gallantry of a Mexican officer, reported that she saw Jim's body tossed from soldier to soldier, each one using the blade at the end of his gun to rip a man past caring.

So, on March 6, 1836, the Alamo fell. But because Bowie had

decided that it must be defended at all costs, and because Travis had carried that choice out, the Texians were given a second chance after the first had been thrown away through the stupidity of the provisional government's guiding council. For the appeals from the Alamo had at last had the effect of bringing citizens together who were in no frame of mind to listen to schemes for self-advancement on the part of spurious commanders in chief. If they gathered too late to try to save the men who died for them at Bexar, they stood behind Houston. Again elected Texian war chief while the siege was still in progress, the Raven at last had a fighting force ready to give ear to military reason.

The news was worse before it got better, though, due to the fatal indecision of Fannin. If ever a man was lucky to be able to hide behind martyrdom because he had been shot by the enemy, it was this fellow.

Purloiner of power without the courage to use it, he had refused to help the men of the Alamo either by sending supporting detachments or creating diversionary action. After Houston had been reaffirmed as the commander in sole authority, Fannin had remained mutinous. Lastly, having insisted upon staying at Goliad against Sam's orders, he lost his nerve at the approach of a strong Mexican force and fled from behind walls which he might have been able to defend against superior numbers and was surrounded where he couldn't effectively resist. Perforce he then let the Mexicans make prisoners of the men he'd kept from making any effective contribution to the Texian cause.

He turned them over to butchers, moreover, although in this case the Judas goat was slain, too. Maddened by the shattering blows which had been dealt his army by the dead men of Bexar, Santa Anna ordered the massacre of Fannin's entire command. On March 26 it was largely carried out by musketeers who made a mass slaughter of prisoners herded unsuspectingly within range.

Herman Ehrenberg survived the carnage, however. Missed by the first volley but dropping as though shot, he managed to creep away through deep grass and brush unobserved.

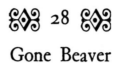

Gone Beaver

DURING THE DOZEN years which followed Ashley's place-
ment of trappers west of the Rockies, the life of the mountain
men had been led under relatively unchanging conditions. The
same Indian tribes, their numbers undiminished, lived as they
had done since they had been first encountered. The white men
had not come among the mountains in sufficient quantity to
alter tribal customs; nor had their advent changed the natural
history of the region in any respect but one. Although beaver
were still plentiful here and there, the streams where they
swarmed in pristine abundance were rare as well as distant from
the original good hunting grounds.

So although the trade was as risky as ever, the take was no
longer what it had been, and the work was harder, because the
readily accessible streams had been the first to be depleted of fur
in quantity. By 1835 there remained only two sectors of the
Rockies where trapping was prime. Of these one was the headwaters of the Missouri, still jealously guarded by the Blackfeet,
while the other was dispersed amidst the terrific jumble of
Colorado's mountains.

But wherever the free trappers turned now, they met the competition of the American Fur Company. Brigade leaders of the
latter were by then experienced mountain men, too; and they
had the wherewithal to buy from the Indians at prices the independents couldn't match.

Such was the background of a quarrel which won a place in
the lore of the West during the year in question. Trapping in the
vicinity of the headwaters of the Platte, Kit Carson was in Arapaho country. So, too, was an Amfurco brigade led by Andy

Drips, once an associate of William Vanderburgh. On the way into the mountains Kit had stayed in an Arapaho village long enough to have fallen in love with a young squaw named Singing Wind. While he was away, one of Andy's brigade had taken a less spiritual look at the same girl. A huge Frenchman, his name has been passed down in several versions, none of them especially Gallic. Some have given it as Shunar, which will serve to identify him as well as any.

This trapper saw his chance to get next to Singing Wind at a tribal frolic called the spoon dance, whose fundamental principles were much the same as the paleface amusement known as post office. Arapaho debutantes, each equipped with a ladle full of soup, would line up vis-à-vis a line of bucks or mountain men who might be guests of the camp. As the fellow who got to mouth the spoon of any girl also got to mouth her, there was considerable maneuvering on the part of both sexes to see that the right lips were first served with soup. As this couldn't be spilled without disqualifying a girl and rendering her uncaressable, the sport was one requiring finesse rather than roughhouse. Shunar, though, had ignored the rules by grabbing Singing Wind and spooning without benefit of spoon.

This had so enraged the girl that she would have nothing further to do with the Frenchman. He on his part watched his time and attempted a rape which was only foiled by the complexities of the leather chastity belt she wore in conformance with tribal dictates.

The Arapaho men were a lecherous lot, but they stood on one point of sexual morality. The squaw of any member of the tribe was fair game for forcing when her husband was away, unless she wound herself up in a tangle of thongs when retiring. It was perfectly good form to sneak into any husbandless tepee to see whether a woman had thought to take this precaution; but if she had, that was supposed to conclude the episode. And the lighter girdle worn by unmarried women at all times was counted as sure a charm against molestation. Shunar's attempted violation of this principle profoundly shocked men who stopped at nothing else; and the Arapahoes darkly suspected that all pale-faces were cast in the Frenchman's mold.

Returning from a trapping session full of honorable attentions, Kit was cold-shouldered by Singing Wind's family. Carson was still looking for a way of getting back into their good graces when the party of free trappers he was with found Andy Drips's brigade camped nearby.

When the servants of a powerful company meet independents whom their concern is bent on putting out of business there is always the possibility of trouble. In this case Shunar chose to aggravate the free trappers by invading their camp with malice in his medicine bag. A man whose mighty thews had accustomed him to shoving people around without getting bruised in turn, he was a flannelmouth who didn't keep the cloth clean; and he waved it about in the course of saying he could lick any American in the mountains.

Abuse from the cause of his broken romance primed Kit, who rose to the stretch of his five foot four and said that if the other meant business, he would take him on with knives, tomahawks or guns. Not expecting a contest in which weapons could countermand his superiority in size, Shunar had to agree or crawfish. He picked a rifle, to be fired from ahorseback, while Carson, also mounted, was armed with a pistol.

Having the piece with the greater range, the Frenchman fired first. A good shot from the saddle, it clipped a lock from Kit's pow; but by the time his shorn hair drifted to the ground Carson was near enough to sling a pistol ball along his antagonist's forearm and into the flesh of an elbow. Having learned about duels from Kit, Shunar begged off and was not around when the mountain man put the approved ending to such an episode by marrying Singing Wind.

But 1835 was not a good year for another aspirant of the fur trade, in the person of Nat Wyeth. What he had counted on, when he had had the brass to commandeer an unused island in the Columbia estuary overlooked by Fort Vancouver, had seemed a sound bet. His plan had been to ship from Boston to this depot goods which he could cordelle up the Columbia and Snake to his post in Idaho. Successful, he would have been able to undersell all competition and beat the other mountain traders at last. But Wyeth's ship was wrecked in transit from the East, and with it his well-conceived and boldly pushed scheme.

In the upshot, 1836 saw the Hudson's Bay Company in possession of Fort Hall, and thus more deeply entrenched in American territory than ever before. Probably because no one else wanted it, Wyeth for long retained title to the island at the mouth of the Willamette, which he never saw again.

But while he was preparing to pull up his stakes in the mountains, others were moving into them. For in June of 1836 Broken Hand Fitzpatrick led out of Fort Laramie an American Fur Company caravan which was trailed by several wagons. In one of them rode Milton Sublette, no longer able to mount a horse but determined to attend a last rendezvous, held that year on Horse Creek.

He did it, and so did the two women who had also crossed the Great Divide on wheels. The first palefaces of their sex to come within hundreds of miles of the Great Basin, these were a curiosity to the natives of the region, who must have regarded the white race as one created monosexually.

One of the pair, a sumptuous blonde, was an abiding delight to mountain men, who had gone for years without seeing a feminine member of their own kind. This was Narcissa, the bride of Dr. Marcus Whitman, surgeon extraordinary to Old Gabe Bridger. A sincere missionary, though no more fond of Indians than was Jason Lee, the Doctor had gone east to wed a helpmeet with whom to share his altruistic drudgery in Oregon.

Major, or Black, Harris, Joe Meek and Fitzpatrick were among those for whom she held court. Southerners on the one hand and an Irishman on the other, they knew how to tell Narcissa she was appreciated; and a genuinely pious woman, who wasn't to have much else in the way of joy in the West, had a splendid time being adored by the hellions of Horse Creek.

Although others were to follow it, this was the last great rendezvous, for it was the last one in which Amfurco showed a major degree of interest. When the books covering the year before were posted, Bill Sublette's foresight in placing Fort Laramie where he did was justified by sales figures which showed that more dollars had been returned by buffalo hides than by beaver peltries. With the price of beaver continuing to drop as the fashion of wearing cloth hats remained dominant, the American Fur Company bought Fort Laramie from Fitzpatrick and his partners. Trading there then overshadowed the once coveted mountain market.

At the close of the Horse Creek gathering, Fitzpatrick took the Whitmans and a companion missionary couple named Parker on to Fort Hall, whence they could proceed west by water. Asked by the Doctor what he meant to charge for his services, Tom wondered aloud how much Marcus had charged Old Gabe for taking iron out of his back. Then they shook hands over a scoreless tie, and White Hair trotted back toward Fort Laramie.

There Milton Sublette died in 1836, as repeated carvings had failed to rid him of the poison which had for two years been draining his once great strength. Mountain Lamb then became the bride of Joe Meek, whom she had also helped to rescue from Shoshone wrath by holding the getaway mounts provided by her father.

Nat Wyeth, still stubbornly trying to win a foothold in Western commerce, was also at Fort Laramie pursuant to the Horse Creek rendezvous. Before the summer was over, though, he was making his way to Bent's Fort.

Charles had been in Missouri earlier, gathering supplies for his store in Taos as well as for the big post on the Arkansas. Although his westward-bound caravan had got through safely, the Comanches had kidnaped two of his mule skinners. Striplings new to the Santa Fe Trail, they had gone hunting against Bent's orders. Only their youth saved them; the Indians would have slain grown men, but they had a policy of adopting male captives young enough to be trained as Comanche warriors. One of the sixteen-year-olds proved a bad investment, but Jim Hobbs made good as a savage, in which capacity he flourished for many months.

Not knowing the fate of his lost drivers, though, Charles had led his ox-drawn wagons on to his fort, and so was present when Wyeth asked for hospitality. He got it, but no accompanying word of encouragement for what he had in mind. The Bents and St. Vrain were no more desirous of competition than the American Fur Company—for which McKenzie now chiefly bought furs from Indians, as in the beginning.

In the fall of 1836, therefore, Wyeth departed from a region on which he had left his mark in a way he never planned. Because of the excitement caused in the East by the freakish Indians he'd brought out of the mountains with the aid of Milton Sublette, Oregon had become a Mecca for a variety of pilgrims with whom the Hudson's Bay Company didn't know how to cope. That odd niche in history is all the West ever gave a hardy adventurer, who went back to Cambridge, Massachusetts, and prospered as before.

His connection with a region he had learned to curse was not quite ended, though. Hall Kelley, the business associate for whom Fort Hall had been named, had become so entranced with various reports of coastal Oregon that he determined to inspect the vicinity himself.

𝕰𝕺𝕭 29 𝕰𝕺𝕭
Old Hickory Has His Way

THE MEN OF the Alamo had never known that they were fighting for anything but a rebellious Mexican province wishful of becoming a state. For a new nation—named, as Long's had been, the Republic of Texas—had not come into being until just before the end came for them. Yet even after they died, they remained the Republic's first line of defenders because of the time for military organization they continued to give Houston.

An army which had lost a fourth of its men in killed alone has to be rebuilt unit by unit. Santa Anna was not ready to push east from Bexar for weeks, and by then the Raven was shaking a steadily growing force into shape.

Veterans of earlier fighting such as Deaf Smith were members, and so were William Oury, recently an Alamo courier, and Herman Ehrenberg, late of Fannin's destroyed command. New to service in Texas, on the other hand, were Ben McCulloch, of Tennessee, Mirabeau Buonaparte Lamar, a poetic *sabreur* from Georgia, and Jacob Snively, claimed for both Pennsylvania and Maryland.

Becoming a staff officer of Houston's Snively was one of the small core of disciplined men which held the Texian army together under a new threat of disintegration. This was owing to the different views, held respectively by the commander and most of his troops, as to how the war should be conducted.

His earlier record of recklessness notwithstanding. Sam turned up, in this crisis, with a Fabian doggedness and willingness to play a waiting game. His strategy called both for gaining more time for training his raw army and for sucking the Mexicans into terrain where natural defenses would help cancel Santa Anna's superiority in numbers and heavy weapons. When the Mexicans at length advanced on the American settlements, accordingly, Houston withdrew slowly toward the bayou-seamed forests along the Gulf.

The frontiersmen-turned-soldiers, on the other hand, had wanted to meet the invaders head on, for reasons which were emotional and economic as much as military. It galled them to be forever in the position of refusing battle to a force they hated as they did the one under Santa Anna of the massacres. Then, as the Mexicans were allowed to proceed unchallenged, they were able to confiscate or destroy whatever the fleeing residents of settled areas had had to leave behind.

There was talk of replacing a commander who wouldn't fight with one that would. Probably only the memory of how things had gone, when Houston's orders had not been heeded in the past, stood in the way of another disastrous division of his army.

Grimly holding sway, Sam drew the enemy into the settlements across the water from Lafitte's old rookery on Galveston Island. Of no military advantage to the Mexicans who seized them, these were surrounded by wooded swamps, ideal for frontier sharpshooters, but never a home at all for massed troops trying to close with a retreating enemy.

Now although the hostile army had been identified with Santa Anna in the thinking of Texians who had no means of following his personal moves, the President of Mexico had not actually been with his troops during their advance to the Gulf. A shoot-'em-on-the-ground lecher, he had begun the second phase of his punitive campaign by taking time out to go through a fake wedding ceremony with a San Antonio señorita whom he had found too prudish to respond to other advances. Having debauched her by this ruse, he packed her off, in the reduced capacity of mistress, to the neighborhood of his genuine wife, and journeyed to take charge of an army which had won everything to be found in eastern Texas except a battle.

By the time he joined his command, some of his cannier lieutenants had become worried at the failure of Houston's force to disperse. The refusal to do so on the part of a foe which had showed every other sign of discouragement was not their sole cause of nervousness. They didn't like advancing farther into terrain which bogged down cavalry and screened the movements of enemy snipers.

Sure that he could drive the Texians east of the Sabine, however, Santa Anna took personal charge of the vanguard, a force of some 1500 men. This was about fifty miles ahead of the main army, numbering 4000 troops, commanded by Vicente Filisola.

Houston's force consisted of less than eight hundred rifles, but it was concentrated where he could use it all when he wanted to. By April 21, 1836, he had drawn the spearhead of Mexican attack across Buffalo Bayou to an encampment not far below the smaller stream's confluence with the San Jacinto River. Deciding that the now-or-never moment had arrived, the Raven moved his men through the woods with a quietness possible only to an army of practiced game stalkers.

Meanwhile Deaf Smith and another skilled axman were circling to the rear of the Mexicans. While the latter were enjoying the siesta to which they felt entitled by virtue of superior strength, the two frontiersmen began whacking down the bridge over which the enemy had passed in order to reach their present bivouac.

Previously, indeed, the Texians themselves had used the same structure, for there was no other span across Buffalo Bayou. Nor was the wide mouth of the San Jacinto bridged at all, while swamps prevented retreat in other directions. So if Deaf Smith was able to complete his mission, the battlefield chosen by Houston would become a cul-de-sac not only for the Mexicans but the Texians, winner take all.

In due course Deaf whispered a report which Sam broadcast when he was ready. Just as his army neared the enemy camp, the word was passed that Vince's Bridge had been destroyed, adding desperation to the other motives which flung frontiersmen at their foes. Knowing the terrain, the Texians knew that if they didn't crush the Mexicans, they would themselves be pressed back into a crotch formed by two streams. And knowing Santa Anna, they knew that in such a case they would be massacred, whether they fought or surrendered.

That awareness filled their minds with the illustrating fates of two garrisons. So they burst from the forest, crying, "Remember the Alamo!" and "Remember Goliad!" and fell upon a largely dozing enemy army.

Mowed down by bullets or slashed by swords and bowies as they tried to reach their stacked arms, hundreds of Mexicans never left camp. Those able to flee found no rallying point, because their officers were killed, out of touch with their commands or, like Santa Anna himself, in downright *sauve qui peut* flight. Because of Deaf Smith's work at Vince's Bridge, retreat to a better place for making a stand was impossible. As unable to regroup as to withdraw, the Mexicans ceased to be an army and died or were captured as individuals.

During the mopping-up operations which followed the storming of the camp 703 prisoners were taken. As, according to Houston's tally, 630 were killed and 208 were wounded, the estimated hostile force of about 1500 men was quite thoroughly accounted for. On their part the Texians lost six men at the Battle of San Jacinto. An additional 24 more were wounded, of whom Sam himself was one.

At first thought to have escaped, Sam's chief opponent ended as a prisoner. Fleeing ahorseback, Santa Anna had been balked by the destruction of the bridge he had counted on using. After his horse had bogged down in mud, he floundered across the bayou afoot, reaching the other side in a uniform no longer resplendent with the glittering braid he favored. By exchanging his tarnished finery for work clothes found in a deserted cabin, he hoped to be able to make his way to Filisola's headquarters; but he was picked up by Texians who had no inkling of his identity until he was brought to where fellow captives identified him as *El Presidente.*

Having just displayed the gambling spirit which was also in his make-up, the Raven once again showed cool foresight. To a man, those under him wished to string up the scoundrel who had had the "Degüello" played at the Alamo, and who had ordered muskets fired at Fannin's helpless men. But what Houston grasped was that Santa Anna executed would become a martyr to be avenged by a nation with the arms to accomplish it, while Santa Anna alive represented political bargaining power.

As matters stood, an occupying force of 4000 Mexicans then held most of settled Texas. To cope with these Houston had something less than the 783 men with whom he had attacked Santa Anna the day before. What he proposed to the latter, then, was his life and freedom in return for ordering, in his capacity as Commander in Chief of the Mexican Army, the withdrawal of all his troops in Texas to positions south of the Rio Grande.

Anxious to get clear of a place where he met bloodthirsty eyes wherever he looked, Santa Anna jumped at the chance to comply; and by the middle of May, 1836, the called-for retreat of his men was in operation. Ostensibly the sovereignty of the Republic of Texas was thus recognized by the nation from which it had been detached.

The Natchez view of where Americans were entitled to live, by virtue of the Louisiana Purchase, had to that extent been vindicated. The Natchez strategy of sending a man to establish an independent country, to be held in trust for the United States, had been carried as far as the halfway point, furthermore. Yet for a time it was pushed no further.

Still in the White House, Old Hickory had been officially correct during the Texas war of independence. Keeping busy with other matters, he ignored the clamors of those who wished to have American troops rushed to the aid of rebels against a foreign government with which the United States was on peaceful terms. Nor did he move to capitalize on the outcome of a conflict which he had foreseen long before the Texians themselves had done so. The key gambit had been successfully made by sending Houston, and Jackson was content to wait for the future to provide an opening for the next suitable American move.

In September of 1836 Sam became president of the nation which his generalship and good sense had brought into being. During March of the following year the United States formally recognized the existence of a third republic on the North American Continent, if by Mexico's count there were still only two. In disgrace because of his conduct north of the Rio Grande, Santa Anna no longer headed a nation whose new government repudiated the war-won verdict that Texas was independent.

ᎦᎸ 30 ᎦᎸ

A Dreamer Reaches Oregon

FOR THREE YEARS after he reached California in company
with David Waldo and Jed Smith's former partner David Jackson, Ewing Young did nothing of great interest to anybody but
himself. In 1834, however, he met a persuasive New Englander
named Hall J. Kelley.

Although this individual had never seen Oregon, he had for
long made a career of finding out about it from sea captains of
his native Boston who had been there. As enraged by Washington's general indifference to the Pacific Northwest as were the
mountain men, he formed a company, largely consisting of himself, for the purpose of founding a settlement which would re-
establish his country's forfeited dominion.

Personally ineffectual, he accomplished things indirectly by
interesting competent men of action in his ideas. He it was, in
fact, who had first directed Wyeth's attention westward. The
colony which Hall wanted Nathaniel to help him found never
came into being, because Wyeth was solely concerned with trying to make money out of the West; but Kelley stuck to his
passion.

In 1832 he had managed to scramble some sort of Oregon-
bound expedition together, but it blew up in New Orleans,
where it had no business being. Continuing alone, he had chosen
to go by way of Mexico, where he was robbed of all the trade
goods with which he had hoped to win the Indians of the Northwest to the American cause.

But if he was ineffectual, Kelley was a barnacle of purpose,
and by 1834 he had made it as far as Los Angeles. There the rock
of action to which he glued himself was Ewing. After listening
to Hall's enlargements on the tales of Boston skippers, Young
agreed to lead an expedition into John McLoughlin's empire.

163

By that time there were a fair number of Americans in California. Some had been brought there by Young himself. Others had come with William Wolkskill and George Yount when they retraced the route to California, arching up from Santa Fe through Utah, known as the Old Spanish Trail. Joe Walker had left a few behind when he went to rejoin Bonneville. Still other American citizens had jumped ships involved in the California cowhide trade. As colonists most of these drifters were of questionable timber; but as they were what was available, Kelley envisioned them as patriarchs of the great outpost of the United States he had traveled so far to found.

The capital of the expedition's members took the form of the horses and mules they began driving north in the summer of 1834. By that time Hudson's Bay Company brigades had found a better route linking California and Oregon than the one picked by Jed. Keeping to higher ground, it avoided the sodden forest in which Smith's party had miserably floundered. Notwithstanding a brush with the Rogue River Indians, the Kelley-Young group reached their destination in good shape; except for Hall, that is. After being doctored for some contracted ailment by a partisan of the British company he had come to fight, Kelley was floated down the Willamette on the flat of his back.

In the meantime a Hudson's Bay Company vessel, coasting north from California, had carried a note from Governor Figueroa to Dr. McLoughlin to the effect that brigands driving contraband horses were heading his way. In view of the experiences of Wyeth and Bonneville, it can be believed that an effort to freeze Young out would have been made in any case. But here was something which McLoughlin could reasonably and conveniently use, and he did so.

Unlike some already named Western adventurers, as it chanced, Ewing not only had come by the stock in hand honorably, but had principles as to how he acquired property. He was therefore doubly enraged when he found that the Hudson's Bay Company refused to trade with him, when he called at Fort Vancouver in October.

164

Contrary to expectations, Young stayed in the vicinity and wrote back to California, demanding the clearance of his name and an explanation of Figueroa's unfounded charge. But postal service when operated through sail-powered trading vessels is not fast; and in this case ships tacking out of the Columbia estuary usually made the Sandwich Islands their first point of call. Months passed before Ewing could gain exoneration on the horse-lifting count, and by then he had made another annoying discovery.

Sailing by way of the Horn and the islands not yet known as Hawaii, missionary recruits had joined Jason Lee on the banks of the Willamette. In these fellow Americans Young had thought to find allies who would take his part in resisting the Hudson's Bay Company's effort to nullify the Oregon occupancy pact, where citizens of the United States were concerned. What he learned was that the missionaries and the company were in cahoots.

If Jason Lee wasn't interested in sharing Christianity with Indians, he was, after his own fashion, religiously bent. In common with many sectarians, moreover, he wished to exclude from his world all who didn't share his particular creed. Where patriotism meant nothing to Jason, Methodism meant a great deal.

Shrewd enough to have perceived that, McLoughlin had made a deal with Lee. Wishing to limit American settlement, as long as he could not altogether stop it, the company factor had agreed to help colonists of Jason's religious persuasion, in exchange for the minister's cooperation in making the area untenable for other comers from the United States.

The Methodists started off by taking the stock-thieving charge at its face value. Young at length obtained a written retraction from the governor of California without improving his welcome in Oregon; for the last thing which either the Hudson's Bay Company or the local theocracy wanted was an independent resident who might draw more such, if allowed to flourish.

His back higher up than ever, Ewing decided that as the allied factions were trying to drive out a man who had asked nothing but a fair chance to make a living, he would carry the war to them. This he now did by declaring his intention of operating a still.

No single other pronouncement could have so hit both his persecutors between wind and water. To the company the emergence of a public liquor dispensary meant the end of any reliable service from the Indians it depended upon for trapping. To the missionaries his proposal was as a threatened visit from Satan. All commenced offering Young the cooperation long denied him; and after giving them plenty of time to cook, he accepted overtures.

Quite a few more months had elapsed while all this was transpiring, though, and in the interim Hall Kelley had exercised his peculiar genius for getting something done by mistake. His achievement in this case was as remarkable as his previous one of having brought about—through Wyeth and the Flatheads—the arrival of Jason Lee in Oregon.

Kelley's take-off in this instance was to blame the ostracism of Young and himself entirely on the Hudson's Bay Company, instead of laying it to a conspiracy in which Americans were equal partners. Out of his muddled understanding of what was afoot, Hall wrote letters to the U.S. Secretary of State, declaring that he and his friends were the victims of British persecution and demanding the protection of American rights.

It was by then 1836. The national administration was that of Jackson, who had been conscious of untoward British activities at the mouth of the Columbia ever since Jed Smith had communicated his findings in the Pacific Northwest seven years earlier. At that time the absence of American settlers had led to tabling the matter, pending further developments. But Old Hickory was not one to leave unnoticed a claim that Uncle Sam's nephews were being abused by overweening foreigners. With Jackson's endorsement, Secretary of State Forsyth sent a naval emissary, in the person of William A. Slocum, to investigate conditions along the great Western estuary.

When Slocum arrived, on December 22, he was cordially welcomed by the master of Fort Vancouver, who wanted to keep an eye on him. The American official, on his part, accepted McLoughlin's hospitality without letting it deter him from finding out what he had been sent to learn.

Appraising the investment of the Hudson's Bay Company in the region, he found that what Jed had prophesied had become a fact. Through Fort Vancouver and ancillary posts on both sides of the Columbia, the company controlled the area politically and militarily as well as commercially. Although nominally insisting only on Britain's claim to the territory west and north of the river which curved down from Canada, it was engaged, among other things, in colonizing a fertile district to the south of it with French Canucks.

Believing that the company's grip must be broken, if all Oregon were not to be forfeited, Slocum saw that colonies of missionaries, even though some sincere ones were then trying to teach the Indians how to farm, could not be an adequate answer. The Hudson's Bay Company, in a word, could exploit and control Christianized Indians as successfully as it had pagan ones. The solution was mass immigration from the States; but if Americans were to come to the region in the quantity needed, they must be lured by something more desirable to most than the hope of teaching a Cayuse or a Walla Walla the story of Uriah.

When he had thoroughly taken in the situation, Slocum talked to the one man who had the knowledge and force to be of any help. Ewing Young had come to Oregon to breed horses, but, having studied conditions there, he saw the possibility of a more profitable stock-raising venture. McLoughlin's minions raised enough meat to take care of their own needs and to sell some to the missionaries. Yet if the country was to grow, it had to have some other source of supply than an opposing company monopoly. What Ewing suggested, then, was the importation of California beef cattle.

This required financing; and as Slocum could arrange it, Young sailed to California with the emissary in 1837. The cattle drive he there undertook, after the complicated business of clearing matters with the Mexican government had been finally taken care of a year later, was probably the ruggedest in even American stock-raising annals.

If there was now a trail of sorts leading from California to Oregon, it wound through a drover's nightmare. Beyond the Sacramento Valley there was steep, forested country where a large herd was hard to keep intact. It was wet country with mud slicks on sharp grades. It was fog country, where cattle could sometimes not be seen, though only a few lengths away. It was Indian country, where strays would be promptly butchered by hovering braves.

It was starving country, too. The difficulties strung the drive out until supplies had been used up, while the noise of their progress cleared game out of their line of march. The men with him longed to kill a steer to alleviate their hunger; but Ewing said he would shoot the first to try it, so that was not done.

Yet if Indian foragers sometimes ate beef while the gaunt drovers did not, Young reached the settlements south of the Columbia with about 650 of the 830 cattle he had started with. Big and tough—they were of the breed which Joe Walker's men had seen pitted against grizzlies—these animals knew how to take care of themselves in the wilderness, as the ordinary domestic kine which the Hudson's Bay Company had introduced did not. Oregon then had an open range steer, suitable for settlers who had neither the time nor the facilities for raising cattle which needed to be fed and guarded.

This was a great frontier accomplishment, but the one initially responsible was not among the cheerers. Hall Kelley had sailed back East while Young was still in California. Some who appreciated what Ewing had done were present, however, for by the second half of 1838 Oregon had attracted other missionaries. And, like Jason Lee, most were more concerned for their own prosperity than for the souls they doubtfully allowed Indians to possess.

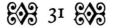 31

A Wandering Opportunist

DEALING IN PAWNSHOP junk bought in St. Louis, a Swiss captain named John Augustus Sutter entered the Santa Fe trade in 1835. During the following year he secured the backing of a couple of German officers, whose native language he spoke, for a venture in Chihuahua. Upon his return to New Mexico, however, he reported that although the expedition would eventually prove profitable, he had been able to do no better than to receive credit from the Mexican merchants to whom he had turned over his goods.

Learning from others that cash was not in short supply in Chihuahua at that time, a Captain Saunders and Sutter's other financer went south to investigate. In Mexico they found that their partner had been paid down to the last centavo, while upon posting back to Santa Fe they were greeted by the news that John Augustus was on his way to Missouri.

The Germans spurred after a man who had taken the branch of the Santa Fe Trail leading north through Taos. At Bent's Fort they were told that the culprit had left but a couple of hours before. Captain Saunders and his associate galloped out of the Bent and St. Vrain station, vowing they would catch up with Sutter. As they were never seen again, it was believed in the Southwest that they had come within gun range of John Augustus, at least. Nothing was ever proved, though, outside of the circumstance that Sutter did not return to New Mexico.

In 1838 he left Missouri, bound for other sections of the West, along with the trade goods caravan led by Andy Drips. He does not seem to have had a particular destination in mind; he appears rather to have been looking the country over, in search of a spot which offered good commercial prospects for a man of modest capital.

Roving traders now served the tribes of the prairies, but Captain Sutter could have found nothing to catch the eye of an ambitious man there. The federal policy of dumping Indian tribes indiscriminately into the region west of the Mississippi Valley and north of the Arkansas was working out to the benefit of none but agricultural Indians such as the Cherokees and Choctaws. Those wholly or partially dependent upon hunting were forlorn wanderers of a region which was being called upon to support many more people than could thrive on its game supply.

Farther west, on the high plains, the same situation was in the making, though for a different cause. The staple of that region's economy, the buffalo herds, had been more or less self-renewing, as long as they had been hunted solely for food, and to supply the material for clothing and tepees. Still seemingly immense, they were dwindling below the point of adequacy, because they were now being hunted for hides, and killed whether there was plenty of meat for all mouths or not.

The situation had not been appreciably relieved by the small-pox plague of the previous winter, which had all but wiped out the Mandans and greatly reduced the numbers of the Blackfeet. Buffalo were being killed off in numbers much exceeding the rate of reproduction, as both Indian and white hunters worked to satisfy the demands of competing traders.

Sutter could have found nothing to encourage him to linger on the plains in what he learned at Fort Laramie. For while the American Fur Company was striving to extend its buffalo-hunting range, so, too, were Bent and St. Vrain. Reaching south and north respectively, the outfits had established a front on the South Platte. For after Charles Bent had sent a well-known mountain man called Doc Newell to establish a trading post along the stream in question, the big company from the upper Missouri had countered by sending Henry Fraeb to do likewise.

Nor were they without challengers on the South Platte. An

Ashley man called Louis Vasquez and Andy Sublette, younger brother of Bill and Milton, had built a station there. So had one Lancaster P. Lupton, who had resigned his commission in order to deal in buffalo hides, after having visited Bent's Fort as a dragoon officer.

Finding no room on the plains, Sutter went on to attend the rendezvous of 1838, which was the year in which Ashley, founder of the great Western institution, died after having served several terms in Congress. Significantly, the gathering place was on the Wind River, on the east side of the Rockies.

Of the mountain men in attendance many were no longer trappers. Joe Walker, for instance, was there to trade off the horses, recognized as superior to those elsewhere obtainable, which he had stolen in California. Some were hide hunters, some were professional meat suppliers for one post or another, or guides for the parties of missionaries heading for western Oregon.

The sight of families wheeling into their loved wilderness out of the civilization they had put behind them must have made some of the mountain men uneasy and resentful. It was probably in protest against the increased number of vehicles at the rendezvous that a gang of Jim Bridger's trappers chose to entertain a group of missionaries with a dance around a fresh Indian scalp.

There was no fortune to be looked for in the declined mountain trade, so Sutter went through South Pass, up to Fort Hall and down the long windings of the Snake to the Columbia. On that river's estuary he didn't find what he was questing for either. Commerce was controlled by a company with which he didn't have the means of competing, while the prospects opened by the arrival of Ewing Young's beef herd failed to entice a man with no farming aspirations.

Toward the end of the year John Augustus sailed west of the West to where the Orient began in the Sandwich Islands. Not thriving there, he took passage to California in 1839, landing at Yerba Buena. The town at the gateway to San Francisco Bay was unpretentious, but Captain Sutter liked the feel of the country and decided to remain in it.

៛◊៛ 32 ៛◊៛

The Fracas in the Council House

OF ALL THE Indian tribes of the West, the people with the greatest territorial range were the Comanches. From the area around Bent's Fort their hunting grounds, as of the 1830's, swung south and east for about one thousand miles to the vicinity of Bexar.

At the northern end of this realm their relations with Americans were relatively genial. For though they robbed, kidnaped and killed palefaces whenever it was convenient, these things were merely what one did in order to secure property or scalps. They were not done with malice toward the people of the United States. With that country, indeed, they had been officially at peace ever since the First Dragoons had made its expedition of 1834—though Philip St. George Cooke had not been impressed by a powwow he rated "as availing as it would be to establish a truce between the howling wolf of the prairie and its prey."

Events proved him right; but the Army undertook no punitive march, and the Comanches still came to trade in amity at Bent's Fort, where the men they would attack when away from it received them without rancor. But this state of good-humored cynicism did not maintain in Texas. There the Comanches were not valued customers but malignant threats to the well-being of settlers with families.

In this capacity they came up against a type of white antagonist they had never encountered before. Elsewhere they had had rough engagements with mountain men, Santa Fe Trail traders, and even Bennet Riley's infantry. Now for the first time they found themselves pitted against professional Indian fighters.

Later famous for keeping obstreperous white men in line, the

Rangers had been organized, a decade before the revolution of 1836, by Texian colonists as a means of keeping dangerous savages in order. At the outset this police force had largely been concerned with the Karankawas, whom James Long had once lessoned. Cannibals, though, the Karankawas always took another chance, for the same reason that unwelcome cats continue to haunt a fish market.

As for the Comanches, the Rangers at first had had no occasion to oppose a tribe which had never raided the eastern settlements. After the founding of the Republic, however, the Mexican settlers of Texas became subject to the protection of what was changed from an organization of local sponsorship to a national military arm.

Just after the Battle of San Jacinto, meanwhile, John Coffee Hays—named for the Colonel Coffee who had sided Old Hickory in his melee with the Benton brothers—had arrived in Texas and joined its army. Pursuant to assignments which included digging graves for the gone men of Goliad, Jack finally found a chance to present to President Houston the letter of introduction he had brought along from Tennessee. Knowing the lad's people from of old, Sam took enough interest in Sergeant Hays to advise him to transfer from the Army to the Rangers. It thus came about that Jack Coffee had the good fortune to be trained as a plainsman by his redoubtable company commander Deaf Smith.

Now if the area patrolled by the Rangers had been extended, so had their sphere of duties. In addition to denying that Texas was an independent country, Mexico retained control of territory north of the Rio Grande, including its valley and the toe of Texas, as far north as the Nueces. From Laredo, as well as posts south of the Rio Grande, garrisons not only conducted raids themselves but gave encouragement and protection to the Mexican banditti who harried the Texian settlements. Not all of these were from south of the disputed river border, for the majority of the Republic's Spanish-speaking inhabitants not unnaturally preferred government by their own people.

In March of 1837 Deaf fought, and took prisoners from, a detachment of Mexican regulars sallying out of Laredo. Smith was in the vicinity because it was rumored that Mexico was going to mount another full-scale invasion there. It turned out to be a false alarm, but the threat was always present because of Laredo's position on the Texas side of the great river.

The bandits were more of a problem than Mexican troops because they were as persistent as flies, and needed no more of an operating base. Not yet in his majority, Jack Coffee was sometimes the leader of small groups, as Smith broke his command into bandit-chasing patrols in order to cover more territory.

Yet Indian fighting remained the true Ranger métier, and on the western Texas frontier, where Hays was on duty, that came to be all but synonymous with Comanche fighting. These Indians had for many years conducted raids into Mexico from which they had usually returned in triumph, laden with loot which included women and children. Now that Texian farmers had begun pushing toward their domain, the Comanches saw no reason why they shouldn't meet them halfway and wreak their customary ravin.

They did that with some, which is to say that they burned whatever they didn't find stealable, tortured to death the men who hadn't died fighting them, slew also the older women, gang-raped the younger ones and bore them and their children off to live as savages thereafter. But when they did so, the Rangers went after them.

This was a new experience for the Comanches, who were accustomed to being the aggressors. The caravans of traders stood them off, if they could; but when the Indians retreated, the episode was over. Mountain men shot their way out of Comanche traps, as Kit Carson, Joe Meek and five others had once done at the cost of forty-two braves, but here again success was measured by escape. Mexicans didn't follow the warriors, who sometimes raided as far south of the Rio Grande as Durango, either. Now, though, the Comanches met men who were not trying to avoid them but were in the business of intercepting them, and retaliating for such attacks on the settlements as they had failed to prevent.

Adding his patrol to the Ranger company led by Colonel Henry Karnes, Jack Coffee took part in the first real showdown between the Comanches and the frontier guards in August of 1837. At a gully with the suggestive name of Arroyo Seco, the Texians intercepted two hundred redskin lance and shield bearers, who lost their commanding chief when Hays raised his rifle.

As a Ranger company was not apt to have more than twenty or thirty men in it, the disparity in strength looked promising for the Indians. At Karnes's command, though, the Rangers scattered afoot through a patch of chaparral. Effective in fending off the arrows of Indians, it did not keep the frontiersmen from picking off twenty Comanches before the rest galloped away.

But the passage of the Texas Land Act in December gave new impetus to the conflict thus temporarily settled. Prior to that time, the western progress of settlement had been limited by the Republic's inability to grant titles to real estate. These still could not be obtained until surveys west of what had been the colonies were made, but land charting was soon being done on an extensive scale. Some Rangers—Jack Coffee Hays for one—doubled as surveyors. With Bexar for headquarters, they ran their lines into territory claimed by the Comanches as well as by the Republic of Texas.

Surveying while living off the country and under constant threat of being jumped by Indians is not the proper work for a man past sixty. Deaf Smith retired, which is perhaps what killed a man who had theretofore been constantly on the go; but at any rate he died at his ranch near Richmond, Texas, in 1838.

Most of the ones who carried on were just rounding into full manhood. In addition to Hays there was the shadowy Mustang Gray, most of whose ascertained biography is contained in a ballad which affirms him to have been a terror to the Indians and the darling of an unnamed Mexican señorita who managed to spring him from prison in Monterey. David Terry, who enlisted in the Texian army at thirteen, was probably a Ranger part of this time. Sam Walker, of Maryland, was assuredly one. Who many of the rest were, there is no way of guessing. The rosters were not kept, and a good few didn't report for duty very long. The grim estimate asserts that during their struggle with the Comanches the Rangers had to replace 50 per cent of their personnel every year.

Numerous Comanches died in the countless skirmishes which featured the surveying of the frontier, but as the Indians far outnumbered the Rangers, the latter were in constant quest of improved weapons, to help compensate for their numerical weakness. It was therefore with great interest that they learned of the experiments of Samuel Colt.

The ingenious but still inexperienced inventor of the revolver bearing his name had turned out a pioneer batch a few years earlier, of which a couple found their way to Texas and eventually came under the scrutiny of the Rangers. They were badly in need of a weapon which would keep barking while they raced after centaurs who usually got away, as things stood. Most of the Comanches so far shot had been killed by men afoot, as single-shot weapons could not be recharged by galloping men. Now the Texians saw the possibility of continuing to shoot as they sped.

The percussion-cap repeating pistol which they carefully evaluated didn't measure up to their needs, though. It had been designed as a light, self-defense weapon, not as a cavalryman's instrument of attack. It had a trick disappearing trigger in place of one available to a man in a hurry; and it was without the guard essential to safety while pushing through chaparral. Nor was it as effective a rapid-fire weapon as was desired, because of the method of reloading. In order to replace the fired cylinder with a charged one, the user had to unscrew the barrel.

The man with the keenest eye for the failings of this primitive Colt was Sam Walker. Belonging to the same company as Hays, he was commissioned to go to New York and confer with the inventor, with a view to having him turn out a revolver tailored to meet the peculiar needs of the Rangers. It turned out that the young mechanical genius was delighted to talk with anyone who took an interest in his generally ignored creation. Walker accordingly presented his notions of what a revolver should be; and between them they produced a hand gun which was the ancestor—except for the fact that it was only a five-shooter—of all those fired so often and so lethally in the West of later years.

Returning to Texas with a few samples of the improved Colt in 1839, Walker found that the Rangers guarding the Republic's western frontier were in need of all the firepower they could muster. By then the Texas Land Office was doing business with settlers on a large scale. Where Bexar had been the hub of a small settlement wheel, it now performed that function for a much larger one. Having taken note of the spreading fire which was eating up their range, the Comanches had jumped in to stamp it out.

A glimpse of their effectiveness can be caught by reading the mortuary statistics for San Antonio as of 1839. Of 140 male Texian residents of the vicinity, 100 were slain before the year was up. Of these violent deaths a few were notched by Mexican banditti, but most were Comanche coups.

The Indians did not steer clear of the town itself. In 1839 a band of Comanche warriors appeared and challenged all Texians present to come out of the city and fight. There weren't too many former Americans on tap in a town which was still largely Mexican; but when eleven of them sallied to meet the somewhat larger group of visible savages, many more braves emerged from ambush.

Yet Bexar and its vicinity were not alone in suffering depredations. For in that same year a band of two hundred Comanches dipped deep into the settlements east of San Antonio, leaving grief and destruction in their wake and making a rich haul of horses and mules.

Aided by a remnant of the Lipan Apaches, whom the Comanches had largely driven west, the Rangers both tried to cope with rising Indian aggression and to help a rebel Mexican group which was attempting to form a Republic of the Rio Grande. If successful, this movement would have put a friendly buffer nation between Texas and hostile Mexico; but though the Texians won several battles for the rebels, they were deserted by allies under ineffective leadership, and the Republic of the Rio Grande rose and fell before 1840 was on its way.

That was the year of the Council House Fight. The episode began when three chiefs sought out Colonel Karnes, under whom Hays and Walker served following the retirement of Deaf Smith, and declared that the Comanches were tired of the warpath and wanted to live in amity with their white brethren. Pleased but desiring concrete evidence of good intentions, Karnes specified that the return of numerous kidnaped Texians would be the only acceptable sign of sincere intentions. To this the sachems agreed, and a date of delivery in San Antonio was set.

Why the Indians chose to put themselves at a disadvantage when perpetrating a mortally offensive joke is beyond understanding. But this is what happened. When sixteen chiefs, together with their families, duly rode into Bexar, they brought along but one Texian infant. Where were the others? The Comanches said they didn't know, as all the rest had been sold to other tribes.

They were in the Council House, dating from Spanish colonial days, when this was divulged. As the enormity of the insolence was digested by the white men present, hot words drew answering anger from the Indians. Belatedly seeing that he and his companions could be held as hostages for the captives they had failed to bring along, one of them drew a knife and sprang at the Ranger guarding a door. Shot, he was the first of twenty-seven Comanches to be slain, while thirty-five were captured. Eight Texians were also killed, while quite a few more were wounded.

This slaughter at what had been looked forward to by the whites as an olive-branch meeting marked the last effort to arbitrate by either side. Not reasoning that they had brought it on themselves, the Comanches spread the word of a massacre committed upon invited ambassadors of the tribe; and members of

178

a far-flung people who had never seen a Texian were taught that such could never be dealt with except by the knife.

Yet this still did not affect the Comanche attitude toward other white men from the States, with whom they would exchange the courtesies of the plains, when encountered in such strength as to make attack or robbery not feasible. Nor did it alter their attitude toward adopted white captives, of whom Jim Hobbs, seized while pot hunting for one of Charles Bent's caravans, remained one.

🙰 33 🙰

No Pretty Boy for Corpse

AT SOME TIME during 1839 a missionary named Elijah White angered Jason Lee by competing for the leadership of the colony founded by the latter in Oregon. In consequence White was ejected from Eden on the Willamette and went back to the Atlantic Seaboard.

Although Jason didn't expect to see White again, even in the Heaven to which he himself confidently aspired, Elijah had determined on a return bout. It took him a couple of years to mature his plans. In the meantime Oregon had gained a couple of nonmissionary citizens and lost one.

In 1840 the last rendezvous was held. There was no money to be earned from trapping now, except by the few with enough capital to arrange for direct liaison with the central wholesale market at St. Louis. Trappers not in the employ of such a brigade leader had the choice of throwing in with Indian tribes or getting out of the mountains.

After Mountain Lamb had been killed by marauding Bannocks, Joe Meek had married a Nez Percé squaw who had divorced him by the approved method of dumping his plunder out of their lodge. It thus turned out that Joe had a motherless little girl, with no stepmother to look after her, when the end of the mountain-man era found him penniless and without prospects. A hard-living, easy-smiling fellow, Joe loved the wilderness as much as any other buckskin wearer; but it seemed to him that the time had come to bite the bullet and return to some phase of civilization. After talking it over with Doc Newell, Meek agreed to go to western Oregon with him.

Prior to that time caravaners to the Pacific Northwest had felt the necessity of abandoning their wagons at Fort Hall. From there on it had been customary to drive stock along the Snake and the Columbia, and to float baggage down those long streams by bullboats. Then at the Dalles both animals and gear were barged the rest of the way with the help of Indian guides.

But Joe and Doc were mountain men, and as such they didn't believe that rough country was necessarily impassable country. Although there was nothing left of the discarded wagon they had reconditioned but wheels and a makeshift floor, they cut, via main strength and determination, the tracks which lengthened the Oregon Trail, as a vehicular trace, by some two hundred leagues.

In the course of doing so, they made a side trip to Wailatpu, in the vicinity of Walla Walla, to visit the mission which Marcus and Narcissa Whitman were directing. Joe had not forgotten the woman whose presence had made a different thing out of the 1836 rendezvous, so to the little flock of Indian girls she was educating he added two half-breed ones. Of these one was his own by Mountain Lamb, while the other was a daughter whom Jim Bridger had entrusted to him for that purpose.

Pressing on down the Columbia, the fugitive trappers muscled their wreck of a wagon as far as the Cascades. Thence, perforce, they rafted to the Methodist colony on the Willamette. The missionaries were not glad to see any of their ilk; but the mountain men had come to settle down, and they stayed.

Before the end of their first winter there they lost the companionship of about the only settler whom they might expectedly have found congenial. The date of Ewing Young's passing cannot be asserted with confidence, but seemingly the stroke or brain hemorrhage which finished him did so in February of 1841.

Not long afterward Elijah White was on his way west again, his purpose to beard Jason Lee. For backing he had a considerable party of Methodists with whom to found a colony of his own. He had had no difficulty in finding recruits for his project, for taking the Oregon Trail had come to be an accepted phase of American life.

From Westport, Missouri, to the Columbia estuary the distance covered by travelers was over two thousand miles. As yet, it should be understood, it had occurred to no one to settle at intervening points. In part this was owing to erring scientific reports, and in part to national tradition.

To take the latter up first, forested western Oregon appealed to Americans as a region where the historic pioneer cycle could be repeated. Ever since Jamestown, settlement had begun with felling trees in order to clear land for plowing. A thickly wooded country had the air of home; a region with trees only along streams or high up in the mountains did not.

Possibly because they had been affected by tribal emotions, too, the investigators sent out by the federal government had also pronounced against the prairies which have since proved so fertile. The assumption appears to have been that since the region did not sprout trees in quantity, its soil was fundamentally unsound. One of the reasons why the government had designated it as Indian territory in 1834 was the consensus of expert opinion to the effect that it would never support a civilized population.

Federal leaders were relieved, too, at having found a section of the nation where settlers would be under no temptation of trying to deprive Indians of their hunting grounds. Nor was there trouble of that sort for several years. During the first half of the nineteenth century the tribes of the country through which the Oregon Trail ran were not crowded by white men but only by each other.

At Westport Elijah White's party was joined by the first non-missionary family to take the trail. Its head was Joel Walker, brother of mountain-man Joe and John of the Alamo. Riding with him was Herman Ehrenberg, once of Fannin's command at Goliad.

After taking part in the Battle of San Jacinto, young Ehrenberg had returned to Germany, there to round out his education as an engineer. In 1840 he was again west of the Sabine, this time as a member of a group of German settlers he had been instrumental in drawing out from under the growing weight of Prussian oppression. Not the settling kind himself, though, Herman had gone to Missouri, met Walker and agreed to trek to the lower Columbia with him.

Their guide along the Platte to Fort Laramie and thence past Independence Rock to South Pass was Broken Hand Fitzpatrick. The pilgrims he led to the proper stopping points for camping, the while he kept on the alert for signs of hostile Indians, did not have the rendezvous as a halting spot this year. But not long after the White-Walker party had passed through the Rockies a remnant of the trappers who still clung to them took part in the last event of note in the history of the mountain men, considered as a group.

In August of 1841 Henry Fraeb, once of the Rocky Mountain Fur Company, was trying to set up a trading establishment of his own by building a post on the St. Vrain Fork of the Yampa River where it crosses the Wyoming-Colorado border. It was hardly more than begun when Old Gabe Bridger got the grapevine tip that the Sioux and some northern Cheyennes were coming to the mountains looking for war. The Dakotas had not formerly frequented that part of the West, but they had shifted to the lee of the Rockies because of Fort Laramie, just as one branch of the Cheyennes had shifted south to be near Bent's Fort.

Getting out of the way himself, as soon as he had learned what was afoot, Jim sent a warning to his former partner. Fraeb, however, got his Dutch up, as he was ancestrally entitled to do, and declared that no redskins were going to drive him from his chosen trapping zone.

The strength of Henry's brigade has been recorded as from one to three score. Even at the top figure the mountain men were badly outnumbered by the several hundred warriors who showed up on August 21 and picked a quarrel about some horses, which they claimed had been borrowed and neither returned nor paid for. Whether their case was a just one or not, it didn't get a hearing from the trappers.

Perched on a hilltop and shooting alike from behind the bodies of slain horses and the stumps of trees, felled to build the contemplated fort, they slew so many Indians that by the next day the Sioux and the Cheyennes were glad to call the engagement off. Fraeb himself was one of the five white men killed at Battle Creek, though. Shot, he remained sitting up with the aid of the stump against which the bullet had slammed him. And he made, in the opinion of a man who had seen enough cadavers to make his judgment that of a connoisseur, "the ugliest dead man I ever saw."

Without taking their wagons as far along the Oregon Trail as had been done in 1840 by Meek and Newell, meanwhile, Ehrenberg, Walker and Elijah White's party reached the Willamette some weeks after the Battle Creek affray. If none was welcome, White, at least, had taken a step which insured him against a second exile.

Assembling influential backers, after having been forced to return to the Atlantic Seaboard, Elijah had persuaded the federal administration that the tribes of the Pacific Northwest were entitled to government supervision. Ever since Hall Kelley's excited letters had led to Slocum's sober report about conditions along the Columbia, Washington had been concerned about the possibility of losing all Oregon by default; and White's suggestion had opened a cheap and easy way of asserting American authority in the nation's most distant dominion. When Elijah went west again, accordingly, it was in the capacity of sub-Indian agent for the United States.

But there were too many missionaries and not enough excitement to be found in western Oregon to suit Ehrenberg. He soon took ship for the Sandwich Islands and other parts of Polynesia, where he sojourned for many months.

His trail companion, Joel Walker, also left before the end of 1841. His destination California, Joel had been preceded there that year by a party including John Bidwell. Making history as they went, they had used a cutoff from the Oregon Trail—doubtless pioneered by Joe Walker and other wholesale horse thieves —leading to the region behind the Sierras.

Not long after his arrival Bidwell found employment in the large trading station being built at the junction of the Sacramento and American rivers by Captain Sutter. Having become a Mexican citizens in 1841, John Augustus had arranged for a huge grant of land which he, as a native of Switzerland, had dubbed New Helvetia. The arrangement was for Sutter's Fort to operate as a frontier outpost of the Captain's adopted country, but in practice it was the capital of what amounted to an independent principality.

𝕰𝕰 34 𝕰𝕰

Scalping for a Living

IF IT CANNOT be claimed that most of the Americans doing business in New Mexico were easy to get along with, neither can that assertion be made in favor of local Mexican officials. Of these the most aggressive was Manuel Armijo. If as objectionable to most of his fellow Mexicans as to citizens of the United States, he was yet successful in leading them toward progressively worse relations with frontiersmen from the neighboring nation.

Out of office as combination governor and customs extortionist in 1837, Armijo started a revolution against the incumbent, whom he succeeded in having decapitated by a mob of Pueblo

Indians. The man who had put them up to it now spread the rumor that the rebellion had been a Texas plot to take over the land east of the Rio Grande, which the Republic had indeed gone along with Napoleon and James Long by claiming. All Americans were suspected of being party to this supposed movement, and Charles Bent, seized at Taos, was among those temporarily imprisoned.

Rewarded for his skulduggery by being made governor again, Armijo fortified his position by having himself also appointed commander in chief of troops in the province. That achieved, he imposed a flat tax of $500 on all wagons, regardless of contents and cargo value, rolling in from the United States.

That was in 1839, the year in which Armijo had released the accused Mexican slayer of an American without even the pretense of a trial. Among the United States citizens in Santa Fe at the time, however, was Jim Kirker, of Belfast, Ireland, a former Ashley man who had likewise served on an American privateer during the War of 1812. Santiago, as the Mexicans called Jim, undertook to tell Armijo that something had to be done about the murderer, and when the Governor called out the militia, Kirker was ready with enough armed frontiersmen to make the Governor prefer concession to starting a fight in his capital.

Pursuant to that incident, Santiago Kirker was captured by Apaches, according to his own story, or turned deliberately renegade, as others affirmed. What is certain is that in 1839 Jim Hobbs at last saw a chance to get out of Comanche bondage.

In the eyes of the Comanches themselves young Hobbs did not then have the status of a captive. Given the chance to qualify as a warrior, he had been trained by Indians recognized as the best among all the savage trick-riders of the Great Plains. Adept with lance and bow, he had gone on the warpath against other tribes and joined forays into Mexico. His prowess had so pleased the chief of the band which had kidnaped him that Old Wolf had awarded Jim his daughter, Spotted Fawn. By the time he was nineteen, Hobbs had sired a son by a young woman he reported as sightly, pleasant of temper and devoted. Yet he had not voluntarily become a Comanche; and upon seeing Kit Carson, he responded to the call of kind.

By then Singing Wind had died, and Kit was hunting for Bent's Fort in company with Peg-leg Smith and an Indian called Shawnee Spiebuck. Traveling domestically, Old Wolf's band was safe to visit, so Carson had ridden into the cluster of lodges to pass the time of day. Because of dark hair and his long over-all exposure to the Southwestern sun, Hobbs was indistinguishable from Comanche bucks of his age. But he found occasion to speak with Kit privately and asked the mountain man's help in escaping from the Stone Age back to the nineteenth century.

It chanced that Shawnee Spiebuck had been with the same caravan as the one from which Hobbs had strayed three years before, never to return. He could thus confirm Jim's story that he had been in the employ of Charles Bent and was not a renegade white who had changed his mind.

Under those circumstances Carson re-entered the camp of the Comanche chief and invited him to visit Bent's Fort. Old Wolf had never been to the great post on the Arkansas, and his plans were such that he felt unable to do so in 1839. But Kit had painted such an alluring picture of the treats in store for sachems who arrived to trade, that the chief promised to make the experiment the following summer.

When keeping his promise, he brought his son-in-law, now four years a captive, along with him. The commonalty were entertained beyond the walls, where trade goods were brought out to them. The chiefs were given the red-carpet treatment, though, and the Bents made a special effort to see that Old Wolf had a good time. Accustomed to pay black-market prices for whiskey, the sagamore was charmed to find that all he wanted was pressed on him free of charge. He stayed so long that his followers, suspecting foul play, gathered by the gates to the number of several hundred and threatened an assault. These were appeased when Old Wolf appeared on the fort's wall and told them, between hiccups, that Charles and William Bent were the best friends a Comanche ever had. When he finally called it a night, though, Hobbs didn't leave the post with him. Jim had been ransomed with six yards of red flannel, a pound of tobacco and an ounce of beads.

Kit Carson and Shawnee Spiebuck were still on the staff of Bent's Fort, while Peg-leg Smith was again there, having returned from the Coast. Eighteen-forty was the year of his greatest equine haul, for he had celebrated its spring by driving three thousand unpaid-for head back from California.

Becoming the joint protégé of the three men who had originally taken an interest in getting him out of Comanche hands, Hobbs fared in their company on hunting expeditions interspersed with sprees floated by the profits from Smith's enterprise. According to Jim, Peg-leg often declared a private war on Mexicans when in Taos or other Spanish-speaking towns. Annoyed by the conduct of such fellow cantina patrons, he would use his removable shank, with which he was remarkably adept at driving the unmannerly out of his presence.

The first to leave the foursome, Carson married again, this time picking a Cheyenne lass named Making Out Road. Peg-leg was the next to go; having drunk up his winnings of the year before, he went back to California in 1841 for more horses.

Jim Hobbs wasn't left at loose ends, though, for Apaches, active along the trade route from Santa Fe to Chihuahua, placed caravan guards in strong demand. Accepting employment in this line along with Spiebuck, Hobbs entered a Mexican state where Santiago Kirker was already in residence.

Whether with the Apaches through capture or choice, Kirker had at length so ingratiated himself with members of one branch of this tribe as to have been made a chief. He had, indeed, become such a successful Indian leader that the governor of Chihuahua had marked him public enemy number one and posted a whacking reward for his scalp.

That offer planted a commercial scheme in Kirker's brain. If Apache hair was turning out to be a better source of revenue than beaver fur had been at the peak market, he wanted to be on the collecting end. Sending word of his intention to the governor, he arranged an interview with that official which ended to their mutual satisfaction. Santiago was known to have been familiar with the trails and gathering places of the Indian tribe which Chihuahuans were anxious to have exterminated. To further this purpose, the governor had agreed to pay a bounty of fifty dollars on each scalp, regardless of the sex or age of the Apache to whom it belonged.

As in the case of licensing Americans to hunt beaver, a Mexican thought in terms of a modest level of enterprise while the man from the States he was talking to had bigger stakes in mind. Doubtless the governor of Chihuahua had visualized keeping Kirker busy and out of mischief while the latter hunted down occasional stray Indians. What Santiago had planned, though, was to raise a band of helpers large enough to raid Apache encampments and reap wholesale.

Hobbs and Spiebuck were still in Chihuahua when Kirker began recruiting early in 1842. Having wintered in a city which offered far more in the way of fleshpots than did Santa Fe, they had been intending to guard a north-bound caravan back to New Mexico in the spring. Instead they rode afield with other blood-money seekers, largely Cherokees and Delawares, in addition to Spiebuck's own Shawnee followers.

As Kirker's band numbered 170, they were more than able to cope with Indians who seldom moved in large parties. Only in country rich in game can nomads afford the luxury of traveling in companies big enough to discourage attack. Not that the Apaches expected attack from Santiago, whom they had raised to a position of trust, until it was too late. It was good hunting on the part of a man who knew just where to look for the wilderness water holes and patches of agave—the Apache staple of diet —where the Indians were to be found. It was not long, therefore, before the raiders were on their way back to the capital of Chihuahua with 183 scalps, 13 live squaws and 1000 head of horses and mules.

As the state's treasury wasn't at all in a position to pay out the sums demanded, the governor looked for loopholes. For one thing, he objected to giving a bounty for the scalps of women who yet had theirs intact. When Spiebuck made as though to scalp them on the spot, however, His Excellency reconsidered. Among the hunters the agreement had been that the bounty money would be whacked up by the leaders, while their followers would be paid by the stock taken over from the Indians. The governor, though, wanted to claim the horses and mules on the score that they had been the property of Mexican citizens before being stolen by Indians. This so enraged Shawnee Spiebuck that in a subsequent council of the hunters he proposed storming the gubernatorial palace for the purpose of scalping His Excellency.

When Kirker vetoed that suggestion, the parting of the ways came. Hobbs, Shawnee and most of the Indians decided to keep what gains they had by driving the stock north. Santiago declared that he would stay on and haggle for what was due on the scalps. When evidence was produced to show that some of the lifted hair was Mexican rather than Apache, the dickering came to an end. Santiago stayed on in Chihuahua, however, garrisoning a ranch from which no one saw fit to try to oust him.

Peg-leg Smith did not return to New Mexico, either, as in 1842 he established a stock farm on Bear River. From it—a useful citizen in spite of himself—he supplied horses and mules to users of the Oregon Trail, or the branch leading to California, many in need of such service.

As for Kit Carson, he was no longer with the Cheyennes, because Making Out Road had been too greedy of foofaraw—the comprehensive term for feminine finery, wilderness style. Customarily the mountain men delighted to load their women with more barbaric splendors than Indians could or would have bestowed on them, but Making Out Road's insatiability had led to quarrels and then quittance.

Still anxious for a mate, though, Carson had fixed his eye on Maria Josefa Jaramillo, Charles Bent's youthful sister-in-law. She was willing, but her people were not disposed to allow her to take care of Kit's half-breed daughter. At Bent's suggestion, then, Carson accompanied Charles east in the spring of 1842, his mission to place his child by Singing Wind in a convent in St. Louis.

As the little girl was not yet of school age, Kit decided to ask some relatives, resident in rural Missouri, to look after her until she was old enough to receive the planned convent education. While he was so engaged, Charls Bent went on to St. Louis, where he was introduced to a Lieutenant Frémont.

৪৩ 35 ৪৩
A Trio of Bad Sendings

THE COMANCHES HAD suffered a severe setback in the loss of sixteen chiefs of note at the Council House Fight; but after devoting the required time alike to mourning and reorganization, they struck for vengeance. Five hundred strong, they by-passed Bexar and dashed for places so far east that even people who saw them coming didn't dream they could be hostiles. After first carrying torch and tomahawk to Victoria, only a dozen leagues in from San Antonio Bay, they surged even nearer to the Gulf and wiped out the town of Linnville.

A blow of that magnitude called out all the resources of the Republic. Major General Felix Huston led as many of the militia as he could promptly muster and rushed west to join the Rangers. Ben McCulloch, of that force, was by then riding the trail of the savages. Due to the fact that the Comanches were driving a large herd of stolen stock, they couldn't return with the speed which had marked their advance, so Ben was able to let pursuit know just about where the reavers could be found.

Although the Army's senior general was nominally in command, Indian fighting was here involved, and strategy was dictated by the top Ranger officer. At this time it was Colonel Matthew Caldwell, whose white-dappled black beard had won him the nickname Old Paint.

Acting on Ben's information, Caldwell intercepted the Comanches at Plum Creek, twenty-seven miles southeast of Austin. Having thus maneuvered to come between the Indians and their own territory, he dug in and was waiting for them with riflemen firing from rests. They needed this advantage as there were but two hundred Texians pitted against two and a half times that number of Indians.

Rare among the tribes in this respect, the Comanches would maintain a cavalry charge against a braced enemy, risking being shot in order to be able to strike with massed lances. Effective against arrows or even the muskets of Mexicans, it did not work against rifles, as about one hundred did not live to reflect.

For many months to come no great war parties were launched against the Republic. Not that the Indians ceased to raid, but they adopted the plan of operating in bands which struck at various settlements simultaneously. Yet these were harassing actions, not threats to the safety of Texas as a whole, nor could such tactics more than slow the steady westward march of pioneer farmers.

The threat from Mexico, on the other hand, grew more severe, following the failure of rebels to detach northern states from the federal government. Having settled internal difficulties, Mexico strengthened her Rio Grande garrisons, making a no-man's land of all southern Texas, from Laredo east to the Gulf.

In an effort to attack a more vulnerable point than the Rio Grande frontier, Houston's successor as president, Mirabeau Lamar, launched the Santa Fe Expedition in June of 1841. It had a commercial as well as a military objective, however, for Texas had long moodily eyed the Santa Fe Trail. Its traffic moved to and from what Texian maps showed to be a Texian town; but none that profited from this trade paid taxes to the Republic. Lamar hoped to tap that revenue source via a wagon road from San Antonio to Santa Fe, which in turn would link Bexar with the trade route running from Independence, Missouri, to Chihuahua City.

The Republic's government must have been under the impression that the people of New Mexico were disaffected and ready to revolt. Certainly no great opposition must have been anticipated, for the invading column mustered only 270 men, and the one cannon they brought along was more calculated to cause trouble to its haulers than to overawe a far outnumbering enemy.

At this point it is necessary to mark time, while glancing at a version which denies the known existence of an enemy. Although the said expedition has usually been referred to as a military one, the record demands mention of the fact that Texians then, and Texans since, have rigidly maintained it was no such thing. According to their claim, its members purposed no more than to invite the citizenry of New Mexico to repudiate Mexico City, and to join the Republic which claimed the territory they lived in. If dwellers in Santa Fe and points adjacent turned down this bid, the Texians were supposed to bow, face about, and trundle their cannon back to Bexar.

It is true that no member of the Santa Fe Expedition was a soldier, as the Texian congress had that year neglected to vote the army sustaining funds. Perhaps the fact that he was automatically out of a job accounted for the presence of former Army Paymaster Jacob Snively. Officers on the loose abounded, moreover, the most distinguished being Colonel Caldwell, the victor at Plum Creek. Old Paint wasn't in command, though, for the column boasted a brigadier general in the person of Hugh M'Leod.

Now although the expedition was rife with veteran frontiersmen, there was none with desert experience. If there had been, the march into northwestern Texas would not have been begun as late as June 22. A few months earlier there would have been pasturage of sorts for the horses as well as the oxen which drew the five wagons loaded with merchandise. There would have also

192

been moisture in streams and water holes, which contained none by the onset of summer.

The Lipan guides seem to have been incompetent and in any case soon deserted, so the Texians had to guess where to sketch a road seven hundred miles long. Losing their bearings in landmarkless plains, they made it one hundred miles longer than necessary. Then, what between ravines and mountains to negotiate or skirt farther on, the trip stretched through so many more days than had been anticipated that supplies didn't last.

Indians of one sort or another harassed them most of the way, but for once that was a minor trouble. Draft animals began dying, first because of a shortage of provender and water, and next because meals had to be made of them.

In hopes of relieving a desperate plight, men mounted on the three strongest horses pushed ahead and reached settled New Mexico in the middle of August. They accomplished nothing, for news of the invasion, a project in which American newspapers had taken a lively interest, had been brought to Santa Fe by traders from Missouri. Governor Armijo had been so alarmed that he had sent for a supplement of one thousand troops; and aid was the last thing he stood ready to give the expected enemy.

When the Texian trio came within Armijo's reach, he first threw them in prison and on second thought had them shot. He furthermore warned the populace that an army bent on slaughter and rapine was on its way. Then as Texians were no more than Americans under a different name, he inspired so much hostile feeling toward citizens of the United States that men who had been doing business in Santa Fe for years saw fit to leave for California overnight.

In his excitement the Governor reached up to Taos for Charles Bent and put him in jail a second time. Through the protests of the United States consul, the trader was soon released; but there was nobody to speak for the next batch of Texians who straggled into Armijo's clutches.

When the rest of the column finally made its way out of aridity, it consisted of skeletons afoot. Back somewhere in the Panhandle were the laden wagons which were supposed to have initiated trade between Bexar and Santa Fe. Somewhat nearer were the bones of the last horses to have been eaten. After dobbin had disappeared from the menu there had been little on it but snakes, lizards and bugs. The cannon was not the only weapon which had been left behind; many rifles had proved too heavy for starving men to carry.

After these near ghosts reached Anton Chico in September of 1841, Armijo sent six hundred troops against them. Not content with the advantage in numbers, though, he had found a means of sucking in the Texians with false promises. His tool was a Captain W. P. Lewis, late of the expedition himself. Terrified at the thought that he, too, might be shot, he had told the Governor that in return for his own safety he would persuade his comrades to surrender without a struggle.

Wan men, the Texians were only too glad to receive the assurance of one of their own number that they would be well and honorably treated if they gave over the resistance they weren't able to offer. It turned out, though, that they were to be marched to Mexico City, there to be dealt with as captured guerillas.

The long march was brutally enforced on men given no time to recover spent strength. Some died, and some were shot when they lacked the force to continue. In Texas, meanwhile, months were to elapse before people knew what had become of the Santa Fe Expedition. By then 1841 had given place to 1842, and the Republic's struggle for survival had entered a new phase.

Texas had been recognized by France, England and several lesser powers, as well as by the United States; but that handshaking did not carry the promise of any of the financial aid which the new nation needed so badly. To get on its feet, it had to have credit, yet its attempts to float bond issues had been so far from successful that when Sam Houston again became president, following his election in December of 1841, he was forced to report to his congress that there was not so much as a single dollar in the national treasury.

Failure on the credit line was owing to the uncertainty on the part of financiers as to whether the Republic could remain autonomous. Some believed that Texas would be annexed to the United States, others that if not so annexed, it would be reconquered by Mexico, while a third group held that the Texians might seek shelter in the British Empire rather than submit to reabsorption by the hated people south of the Rio Grande.

Early in 1842 Mexico made its boldest move yet against the Republic, at that time not only bankrupt but militarily weakened by the absence of numerous officers on the Santa Fe Expedition. Moving out of Laredo, General Vásquez led seven hundred men against Bexar. In command at San Antonio at the time, Hays could muster no better than ninety-odd. After skirmishing with the vanguard, Jack Coffee withdrew to find reinforcements, leaving San Antonio and the Alamo once again in Mexican hands.

In the meantime Caldwell, Snively and the other survivors of the Santa Fe Expedition had made their painful way to Mexico City, where Santa Anna was again in power. Whatever he might have liked to do to men he hated as he did all Texians, he could not prove that these had done anything more than walk into New Mexico and submit to arrest. Through the intervention of the American and British ministers to Mexico, the prisoners were released in batches; and by April of 1842 they had begun re-entering the Republic.

Vásquez had withdrawn from Bexar by then, but it was believed that his reconnaissance in force would be followed up, as such moves usually are when as successful as his had been. So the men who had gone to Mexico City by way of Santa Fe were doubly welcomed.

Not much account was taken of the fact that the many former army officers among them had gained their liberty at the expense of agreeing not to bear arms against Mexico in the future. As most of them looked on this as belonging to the same phylum as a confession extracted by force, they were again available for service. For Texas had corrected the omission of the previous year and once more had a military arm.

A part of it saw action along the Nueces in July, at which time Ewen Cameron crossed the path of General Antonio Canales the second time. The first occasion had taken place in 1840, during a temporary cessation of hostilities for all but Ewen.

A native of Scotland, Cameron was a physician. In Texas he acted as a line officer, not as a member of the medical corps, however; and his original meeting with Canales showed why tough frontiersmen thought he was a man worth following.

Missing a horse he valued, Ewen had tracked it to the bivouac of the force Canales commanded, entered the camp alone, found the mount he was looking for, and separated the man on it from the animal. Among those who tried to interfere on the Mexican soldier's behalf had been the General himself. He was also among those who had backed off when Cameron drew his Colt and announced he'd plug any bairn of a bitch who didn't have sense enough to get out of his way; but Canales did not let the incident slip his mind.

He remembered it with especial vividness when a Texian force attacked and defeated him near Lipantitlan in 1842. Present and particularly active were one hundred riflemen under Ewen, whose height and bulk made him easy to recognize.

But if the Mexicans were driven back elsewhere in July, they advanced again from Laredo before the summer was over. On September 11 General Adrian Woll entered Bexar at the head of twelve hundred men. Unlike Vásquez, moreover, he was prepared to hold on and meet the Texian force which wasn't long in arriving.

Back from Mexico City, Old Paint Caldwell was in command. In so acting, he was putting his life twice in jeopardy, for as a breaker of parole, he would certainly have been shot out of hand, if captured.

Colonel Caldwell had only 220 men, but the veteran Indian fighter knew how to use them. Posting his rifles along a stream six miles east of San Antonio, he sent Major Hays with a detachment of fifty horsemen to draw the enemy into his trap.

What happened, after Jack Coffee had aggravated General

196

Woll to the point of following him with eight hundred at his back, was told by Old Paint himself in a report dated September 17. "At the Salado, two miles above the old crossing," it ran in part, "we commenced fighting at eleven o'clock today. A hot fire was kept up till one hour by the sun, when the enemy retreated, bearing off their dead . . . We have a glorious band of Texas patriots, among whom only ten were wounded and not one killed. The enemy are all around me, on every side, but I fear them not."

He didn't need to fear them, for Woll had had enough and retreated south from Bexar the following day. The Mexican garrisons still made the Rio Grande Valley uninhabitable, though, and before the year was out an effort to dislodge the enemy soldiery was launched by the Texians.

Laredo was at last incorporated in the Republic as of December 9, 1842. General Alexander Somervell then took the Mexican garrison town of Guerrero; but having found himself unable to control an element in his command which broke ranks to plunder, he ordered withdrawal. Hays was among the two hundred who turned back to Texas with the General. He tried to persuade Sam Walker and a younger member of his Ranger company called Big Foot Wallace to stay with him. They, however, joined the three hundred—in part hot-blooded patriots who sincerely wished to carry the war to Mexico, and in part ruffians who sincerely wished to go in quest of more loot—who chose to go on down the valley toward Mier.

36

Tom Benton Eyes the Pacific

HAVING SURVIVED a stray Jackson or Benton bullet in 1813, John Charles Frémont had gone on to graduate from a college in Charleston, South Carolina, where he had shown an aptitude for mathematics which had eventually earned him an appointment as an officer in the U.S. Army's Corps of Topographical Engineers. Assigned to assist a man who was in the business of mapping the country between the Mississippi and the Missouri, Frémont soon met Thomas Hart Benton, whose pervasive interest in the West was the driving force behind the project.

Later to wish that either he or Old Hickory had shot John Charles while the latter was an infant sojourning in Nashville, Benton began by favoring him, because of the good reports of him made by the man whose protégé he had become. Jean Nicholas Nicollet was the best topographer in the nation at the time. In 1838 and the following year he took Frémont on field trips to the upper Missouri country. As their guide on the second of these was none other than Hugh Glass's old associate, Etienne Provost, Frémont received excellent instruction in the art of taking care of himself in the wilderness.

He made progress in other respects, too. By 1840 Senator Benton regretted having introduced John Charles to his daughter Jessie. Tom was convinced that she was far too young to get married; but as she thought otherwise the wedding took place in 1841. Given the choice of liking her marriage to an unknown junior officer and losing touch with a child to whom he was devoted, Benton got over his grouch and was Frémont's backer from then on.

Their shared enthusiasm for the West and Nicollet's declining health made pushing Frémont forward a natural act rather than one tainted with nepotism. Having taken charge of a field trip in 1841, Frémont was the man best qualified to step into Nicollet's shoes; and when, the following January, the aging topographer had to confess himself physically incapable of carrying out the plan which he and Benton had so long discussed, John Charles was inevitably put in charge of its execution.

To the scheme in question, mapping the northern plains had been merely introductory. Tom Benton wanted the Pacific Coast for the United States; and as he had thought all around the problem of acquiring it, he was proceeding in a logical manner.

198

Although California was a Mexican province, the Senator felt that Mexico's grip on it was so tenuous as to be disregarded. In his opinion the British Empire would acquire California, just as it had already managed to get tentative control of the Pacific Northwest, unless America moved in. Lacking a cat's-paw like the Hudson's Bay Company, the United States could only rely on occupation by settlers, and up until 1842 emigration to the West Coast had been inadequate. What was needed by way of opening the throttle, Benton reasoned, was the dissemination of accurate knowledge about the trails to the West and the country through which they passed. While it was true that quite a few works on the subject had been published, they had been written by amateurs who had left out the very information calculated to give prospective immigrants confidence in their ability to negotiate the long wagon roads to Oregon and California. What Benton wanted his son-in-law to provide, in a word, was a trained observer's guide, together with illustrative maps.

Having made preparations for his first trip west of the Missouri, Frémont cruised up that river as far as Westport Landing in May of 1842. His daughter deposited with relatives and his sinews oiled by a spree in St. Louis, Kit Carson was on his way back to New Mexico, traveling on the same boat. The mountain man was exactly the cicerone of the Far West the officer needed; and as they found themselves congenial, Carson accepted the proffered post of guide.

From then until October, Frémont's first expedition surveyed the Oregon Trail as far as South Pass. It also examined the environing Rockies. Employing astronomical observation, John Charles established heights, distances and the relative positions of landmarks which had been matters of guesswork before. He also took barometric as well as thermometric readings which showed the climate and weather conditions were not causes for alarm. Lastly he described the vegetation and the mineral consistency of the mountains in a way which took the region out of the mysterious category, where much previous writing had pegged it, and brought it comfortably into focus as an unintimidating section of mother earth.

If Frémont's accomplishment was thus far solid, the contention of some was that the man himself was not. He has also proved a figure capable of posthumously giving apoplexy to historians who never walked the world he did. Still others have exulted in him as though they were on his payroll; and between the two clouds of dust the man has been harder to discern than most. But it can be said of him that he dared much, achieved some of the great things he aspired to, held the love of a remarkable woman as long as they both lived and won many friends as well as making enemies of some beside his chroniclers.

In his train in 1842, for instance, was one Charles Preuss, a German cartographer. A genius in his line, he kept a journal which revealed his fierce hatred of everything and everybody he met in the wilderness, beginning with Frémont and Kit Carson. But unwittingly he demonstrated the enterprise of a man he never tired of reviling by making fun of Frémont's efforts to make daguerreotypes of Western scenes in 1842. According to some authorities there is no earlier record of an American attempting outdoor photography.

Failing in that, but successful otherwise, John Charles spent a few months with his wife before packing for the West again. Kit Carson also left a bride (for he had married Charles Bent's sister-in-law in January 1843), in order to take part in Frémont's second expedition. He was not in this case the primary guide, though, for Tom Fitzpatrick led the way across the Great Plains to the mountains.

Frémont had left Missouri toward the end of May, starting somewhat earlier than he had intended to, because he had received a letter from his wife urging him to go afield without further delay. Jessie Benton Frémont did not explain why, because if her officer husband had complied with her injunction while knowing what was afoot, he would have been guilty of mutinous conduct. What his wife had got wind of from her post in Washington was that Colonel John James Abert, commanding officer of the Corps of Topographical Engineers, had planned to recall John Charles. Her messenger was faster than the Army's, so the lieutenant was up the Missouri and out on the trail by the time the change of orders reached St. Louis. The route of the second expedition coursed along the Kansas River to the Republican Fork and thence up to the Bent and St. Vrain's fort on the South Fork of the Platte, where they arrived on the Fourth of July. Given the job of jockeying the baggage trains across the mountains, Fitzpatrick proceeded to Fort Hall, while Carson, who had arrived with supplies from Bent's Fort, led the exploring expedition proper. In the course of examining the Great Basin, Frémont paddled about in Great Salt Lake, using a rubber boat brought along for just such emergencies. Surveying the Oregon Trail as fas as the Dalles was then resumed.

Anew in the wilderness he hated, the cartographer Preuss was among the few whom Frémont took downriver to Fort Vancouver in November. The lieutenant's purpose was to bring back supplies in the canoes belonging to the Indians hired to pilot them. So much was necessary.

As John Charles had a soldier's eye for neatness, though, this business mission was salted by a comic episode. According to the unforgiving cartographer, Frémont asked Preuss to trim a beard which he had let grow wild, in order to make a more presentable appearance at the Hudson's Bay Company post. When the German refused, the officer challenged him to a duel, which was also indignantly declined.

Inasmuch as Dr. McLoughlin was a shaggy man himself, Frémont's concern for his views was in this case needless. And as the Hudson's Bay Company officer was always ready to help Americans who were on the way out of Oregon, these found no difficulty in getting what they wanted. So after a pleasant visit with the man who had starved Captain Bonneville out of the region, Lieutenant Frémont was east of the Cascades again with the supplies he needed in order to carry out his further plans.

For the first two months the hardships of the explorers were not great, as they moved south ahead of severe weather and stayed clear of the mountains. In mid-January of 1844, though, Frémont decided to strike across the Sierras, his destination Sutter's Fort. If he wasn't quite sure where that post was in relation to his starting point, Frémont had one thing definitely in mind. Knowing that his long-thinking father-in-law was hopeful of spanning the continent with a railroad, he wanted to prove that California's mountains were passable in winter.

There can be no doubt that John Charles liked to pit his strength against rough country and fierce elements. The Sierras now served him both. From the moment he and his men began working their way up the valley of Nevada's Truckee River, every day's hardship was mild compared with that offered by the next calendar point.

The going got too tough for their Chinook Indian guide, who cleared out one night, never to return. Even Frémont began to wonder if his experiment would fail, when the snow got so deep that walking was an exhausting struggle for men, let alone pack-laden animals; but Broken Hand Fitzpatrick had wintered with the tribes of the northern Rockies. Making snowshoes, he led a party which included Frémont and Carson up to the notch of a now not certainly identified pass. From this lookout point they beheld, on February 6, a snowless region to the west backed by a horizon formed by low mountains. Having seen them fifteen years earlier, when he had come to California with Ewing Young, Kit identified these as the Coast Range, and the intervening lowlands as the Sacramento Valley.

But if men could use snowshoes, the horses and mules weren't up to it. A way through the giant drifts had to be cleared and given a sustaining surface by a combination of trampling the snow and thatching it with evergreen branches. It took two weeks in the terrific cold of that season and elevation, but on February 20, 1844, the animals were brought to a place whence the downhill haul toward the district watched over by Sutter's Fort could begin.

Certainly a thief and very possibly a murderer, Captain Sutter was a man of great business competence. On the 49,000 acres he had received as a grant he had planted a flour mill, a blacksmith shop, a blanket factory, a tannery and a distillery in addition to a general trading station. Frémont, in short, could not have found a place in the West better equipped to meet his requirements at every turn.

But, unsparing alike of himself and his men, he resumed his task of studying approaches to the Coast at the earliest moment possible. Without turning aside to visit the sea-hugging towns, he looped south of the Sierras and cut northeast across the desert with a view to reaching Great Salt Lake from the south. Although he might have got into trouble in this land of small water, luck caught up with him in the person of Joe Walker. Tired of the mercantile caravan he had left Los Angeles with, Joe had learned of the expedition's passing from either Mexicans or Indians and hurried to join it.

Walker knew the country southwest of Great Salt Lake better than anybody, having first traversed it as a lieutenant of Bonneville's a decade earlier. Under his guidance the desert was passed through without difficulty.

Zigzagging back and forth across the Rockies first, John Charles reached Bent's Fort on July 1. As only the Santa Fe Trail remained to be negotiated, Walker and Carson left the expedition there and went on to Taos. For once doing what the dour Charles Preuss wanted him to, Frémont easted as rapidly as possible, his goals being first a reunion with Jessie and secondly the preparation for publication of the reports desired by Tom Benton.

⚜ 37 ⚜

The Renegade Missionaries

ONE OF THE strange episodes in the history of a region, where Christian zealots were otherwheres faithfully at work, is the change of heart which visited the majority of those who had come to convert the Indians along the Willamette. What makes the story all the odder is that the people involved were undoubtedly sincere in the beginning. Convinced that they would be counting heavenly coups, they fared far and perilously to save the souls of Indians by rescuing them from paganism. They ended by joining Jason Lee as embezzlers of the money which the Methodist Church had raised to further their pious ambitions.

After the first few years there was hardly a pretense of bettering the tribesmen. Concerning them the only interest shown was the jail for redskins built with funds purloined from the estate of Ewing Young, together with a code of punishment designed to discourage the Indians from robbing white farmers. The latter meanwhile were devoting energies on furlough from piety to staking out huge property holdings and devising means of having possession confirmed in an as yet unorganized territory.

Originally in alliance with McLoughlin against nonmissionary Americans, Lee cut the Doctor's throat in secret while professing friendship outwardly. So did others of these apostates, gouging a man by whose sufferance they had so far thrived.

Sure that all western Oregon, at least, would become part of Canada, McLoughlin had laid claim to real estate south of the Columbia before the missionaries arrived. In particular he had staked out property which included a falls on the Willamette suitable for operating a mill. When the land fever hit them, though, the backslid Indian converters jumped their benefactor's claims and surreptitiously made improvements calculated to render their own of greater validity.

Inevitably their point of view changed, and they that had been indifferent to American interests in the region became patriots. For if what they had done cut at McLoughlin as an individual, it yet set the forsworn apostles against the Hudson's Bay Company and all it represented. As they saw that if the company succeeded in holding Oregon for the British Empire, McLoughlin's hopes and not their own would be realized, they began to work for its downfall by invoking the only power big enough to defeat it. That is to say, they began sending political figures in the States complaints about the company's conduct in Oregon as virulent as those once composed by Hall Kelley. If not much came of this at the outset, the written sentiments turned up as the voice of local public opinion; and bucking the Hudson's Bay Company grew to be a popular activity. The movement waxed in boldness when, in 1842, the population was increased by the first considerable influx of nonmissionary settlers, many of them tough backwoodsmen. During the following winter, moreover, Oregon City was founded. Well up the Willamette, it was a focal point which eclipsed the centrality which Fort Vancouver had up to then enjoyed.

This warning that Britain was losing her grip on the grabbed territory over which it had held undisputed sway since the War of 1812 was not the only one given McLoughlin in 1843. Old Bill Williams led a party of trappers west of the Cascades that year. In the course of a debate with the Doctor, as an auditor recorded, Bill showed himself perfectly familiar with the political history of the region and wound up by telling the Hudson's Bay Company factor flatly that the Empire's line would be rolled back to the 49th parallel.

Following this pronouncement Old Bill, who was one of the last of the mountain men to trap on a large scale, moved on down to the Tule Lake region. The rugged Modoc Indians tried to eject him, but with Williams as strategist forty trappers killed fifty of the two hundred warriors of the tribe—notorious for using poisoned arrows—while losing only three to death themselves.

In the Oregon settlements, in the meantime, a step was being taken which showed that Old Bill had spoken from knowledge of his people when arguing with McLoughlin. In May of 1843 a convention was held along the Willamette at which a motion to launch a provisional government was made. In back of it was the tentative show of United States authority represented by the presence of Elijah White as a sub-Indian agent; and only Americans took part. The French Canadians settled south of the Columbia by the Hudson's Bay Company had been invited to participate, but their own inclinations as well as the urgings of McLoughlin counted them out.

Not even all the men from the States favored the movement, for some were opposed on the principle that there could be no proper organization without federal authority, while others feared British intervention, or unfavorable trading relations with the commercially dominant company. For a moment, after all at the convention had been asked to walk to one of two indicated positions or the other, by way of showing how they stood on the matter, the measure seemed to have no confident backers. Then Joe Meek sounded a political battle cry and led to the yea post a band which had enough strength to carry the day for positive action.

Joe became sheriff under the makeshift Oregon administration, which had a nine-man legislative committee rather than a governor as its head. After this body had presented a constitution which won poll approval in July, Meek had the task of dealing with those among the frontiersmen who didn't take the government's edicts seriously. But as he had a pleasant personality as well as a mountain man's training in the use of weapons, he succeeded in handling matters both effectively and in a manner which earned the orphan organization both good will and respect.

There remained the opposition of the Hudson's Bay Company. McLoughlin, however, had been caught short by this development, for nothing in the experience of a man bred to paternalism had prepared him to understand the political self-reliance which was one of the strongest characteristics of American pioneers. Had the situation remained unchanged, he might have been able to undermine a republic so poor in citizens; but late that summer its population doubled.

Marcus Whitman had gone east during the previous winter in order to persuade his Presbyterian directors not to carry out their threat to withdraw support from his mission. Accompanying him was a man named Lovejoy, one of two pilgrims whom Fitz-patrick had talked the Sioux out of murdering the year before. Cutting south in order to avoid the Dakotas, the pair from Oregon had made Bent's Fort a way stop. Lovejoy had stayed there, rather than take the Santa Fe Trail in January and February, but the urgency of his purpose had led Whitman to push on by himself.

But if differing from Jason Lee by remaining faithful to the missionary ideal, Marcus resembled him both in being enthusiastic about Oregon, and in being determined that the United States should regain it. So in addition to persuading the synod that the work of converting Cayuses and Walla Wallas should continue, Whitman was instrumental in organizing the party of one thousand immigrants which assembled in Missouri at about the time that Oregon's provisional government was being formed.

Captain John Gantt, a cashiered Army officer who had gone west to operate as a fur dealer in the great days of the trade, guided what was known as the Oregon Company. Across South Pass, he put a new wrinkle in the trail by detouring to the post which Old Gabe Bridger had just built on Black's Fork of the Green. Not serving any other purpose, this station catered to wayfarers bound for California and Oregon, to whom it offered the only repair and supply point between Forts Laramie and Hall.

At the latter post Hudson's Bay Company hands tried to stem the immigration tidal wave by insisting that wagons could go no farther. Whitman, though, had seen Joe Meek and Doc Newell prove otherwise three years earlier. Thus the strong band of Oregon recruits reached the Dalles and from there barged down the Columbia, complete with their belongings and stock.

That bad news for the company was soon supplemented. Through 1843 American interest in the Pacific Northwest had been focused on points south of Columbia. Nor had United States diplomats got anywhere, during a quarter of a century, when requesting that the 49th parallel should form the international boundary. In 1844, though, some wild-eyed journalist staggered British diplomacy as some of America's great statesmen had found themselves powerless to do.

Reviewing the territorial claims registered by various nations with respect to the continent's west coast, this nameless champion allowed possession solely to Mexico, the United States and Russia. As Muscovy in America extended south only to the latitude of 54 degrees and 40 minutes, it followed that United States territory ran up the map from California to that point.

Tossed out during a presidential year, this firecracker was the hit of the electoral campaign. The desire to own the Pacific Northwest became a national desire; and after one of James Polk's handlers had wrought the alliteration, "Fifty-four forty or fight," it became a passion.

Thus Britain, long so confident of enlarging the western coast line of her great American dominion, suddenly found herself confronted by a nation whose people cried that Canada didn't abut on the Pacific at all. To hold on to what was properly the Empire's began, in consequence, to supplant encroachment in Oregon as a London policy.

Among further results of the national interest in the West was the return to it of one who had been long absent. After the Black Hawk War, Jim Clyman had gone to the Wisconsin frontier, where he had been the victim of a surprise attack during a rising of the usually peaceful Winnebagos. One shot had broken his arm and another had given him a nasty wound in the thigh; but he had outdistanced pursuit and lived to hark the clamor about the Pacific Northwest.

Arrived in Independence in the spring of 1844, he found there two sharers of his mountain-man adventures. Bill Sublette, rich and with time on his hands, had contracted to take a party of health seekers—accompanied by guards to ward off the Sioux, it can be assumed—to that part of the valley of the Green known as Brown's Hole.

Black Harris was also at the eastern terminus of the Oregon Trail. Some years earlier, when the fur-trading wars were at their height, Harris had advocated a filibustering expedition into the Columbia River region as a means of putting an end to the competition of the Hudson's Bay Company. Now he was the guide of one of the strong contingents marching to seize the territory through farming it.

Traveling with the party guided by Major Harris, Clyman next had the experience of seeing a long train of wagons roll along the Platte, bringing white women and children through the valley he had found empty of all but hostile Indians and dead trappers twenty years before. He likewise saw the great canvas-covered vehicles known as prairie schooners roll up and over the pass through the mountain which he had penetrated, in pursuit of beaver, when riding with unscarred Sublette, unmaimed Fitzpatrick and alive Jed Smith.

One more of that pioneer mountain-man foursome was soon to cross the mortal Great Divide. His trip to the Great Basin had made Cut Face anxious to live in the wilderness again. He therefore decided to retire from business and put his knowledge of the West and its natives at the service of the Office of Indian Affairs. In order to get the agency appointment he had in mind, Bill began a trip to Washington which didn't extend beyond Pittsburgh. In that prosperous city a man who had thrived on hardships had caught cold while traveling de luxe and died in August of 1845.

𝕰𝖁𝕽 38 𝕰𝖁𝕽
Old Hickory's Source of Content

FROM THE DAY of its founding, the Republic of Texas had been a subject of debate, conducted by those in America who wished it to be annexed to the United States and those who didn't. With rare exceptions this argument was not honestly carried on by the spokesmen for either course of action.

There was much talk in Northern political circles of the expense of taking over an impoverished nation and of the sinfulness of trying to take advantage of Mexico's territorial loss. What the speakers meant was that Texas lay below the Mason-Dixon line and would amplify the agrarian South.

There was rhetoric in Southern political gatherings dealing with the obligation of sheltering former Americans who had shown their worth by winning independence exactly as the Founding Fathers of the United States had done. The thought behind these declarations was that Texas could provide the South with two more senators, needed to vote the industrial North down in the increasingly bitter struggle for dominance between the two.

As they were then about equal in Congressional strength, a stalemate developed which favored the exclusionists. It might have been prolonged indefinitely except for the fact that popular sentiment disrgarded both false and true issues and settled the problem on an emotional basis.

Sympathy for Texas began to be a force to reckon with after the tale of the disastrous Santa Fe Expedition became a known one in the States. It gathered more power after the Texians who had refused to obey the orders of General Somervell organized their own army.

With the wishes of the Republic's war department kissed goodbye, commissions were ignored and rank was established by election in the usual frontier manner. Popularity won the commander's spot for one William S. Fisher, while Sam Walker and Ewen Cameron were among the company captains.

Their first target, the Mexican town of Mier, turned out to be strongly garrisoned. The Texians had, in fact, moved into a district swarming with hostile troops. The invaders suffered heavy casualties in the battle which developed; and after a wound put Fisher *hors de combat*, they surrendered to far superior numbers.

The pledge here, as in the case of the Santa Fe Expedition, was that they would be given the consideration accorded prisoners of war. History again repeated itself after they had put down their arms, though. They were treated as felons, pending the receipt of orders as to their disposition, which arrived from the capital in February of 1843.

The doom of the 261 able to do so was to be led afoot to Mexico City, just as the Texians captured in New Mexico had been. The situation was different in one important respect, though. The men of the Mier Expedition had not been enfeebled to the point of impotence by starvation.

They proved this at a stopping point called Hacienda Salado, one hundred miles south of Saltillo in Coahuila. There Cameron and Walker personally took care of the two sentinels guarding the exit to the building in which the prisoners had been herded. Quiet men, they had strong hands.

Outside in a rush, the Texians seized arms and ammunition from troops stationed in the court beyond the door. When their guns had routed a supporting cavalry squadron, the fugitives forced the surrender of the infantry units which had been guarding them and set out for the Rio Grande.

Knowing that they would be run down by horsemen if they stayed on the road, they struck across country. Men they might have defeated, but the waterless barrens into which they plunged were too much for them. There were only 160 out of 261 left when Mexican troops finally cornered them eleven days later.

Marched back to Hacienda Salado, they there received Santa Anna's special decree. The author of Fannin's Massacre had first ordered death for all of them; but the publication of that command had resulted in such vigorous protests from foreign members of the capital's diplomatic corps that he had modified his ukase by calling for decimation instead.

Life and death hinged on white and black beans respectively, with each man picking his own fate from an urn holding the vegetable lots. After the sixteen who drew black beans had been subtracted by gunfire, the rest were walked to Mexico City. Among its residents then was General Canales, who saw an enemy for the third time.

In common with Walker and Big Foot Wallace, Dr. Cameron

had drawn a white bean. But when Canales learned that Ewen was among the Texians brought to the capital, he asked Santa Anna to have him shot anyhow, as a favor to a friend. After Santa Anna had cheerfully obliged, the 144 left of the 300 once belonging to the Mier Expedition were sentenced to hard labor under chain-gang conditions and sent to wherever the government found use for their services.

The outcry raised in America by Mexican treatment of the men captured at Mier shortly had echoes caused by the U.S. Army's treatment of yet other Texians. This time it was questionable whether they were trespassers, for equally positive historians have decided the matter both ways.

Back from his harrowing experiences with the Santa Fe Expedition, Jacob Snively thought of a way to cut back at Mexico. Having been the Republic's acting Secretary of War, as well as having served as paymaster and inspector general of its army, he had the influence to be commissioned commander of a third Texian expeditionary force. The purpose of this one was to lift the cargoes of Mexican merchants in transit on the Santa Fe Trail.

His scheme horrified American politicians, unable to draw the analogy between sea and land warfare; for in principle it was no different from the normal naval practice of preying on the merchantmen of hostile nations. Yet because the notion was novel, the United States government became gravely concerned about the necessity of protecting Mexican merchantmen in the American sector of the Santa Fe Trail, and Captain Philip St. George Cooke galloped west with three hundred dragoons in tow.

This anticipatory move could easily be made. For although Jacob got his authorization in February of 1843, he first had to find volunteers willing to brave the desert which had ruined the column bound for Santa Fe, and then make the long, rough journey to the trail of that name. The time lag of three months allowed American newspapers to spread the word well before the Snively Expedition reached the Arkansas.

The screams of "land piracy" notwithstanding, the rights and the wrongs of the case depended on the maps of the three countries involved. According to those of the United States and Mexico, the Santa Fe Trail coursed directly from one country to another. Yet according to the Napoleonic ones of Texas its Panhandle extended to the Arkansas in addition to stretching west to the Rio Grande.

But in any case Jacob's expedition had been preceded by an out-and-out filibustering one, raised in Missouri by a Colonel Charles Warner for the express purpose of invading New Mexico. This had been done with the consent rather than the authorization of the Republic, which did no more than tell Warfield that he was welcome to enlist as many as he could for the purpose of harrying the enemy.

Having drawn only two dozen men to his banner, this free lance didn't loom as much of a threat, but Governor Armijo had sent a number of detachments, amounting to several hundred men in all, to round the invaders up. The filibusters had taken the first bout by catching a body of cavalry camped near Mora off guard. After killing some and chasing off most of the rest they had let their eighteen captives go, while retaining all the mounts, pack animals and gear belonging to the routed unit.

Armijo's men had won the return engagement, however, getting back the seized stock as well as the steeds of the Americans. Cooled off by having to make it back to the Arkansas afoot, about half of these had quit the game; but Warfield and the rest of his command threw in with that of the newly arrived Snively.

It was no great army. Jake had been able to enlist but an even 180 men. Traveling at a more favorable time of the year, though, than had the Santa Fe Expedition, they had reached the Arkansas in good condition and gone into bivouac forty miles east of the Santa Fe Trail crossing.

Snively's purpose was to wait until the first caravans of the season, then plodding east from Missouri, should roll south of the Arkansas. The Mexicans would then be where he could take them over without infringing American neutrality.

213

While he was lying in wait, however, he learned that Armijo was leading an attack force, and sent a detachment under Warner to meet the vanguard. This the filibuster and his men destroyed, killing a number variously estimated as from twenty to forty and capturing the rest.

Now while having no reason to like Armijo, Charles Bent had been an unhappy ponderer of the effect of Texian military activities upon his mercantile affairs. Inside New Mexico—for Charles still had a store and supply depot at Taos—these had been not only difficult but dangerous to conduct, because of the Governor's hostility. Remembering the blowup at the time of the Santa Fe Expedition, Bent feared that reprisals would be visited on himself and other local Americans, with whom Texians were inseparably associated in Mexican thinking.

Warner's victory over troops personally led by Armijo was the last straw for Charles. Couriers from Bent's Fort sped word of the Snively Expedition's initial coup to the caravan which Cooke was escorting to the Arkansas. The news created general panic among the traders, for if the Mexican ones feared Jake's men, those from the States were afraid of what would happen to them in Santa Fe should their Mexican colleagues be pillaged by the Texians.

Beset by merchants pleading for help and unwilling to exceed his orders by escorting them into New Mexico, Philip St. George hit upon an arbitrary method of seeing to it that the traders could proceed in such safety as the Comanches might grant them. That is to say, he made the decision that Snively was camped a smidgen east of the 100th meridian and was therefore trespassing on United States territory.

As historians have proved Cooke both right and wrong, the chances are even that he was the ill-doer himself. But having justice on his side, if he did, didn't help Jake. Overwhelmed by a much larger force, supported by caravan guards, he surrendered to an officer who returned only one rifle for every ten men.

There's nothing to be said about Cooke's act except that it was left-handed murder committed by one fully cognizant of the perils he was forcing upon men whom he had by no means caught in any overt criminal act. The United States in due course paid for the confiscated rifles; but that didn't save the lives of those who were killed while making their way through hostile Indian territory without guns. The barbarity served Cooke's purpose, however. Hearing of his injustice, Armijo pronounced him the only just American he had ever heard of. Official wrath no longer threatened the merchants of Cooke's country, who proceeded to cross the Arkansas with the also cheered Mexicans.

But Texian protests were taken up by angry American citizens not at all reconciled to the idea of having United States troops used to help foreigners at the expense of people of their own ilk. Then as news of the enslaved members of the Mier Expedition was followed up by a bitter report on the outcome of the Santa Fe trek, written by one of its members, the sighs of sympathy were in undertone to a clamor for annexation which crossed sectional lines.

As soon as people grew seriously interested in the subject, moreover, the advantages to the nation became obvious, and the delay in seizing them, on the part of the government, became a source of pained wonder. Sensing as much, President John Tyler accepted overtures from the younger republic which resulted in a treaty calling for a merger of the two nations. Adopted in April 1844, this was defeated in the United States Senate two months later. The outcry against this Congressional action was, nevertheless, so loud that James Polk was encouraged to run for the presidency on a platform calling for the annexation of Texas and won the nomination of the dominant Democratic party largely on that plank.

Not waiting for Polk's inauguration, a chastened Congress passed a joint Senate and House resolution approving annexation on March 1, 1845. On the following day, or forty-eight hours before he stepped out of office, President Tyler made the invitation to Texas official by signing it.

Mexico promptly broke off diplomatic relations with the

United States. France as well as Britain lodged vigorous protests concerning the planned union because they resented the extension of America's Gulf of Mexico coast line. Neither of the involved nations paid them any mind, though, and Texians, hereinafter to be known as Texans, celebrated the Fourth of July by voting to join the Union.

Andrew Jackson had gone under by then; but he had lived long enough to know that what he had looked forward to thirteen years earlier was due to become an accomplished fact. Having had the satisfaction of exchanging letters on the subject with Sam Houston, the hand which had justified the trust he had put in it, Old Hickory died on June 8 in the house he had built on land bought from the grandfather of Jack Coffee Hays.

৪৩৪ 39 ৪৩৪

Looking for a Home

AS BRIGADIER GENERAL of the Missouri militia, Alexander Doniphan had disobeyed orders in 1838 by allowing the Prophet, Joseph Smith, to lead the Latter-day Saints east of the Mississippi instead of exterminating them one and all. The Mormons prospered in Illinois but only for a time. The Prophet didn't startle anybody by coveting a woman other than the one to whom he had long been espoused, but he created a furor by thinking of a way to ease both his body and his conscience.

As in the case of Mohammed before him, what the man of Nauvoo saw where he had previously been blind, was that Heaven blessed polygamy when practiced by members of the true faith. Yet Joseph did not try to make the prerogative popular; in his view it was one to be enjoyed only by the hierarchy.

Still some of the women propositioned to become "spiritual wives" not only failed to take kindly to the idea but spread the news that alien ethics had invaded Illinois. It therefore wasn't long before a practice of limited applicability had been vocally ballooned into general orgies which would have been banned in Gomorrah. So in 1844 some from the neighboring countryside broke into the jail where Joseph had earlier been placed and administered the martyr's death by which prophets best serve the cause of their respective beliefs.

The most remarkable among those who shared Smith's was Brigham Young, also from Vermont. Unlike the imaginative and erratic Joseph, he was as tough and practical as a slab of Green Mountain granite. As the interest of an all-business brain in spiritual intensities cannot have been great, it can be assumed that Young became a disciple of Smith's because he saw among the Mormon community a chance to use the qualities he knew he possessed. If so he was not the first man of extraordinary ability who seceded from the norm of society on account of its failure to make room for his talents. In seed a captain of industry, he had been relegated to the trades of house painting and window glazing until Joseph Smith found gold plates in a western New York well and transcribed their else unreadable messages with the aid of magic spectacles. But though he read opportunity in the Book of Mormon, Brigham had to wait until he was forty-three before the citizens of Illinois shot the Prophet and gave an abler man the freedom to use his powers.

Young was not in Nauvoo at the time, as in 1840 Smith had dispatched him to England, where he functioned as a missionary and recruiter for Mormon colonies in America. In this he was successful not only because of his personality but because of conditions abroad. Far more advanced in Europe than in America at that time, the Industrial Age was covering former farming areas with cities which spread like spilled water. And many of those uprooted by this process were glad to be told of rural areas in America where they could expect to be welcomed as co-religionists.

A Latter-day Saint called Rigdon had inherited the Prophet's mantle; but Young had taken a rear seat long enough. Hastening back from England, Brigham not only exiled his rival physically but used his usurped authority to pronounce a spiritual ban. Rigdon, as he assured followers who had once looked upon the former as Joseph's alter ego, would be "buffeted for 1,000 years" by agents of offended Heaven.

At last in full command, Young faced the problem of what to do with his people. It was clear that Mormons could not flourish in Illinois, where sentiment hostile to them continued to mount. Nor could they count on being well received elsewhere in the States, where their assumptions of sainthood had aroused storms even before Smith had triggered the hurricane which blew him into the Great Beyond. Believing that saints were post-mortem creations, other sectarians were hot against what they regarded as impious imposture.

As the prejudice was national, the problem it caused was national. The question troubling Brigham was also being discussed in the East, where some lesser Mormon communities were struggling for survival. These held a convention in New York City, in the fall of 1845, at which the man most listened to was Sam Brannan.

Like Brigham, Sam was possessed of abilities which had not yet found fruition. Otherwise the Downeaster bore no resemblance to the man from Vermont. Where the latter was a long thinker who kept his own counsel, Brannan was a loud spur-of-the-minute man, and one who liked liquor for bright lights to twinkle in. Junior to Brigham, he matched him in a grasping ambition, which had so far done no more than wince at a couple of failures as a newspaper publisher.

At the convention in New York the delegates agreed that it was useless to seek acceptance among their fellow countrymen any longer. Some wished to try to form a Mormon colony in Oregon, but Sam talked that notion down by pointing out that they couldn't expect to be any more welcome to the settlers established in the Pacific Northwest than they had been to any other unsainted Americans. The thing to do, he insisted, was to get entirely out of the United States, or any territory it claimed, and emigrate to Mexican-owned California. And before the meeting broke up he had so far carried his point that he was given authority to recruit volunteers for a trial colony, and to charter a ship in which to conduct them to the West Coast.

Although Brannan thought he had hit upon the one promising solution of the problem confronting the Church of Jesus Christ of Latter-day Saints, Brigham Young had not only been thinking, he had been reading. A literary sensation of 1845 was Frémont's report of his first two exploring expeditions.

One of the strong moving forces in the history of the West, it had accomplished what Tom Benton had hoped would happen. No longer feeling that they were wheeling into terra incognita, pilgrims bound for Oregon and California crossed South Pass in unprecedented numbers.

Brigham, however, had taken note of an important aspect of Frémont's descriptive analysis of the West to which others had not given the attention it deserved. An all-around scientist, John Charles was both a botanist and a student of soil composition. Among the things he stressed was the fertility of many portions of the West where previous investigators had declared the earth to be too barren for agriculture.

Although agreeing with Brannan in not wishing to go to Oregon, Young didn't wish to go to California, or any place where he and his people would be subject either to governmental direction or social pressure. What he wanted to find was a point of settlement with a minimum of communications with the rest of the world. The Great Basin south of Oregon offered him that, as it was a place where Washington's law didn't run, while Mexico City had shown no interest in it; and now Frémont had declared it a feasible refuge by warranting much of its soil prime.

While finding out all he could about the region beyond the Rockies from those who knew of it at first or second hand, Brigham kept his thoughts to himself. Nor had his colony attained the strength he deemed necessary for his contemplated venture when an edict forced the Mormons out of Illinois in February of 1846. Leading them across the frozen Mississippi, Brigham didn't call more than a temporary halt until, in the Council Bluffs vicinity, he founded a depot city named Kane.

During the same month Sam Brannan, in company with some three hundred other Saints, started around the Horn in the sailing craft *Brooklyn*. He felt confident that the exiles from Nauvoo would join him in a coastal region, where he would have the status of seniority as a patriarch. And mentally looking west up the Platte Valley from Kane, its residents thought the future would find them beyond the Sierras, too.

Young did nothing to unsettle this theory, even when the outbreak of war with Mexico led to a draft of some of his followers. Selecting the ones to go, he cooperated out of a need for money, not out of love for the country from which he was determined to escape. As the Mormons were a communist organization at that stage of their development, he could arrange to have the pay of those detailed as soldiers deposited to the account of his community's general fund. As for the draftees, Brigham bid them a prophet's farewell, without bothering to tell them that he wouldn't see them in California.

𝕊𝕍 40 𝕊𝕍
Incorporated Claret Takes Santa Fe

THE INDIANS OF the Great Plains had become, by the middle 1840's, increasingly restive. After the last of the tribes shifted from the East had been thrust beyond the Mississippi Valley, crowding had become acute in some sectors. Creeks, Chocktaws, Chickasaws and other Muskogians, as well as the Cherokees, dug in as slaveholding planters in Oklahoma. The expansion of white settlement in Texas pushed tribes which had been resident along the Trinity back to the Red, thus causing further adjustments, as well as further demands on the game supply of a narrowing range.

Some of the smaller nations had been ground to pieces in the friction or lost their identity by joining larger ones. Some of these were no longer autonomous. Having found the problem of meeting current conditions too much for them, they had accepted the establishment of regulating agencies.

West where the mountain tribes ranged, the pressure from the East had been felt only slightly; but the increased use of the Oregon Trail worried thoughtful Indian observers, who began to have the feeling of being surrounded. The Sioux in particular had become irritated by the sight of the vast wagon trains rumbling across their hunting grounds toward who knew where? The very fact that they couldn't envision a destination made the immigrants a source of nervousness. The feeling that something was going on which ought to be stopped caused protesting attacks which attained alarming frequency.

In consequence the First Dragoons, Stephen Watts Kearny commanding, went up the Oregon Trail in June of 1845. Their first port of call was Fort Laramie, whose inmates won no approval from Captain Cooke. Commenting on the families of the squaw-mated residents, he marked the place as an arena where barbarism and civilization were at it dingdong. "The struggle," Philip St. George wrote, "is at close quarters; civilization, furnishing house and clothing; barbarism, children and fleas."

The fort was, nevertheless, the site of an international council. After the chiefs of the Oglala Sioux had responded to an invitation, Kearny pointed out that the Oregon pilgrims were not really invaders but people who were hurrying through Dakota hunting grounds as rapidly as possible. Adding gifts to reason and the argument offered by his troopers, he won promises to leave the trail farers alone.

In itself the agreement meant nothing, and for the very same reason that promises made to Indians by the federal government meant nothing. However well-intentioned, political leaders at Washington were powerless to control the actions of self-sufficient pioneers who made their own rules. By the same token, the pledge of any Indian chief was only binding upon himself and any present who consented to have him speak for them.

But as the parading of a considerable body of armed white men appeared to have a sobering effect on warriors told that many more would arrive, if necessary, the dragoons went on to South Pass. Crossing it under the guidance of Tom Fitzpatrick, they displayed their weapons to the Shoshones and Bannocks with like success.

Yet if the soldiers inspired the Indians with sufficient awe, they tickled the risibilities of Old Bill Williams, who took note of them as they were returning via Bent's Fort. Having a maverick's scorn for men bound together by organization, he undertook to amuse himself at their expense.

On a series of occasions he caused alarms which waked the whole visited camp by showing himself guised as an Indian. Then while everybody stood to arms, Old Bill would disappear to enjoy his laugh.

On detachments officered by men of less experience, he pulled this stunt scathelessly; but then he tried it on the encampment of Captain Cooke's troop. By that time Philip St. George had been a plainsman for sixteen years. Tracking Williams down, he caught the old rapscallion, while the latter was taking it easy in the belief that he had left pursuit behind.

As Bill was still in Indian getup, he was booked as a renegade. Although the mountain man tried to explain his joke, the Captain was not entertained. A dragoon detail hustled Williams east to Fort Leavenworth, where he did time for a while before he could clear himself.

At Bent's Fort, meanwhile, Colonel Kearny questioned Charles Bent exhaustively about New Mexico. For in annexing Texas, the United States was in the way of taking over the Republic's claim to the settlements along the Rio Grande; and Army leaders foresaw the chance of action there.

When Congress made this thinking valid by voting to uphold the Texas view of Western geography in full, the effort to drive out Americans settled in New Mexico was naturally intensified.

George Bent, junior to Charles and William, survived being mobbed in Taos, but some who were attacked did not. Originally opposed to any show of hostility against Mexico, on the ground that it would make trade hazardous, the merchants from the States came to hope for belligerence as the only means of relieving them from harassment and worse.

Help was on the way, for in "Fifty-four forty or fight" Polk, Tom Benton had found exactly the President to support the scheme he had in mind when he had first sponsored the mapping of the West by Nicollet. Not content with claiming New Mexico as far as the Rio Grande, Tom wanted the rest of it as a land bridge to California. Concurring, Polk ordered the formation, in the spring of 1846, of the Army of the West.

When war with Mexico was officially declared in May, Captain Cooke was happy to receive orders which started him for Texas and presumptive service with a force being assembled to invade Mexico from there. But Kearny had been given command of the Army of the West, and he prized Cooke too much to be willing to lose him. He therefore fired a protest which had the effect of forcing the disgusted Captain to go where he had already been too often for his satisfaction. As his chief had left Fort Leavenworth by then, Philip St. George found only instructions to follow an already marching military expedition.

Always at hand wherever history needed him, Broken Hand Fitzpatrick led the vanguard, showing short cuts to a flying column whose purpose was to warn American traders along the trail that it would be unsafe for American civilians to enter disputed New Mexico. Colonel Kearny, whose brigadier star was on its way after him, had ordered the main body to set out on July 3. As Bent's Fort was the designated rallying point, Cooke had been instructed to meet his commander there. Arriving the last of the month, the Captain found not only the Colonel but James Magoffin of Kentucky.

A prairie trader of long standing, Magoffin knew a great deal about Mexico, where he had done much to relieve the sufferings of the Santa Fe Expedition. Additionally he was known to Tom

Benton, who had brought him to Washington to expound matters Mexican to the President. Viewing him as serviceable to Kearny, Polk had asked him to report to the commander of the Army of the West.

In spite of its imposing title, the force consisted of no more than eighteen hundred men, of whom only the dragoons were regulars. Governor Armijo, on the other hand, had shown himself able to put several thousand in the field. Deciding to avoid pitting his raw volunteers against superior numbers, if he could, Kearny emerged from his conference with Magoffin with two plans. One entailed a bribe, which the trader was authorized to offer Armijo. The other was to try to run a bluff through the agency of Cooke.

Philip St. George had been chosen because of his unique standing with the Mexicans, earned when he had protected merchants of that nation to the cost of the Snively Expedition. He could therefore have a reasonable hope of entering Santa Fe without being shot, as well as of getting a respectful hearing from Mexican officials.

Leaving Bent's Fort on August 1, Cooke and Magoffin hit it off well. The trader was not only excellent company in himself but was supplied with enough claret to make the journey one for Anacreon, or even a thirsty officer from Virginia. They arrived at Santa Fe twelve days and innumerable pulled corks later; and after Philip St. George took thought to wave a white handkerchief, tied to the point of his saber, they were admitted to parley.

Kearny had authorized Cooke to proffer Armijo a choice between knuckling peacefully and being crushed by an invading force of overwhelming power. Magoffin then talked to the Governor in private, jingling coin, it has been assumed, for a man known to have enjoyed such music. And because of either or both of these interviews Armijo announced that his troops would evacuate a highly defendable approach to New Mexico's capital.

Kearny had in the meantime gained the rank suitable for the commander of an army. The largest unit of his invading column was a regiment of Missouri volunteers led by the Colonel Doniphan who had once spared the lives of Joseph Smith, Brigham Young and others of their sect. An officer in his outfit was Richard Weightman, who had taken a bowie knife with him when appointed to the U.S. Military Academy and had been sent back to his home in Washington for using it on a fellow cadet. Subsequently becoming a lawyer in Missouri, he had been elected captain of a light artillery battery. As sickness had forced him to lag behind at Bent's Fort, he was at that post when Kearny's star of command had arrived, and had nominated himself as the one to give it to his superior.

Apprised by Cooke of Armijo's intentions, the advancing General spoke as a conqueror at each town he reached, announcing to puzzled Mexicans, as though it were an uncontestable fact, that they were now inhabiting United States territory. He also enfranchised them in a manner which stirred grim amusement in Philip St. George. "The great boon of American citizenship," he noted, "was thus thrust, through an interpreter, by the mailed hand, upon eighty thousand mongrels who cannot read."

At the same time the Captain fully appreciated the deft coolness with which his commander was operating, as indeed he should have. For Kearny's show of confidence, plus the respect for the rights of a civilian population which he forced his troops to maintain, kept the noise of conquest down to the level of parlor conversation. The rioting which might well have developed did so at no place along the line, and on August 16, 1846, Cooke found himself commanding the captured but peaceful city of Santa Fe.

Territory which had been well settled by Spaniards and their Mexican successor for many decades was thus bloodlessly taken over by America as though by sleight of hand. After handling the business in this admirable manner, General Kearny took notice of orders which called for marching on west. New Mexico had to be administered, however, and Kearny did not wish to impose military rule on a people who had accepted their change of nationality so docilely. Remembering the man whose detailed knowledge of the province had impressed him the year before, he appointed Charles Bent as governor.

৪৩ 41 ৪৩

A Grizzly on a Flag

LEAVING OREGON WITH a party which included a James Marshall, Jim Clyman rode south in the spring of 1845 and checked in at Sutter's Fort in June of that year. Finding opportunity in the commercial hub by the Sacramento, Marshall stayed there, but Clyman resumed his wanderings.

He visited George Yount in the course of them, for this quondam associate of Hugh Glass, Milton Sublette and Ewing Young had settled down and was thriving as a rancher. After leaving George, Jim once had to flourish his sword and gun to shoo off Indians who were engaged in trying to cut him off from his companions; but having a gift alike for getting into trouble and out of it, he managed a tour of California which included the capital, Monterey.

Noting that if this city was fortified, he couldn't find the fort, Jim became convinced of two things. One was that California could be seized by Americans, granted a competent leader, and the other was that the province would be no fit place for a man of free leanings to reside until it was under United States rule. This latter conviction was owing to the rub between Americans and Mexicans, which duplicated the friction in New Mexico in origin as well as nature. Then the natives quite reasonably feared that what had happened in Texas would be repeated, if Americans were allowed to settle in quantity and follow their independent bents.

While Clyman was moodily drifting around California, Frémont commenced his third expedition with Kit Carson and Joe Walker as his principal guides, though Old Bill Williams was with him part of the way. Pursuant to making a further examination of the Great Basin and blazing a new trail across the Sierras, John Charles returned to Sutter's Fort on December 9, 1845.

Just what instructions he had received from Benton before he left the East, or what he learned in the course of the visit he paid Larkin, the American consul at Monterey, are not certainly known. It can be assumed from his actions, though, that he was this time in California with more on his mind than looking the country over.

Whether or not Mexican officials understood his relationship with a prominent United States senator, they didn't want him around. Because of his status as an Army officer, they took the position that Frémont's was a military party and ordered it to leave.

Cheered when John Charles showed signs of resisting, Jim Clyman offered to rally American volunteers to his aid. Eventually, however, Captain Frémont disappointed Jim by abandoning his stand at San Jose. Probably he had been instructed to do nothing overt until war between Mexico and the United States had been definitely declared. As news of it still didn't break, he ordered a withdrawal, in February 1846, to Klamath Lake, in Oregon.

More dissatisfied with California than ever, Clyman decided to return to the States again. For companion he had a journalist named Lansford Hastings, whom Fitzpatrick had formerly rescued from the Sioux along with Whitman's associate, Lovejoy.

A promoter who meant to boom the advantages of California upon reaching the East, Hastings was enthusiastic about a short cut they took. From the Nevada side of the Sierras it ran through seasonably passable country. That is to say, it had offered enough moisture and grazing when Frémont's party had used it the previous fall; and conditions were also favorable in the spring. What Jim as a veteran mountain man realized, though, was that summer heat would turn the region into one which travelers had better avoid.

He said that to James Reed, with whom he had served in Black

Hawk's War, when he encountered him at Fort Laramie. Clyman advised Reed and other members of the Donner Party to continue on the Oregon Trail to Fort Hall's vicinity, and take the regular trace to California from there. But the immigrants were more impressed with the cheerful voice of the promoter; and beyond the Rockies they took the so-called Hastings cutoff, running south of Great Salt Lake.

In the province toward which their ox-drawn vehicles were creaking, events of moment had been taking place in the meantime. On May 8, 1846, a lieutenant of the U.S. Marine Corps named Gillespie had arrived in Frémont's Oregon camp with a message from United States Consul Larkin. Its tenor was to the effect that on the one hand there were indications of a plot to turn California over to Great Britain, while on the other Governor de Castro was suspected of a plan to destroy some American settlements strung along the Sacramento.

Returning to that area with battle in his eye, Frémont did not make the master of Sutter's Fort happy. John Augustus held his immense patent under Mexican authority and was understandably not anxious for a change in government. But he became involved with a movement aimed at such a shift. Although the preserved grumblings of Sutter's man, Bidwell, hint an effort to hold back, Sutter became Frémont's supply agent and his fort the headquarters from which John Charles worked to detach California from Mexico.

Another not cheered by Frémont's return to California was Commodore Sloat of the U.S. Pacific Squadron, then anchored at Monterey. A cautious fellow who didn't like to hear sabers rattled out of official turn, Sloat answered Frémont's request for cooperation with the word that he would sit tight pending Navy Department instructions.

Thus forced to act alone, Frémont promoted the gathering of armed Americans. Some were settlers whose ranches or what not they wanted to defend against expected California aggression. Some were quasi settlers like Bill Bradshaw, who had come to northern California after felling a sword-wielding hidalgo from the southern part of the province with a picket. Some were guaranteed nonsettlers like Herman Ehrenberg. After spending some seasons as the consort of a Kanaka queen, Herman had returned to the West.

As of May 23, both the United States and Mexico had formally recognized a state of war; but for all the embattled men under Frémont knew to the contrary, they were a rump insurgent force. Needing a banner and not feeling able to fly the one of their native country, they hoisted one whose device was a grizzly, gules, on a white field. Going into political caucus next, they declared the independence of the Bear Flag Republic.

Under it and John Charles, the new nation's army captured a Mexican post at Sonoma Pass in mid-June. A week later they advanced to meet de Castro, bent both on quelling insurrection and destroying American settlements, as earlier threatened. As the Bear Flag again triumphed, Frémont was unanimously elected the Republic's president on July 5.

The land of the Bear Flag enjoyed its sword-earned autonomy for two days. On July 7 the news that war had broken out finally reached Commodore Sloat, whose men-of-war then pointed their guns at Monterey. Inasmuch as Jim Clyman was not the only one who couldn't find a defending fort, the capital of California capitulated.

After the Stars and Stripes had been raised ashore there, Sloat sent a ship to Yerba Buena, by the mouth of San Francisco Bay, where its commander saw to it that the same service was performed. But that was all the Commodore would do in the way of conquest although he did turn one man-of-war over to the officer, already on deck, who was scheduled to replace him in short order.

Pioneer in advocating steam vessels for the Navy, Commodore Robert Stockton was a let's-get-on-with-it officer in marked contrast to Sloat. In his pocket were orders to conquer California, and to administrate it in the name of the United States government. This, without waiting for his colleague to pass the command to him, he moved to undertake.

If Sloat hadn't wanted Frémont's cooperation, Stockton very much did. Southern California remained in Mexican hands; and the Commodore used the blanket powers which had been given him to offer John Charles a lieutenant-colonelcy in a joint sea and land force.

Notwithstanding the tentative advance in rank, Lieutenant Frémont hesitated. He would have preferred to maneuver his volunteer legion independently. Having his own views of what should be done, besides, he wanted to advance south by land and disperse any bodies of Mexican troops found en route. Still Stockton ranked him, albeit of another service, so Colonel Frémont, Major Ehrenberg, Lieutenant Bradshaw and the other Bear Flaggers put to sea from Monterey in mid-August, their destination Los Angeles.

A crack Navy commander, Stockton did not understand that seizing the coastal cities, even though they were the primary population centers, did not constitute conquest of a ranching people. After he had taken San Diego as well as Los Angeles, therefore, the Commodore considered his task done.

That being the case, he next wanted the Navy Department at Washington to know what he had accomplished. For this purpose Stockton borrowed Lieutenant Carson from Frémont and sped Kit eastward with dispatches.

⚘ 42 ⚘

Sam Walker's Dime

WHILE A PRISONER as a consequence of taking part in the Mier Expedition, Sam Walker had undertaken to tell his guards at the castle prison of Perote that the American flag would some-day fly over it. In rebuttal, his wardens had made him and some fellow Texians erect a pole up which to hoist the Mexican banner. Possessing a ten-cent piece, Sam showed it to his overseers before dropping it in the hole he had just helped dig. "I'm coming back to get this," he promised; and then assisted in seating the flagpole atop the wagered coin.

Released, following a year of servitude, Walker rejoined the Rangers, whose senior officer was then Major Hays, his age twenty-seven. Not tall or powerfully built, as were so many frontiersmen, Jack Coffee had earned pre-eminence through the possession of explosive energies, under marvelous control, and an endurance no less extraordinary. On one occasion he had kept pace for three entire days with a party of Delawares running down afoot the Comanches who had lifted their horses.

Under Hays the Rangers were all, for the first time, armed with the multiple-fire hand guns which Walker had helped Colt to produce. They needed some advantage, for the indications that the United States was planning to annex Texas had touched off furious bandit raids. Encouraged by Mexican emissaries, too, the Comanches were taking the aggressive as they had not since Old Paint blew them down at Plum Creek.

But though the revolvers gave the Rangers firepower superiority, they were effective only at near targets. That meant getting so close that the Comanches could use their bows effectively, and sometimes even their lances. In a melee forty miles north of Bexar, for example, Walker had a shaft thrust in his back by one brave while he was warding off the weapon of another Indian. Sam survived and was soon active again, however, for the Rangers were as tough and hard to kill as the mountain men.

Still the real threat to the safety of Americans in Texas was the renewed hostility of Mexico as annexation by the United States neared accomplishment. Nor did completed annexation change the fact that south of Corpus Christi settlement was denied by Mexican garrisons.

It was to correct this situation that General Zachary Taylor went to Texas in July of 1845. In command of 1500 troops, he reached Corpus Christi, full of grit and good intentions but short of any clear notion as to what he was going to do about the outnumbering soldiery at Matamoros, abetted by guerillas.

Governor Henderson of the new State of Texas offered him

the services of the Rangers, but Taylor asserted that he could depend on his own dragoons to scout for him. Under pressure he consented to incorporate the local force but created an "as you were" situation by putting the accepted companies on detached service as wardens of the frontier. They were needed, as it happened, for during the ensuing months they were engaged in Indian fighting, climaxed by the Battle of Paint Rock.

In February of 1846 Comanches struck the settlements southwest of San Antonio six hundred strong. Gauging their line of withdrawal, Hays led the forty men with him across country to the landmark in question, at whose foot was a pond which was a favorite watering point for the raiders. Jack had guessed right, and as the Indians were driving off stock which had to be herded over a more roundabout route, the Rangers reached the little lake first.

Below the mottled surface of Paint Rock was a thicket which offered not only concealment but—against arrows—pretty satisfactory cover. Here they not only ambushed the Comanche vanguard but stood off assaults which took the form of repeated charges, while archers mounted on the rock simultaneously tried to pick the white men off.

Unusually determined, the Indians kept at it, in the face of very heavy losses, until Hays managed to shoot the commanding chief. The Comanches then at last fled, leaving men, of whom only one was so much as wounded, to collect the booty abandoned by the savages.

This was the last Indian fight which the Rangers handled as the service in charge. For, as on other frontiers, keeping the tribes in order became primarily the responsibility of the United States Army.

With that military branch the Texan border guardians soon afterward became actively associated. For in anticipation of war Jack Coffee was asked to raise the First Regiment of Texas Volunteers. Only official reports so styled them, however. Commonly they were called Hays's Rangers to distinguish the frontier Indian fighters from a second regiment, drawn from more settled eastern Texas.

Although the Rangers refused to wear uniforms, they had adopted a general style of dress and equipment which marked them a body. From Mexicans they had borrowed not only the sombrero but the serape, a wrapper much resembling the Highland plaid in shape, colorfulness and all-purpose serviceability. As to weapons each man was a riding arsenal, for in addition to rifle and bowie knife, every Ranger carried a minimum of two revolvers as well as a couple of single-shot weapons for emergency purposes. One was to shoot himself, if wounded and about to be captured.

David Terry was a lieutenant in Hays's Rangers. William Oury belonged in some capacity, while John Glanton, said to have been a protégé of Mustang Gray, was a captain. Second in command was Lieutenant Colonel Sam Walker.

He was first in the field, though, as Colonel Hays was still busy recruiting when Taylor sent out a call for all available local volunteers. Old Rough and Ready, who was only ready in the sense of being willing to fight, had bumbled his way into a bad situation.

Still the more truculent of the two not yet warring governments, that at Mexico City had sent word that any American soldier found south of the Nueces River would be considered an armed trespasser on Mexican soil. As a countermove Taylor had been ordered to assert the American view as to the stream which marked the international boundary line. In accordance with that command the General advanced toward the Rio Grande in April of 1846, his tactics original if nothing more.

Having ordered a Major Brown to supervise the building of a fort opposite Matamoros, Taylor left the main body of his troops to follow and led the vanguard toward Point Isabel, his chosen coastal supply depot. As the intervening country was a chaparral jungle in which only the experienced could maneuver, his newcomers couldn't find their way about, while guerillas snapped up the General's unaccustomed couriers. There was therefore no liaison between the various parts of his divided command.

Old Rough and Ready had tangled himself in this ball of yarn when Sam Walker appeared on the scene. After putting Taylor in touch with his main body, Sam ascertained that General Arista was moving large units across the river in order to take advantage of American blunders.

Although Walker lost most of his command of 75, when he found 1500 enemy cavalry between him and Point Isabel, he got through and back himself, only to be ordered to report on the situation at Fort Brown. Outmaneuvering swarms of guerillas and Mexican scouts, Sam brought back the assurance of Major Brown that he could hold out against the siege then in progress.

With his command thus coordinated, and enemy surprise nullified, Taylor was able to hammer out a victory at Palo Alto on May 8. After he had won a second victory at Resaca de Palma the following day, the relief of Fort Brown was automatically achieved, for the shattered Mexican army fled to Monterey.

War wasn't actually declared until two days later by the United States and two weeks later by Mexico. When the news reached Texas, gratified Rangers, whose worth had been established by Sam Walker, were at last able to do what they had joined the Army for.

To these young men the war was the long-prayed-for chance to fight Mexico on even terms. It was their opportunity to square accounts for a string of brutalities stretching from the Alamo massacre to the murder of Ewen Cameron. Their feeling that they were engaged in a crusade was exactly expressed by the refrain of one of their songs: "Cry vengeance for Texas! and God speed the right."

They got their vengeance; and found more to avenge, too. For the guerillas who got hold of an American foolish enough to be taken alive had a way of stripping him and dragging him through cactus behind a galloping horse. It was not a generously fought

234

war; and if the Rangers did not act in kind, neither did they take any prisoners.

They horrified Old Rough and Ready alike by their bloodthirstiness and their contempt for military decorum. Yet they pulled his fat out of the flames for him, after he'd bulled into a position at Monterey which put his army under fire from two heights and a fortified structure.

Operating at night in the rain, Hays led a band of old Indian fighters who located and removed the pickets guarding the lone approach to Independence Hill. Then Jack Coffee and Walker led the two shock-troop units which spearheaded a successful surprise attack. Under cover of fire from the taken point, they next led assaults which pried the enemy's grip loose from the strongly defended city, which Taylor finally entered on September 23.

The Rangers wanted to carry on; but when their general outraged them by granting the enemy eight weeks of truce, they told him they wished to be no part of a do-nothing army. Not himself desiring the peacetime company of men of whom he was so doubtfully in control, Taylor acceded to their request for release from service. By early October, accordingly, Hays's Rangers were on their way back to Texas.

When it seemed as though activities were about to be resumed, Hays was asked to assemble another regiment in 1847, although not for service with Taylor. American strategy had by then changed, with the emphasis shifted from the campaign in northern Mexico to attacking its population center through the southerly seaport of Vera Cruz.

As there was some delay in assigning the Rangers to that sector, Sam Walker was not with the regiment which Hays led aboard ship with orders to serve under General Winfield Scott. Vera Cruz was not far from Perote, where Sam had a ten-cent piece on deposit; and eagerness to be in action thereabouts had led him to join another unit at the sacrifice of two degrees of rank. Months before the Rangers were reactivated, he had become captain of a company of mounted riflemen. But because of the fact that Sam was their commander, these, too, were known as Rangers, whose functions they performed by rooting out the guerilla bands which were forever harrying supply trains and preying on stragglers.

🙾 43 🙾

A Dragoon Gets a Baggage Train

UNLIKE IN SO many respects, Commodore Stockton and General Kearny had one thing in common. Each had been given instructions to conquer California and set up a government there by the chiefs of their respective commanding departments. In writing orders which couldn't well have been carried out by both men, moreover, the War and Navy Department secretaries did not think to consult each other.

Getting to California first for the Navy, Stockton conquered the province, and then had to do it once again. The second conquest was necessitated by the failure to follow Frémont's plan of advancing south by land as well as by sea. Mexicans in southern California's interior were thus given time to organize and draw recruits from Mexico proper. The Commodore had hardly dropped anchor again in Monterey, after having taken the cities to the south, when de Castro and a pair of brethren named Pico began putting a revolutionary movement on the road. As the small American garrison couldn't begin to challenge the force they led, Los Angeles was recaptured in October, 1846.

While this was going on, General Kearny was making brisk preparations to take over California himself, using but a part of the Army of the West. Colonel Doniphan's regiment was due to cooperate with the command of another general and meanwhile was on detached service against Indians. Other troops had been assigned to Colonel Sterling Price, the next commandant of New

Mexico. With only the First Dragoons, Kearny rode west in October, Fitzpatrick his guide.

He had no more than got well started than he received word that the Mormons whom Brigham Young had turned over to the Army at Kane were nearing Santa Fe. To this uninspected force of battalion strength had been allotted the task of bringing the supply train to California. The veteran officer placed in charge, however, had died en route, leaving only a youthful shavetail to carry on. Robbed of the chance to serve on the main front in Mexico, Captain Cooke had been looking forward to being one of the conquerors of California. To his unspeakable horror, though, Kearny breveted him a lieutenant colonel and gave him rear-echelon service which included making a wagon road where none had existed before.

Without his best troop commander, the General marched down to the Gila. He was westing in the pass it cut through the mountains when he met Kit Carson, himself heading east with Stockton's dispatches.

At this point the man who had shown so much wisdom in New Mexico went mad. Although Carson had informed him that California was already in American hands, Kearny was determined that he was going to govern the province, as allowed for in his orders. In his frenzy to realize this ambition, he sent all but one troop of the dragoons back to the Rio Grande Valley. The better to speed, too, he broke all rules of military etiquette by taking the Commodore's messages from the one to whom they had been entrusted and ordering the man to return to California with him. Fitzpatrick, who had never been along the Gila before, was handed the dispatches, while Carson became the General's guide.

Back at Santa Fe, as this was happening, Lieutenant Colonel Cooke was disconsolately looking over the Mormon Battalion. Seldom in history, it can be guessed, has a dedicated and thoroughly trained soldier found himself in command of a unit less likely to inspire his hope and pride.

All its members were religious zealots, antagonistic to him as a man placed in power over them while not of their faith. All were, of course, resentful of having been forced to serve in the army of a nation which they had been anxious to flee when conscripted. About a hundred were either too old or too young, or were otherwise disqualified for effective service. Some had brought along mates and progeny, and were counting on taking them to California.

After he had weeded out the absolutely impossible elements of his command and shaken the remainder into some sort of military shape, Philip St. George gloomed at his marching orders. By command of the War Department, he was to lay out a wagon road from Santa Fe to San Diego. There was a sound enough reason for the injunction. The known vehicular route swept north through Utah and could be blocked by snow. But against the need for a road usable in all seasons could be set the fact that nobody in Santa Fe knew of a pass leading to Arizona over which wagons could travel.

The only course open to Cooke was to proceed down the Rio Grande in hopes of finding mountains to the west which were less formidable than those in northern New Mexico. Doing so, he began probing the serried ranges near the present Mexican border with the aid of a couple of guides picked up along the way.

As one of these was a wight called Pauline Weaver for reasons not clear to later-born contemplators of his beard, Philip St. George had knowledgeable guidance. This mountain man had been roving the Southwest for fifteen years or more. The trouble was, though, that a habitual rider of rough trails wasn't the best judge of where wheels could be rolled. But by trial and error, a way was found over the Great Divide not far from the much more satisfactory Guadalupe Pass.

In the course of getting their wagons through to Arizona, Philip St. George had become reconciled to his Mormons and they to him. Sour while they were being led south, instead of the direction in which they felt that Brigham Young wanted them to go, they had cheered up when ordered to push west.

238

That decided them that their colonel knew his business, so they had put their backs behind the chore of getting the wagons through the mountains. Justly proud of that accomplishment, they were soldiers by the time they had dipped south into Mexico and marched north down the San Pedro Valley early in December.

Kearny was by then nearing San Diego, where Stockton was preparing to crush the revolution. A naval officer's failure to understand the worth of cavalry had kept him from promptly dealing with the insurgents. When he finally learned that Frémont was right in asserting that the Mexicans couldn't be coped with by sailors acting as infantry, he discovered that the rebels had also had the forethought to sweep coastal Southern California all but clear of suitable mounts. While enough were being rounded up to make the Commodore's command mobile, the Mexicans retained Los Angeles and held the interior, high in morale.

That was the situation with which Stephen Kearny collided; not in ignorance, either. Having sent a messenger ahead to San Diego, he received a briefing on December 5, together with a detachment of marine reinforcements. Led by Lieutenant Gillespie, these brought the General's strength up to 160 men.

With these he attacked a much smaller force, encountered at San Pascual, northeast of San Diego, the day after Gillespie's forty devildogs joined him. How an able campaigner, operating with the advantage of numbers and superior weapons, could have fared as badly as the General did can only be answered by assuming that his bloodless sweep of New Mexico had convinced him that Mexican opposition was never to be taken seriously. If that was indeed his notion, he learned otherwise.

The battle began when Kearny ordered Captain Johnston to lead a charge which turned out to be his last one. The General then himself led an assault which had the desired effect of making the rebels flee. But in giving chase, Kearny failed to keep his command together. Observing that pursuit was strung out and disorganized, the Mexican commander wheeled his own compact force of lancers and began mowing the startled hunters down.

Captain Moore followed Captain Johnston into the great question mark; so did eighteen from the ranks. Kearny, Gillespie and seventeen others were put out of action with wounds. To cap the disaster, the mules towing one of two cannon bolted toward the Mexicans, who slew another American, kidnaped by the runaway beasts.

Captain Turner, in command after the General had been side-lined, ordered the dead to be buried at night, so that the enemy could not ascertain the extent of the losses which had been inflicted. Meanwhile the insurgents had collected reinforcements, and a camp which was half a field hospital was surrounded in depth.

The first messenger sent to Stockton did not get through, so Kit Carson was ordered to try to establish liaison. He succeeded in leading a set of alternate couriers, of whom Lieutenant Edward Fitzgerald was one, through besieging lines in the dark, though at the cost of dispensing with boots in cactus country. In spite of thirty-six hours of forced marching on tortured feet, Kit's mountain-man training enabled him to assure the Commodore that he stood ready to guide a rescue force back to where it was needed.

Stockton was surprised but not pleased to find at his side a man he thought well on the way to Washington, bearing word of the naval officer's successes in California. Understandably, he was miffed at the General's effrontery in taking over his courier; but he nevertheless sent all the men he was able to provide with mounts to the aid of the beleaguered command at San Pascual.

Two weeks after what was left of Kearny's dragoons reached the Coast, Stockton was ready to advance on Los Angeles, toward which Frémont's California Battalion was marching from the north. Kearny took the field, too, but as the troops he contributed numbered well under a hundred, his presence had no effect on the outcome. The Commodore's sailors and marines, and the men of the Bear Flag, could have easily accomplished what took place alone, just as they had managed the original conquest without help.

The Mexicans, as it developed, were no longer disposed to make a contest out of it. At San Gabriel, east of Los Angeles, they made what can be called nothing better than a show of arms; for the skirmishings which took place there on January 8 and again on the following day were of such a desultory nature that the Americans lost but one man. Opposition to the recapture of the revolutionary stronghold then dissolved.

There remained one thing to be done, however, and Frémont did it. On January 13, 1847, John Charles met the insurgent leaders, Flores and one of the Pico brothers, at Couenga and there signed a treaty on behalf of the United States which ended hostilities. He furthermore recovered the government-issue property, in the form of a howitzer, which Kearny had lost at San Pascual.

Three days later Commodore Stockton, acting on the authority which had been given him by George Bancroft as Secretary of the Navy, carried out his delayed purpose of appointing Frémont Governor of California. Thus it seemed that the man who had initiated the conquest of the province would have the gratification of reaping due honors.

The unsuspecting explorer, however, was hardly confirmed in office when Kearny produced the orders which he had been given by William L. Marcy, as Secretary of War. These authorized him to follow up his conquest of California by acting as governor, and the General made it clear that he intended to obey his instructions.

⚜ 44 ⚜

Kirker Gets Even for a Bilking

EVEN ALLOWING FOR the discovery of Mexican scalps among the Apache ones he had contracted to collect, Santiago

Kirker had counted on being paid a considerable sum of money by the State of Chihuahua. When he received only about $2000, he considered himself badly used. He was offered no chance to square the ledger, though, until years after he became a Chihuahua settler, raising cattle which may have been his for all the evidence to the contrary.

Santiago's debt-collecting agent was Colonel Doniphan of the Missouri Volunteers. Following the departure of Kearny, Doniphan briefly commanded in New Mexico, pending the arrival of assigned occupation troops under Colonel Price. Later due for other service, he first dealt with the Navajos. The tribe had long made a practice of raiding the towns along the Rio Grande, then losing pursuit in the great maze of canyons which made their homeland a splendid robber's haven.

The Navajos could doubtless have evaded the force Doniphan took into their scenic warren, for as Missourians, the Volunteers were unused to the complexities of Western mountain country. The Indians were impressed, nevertheless, by the sight of more white men under arms than they had ever seen before. So they agreed to a treaty which they might have kept, had Doniphan stayed to enforce it. Pendant for him, though, were orders to proceed into Mexico proper, there to combine forces with an army supposed to be pushing toward Chihuahua from San Antonio. Late in November, accordingly, he marched down the Rio Grande Valley without returning to Santa Fe.

The Missouri Volunteers celebrated the Christmas season by defeating a force which had sallied from Presidio de San Elizario, generally called El Paso, and met them at a spot called Bracito, because there the river made a small bend. Led by an officer with the luckless name of Ponce de León, the Mexicans left ample proof that the frontiersmen were dead shots. And as a bonus for this victory, Doniphan was called on by Santiago Kirker.

The scalp hunter had ridden out the war, in Chihuahua, until the rumor of Doniphan's advance had launched a violent anti-American movement. Even James Magoffin, long liked and respected in Mexico, had ended up in prison; but catching an old mountain man like Kirker was something else again. He had led a small party through scouting patrols and now was anxious to strike back at the state which had welched on paying him due blood money.

Volunteering on the part of Kirker was good luck for Doniphan, as there was no other American so well equipped as he to give an account of the geographical, man-made and human obstacles to the taking of Chihuahua City. He began proving his knowledge by predicting that the outnumbering force still in El Paso would not defend that town.

Although he was right, the Missourians were yet delayed for some weeks, waiting for their artillery. At the request of Governor Bent the big guns had been kept in Santa Fe till quiet had been restored following an attempted rebellion.

Belatedly there had been strong opposition to the American conquest of New Mexico—an opposition which had failed to take concrete form at the beginning only because Armijo's treachery had denied it leadership. An underground movement had been organized, though, and the departure of most of the Army of the West had encouraged the belief that gringo domination could be unseated.

Discovering the plot, Charles Bent and Colonel Price had quashed the coup which had been planned by former officers of New Mexico's disbanded militia. These had been counting on support from Chihuahua, a hope which had been blasted by Doniphan's seizure of the key Rio Grande crossing at El Paso.

As Charles then reasoned that the insurrectionists must have perforce lost heart, he released the retained artillery for service with Doniphan. The plotters did not indeed try again, but the revulsion against Americans with which they had inspired Mexican peasants and the Pueblo Indians had not abated. Unaware of this underground storm, Governor Bent decided to go from garrisoned Santa Fe to unpoliced Taos in mid-January of 1847.

What happened after he reached the latter town was probably not planned. Rather it can be judged that the sight of the Governor unstoppered the accrued hatred of foreign rule of which he was the symbol. They were savages whose pressure gauge had been tampered with, and the extra steam-thrust caused by the presence of Charles sent them amok.

Except for one outbreak, by then nearly 170 years in the past, the Pueblos had been the perfect Indians from the white man's point of view. Accepting submersion, without ever trying to compete with those who had made serfs of them, they had long seemed too spiritless to make trouble of their own volition. But now the stolid draft horses snapped their harness, shook the blinders off and kicked the cart to pieces.

Boiling out of San Fernández Pueblo, the Indians sought the blood, not of the people who had demeaned them but of the new conquerors who had done them no harm. Among their ways of dealing with these, as well as with any Mexicans suspected of being in alliance with them, was to shoot them full of arrows while being careful not to kill. In all cases possible they scalped while full consciousness remained.

After working themselves up to it by horribly torturing others, they went to get the Governor. There was no one with him at the time except women of his household, including the wife of the absent Kit Carson, and children. The men who would otherwise have rallied were either dead or wishful of that release.

The one chance for escape, after the mob commenced beating on the door, was to dig through the adobe partition separating Bent's house from another, offering an exit which the attackers might not think to block. Charles tried to parley with the Indians while his companions frantically clawed at the tough mud with anything handy; but he was shot in the stomach by a bullet fired through the door even before it was finally bashed in.

His household did manage to squeeze through the hole, granting access to escape; but the Indians caught the Governor. He, too, got the pincushion and scalping treatment, though he may have been so far gone that he was not aware of it. In any case, so died Charles Bent on January 19, 1847. He had survived dealings with most of the great warrior tribes of the West, only

244

to be given the deep six by a traditionally long-suffering one. Retribution for his murder was swiftly awing. Although the Cheyennes, into which tribe William Bent had married, were overruled on their bid to carry the tomahawk into New Mexico, palefaces girded for the warpath. They trod it gingerly, however, for the Taos revolt had sparked an uprising which was province-wide in scope. More Americans were slaughtered, by Mexicans as well as Indians, while others saved themselves only by taking to the hills in the dead of winter.

Because of the danger of an assault on Bent's Fort, William stayed in command there. But he sped a detachment of blood-eyed mountain men toward Taos, which had become the site of a new type of rendezvous.

After first sending down the Rio Grande for a troop of the dragoons which had been left behind by Kearny, Colonel Price started north on January 23. And with him went a pickup company led by Charles's partner, Ceran St. Vrain.

Price had to risk the loss of undefended Santa Fe to rebels who might close in behind him. With only 350 men—including St. Vrain's detachment—he couldn't afford both a holding and an attacking force. Reasoning that delay would only serve to strengthen the enemy and increase the odds against him, he made for a Mexican rallying point called La Canada with every gun he could muster.

General Tafoya had a command of 1500 Mexican and Indian rebels, holding strong hill positions as well as the town. The hope of being able to loot the American baggage train drew many out of their advantageous positions, though; and after St. Vrain's frontiersmen attacked from the rear, while Price was making a frontal assault, La Canada was abandoned. No longer commanded by the late Tafoya, the still numerous survivors retreated to a defile known as El Embudo.

There (the dragoons now aiding), Price beat the insurgents anew with even more disastrous results to the latter. Most of the Mexicans decided that they didn't want to be rebels any more; but the mania which had twisted the Pueblos out of character had not yet run its course. Retreating to the scene of the original crime in Taos, they holed up in their village and prepared to make a badger fight of it.

Surrounded by a stockade and built of thick adobe, piled to the height of five windowless stories, the beehive of a pueblo offered no good targets. Even cannon proved of no avail. Price's three weren't equal to breaching even the walls of the connected church, which was at once the most vulnerable point and the bastion from which the defenders were launching their hottest fire.

The nut wasn't cracked until a dragoon captain named Burgwin led a charge afoot which he died without finishing. Some who did complete it were killed by Indians whose marshal was a huge Delaware chief who had taken the name of Big Nigger; but the attackers had gained a foothold which they widened with rifle butt, bowie knife and tomahawk.

The fury which had been sustaining the Pueblos broke like a fever then. They wanted to quit but were not allowed to by men whose friends they had mutilated and slain. St. Vrain led the mop-up which served in place of funeral games for Charles Bent; but it was not safe play. Bending to identify a half-recognized chief, Ceran was throttled by a man he thought dead; and he would have been stabbed had not a mountain man called Dick Wootton leaped to side him.

By dark of February 3, 1847, the revolt had ended where it had begun two weeks earlier. Four days before that Doniphan had finally been reinforced with the battalion of artillery he had been waiting for. In command was Major Meriwether Lewis Clark, the namesake of one of the West's primary explorers and the son of the other. Of his two batteries of light howitzers, one was commanded by Captain Richard Weightman.

According to War Department plans, Doniphan's regiment was to have been but a supporting force, cooperating with the already mentioned command thought to be advancing from Texas. General John Wool, however, never managed to assemble the force considered necessary for the purpose, and eventually was ordered to reinforce Taylor instead. The intention of the departmental commander was to notify Doniphan of the change in plans and send him elsewhere. But before new orders could reach him, Doniphan had tired of inaction and decided to take Chihuahua City himself.

The Doniphan Expedition, as it came to be officially known, mustered 1200 men, including the scouts directed by Kirker. Yet Santiago had a challenger in the person of a Kentucky plainsman named James L. Collins. As the climax of a quarrel as to who knew most about the country through which they were guiding the Volunteers, they agreed to fight a duel. The Colonel succeeded in putting a stop to that but not to their animosity, which hadn't softened by the time the Battle of Sacramento was fought on February 28.

General Heredia, the Mexican commander, chose to meet the Americans here, rather than at Chihuahua City, for sound military reasons. The locale was eminently defendable, and he had something better than three men for every member of the attacking force.

The battle didn't start well from the American point of view, because of conflicting orders. After the Colonel had given the word to charge the enemy's center, forward movement was checked at the command of a major full of Dutch courage to the point of not knowing what was going on. The resulting uncertainty left the Americans hesitating at a point where Mexican artillery could have broken them. The only reason this didn't materialize was the rivalry of Kirker and Collins.

Just before the swacked field officer threw the Volunteers into perilous confusion, Santiago had challenged James to see how near to the threatening enemy battery each could penetrate the Mexican lines. As Collins instantly took him up, the two scouts swooped ahead of the infantry and galloped toward the musketeers protecting the Mexican artillery. This unexpected development not only diverted the cannoneers from what should have been their purpose but excited the musketeers, who all began banging away at the two horsemen in place of firing at the wavering Missouri riflemen.

Inexplicably Kirker and Collins escaped unscathed, and meanwhile their diversionary action had given sober commanders time to patch the morale which had been cracked by the fuddled one. The charge was resumed and with a picked-up tempo. Some officers forgot about their men in the anxiety not to be outdone by a pair of civilians and rushed after Santiago and his rival instead of leading their units. Then the race between the two scouts was grotesquely duplicated. Captain Weightman was supposed to have supported Doniphan's detachment of cavalry when it rushed enemy gun positions, but he and his light howitzers kept pace with the horsemen, who proved unable to draw ahead.

This display of *élan*, in combination with perplexing tactics, routed the Mexicans, who finally fled in such disorder that Weightman and Kirker captured the wagon carrying General Heredia's personal gear. Chihuahua City then became Doniphan's prize. It is true that an effort was made to oppose his entry into the local mint, but after Weightman rolled his guns in front of the door, a less destructive key was supplied.

After accomplishing what it had never occurred to the War Department to ask them to do, the Missouri Volunteers marched east through Mexico and returned to their home state via New Orleans. New Mexico had taken Richard Weightman's fancy, though, and he once more rode west on the Santa Fe Trail, as did Kirker.

৪৹৪ 45 ৪৹৪

Joe Meek Meets a Cousin

WHILE OTHERS IN the West had either voluntarily taken part in the Mexican War or had been drawn into it willy-nilly, the settlers of Oregon remained absorbed in their own problems. They dwelt, indeed, in a singularly isolated world. For though Black Harris and others had searched diligently, a good wagon route across the Cascades was long in being developed. And although there was a frequented trail to California, hundreds of miles of forested country intervened between the inhabited portions of the two regions.

Dead in 1845, Jason Lee had ceased to function—quite a few months before his demise—as ambidextrously as he once had. Warned probably, Methodist leaders back East had in any case smelled a rat and sent somebody to find out just what the supposed missionaries west of the Cascades were doing with the money which had been raised for them. Jason, as it chanced, was in the act of returning to the Atlantic Seaboard in order to shake church chieftains down for more cash to divert from holy to secular uses. But in Hawaii, whither he was deposited by a Hudson's Bay Company trading vessel, Lee met the man dispatched to relieve him of his post.

Trying to accomplish something, the new man found that what had been blamed on Jason Lee was a general condition, i.e., a lack of zeal for conversion and a plethora of interest in land exploitation. Due to his report, the religious embezzlers on the Willamette had their water cut off; and the so-called Indian mission—which yet could be credited with the fine accomplishment of opening educational facilities for white settlers up through the college level—was closed down. Of those who had once called themselves missionaries, only Elijah White had anything to do with Indians; and the property of palefaces was his concern rather than the souls of redskins.

Debauched by the North West Trading Company which had originally exploited the region, and pushed out of the way by the settlers, the savages of the vicinity were a sullen lot of pilferers, given to extortion, when they were numerous enough, as well as begging. White tried to instigate better behavior by giving them legal and penal codes, usable by themselves against their own people. If more or less sound in principle, in operation this only served to irritate the natives, because of the differences separating their viewpoints and those of the newcomers.

In the first place the punishments were chiefly prescribed for larceny, whose skillful practitioners the Indians admired. Second, the concept of private real estate was foreign to the thinking of savages, who couldn't see why they didn't have the right to wander where they wished, and take what they found along the way. Third, they could understand the law only as some sort of god or demon, which they were helping to placate by letting themselves be whipped. According to their way of thinking, they deserved to be paid for this cooperation; and when rewards were not forthcoming, they felt themselves swindled.

Through a remarkable irony, the lid finally blew off in the bailiwick of the one man who had labored unceasingly to help the Indians. Nor had the immediate cause anything to do with Marcus Whitman.

Accompanying settlers who had made a trading expedition into California, a Walla Walla had been killed in the vicinity of Sutter's Fort by a white man. As nothing satisfactory to the Indian's fellow tribesmen was done in compensation, they brooded about it and talked the matter over with their neighbors, the Cayuses.

After ten years of striving, in the meantime, Whitman and his equally dedicated wife could count only a score of indifferently dependable converts. Finally even the Doctor had become convinced that nothing could be done to move the Cayuses and the Walla Wallas nearer to grace. Having devoted the cream of his maturity to thankless work, he had decided to give it over and move his family west of the Cascades to Oregon City. He had not concluded his arrangements, though, when the Cayuses descended on his ménage on November 29, 1847.

They gave Marcus a mortal blow before he knew what was afoot. They slashed and belabored Narcissa, killing her after she emerged from unconsciousness and tried to crawl to the aid of her husband. They murdered Joe Meek's young daughter and that of Jim Bridger. They killed nine or ten other inmates of the mission. Then they went on to participate in a general rising of the region's natives.

The pioneers of Oregon were in a desperate plight because of what had been done and what had not been done by the United States government. Pursuant to nearly thirty years of debating the subject, Washington had insisted upon fixing the international boundary of the Pacific Northwest. As cards in forcing this issue, American diplomats had more than the fact of settlement along the Willamette. For one thing, Americans had moved north of the Columbia, in spite of the Hudson's Bay Company's efforts to discourage them. Then there was the knowledge—at first pointed out to the War Department by Jed Smith, and later amplified by Bonneville and Frémont—that the United States was in a stronger military position than Great Britain. If no American troops had so far marched nearer the Columbia estuary than the Great Basin, an overland expedition would have been able to reach the region well ahead of any British effort to mount an occupational force by sea.

At the same time England would have been pushed too far, had the absurd claim to a part of Canada implicit in the "Fifty-four forty or fight" slogan been insisted upon. When it was withdrawn, the 49th parallel was agreed upon, becoming official as of August 5, 1846.

But having acquired Oregon, the United States government had let it dangle, taking no steps to administer it. And it was this sin of omission which spiked resistance when the Whitman massacre detonated a general Indian revolt.

Because nothing had been done toward organizing the territory, the troops which would ordinarily have been sent to guard frontier settlements had never been dispatched. The settlers were themselves in a poor position to deal with an uprising, as their provisional government had been disbanded on the theory that an official one would be established. As for the Hudson's Bay Company, although it still occupied its Oregon posts, it no longer wielded its old authority over the savages.

Nor was that all. The failure to organize the territory entailed a failure to validate the so far tentative titles to land claims. The consequence had been a growing loss of faith in the region's future. Not only had immigration fallen off, but disgruntled investigators of conditions in the Pacific Northwest had streamed back east along the Oregon Trail. Indians could be fought where it was worth while, but the feeling was that people couldn't be expected to put up with that hazard where they couldn't be guaranteed freehold.

Realizing that the Oregon settlements would collapse entirely unless the federal government took responsible action, former members of the provisional government convened and decided to use the Indian outbreak as the basis of a dramatic appeal. Winter offered wilderness travel conditions with which not many were prepared to cope, but the season didn't intimidate Joe Meek. Calling on all the experience and knowledge of short cuts collected in his years as a mountain man, he took a lone companion on an epic forced march.

When blizzards forced them to forgo horses, they traveled on the snowshoes Joe had made before they left. They were nearly starved when they reached Peg-leg Smith's camp on the headwaters of the Green; but as Peg-leg knew Joe, he provided the wayfarers not only with a supply of provisions but fresh mounts.

At Fort Bridger Joe had to break the news to Old Gabe that their daughters had been murdered by the Cayuses; but Meek and Squire Ebbert were outfitted anew by Jim. Across South Pass they stumbled into an Indian camp while another snowstorm was raging. Luckily the first person they met was a French old-timer who warned them they were in a Sioux village and that the Dakotas had knives out for Americans then.

They were destitute and phenomenally ragged by the time they'd crossed the plains, but Joe wasn't dismayed. He sent a collect telegram to President Polk that a delegate from Oregon was on his way to Washington. Arrived there still in his bedraggled mountain-man gear, he went directly to the White House, where he had no difficulty in gaining admission. Unknown to

Joe, a Virginia cousin of his called Knox Walker had been made Polk's secretary.

After Meek had laid the case of the Oregon settlements before the President and both houses of Congress, organization was scheduled, but could not be created overnight. First the terms of administration had to be argued over, and next the allotment of patronage arranged. As territorial posts were filled by presidential appointment, the officers consisted of either political or military figures who had earned consideration through active membership of the party in power. There was an exception, however. When the organization of Oregon Territory was finally ratified in August of 1848, the position of United States Marshal for the region was awarded Joseph Meek.

By virtue of his exploit, the Hudson's Bay Company was at last forced to prepare for withdrawal from the country it had so long exploited; but it did so without the aid of a valued hand. Forced to choose between the organization he had faithfully worked for and the land he had fallen in love with, Dr. John McLoughlin became a citizen of the nation whose occupation of Oregon—but always with fairness—he had doggedly fought.

🙂 46 🙂

Santa Anna's Wonderful Dress Coat

IN NORTHERN MEXICO, after the truce which followed the fall of Monterey had lapsed, certain Rangers again served with Taylor. Colonel Ben McCulloch led the regiment of Texans whom the General was willing, if not glad, to welcome back; for by that time the latter needed every man obtainable. As commander of the new main expeditionary force, Winfield Scott had asked for so many units of Old Rough and Ready's army that it had been pared down to five thousand men.

With four times that number at his back Santa Anna marched north to destroy Taylor's weakened command. If successful, he would have been in a position to invade the United States, which had gambled so many troops on Scott's projected strike at Vera Cruz that it would have been vulnerable.

A man of many vicissitudes, Santa Anna had fought at Vera Cruz himself some years earlier. At that time the port had been blockaded by the French, anxious to collect indemnities for destroyed shipping. In resisting that demand, Santa Anna had not only lost the deciding battle but part of his left leg. Like that of Smith it had been replaced with a wooden shank.

Santa Anna resembled Smith, too, in being an active and confident peg-leg. Although he seldom won any battles other than political ones, he was always both eager to try and sure that his next effort would be successful. On this occasion he had rushed back from exile in Cuba to redeem himself by putting America on the defensive.

Having wintered in Coahuila, Taylor elected to meet Santa Anna at a place called Buena Vista, which turned out to be the scene of a very stiff battle. Fought on February 23, 1847, it marked the entrance into history of a character known as the Great Western.

Some of the functions since performed by rear-echelon service units were then allotted to a corps of women designated as "camp followers." In addition to taking care of laundry, giving medical attention and the like, its members bunked with soldiers, sometimes even with legal sanction.

Sarah Bowman, a Tennessee mountain woman of enormous proportions and a blacksmith's muscles, was a camp follower whose husband had been an army sergeant. He seems to have been an early casualty, though, for there was nothing to suggest domesticity in the actions recorded of her while with Taylor's command. Whatever of womanly devotion there was in her make-up she gave to Old Rough and Ready, who was perhaps not aware of being the star in such a rugged life, prior to the Battle of Buena Vista.

It was subsequently said of Sarah Bowman that she was the toughest rough-and-tumble fighter along the Mexican border. Exaggeration or not, her thews and skill in using them impressed the young engineers, just out of West Point, who were serving under Taylor. Before the cable-laying *Great Eastern* was built, the biggest thing in the mechanical world was another steamship called the *Great Western*. With this marine monster in mind some member of the corps saw Sarah Bowman and told his thought to his fellows. The name so stuck that in chronicle after chronicle she was referred to simply as "The Great Western," with no other noun given, or perhaps known.

During the Battle of Buena Vista the Great Western strode back and forth under cannon fire, going out empty-handed and returning with a wounded man, carried easily and unaided in her arms. She was also credited with restoring the morale of a volunteer regiment, which had just been assigned to Taylor's army. Breaking under the pressures of a fierce contest, some fled, shouting that the Americans were being routed.

But if they wished to retreat, they shouldn't have gone near where the camp followers were taking care of the wounded. Horrified at the thought of anybody deserting Old Rough and Ready in his hour of need, the Great Western knocked the leading fugitive down and told him to get back in the lines or she'd kill him. She also voiced her personal confidence in her hero. "You damned son of a bitch," she told the stopped deserter, "there ain't enough Mexicans in Mexico to whip old Taylor."

As there were not in that part of Mexico, at least, Old Rough and Ready and the Great Western remained in Coahuila, while Santa Anna's shattered army fled south. There, following Doniphan's soon capture of Chihuahua City, the rest of the Mexican War of 1846–1848 was fought.

After Vera Cruz was taken, at the conclusion of rough amphibious action, late in March of 1847, the American army was faced with the problem of extending its bridgehead in terrain which ran steeply up from the sea to Mexico's interior plateau, with its mean level of 8000 feet. This was achieved by forcing the pass at Cerro Gordo three weeks later. As several protecting strong points were next captured, the American flag was raised above the Castle of Perote, where Sam Walker had been imprisoned.

Busy fighting the guerillas who proved more of a threat to American supply lines than the Mexican regulars, Walker does not seem to have been present when the first part of the bet he had made with his jailers was won for him. On May 25, however, he found time to win the second portion of his wager. Entering as a conqueror the city where he had been enslaved, Sam had the flagpole he had helped to erect uprooted. After exhibiting the dime he had sworn to come back and collect, he went about less personal business.

"Old Fuss and Feathers" Scott now marked time for months, pending the arrival of the troops and supplies he needed for his projected advance on Mexico City. This was taken in September, in spite of some rough opposition and a false truce, through which Santa Anna had sought to lure the Americans into a trap; but the war was not over.

Though defeated, a fugitive and leaving a leg as the trophy of a happy Illinois regiment, Santa Anna was still dangerous. What he had been shrewd enough to see was that Scott's weakness was his supply line, stretching 263 miles west from Vera Cruz. To break it, the Mexican laid siege to the American garrison which had been left at Puebla.

The approach to this control point was in turn protected by Huamantla, which Santa Anna already held, and where he had left men and guns in strength. For as long as this bastion stood, his position at Puebla was secure.

By that time in southern Mexico, Hays and his Rangers formed part of the force with which General Joseph Lane surged against Huamantla. Also in his command were two companies of mounted riflemen under Walker. Lane's shock troops, these were flung forward to take the defense barrier which was the core of Mexican strength. Leading the charge, Sam accomplished his mission but was shot to death on October 9, 1847.

Remarkably, in view of the fact that the Rangers were forever in front-line action, Walker was one of the only two famous ones who did not survive the Mexican War. Doubtless mourned by the Monterey belle who had once helped him escape from prison, Mustang Gray had earlier fallen at Camargo, in a minor engagement of the northern campaign of 1846.

But for the Rangers as a whole the war was almost a complete success. They shocked Scott as they had Taylor by their ruthlessness, but they piled up corpses which more than equaled the heaps of Texans slain in the course of Mexican massacres. Sitting their horses any old way, for many were young enough to make clowning forgivable, they rode into the capital of Mexico. This was a city, too, which they voluntarily policed when American soldiers, after relaxing in cantinas, were knifed as they made seaway back to their billets. There were fewer residents but better-behaved ones, once the Rangers had combed the districts where the attacks on gringos had taken place.

The riders from Texas had two disappointments to score against these satisfactions, though. They failed to get Canales, who had been the agent of Ewen Cameron's murder, and they failed to lag Santa Anna.

Yet they almost did that. Peg-leg or not, the man whose name was a Texas curse word was so elusive that three months after the taking of Huamantla he was still at large. Anxious to get at him before he surrendered to somebody who would let him live, the Rangers responded with alacrity to a tip that Santa Anna was skulking at a place called Tehuacan, south and west of Puebla. Swiftly though Hays acted, Santa Anna had learned of his danger and vanished; but the miss was such a near one that he had left his personal effects in the quarters soon ransacked by the Texans.

Prizes among the loot included a richly jeweled cane and Santa Anna's gaudily bespangled dress uniforms. The first of these was ultimately turned over to President Polk, but Hays bore off a garment so covered with gold braid that the cloth was hardly visible.

When the Mexican general was finally cornered and allowed to leave the country in the spring of 1848, there was justifiable fear on the part of American commanders that the Rangers would "cry vengeance" to the extent of waylaying and lynching him. Appealed to personally—for the regulars had no way of fencing his mobile force—Jack Coffee reluctantly conceded that it would not be proper to make way with a man who had been promised safe conduct. He therefore persuaded his men that such an act would be a blot on the escutcheon of Texas, which was probably the only argument that could have induced them to abandon their plan.

Still Texas had the gratification of seeing a symbol alike of its arch foe's defeat, and of the part in it played by its Rangers. For when Colonel Hays stepped ashore from the homing transport a few weeks later, he was clad in Santa Anna's dress-parade coat, resplendent with medals as well as with gold frogs and majestic epaulettes.

Reaching San Antonio on May 20, Jack and those with him left the national service but did not re-enter that of their state. For the Army's insistence upon taking over Indian policing left the Rangers, as originally constituted, without function. Men of action had returned from war, in a word, to find no ready outlet for their aroused energies.

𝕰𝕰 47 𝕰𝕰

Prophets and Profits

ROUNDING THE HORN in the *Brooklyn*, Sam Brannan had been looking forward to settling his flock of Mormon home seekers where citizens of the United States couldn't feel free to persecute them. As the chartered ship had called at no intervening ports, Brannan's last knowledge of international developments was datelined February 1846. When the brig finally trudged

258

toward the entrance to San Francisco Bay it was July and a United States naval vessel had made a visit.

Unbelievingly Sam gazed at Yerba Buena and the American flag flying above it. Understandably, he felt outraged at the trick history had played him. After he had landed, however, he found that American occupation had not yet filled California with enemies of his sect. Most of the little town's inhabitants were Mexicans who had never heard of Mormons, and wouldn't have been interested if they had. The few American residents were former seafaring men or trappers, who didn't mind if people called themselves saints, even if it wouldn't have occurred to them to do so.

Actually the arrival of two or three hundred newcomers was a cause of pleasant local excitement. Finding themselves unexpectedly welcome, the Latter-day Saints decided that they had found their promised land and began looking around for means of prospering.

The most adept at this was their leader, whose instincts moved him toward commercial prominence with a minimum time lag. Among other enterprises of his was the founding of Yerba Buena's first newspaper early in 1847. In this journal he denounced, incidentally, the changing of the town's name, later that year, to San Francisco.

Sam's objection appears to have stemmed from no more than the fact that he wasn't consulted when identity between the town and its great harbor was established. But he was quite often elsewhere due to business and other reasons.

He had not forgotten that he had originally come to California as a religious magnate, and town life was not best suited to the needs of many of his followers, farmers by trade. On the lookout for a suitable place for them to till soil, Brannan had visited Sutter's Fort. Impressed by the advantages offered by the industries of New Helvetia, he established a Mormon colony nearby, the time 1847's plowing season. He didn't plan for John Augustus to get all the Saints' business, though, for Sam himself opened a store on the Sacramento.

His confidence was that Brigham Young would swell his coffers (and forfeit to Sam much of his leadership) by bringing the great Midwestern group of Mormons to the Pacific Coast. Brigham, however, was brooding over the unseen shores of a different body of salt water.

Aware that a prophet can't afford to be wrong, Young had told nobody that the country around Great Salt Lake was filling his mind. From hundreds of miles off, though, it appeared to have the makings of a sound inspiration. On the spiritual side, the parallel between the lake and the Biblical Dead Sea made the region about the former a desirable prophet's choice. As for practical advantages, it was isolated, and in nobody's political sphere, while the climate was said to have been found as healthy as the soil was fertile.

When the Oregon Trail became passable in 1847 Brigham decided to lead a trial run of Saints to the Great Basin. His announcement said nothing about a geographical goal; it was understood that revelation would decide whether or not the Mormons' Canaan would be discovered that year.

Brigham was by then so well informed about the West that he knew where its prominent personalities had wandered. Upon meeting Black Harris, as the latter was riding out of the mountains for the last time, Young queried this landlocked Odysseus exhaustively. He also catechized Jim Bridger, whom he recognized as the discoverer of Great Salt Lake, while tarrying at Old Gabe's fort.

That interview marked the beginning of a feud which proved deadly to many others, if to neither of its principals. Brigham thought Gabe was deliberately trying to discourage him, and he was undoubtedly right. As the Adam of Great Salt Lake, Jim took a proprietary interest in the region around it, which he naturally did not wish to have overrun with settlers who would scare the game away. Wherefore Bridger jeered at Young's notion that the area in question could be made productive; and prophets like to be jeered at even less than other people, for their professional standing is wrapped up in the tinfoil of inspired solemnity. But because of Frémont, Gabe gained only a killer whale for an enemy. Sure he was heading for what he wanted, Brigham left the Oregon Trail and stamped off southwest, trailing clouds of hard-boiled mysticism.

Young had one arrow in his quiver that Bridger could not have been expected to know about. In reading anent the Near Eastern fountain of Christianity, as well as of the Hebrew tribes to which he likened the Latter-day Saints, Brigham had run across descriptions of farming by irrigation. He was therefore not discouraged when he saw the scrawny corn stand which a lone experimenter had planted in the vicinity of Great Salt Lake that year.

As for the surrounding region, it was perfect. A good many other men, including some not religiously gaited, had been inspired with a special feeling for the lake's basin, with its Wagnerian backdrop of mountains. It is thus not surprising that Brigham felt the spell of a region tailored to make a prophet look as though guided by portents. "This is the place," he boomed to his awed followers.

There were no contradictions from those assembled with him in that July day, but there was one Mormon elsewhere who had a different idea. Learning from travelers through to California that Young's party had halted east of the Sierras, Sam Brannan hurried over that range. Feeling perfectly capable of being a prophet himself, he was bent on persuading Brigham to join the colony on the Sacramento of which the former was the directing force.

The two had perhaps met earlier, when Brigham was passing through New York on his way back from England several years before. Whether that was the case or not, they now took a good look at each other; and neither liked what he saw, because it was his own ambition in another man's skin.

As neither had the slightest intention of going where the other held the reins of power, the clash was a draw, but here was the beginning of another blood-marked feud. For the moment, though, all that happened was withdrawal to California on

Sam's part, leaving Brigham to go ahead with the best-worked-out scheme in the long and amazing history of American real estate development.

To do so, he left the vanguard of the migration he was planning—after first showing them how to start farming operations along the stream connecting Utah and Great Salt lakes, which he christened the Jordan—and returned to Kane. The spring to which he was looking forward had not yet opened the Oregon Trail again, however, when his rival became party to an event which altered the nature and tempo of the West's development as no other single episode could have done.

Deciding to add a lumber mill to his coterie of enterprises at New Helvetia, Captain Sutter had taken on, as partner and builder, the James Marshall with whom Jim Clyman had come to California from Oregon. On January 24, 1848, this man saw John Augustus privately and announced that, in digging the race to provide the mill with water power, one of his laborers had turned up what he was positive would prove to be precious metal.

Quite naturally they wished to keep the matter secret, so that they could exploit the find without drawing a foreseen swarm of rivals; but murder isn't the only thing that will out. How Brannan learned what was in the wind isn't in writing; but a few days later he came dashing into San Francisco. His purpose was to give the scoop to the paper he owned, yet the story was too big to be contained. So as he charged along the little town's main street he shouted to everybody he saw, "There's gold in California!"

The news was so slow in percolating back East that it did not gain currency there until late summer. It therefore did not affect the direction taken by covered wagoners bound west in the earlier months of 1848. The caravans leaving Westport were still manned by people with no thoughts but of farming along the Willamette or of raising stock in the Sacramento Valley. And from Kane, Brigham led his people toward a section of the country whose continued isolation he heavily counted upon.

Having developed in his followers the kind of obedience given a queen ant, he was able to implement a marching plan whose call on discipline would have shocked Doniphan's stride-at-your-whim volunteers. Where he had learned logistics is a mystery of talent; but Young grasped what had to be done in order to get his tribe over the mountains with a minimum of waste motion. When the summer was yet new, accordingly, they were all in the region he had determined to turn into a theocratic state, and before long many were hard at work on its capital. Strangely enough, this was not given any of the real or pseudo Biblical terms in which the sect delighted. Speaking straight American, for once, the Mormons named their town Salt Lake City.

A section of it watered by irrigation meanwhile, the area had turned out to be as fertile as Frémont had promised. Of all that Brigham had planned, as a matter of fact, only one thing had not worked out to his liking. Hoping, as Brannan had done, to leave United States territory, he also had failed. On February 2, 1848, the Treaty of Guadalupe-Hidalgo, which formally ended the Mexican War, had ceded to the United States all the northern provinces of the losing nation.

〄 48 〄

A Mulligan of Disasters

As THE MORMON Battalion was too numerous for Indians to attempt to halt, its march from Santa Fe to the Pacific was not marked by any battles with savages. Yet the cattle found grazing in the San Pedro Valley showed themselves to be of sterner stuff than the Apaches.

Of the same hardy breed which fought grizzlies in California, these bovines had been roaming the vicinity since efforts to ranch this tributary valley to that of the Gila had been made during the eighteenth century. After Apache expansion south had rendered the San Pedro's banks untenable for stock raisers, the cattle had carried on without owners. Not thoroughly domestic to begin with, they had lapsed into complete ferality by the time Philip St. George Cooke led his men north and downstream late in the fall of 1846.

As in the case of many wild animals the males not only moved separately from the females, outside of the mating season, but congregated in large herds. Hundreds of bulls belonged to the one whose members were annoyed by the sight and sound of vehicles being driven past a grassland where they had been wont to graze uninterrupted.

Being bulls, they turned irritation into action, and before the startled soldiers could get their rifles into play, a horde of snorting, great-horned monsters was charging near. Colonel Cooke himself had a close squeak, for only fast shooting by one of his men kept him from being run down. A few of the Mormons weren't that lucky, being ripped or bruised; but mules were alone in being fatally gored by the attackers, which left behind casualties of their own, as they rushed on.

Fought on December 11, the Battle of the Bulls was won by the Mormon Battalion, next to take Tucson at the expense of no blood-letting. After the small garrison of this northernmost Sonoran town withdrew south, the American flag was raised over it on December 17.

Rafting wagons over the Colorado took some doing, but it was accomplished, and the battalion rolled on toward the Coast, in January of 1847, well pleased to a man. As a unit which had put a difficult undertaking through in much less time than Kearny had reckoned that it could, the Saints had their chests out and admired the man who had directed them. Having made military points through the energy his men had shown, Cooke was proud of his outfit.

Both the commander and his troops, moreover, looked forward to their arrival on the Coast as a goal where they would be rewarded by being allowed to do what they wished. For Philip

St. George this meant a chance to serve on the main Mexican front. For the Mormons it meant release to go to whatever part of California Brigham had brought the people of Kane to, or would during the coming summer.

But California was not a land of kept promises that year, as the party led by George Donner had found out. Ignoring the advice not only of Jim Clyman but Joe Walker, the pilgrims had taken the short cut running south of Great Salt Lake.

The sparse water and grazing of Nevada in summer did not sustain their draft animals. Where these didn't die outright, they became too weak to move more than a few miles at a time. It took the party months instead of weeks to cross the desert. The result was that they didn't reach the Sierras soon enough.

Pinned down by snow, the Donner Party wintered high in the mountains. As they had not brought supplies enough to last them that long, some died, and some ate the ones that died—if they waited for natural death. As the West's one great horror story, it has been a sphere for gruesome speculation.

In the end some were able to leave Donner Lake and win to safety, in part through their own efforts and in part through the visionary powers of George Yount. Possessed of second sight, the former mountain man became aware of the Donner Party's plight and sent younger men to meet a few of the pilgrims who were struggling out of the Sierras in search of help. Some historians, not personally acquainted with him, have undertaken to declare that Yount wasn't geared for telepathic communication; but George, far from boastful when otherwise writing of himself, claimed that he was.

At all events only about half of the eighty-one originally on the roster reached the California settlements. Arriving destitute, many of the survivors yet had a possession they could have dispensed with. This was the burden of knowing themselves the living tombs of former companions.

But before the spring of 1847 saw the sorry end of their adventuring, there had been man-eating in California among the well fed. The cannibal in this case was Stephen Kearny, whose bad management had already caused the death of not a few men at San Pascual.

Unabashed by this, or perhaps because his failure had rankled him into feeling the need of asserting himself, he undertook to pick a quarrel with the man who had pulled him out of the trouble into which he had blundered. The Mexican rebellion had hardly been put down by Stockton's sailors and the allied volunteers led by Frémont when Kearny started urging the Naval commander to stand clear and let him handle affairs in California.

It seems reasonably plain that Frémont was not at first a target of the General's. John Charles only came into Kearny's line of fire after the Commodore affably pointed out that most of the conquering of California had been accomplished before the General was so much as in the province, while it had been completed with forces of which he was in paramount command.

Without ceasing to bark at the unperturbed Stockton, whose cool citation of facts further enraged him, Kearny then flung at Frémont a War Department order which authorized the General to take charge of all Army troops in California. To this he added the rider that he wished no changes to be made in the personnel of the California Battalion.

The point of this infighting was Stockton's naming of John Charles as the province's governor. Remaining at the head of his military command, Frémont would not be able to accept the administrative position.

From then on the man who had led the Bear Flag revolution was damned no matter what he did. Morally he was bound to Stockton. Against his original inclinations he had agreed to serve under the Commodore and had accepted a commission from him. But once having taken those steps, he could not have refused to go along with Stockton even if he had disliked the idea of being governor of California, which, of course, he didn't. He had come by his appointment fairly, and through merit, and he meant to hold on to it.

The snag was, though, that if he owed his lieutenant-colonelcy to a Naval officer, it was an Army commission. In that service Kearny ranked him, so refusing to comply with the General's orders was risking trouble.

As long as Stockton remained in power militarily, Frémont was secure, but the former was replaced early in February by Commodore Shubrick, who had neither orders bearing on the matter nor a personal stake in the controversy over the governorship. For a time Kearny and Frémont both operated as warring chief executives of California. At length, though, the General got confirmation of his standing as military commandant and placed John Charles under arrest at a camp established near Sutter's Fort.

In holding him there Kearny was himself insubordinate, for Polk had given him ignored orders to allow Frémont to proceed elsewhere. But the ambition to be known as the conqueror of all the Mexican West, and not merely the portion which he had deftly taken over, seems to have maddened Kearny for keeps. And as he was a general in wartime, he was supported in bad acts as well as good. So he was permitted to subject a more generous man, and one of far greater achievements, to insulting treatment for months. Then at the end of this period, for the General was relieved of his ill-gotten governorship in June, he dragged John Charles across country, to be rewarded for raising the Bear Flag by court-martial and dismissal from the Army in October.

Philip St. George Cooke was another disappointed man who became entangled in the consequences of Kearny's fury at frustration. On his way to the front in southern Mexico at last, he was called back to testify at Frémont's trial.

Due to Stockton's strong backing of John Charles, the generals who condemned the latter could yet do no less than to recognize mitigating circumstances and forward a recommendation of clemency to President Polk. The latter accordingly offered Frémont reinstatement, which the latter refused on reasonable as well as emotional grounds. Under a high command which had once black-tagged him, he had no future in the service.

The man who left it, though, was not the same as the one who had led the California Battalion. He was as cracked as Kearny by the time his ordeal of humiliation was ended. Desperate for some gesture that would vindicate him in the eyes of the public, he emerged with a harebrained scheme for a fourth exploring expedition, which drew him west again in the fall of 1848.

⚜ 49 ⚜

Good Riding and Bad Planning

IN A REGION renowned for horsemanship there were three riders who established phenomenal long-distance records. The first of these had been racked by Frémont in the course of his feuding with Kearny in California. Responding to a summons from his antagonist, John Charles had used part of his spleen to astonish the General by his military promptness. Charging over rugged country separating Los Angeles from Monterey, Frémont had covered the 420 miles in four days. What's more, he had duplicated his time on the way back, pursuant to only a day's stopover, making 840 miles in nine suns.

Of the other great riders, Jack Power, or Powers, was newly arrived in California as of the same year in which John Charles burned the coastal mountain trails. A member of the Stevens regiment of New York volunteers, he was not immediately free to go his own Western way. The third was Felix Xavier Aubry, who matched Frémont's hand and raised it the very next year.

The endurance riders weren't rangy men; loosely knit frames couldn't stand the incessant brutal shaking to which long-distance racing subjects bodies. Aubry was short, but somebody remarked of him that he was built like that sturdy engine for lifting great weights, a traversing screw jack.

A French Canadian from Quebec, Felix had arrived in New

Mexico in 1846. By way of promptly showing his bent he had begun by making two round trips of the Santa Fe Trail, where one was considered a season's work by most.

In 1848, however, he scored the feat of coursing from Santa Fe to Independence and back three times. On the out leg of his last one he was racing against time, the wager being that he could cover the better than eight hundred miles in six days.

With $1000 to win or lose, he left Santa Fe in September of 1848, riding at a gallop on a mare called Dolly and driving several spare mounts. These worn down, he was counting on leaving them and obtaining others at the various trading stations by then strung along the trail. Dolly he kept with him by shifting to other horses until Indians caused a change in his schedule.

The station on Rabbit Ear Creek, where he had counted on relay mounts as well as refreshment, had been attacked and plundered. His other horses spent, he reached the Cimarron on his blue-chip mare, but Felix had to leave her at that point.

Seasonal rains were the next obstacle. The three horses he got at the Cimarron should have seen him through to the Arkansas handily, but the customary dust had become a bog which foundered the last of the trio before he reached the latter river. Afoot, he jogged twenty miles in the heavy going, and then had to swim the rain-swollen stream to reach the station on the other side.

There was one more untoward delay, when he had to pause at a caravan to leave used-up mounts and buy replacements. Blood from sores smeared his saddle by the time he reached Independence; but he triumphantly fired a gun when he did so, for he had made his ride and won his bet with almost eight hours to spare.

His achievement, it should be pointed out, was undertaken on a more important count than just the wish to show his equestrian prowess. Possession of new, inhabited regions of the West had brought with it an urge for improved communications between them and the United States proper; and Aubry's feat, by drastically cutting the time gap between New Mexico and Missouri, was a contribution which excited men on practical grounds.

In Texas during the same period Jack Coffee Hays was engaged in trying to locate a wagon route which would connect San Antonio with Southern New Mexico. For the state was without a road link between its settled eastern section and towns along the upper Rio Grande which it now counted as its own beyond question.

Starting late in August, Hays first made the error of trying to ascend the river to its northward turning point. But the country grew progressively more impassable; nor was rough geography all they had to contend with. By turns or both at once, they nearly starved and died of thirst before they reached the Pecos River; for they had mistakenly counted on being able to live off the country, while their efforts to find a passageway for wagons took them far from the Rio Grande and into desert.

Although they never reached El Paso, as planned, they learned from a hardy rancher who had pushed down the Pecos from New Mexico that proceeding to the town from where they were would be no serious problem for vehicles. On the way back east, then, they charted a route which dipped down to San Antonio from the northwest. As this offered few harsh stretches, Hays felt able to report that he had found the course of the needed wagon trace; and he was almost right. With some modifications, supplied by a federal party which was operating more or less at the same time, the way recommended by Jack Coffee was the one which wheels began to follow.

But Tom Benton was thinking not of wagons, but of railroad cars. He wanted them for the West, moreover, without forgetting that he was a senator from Missouri. The transcontinental line which he hoped to see established would run through St. Louis. It followed that a feasible crossing of the Rockies as nearly due west of it as possible would have to be located. And that meant finding a suitable pass through the Colorado Rockies, the most formidable mountains in America.

What had to be proved, though, was that snow wouldn't

270

seasonally block any pass which might be found usable otherwise. This could have been determined by finding mountain crossings in good weather and building sturdy observation posts at which snow tables could be kept and compared with others. It was not the way which appealed to the usually scientific John Charles Frémont.

What he saw was a chance for a dramatic exhibition of his abilities which would serve at once to assert his worth and to measure the smallness of those who had wrecked his military career. He therefore proposed to Benton and his railroad-minded associates that they should commission him to captain a midwinter exploring expedition.

Yet even as he neared Bent's Fort early in October of 1848, one hoped-for result was doomed to failure. Frémont would not be able to shine as a means of casting Kearny's worth in comparative shade, for the General had been dying in St. Louis when the explorer left that city.

The state of John Charles's mind can be gauged from the fact that he had not arranged for a guide before taking the Santa Fe Trail. He had counted on obtaining Carson's services, but Kit was developing a ranch, on which to raise a family among other things; and he would go no more exploring.

Tom Fitzpatrick now made his headquarters at Bent's Fort, but he wasn't free to accompany Frémont, either. In 1847, following his delivery of Stockton's dispatches, he had begun serving as Indian Agent of the Upper Platte and the Arkansas.

Frémont was warned by Carson and William Bent to stay out of the mountains at that season. And he was warned again when Dick Wootton, who had agreed to act as pathfinder, changed his mind. He did so upon finding that snow was that early piled high on the shoulders of the Sangre de Cristos; but John Charles was in no trim to heed advice or pay attention to anything but his need to prove himself. Continuing his search for a guide, he found that Old Bill Williams would undertake to brave the coming winter in that capacity.

There was a story behind his acceptance of the post. Settling down with three squaws at last, the former Methodist circuit rider had been a Ute medicine man for some years prior to the summer of 1848. He had then undertaken the responsibility of packing peltries belonging to his adopted clansmen to Taos. The supposed purpose of his trip was the acquisition of trade goods needed by the tribe; but habit triumphed, and Old Bill exchanged the furs for whiskey.

Recovered from his spree, he was shrewd enough to reason that he could not safely return to his tepee until time had blunted the just wrath of the Utes. These in the meantime had teamed with Apaches in order to raid New Mexico's expanding northern frontier.

There were, at the time, detachments of troops at Taos, which received orders to bring the troublemakers into line. Out as a medicine man and in need of other employment, Bill had agreed to be one of the guides they sought. Also at loose ends, Santiago Kirker had become the other.

Utes and Apaches, to the number of four hundred, had dug in at Cumbres Pass, just over the Colorado border, but Williams and Kirker found a way to outflank them. Thirty-six Indians were slain here, at least half of them Old Bill's chosen people. As Williams was cited in official dispatches for the energy and skill he had shown in pressing the attack, he must have been recognized, and known he was recognized, by redskins whom he had already betrayed financially. Old Bill had thus emerged from the battle not only with a wounded arm but as a Ute without a country.

Again in need of employment, he took the job as Frémont's guide which nobody else wanted. In so doing, he became involved in a story which is told in different ways by different people, all positive of holding the correct sum of facts.

The great immovable one is that the expedition was a gruesome failure. Ten of thirty-one did not win past an obstacle course featured by starvation as well as blighting cold; and those who did stagger over the finish line had nothing to their credit but a retained grip on life.

At best this expedition, as conducted, would have proved little. If the men and their mounts could have easily negotiated passes through the jumble of Colorado's great mountains, it would have demonstrated only that they had traveled at a time when the snowfall was unwontedly light. But the reverse was true; the snow came early, continued to fall and attained depths which reduced the men contending with it to chilblained futility.

For Frémont, who had hoped for increased stature as a means of confounding his enemies, the disaster was crushing. Beside himself, he laid the blame for his ill success on the poor guiding of a man whose infallibility as a regional pathfinder had become a byword. The countercharge hurled by those who could not believe that Williams could lose his way asserted that Old Bill could have led the party through negotiable passes but that John Charles overruled him.

For more than a century the decision as to who was right has been tied to partiality, on the part of the respective judges, for either Frémont or Williams. But this pattern of biased speculation has finally been broken by the discovered journal of cartographer Charles Preuss. Unlike other writers on the subject, he got his information at first hand, for he was a member of the expedition. Unlike them, too, he was impartial, for he heartily despised both the men in question. According to this Rhadamanthus, Old Bill acted as though he didn't know one bearing from another.

If that would appear to vindicate John Charles, it doesn't choose between the theories advanced by Frémont's defenders concerning the cause of Old Bill's misguidance. Of these one has run to the effect that Williams had become senile and thus mentally confused.

That Bill was to a degree insane there can be no doubt. He had, notably, a host of fetishes, capped by a heart affair with the mountain in Arizona which bears his name today. Yet his frequently demonstrated balminess had never interfered with his efficiency before, nor is there reason to believe that it did so now.

The alternate theory has held him guilty of deliberately lead-

273

ing the party astray in order to bring about a state of affairs which did indeed materialize. This was the caching, in desperation, of expensive instruments and other excess equipment, in order to make withdrawal from a snow-smothered area possible. In this case the prosecution assumed that Bill planned to retrieve this stockpile with a view to selling it; and not without grounds.

Whether Williams ate one of the members of the party, as Frémont charged, is neither here nor there; but, as has been pointed out earlier, this was not the first indictment to such an effect. If that charge can now neither be proved nor disproved, it can nevertheless be stated that Old Bill did have his bearings while with Frémont in Colorado's mountains, whether he was willing to let John Charles know it or not. For after survivors of the broken expedition straggled out of high country in February, Williams and a Dr. Kern made for the above-cited cache and found it, without bothering to tell the man to whom most of the contents belonged that they were doing so.

Exactly what Old Bill's intentions were can't be told, because —as Mexican mule packers survived to report—Utes learned the whereabouts of their recreant medicine man. Bristling with arrows fired by Indians who came suddenly out of the night, he fell by his campfire in the Rockies on March 14, 1849.

𝕾 50 𝕾

The Golden Catchall

IT MIGHT HAVE been thought that James Marshall and John Augustus Sutter would have profited from the discovery of gold on property belonging to the latter. It led to greatly raising the per capita wealth of the country. It totally changed the level of individual expectations, both as to the size of possible fortunes and the speed with which they might be accrued. It supplied the capital to boost the United States fully into the Industrial Age. It started the nation on its way to becoming the most prosperous one in modern history.

But for Sutter and Marshall the finding of gold was disastrous, for they never located any in quantity themselves, while nothing else went right, either. New Helvetia was ruined, beginning with the mill whose erection had led to the discovery of buried treasure. Nobody wanted to accept modest wages for either building a mill or helping to operate it when there was a possibility of finding in the course of a single day more than could be earned by years of hard work. As for the cultivated fields and pastures along the Sacramento, they were turned upside down by the spades of farmers who had become prospectors at home before trotting off in search of other gold fields.

But although the treasure-hungry locusts began destroying, early in 1848, the economy which had made Sutter's Fort a thriving enterprise, the news of gold for the picking was slow to reach other portions of America. Ships bound for the East did not sail from the quiet little port of San Francisco very often, and they were long in transit. It was fall before newspapers of the Atlantic Seaboard received enough confirmation to take the tale of gold in California seriously. Some people who had actually seen, and could produce samples of, free gold had by then turned up; but even then Americans as a whole were slow to believe. The notion of easily gained wealth was foreign to the thinking of a still essentially pioneer people, used to working very hard for any prosperity they might finally boast.

The first to be willing to credit the existence of a natural Western mint were those who found nothing to their liking in the existing state of things. In the main they were either youngsters gazing glumly up the long, slow road to attainment or older men looking for a way out of settling down.

These were particularly numerous among veteran Rangers. For years they had rushed to and fro, fighting Comanches and bandits; and then there had been the campaigns of the Mexican War in which they had won national acclaim for their dash and daring. But in 1848 they had returned, unemployed, to a state where farming was the accepted way of making a living. Nor were they on a par with their coevals, who had been clearing and tilling land during years in which the Rangers had called their saddles home.

Jack Coffee Hays was one who saw California as a chance to get a new start in life. William Oury came to the same conclusion, and so did David Terry, younger than the other two but still a late starter as careers were reckoned on the frontier. Numerous other Rangers of lesser note also decided to try for fortunes on the Pacific Coast, while John Glanton seems to have been headed for the gold fields, even though he ended by plucking wealth from different sources.

But 1848 was not the migration year for any of these. Hays, for example, could hardly have heard of California as bonanzaland until he returned from his wagon-road exploring trip in December. It was the spring of 1849, in fact, before the surge to California became more than a sporadic movement anywhere in the nation. "The spring fret," or the primal urge to respond to the rebirth of life by moving, was a cogent force among a people still generally close to nature; and in combination with the call of gold it drove thousands upon thousands west from wherever they were.

In addition to the water route around the Horn, there were two amphibious ones to the aureate promised land. Those using two ships took one as far as the Isthmus of Panama, crossed it on mules and then boarded a north-bound vessel. Others struck overland for Mexico's western coast and put to sea from either Guaymas or Mazatlán.

Most, however, fared by way of one of the overland routes, of which there were likewise three main ones. Supplementing the Oregon Trail, and the road to New Mexico, with its Old Spanish Trail continuation, was a southerly trace. In part charted by Hays and in part composed of Cooke's wagon road, it linked San Antonio and San Diego.

The gold lure drew old trappers as well as Texas plainsmen

276

and hordes of newcomers to the West. Black Harris did not respond, as he died in Missouri of cholera in 1849; but James Ohio Pattie returned to California. So perforce did Peg-leg Smith, concerning whose morality a word is in order.

Grand stock-lifter though he was, Peg-leg did not look upon himself as a thief, nor was he so regarded by most Westerners, as long as he preyed only upon Mexicans and Indians. Horse stealing was the act of taking an equine from a white man. For this reason the raising of the Bear Flag had foretold the downfall of Smith's business. Raiding Mexican California had been, in his eyes, legitimate; but once the region beyond the Sierras had been ceded to the United States, Peg-leg did not feel that it would be right for him to continue his raids, so he dropped the business. For a time he had been able to carry on with the stock in hand, but by 1849 he was ready to turn prospector.

Cities as well as rural districts and the mountains lost men to California. William Walker came from Nashville, William Tell Coleman from St. Louis, David Broderick from New York, Joseph Stokes from Albany and Edward McGowan from Philadelphia. Then there was Billy Mulligan, seemingly of New York in the first instance, though a Ranger who had served under Hays with distinction during the Mexican War.

No doubt they all had adventures of one sort or another on their way to Eldorado, but the most remarkable deeds wrought by the converging Forty-niners are laid to the score of a man who didn't go the route. Although it was said of John Glanton that he left a beautiful bride in San Antonio, in order to find gold for her, it can't be demonstrated that such was his motive. But he set forth, at all events.

The protégé of Mustang Gray, John had won admiration as a Ranger both before the Mexican War and during it. He was therefore able to gather a following when he decided to go farther west; and he must have picked his men with care, for they turned out to be a singularly broad-minded lot.

Their first recorded exploit, though, showed them on the side of whatever angels were resident in Tucson at the time. The

277

Texans arrived at the little walled city on the Santa Cruz to find it besieged by warriors of the Apache confederacy founded by Mangas Colorado. Warned that Glanton's men would help the Mexicans, Mangas agreed to withdraw on the face-saving consideration of a carousal hosted by, and held in, the town. Its plaza then became the scene of barbaric revelry, from which the participating Apaches and Texans staggered away at the end of seventy-two hours.

In spite of the fact that Cooke had raised the American flag over the tequila-ransomed pueblo, it was not waving aloft at the time of Glanton's visit. As the Treaty of Guadalupe-Hildalgo had established the Gila as America's southern boundary in that zone, the town which he had saved at the expense of a hangover was in Sonora.

No doubt the former Ranger had been told in Tucson that Mexican authorities were willing to pay Apache-exterminators. Remaining in Sonora, in any case, John imitated Kirker in becoming a professional scalp hunter. As in Santiago's case, the agreed bounty was fifty dollars; but when his wanderings in search of hair to be lifted had taken Glanton as far as the Colorado, he found an additional source of revenue.

The biggest natural obstacle along the southern route to California was the Colorado. Probably using the rafts with which Cooke had floated his baggage train across this river, the Yuma Indians had begun a ferry service, maintained as a tribal monopoly. As they were tough savages with no prejudice against extortion, they had done well in 1849 until Glanton showed up late in the fall. Ambushing operators which included one white man, he and his followers took over the ferry fleet.

Floatation fees were not all that they gained. They killed, and robbed the corpses of, any traveling in parties small enough to be conveniently attacked. And meanwhile there were scalps to be plucked.

But Glanton's own turn came at the hands of the Yumas, whom he had come to consider too overawed to be dangerous. Watching for such a chance the Indians struck while the gang of whites was celebrating on borrowed whiskey and wiped out John, together with fourteen of his henchmen on April 23, 1850.

No such definite date as that reported by a survivor or so of the Glanton massacre can be assigned the death of another Western adventurer. During the previous winter James Ohio Pattie had visited the California holding of David Waldo, whom he had known in their mutual Taos days. It was believed that either Indians or the blizzard which belted the area a short while after he left Waldo's ranch did for him; but all that is known is that no trace of Jacova's rescuer was ever seen again. He vanished in the wilderness, at some time during the winter of 1849–1850, with the completeness of dissipated smoke.

51

Saints and Killers

SOME BESIDES SUTTER and Marshall were troubled by the finding of gold in California. Two so bothered were men as different in their desires and methods of procedure as Brigham Young and William Bent.

To begin with the former, the call of Eldorado drew thousands of covered wagons along trails which cut across the region he meant for his people to have in uncontested possession. He had also wished them to have no contact with the Gentiles—the Mormons had long likened themselves to the Jews—from whom they had sought escape when crossing the Rockies.

To raise his fence as high as he could about his religious commonwealth, he drew up the constitution for the State of Deseret in March of 1849; and on the 12th of that month he didn't lose a vote when successfully running for governor. Thereafter he forwarded the information that he was chief executive of one of the United States, together with the instrument of government which he had composed, to Washington.

Had the constitution been accepted there, Young would have established a privately owned component of the American commonwealth from which all but Mormons could have been excluded. For something over a year, in fact, he did rule over a sovereign entity of some kind, though it was debatably a part of the country to which he claimed that Deseret belonged. The principle of theocracy has always been foreign to American political thinking as embodied in the nation's great administrative document.

Inevitably Brigham's proposed state was turned down by Zachary Taylor's administration, which nonetheless recognized that political organization of the region in question was due. As for Young himself, the federal government was realistic enough to accept the fact of his dominant role. When the Territory of Utah was at length formed in September of 1850, therefore, the practice of awarding the governorship to someone in good standing with the party in power nationally was set aside.

Appointed chief executive of the new territory, Brigham got much of what he had tried for, if by no means all. In particular he could hand down laws which an all-Mormon legislature was bound to pass; and he could give his private police force legal sanction by ascribing territorial duties.

While Joseph Smith was still alive the Saints had developed a military arm for both internal and external use. If the Mormons were religious zealots, many of them were yet American frontiersmen and not necessarily always disposed to do as they were told. As prophets flourish only in an atmosphere of implicit obedience, there had to be a means of enforcing it on willful members of the sect. To bring this about, Smith had formed an order called the Danites, answerable only to him.

Whether or not the Prophet had heard about the Old Man of the Mountain and his Assassins, the Sons of Dan functioned like the latter. They would murder at Smith's word and count it unto themselves for righteousness. Danites tried for Governor Boggs of Missouri, for example; and it was not for nothing that they were also called Avenging Angels. One of the reasons for the unpopularity of the Saints elsewhere was the penchant of this force for disposing of settlers who had opposed Mormon domination of any district into which the sect had chosen to move.

Within the Mormon community the Danites saw to it that the will of the Prophet was obeyed, using the methods usual to strong-arm squads. So it came about that conformity as to habits was achieved and respect for the hierarchy established. Then it was likewise brought about in this way that tithes were paid in full and on time.

After getting rid of Rigdon and usurping the role of Prophet, Young had taken over the Danites as his own. In the States the Avenging Angels had been something curbed, as sheriffs' posses and other bodies of armed Gentiles were possible opposing forces. But after the removal to Utah there was none to limit their violence—at least while they stayed in their own bailiwick.

To be the leader of such a group required a viciousness with which Bill Hickman seems to have been amply furnished; yet he and his minions failed to overawe Sam Brannan. The latter reported an illustrating episode, though without giving dates. Evidence points to the fall of 1849 as the time of the first clash, however.

Needing funds for his growing commonwealth, Brigham decided to tap California's gold supply himself. Feeling that Brannan's colony on the Sacramento must be wallowing in wealth, he sent messengers beyond the Sierras who demanded the payment of tithes to the central see in the Great Basin.

That was cool gall. Young was recognized as the new Prophet of Latter-day Saints only by the Utah branch of the sect. A son of Joseph Smith had assumed the leadership of those remaining in the Mississippi Valley; a man called Levi Wright had led a migration into Texas, in 1845, whose members looked only to him; and in California Sam was supreme.

His colony, which had been strengthened by the members of Cooke's Mormon Battalion, when they had found no Saints from Nauvoo to join, was indeed doing well. For those were flush times, and Brannan had developed the knack of dropping one dollar and picking up ten. A charity-begins-at-home advocate, though, he wasn't in the least inclined to honor the claims of the man who had refused to join him in California.

Accordingly he listened unmoved to a request for church taxes made in the name of the Lord. "You go back and tell Brigham," he suggested to the Prophet's messenger, "that I'll give up the Lord's money when he sends me a receipt signed by the Lord."

Excommunicated by Young, Sam possibly joined Rigdon as one doomed to be buffeted for a thousand years. What certainly happened was that a detachment of Hickman's Avenging Angels swooped over the Sierras and down on the Sacramento Valley.

Brannan appears to have been caught short the first time and forced to disgorge; but when the next tithing season rolled around, he was ready with a goon squad of his own. Dubbed Angel Exterminators by their sponsor, these lived up to their name by laying for the Danites, as they rode off with politely paid taxes, and rubbing them out.

Giving up on the Mormons of California as a source of revenue, Brigham next recognized that the westward-bound Gentiles could be useful as well as irritating. His farmers and artisans needed a market for their products, and the caravaners formed one. The dead mouse in that jug of wine, though, was that the pilgrims reached Fort Bridger, where they were served with all they required, before entering Brigham's domain.

While Young was making up his mind what to do about this unfavorable trading situation, a commercial decision had already been arrived at in another section of the West. The firm of Bent and St. Vrain no longer existed.

William and Ceran had not made a good team since the passing of Charles Bent. Prematurely fearing the end of the buffalo-robe trade, St. Vrain had wished to shift the company's headquarters to Santa Fe. A plainsman who hated towns, Bent had refused to consider leaving the upper Arkansas.

His trading zone was shrinking, though. Resenting being crowded, as their free range was gnawed away by white settlements and displaced tribes alike, the Comanches, Kiowas and Lipan Apaches had become so difficult to deal with that William had ordered abandonment of a Bent and St. Vrain outpost on the Canadian River in 1848. To keep others from getting any joy out of it, he had personally blown it up, moreover, leaving only a landmark known to the rare white travelers of the region as 'Dobe Walls.

When St. Vrain left the firm early in 1849, William Bent had thought to carry on as before; but then the gold seekers came. In the past most pilgrims had been farmers looking for better land and more of it than they could acquire where they came from. But the Gold Rush was manned in at least equal measure by men from the cities. Cholera was rampant in New Orleans, St. Louis and other large towns, whose citizens took to the plains in 1849. They brought it with them, and the plague raged through the Indian tribes.

It killed off half the southern Cheyennes, who had been both the commercial mainstay of Bent's Fort and its means of keeping other savages reasonably well behaved when in the post's vicinity. To be sure, the guns of the fort could have taken care of the Indians who began making warlike demonstrations in front of it. But aside from the fact that killing customers wasn't a trader's proper occupation, William knew that the hostility was not really directed at him. There wasn't food enough to go around at times, now that many thousands of immigrants had been added to those trying to live off the buffalo herds. In consequence, tribes were staging wars of survival with each other; and they were ready to strike at any target.

Although they had not yet combined for the purpose of making mass attacks on the immigrants, the Army feared a general uprising of the tribes. In preparation, the service was building new posts on the plains, in addition to having bought Fort Laramie from the American Fur Company. It had sought to buy Bent's Fort, too, but William had turned down whatever was offered. If his claim was that the amount was too low, his real motive seems to have been an unwillingness to have the struc-

ture stand for war against the Indians instead of the friendly relations with them—taking the picture as a whole—which it had
long represented.

The Army didn't get a chance to make a second bid. Seized by
an entirely uncommercial whim, the merchant cleared out the
old caravanserai, less a certain number of barrels of gunpowder,
on August 21. Torch in hand, he went from point to point of the
post and then rode off to await the sky-blackening results. After
he got them, he must have felt better, for he proceeded to a
point called Big Timers, a few leagues down the Arkansas, and
there matter-of-factly set up shop on a smaller scale.

Broken Hand Fitzpatrick joined him there in the fall of '49,
pursuant to a trip to Washington. At the capital Tom had advocated the calling together of all the tribes of the plains for the
purpose of thrashing out current problems and agreeing on plans
for meeting future ones. White Hair had hoped that the redskin
convocation would be scheduled for 1850, but as Congress failed
to vote the necessary appropriation, it did not materialize that
year.

𝕰 52 𝕰

The City Gold Built

NOT A FEW of the many who quested for treasure in California found an appreciable amount of gold. And some did what
almost all had planned; that is to say, they returned home to invest it in land or some commercial venture. More stayed on the
West Coast, either because they had squandered their troves or
because they had found in prospecting a way of life which appealed to them.

Some who failed to make a strike grew disgusted with the land
and their folly in traipsing to it. But if these left, more that made
no immediate fortunes pressed on elsewhere, unwilling to go

back to the past and make terms with it empty-handed. In time they sifted all of California's valleys, wandered through all its forests and probed all the gulches in its mountains. While so doing, or while sojourning in the various bonanza camps they pitched together in the wilds, they had adventures enough; but the great story of the Gold Rush is not a matter of treasure seeking in the wilderness but of the city which was its by-product. Even in the United States there had previously been no sudden city. But San Francisco was one, as of 1849. A year after Sam Brannan had raced along its main street, bawling that gold had been found in California, the little town on the great harbor was still one. And then the Forty-niners began piling on the scene. With gold so plentiful that any price asked was paid, they rushed through the cycle running from tent town to modern metropolis in seven tempestuous months.

At the end of that time the city boasted rows of office buildings, well-stocked stores and hotels whose accommodations were reckoned excellent by men used to the best that the Atlantic Seaboard had to offer. Much more was promised, for the hurry of building was going on unabated, when Edward McGowan reached San Francisco late in October.

An attorney from Philadelphia with a flair for journalism, a passion for politics and a penchant for lively company, McGowan had come west with a letter of recommendation to California's current military governor, General Bennet Riley. Behind him lay participation in Pennsylvania's Buckshot War, expulsion from the state's legislature because of a brawl while it was in session, a charge of accessory to theft of which he had been cleared a year earlier and a trouncing administered to Ned Buntline—on the score of a scurrilous journalistic attack—as recently as the previous May. Then somebody had shown him a specimen of California gold; and the sight, as he wrote, had fired him with the desire to be a prospector.

Yet he never looked for metallic gold, once he had reached the Pacific by way of Panama and sailed through America's Gates of Hercules. For the vitality of nonesuch San Francisco spoke to

285

the equally remarkable vitality in Ned McGowan. It was love at first glimpse, and, except when political errands took him to some one of California's several capitals, he never stayed otherwheres for some years.

He never presented his letter of introduction to Arikara-siege Riley, either, for reasons descriptive both of him and the community he had promptly embraced. Upon checking into the well-appointed Parker House, he had been approached by the owner of a roulette wheel, anxious for an operator. Ned had not earlier been a croupier, but as all phases of life interested him, and as he needed some source of income while finding where to plant his feet in a strange land, he briefly became a professional gambler. During his tour of duty in this capacity, as it chanced, he was stunned to find that one of his clients was Governor Riley. Everybody gambled in San Francisco at that time, but as Ned wasn't sure how the General would react to a wheel spinner who asked for patronage, he didn't try to find out.

Following his natural bent, he became involved in the politics of a region which was not fully organized as a territory, albeit confident of becoming a state. It had the assurance of gold behind it.

In January of 1850 Ned had friends carry him from the sickbed to the polls so that he might vote for David Broderick. In this way he came to the notice of a demonically ambitious man who had come to California from a Bowery Boy precinct of New York so that he might return to his native Washington, D.C., as a United States senator. When McGowan first voted for him, though, Broderick was running merely to represent San Francisco in the territorial senate.

The county he spoke for, so hastily and erratically were things being done, was not organized until the following April. Contending for the sundry offices were slates of Democratic and Whig candidates, as well as a few independents such as Jack Coffee Hays, who wished to be San Francisco County's first high sheriff.

Still riding the crest of his war-earned fame, Hays campaigned by making personal appearances ahorseback. If his method did little to show his political worth, it turned out to be more effective than the fervent oratory of more experienced candidates. In particular, as Ned moodily watched, he appeared in San Francisco's plaza in dashing Ranger attire and put his horse through circus-act gyrations, while the prospective voters roared applause.

With their reaction for warrant, McGowan advised other Democratic leaders that if they wanted to be sure of carrying the day they should dump their candidate for sheriff and take on Jack Coffee. Done, it worked out as Ned had predicted. Most of the voters didn't care about any of the other candidates, as he later noted; they just wanted to be sure of having a ballot bearing the name of the fine rider with a clever horse.

After the Democrats had stunt-ridden to victory with Ranger Hays, Ned was appointed a justice of the peace. Then, when a higher tribunal was established in June 1850, he was made an associate justice of the Court of Sessions.

If a position promising quiet dignity elsewhere, it did no such thing in San Francisco. For the duly constituted judges immediately found themselves arrayed against a citizenry which felt that the function of the courts was to convict prisoners. The city's burghers also believed in capital punishment in cases where the law didn't demand it; and when judges didn't go along with them, they raised the hue of undue lenience.

In back of this attitude was the fact of people converging in quantity on an area which had not been legally and politically prepared for their advent. To begin with the gold seekers, they were illegally in business to a man, inasmuch as the federal government had not paved the way by setting up any system of laws by which land could be held for the purpose of extracting the minerals on deposit. The Forty-niners gathered at the various mining camps made up their own laws and, borrowing from Spanish politics, chose alcaldes, or officials with both executive and judicial functions, to see that they were enforced and to adjudicate upon disputed claims.

The power of the alcaldes lay in the mass of men supporting them, all jurors in their opinion but hard to tell from a mob when excited. At first organized to act in civil cases related to mining, these popular courts began to handle criminal matters, too, for there was no judicial system. Neither were there legal and penal codes to offer guidance, so these were also made up by men who had no jails for correctional purposes. Punishment was thus always physical. For minor offenses they flogged the perpetrators; for major ones they hanged them.

Sometimes they tried to consider the case quietly, and to hear whatever there was to be said in favor of the accused. More often the law of Abingdon prevailed; they acted first and talked it over later. For they were not a court then, whatever their pretensions, but a blood-stirred crowd, and at such times any who might try to put in a word for the accused were themselves in danger of mob violence.

Many who were in San Francisco, as of the second half of 1850, had taken part in popular tribunals and emerged with firm juridical convictions which were entirely alien to the principles basic to proper American legal procedure. The city itself had a heritage of popular action, moreover, though for a somewhat different reason.

When claiming California as a United States territory, the national administration had not troubled to supplant the system of governing towns which Mexico had inherited from Spain. Set up to administer colonial villages, it was completely inadequate for a cosmopolitan city which had drawn its full share of the feloniously inclined. There was no grand jury, no judicial system, no law-enforcement body to speak of, and no authority to provide these things.

Taking advantage of the situation, a gang calling themselves the Hounds began operating. Pretending to be volunteer police, and making a show of disciplined organization by holding parades, they were vicious predators.

Something had to be done about the Hounds, who also referred to themselves as Regulators, and this was accomplished in

288

July of 1849 by citizens who had no other recourse. But after California became a state on September 9, 1850, and after Frémont and Dr. William Gwin took their seats in the U.S. Senate, the residents of its metropolis had all the political advantages as well as all the administrative tools enjoyed by any community in the nation.

But the feeling persisted that the people and not their duly delegated agents should handle legal and judicial matters directly. So when courts manned by trained personnel did not arrive at the prompt arbitrary decisions favored by popular tribunals, they were challenged and then actively fought, with Sam Brannan taking the lead.

By the beginning of 1851 the controversy had come to such a pass that the court's critics were stamping their feet and catcalling while attorneys were attempting to defend their clients, or whenever judges opposed the prosecution on any point. Mass meetings were held, besides, at which the courts were excoriated because the judges wouldn't allow themselves to be dictated to.

Yet in spite of this hooliganism, these men considered themselves the town's most respectable element and so unabashedly dubbed themselves. For associated with Sam were other climbing merchants of a booming community as well as bankers such as James King. Hailing from the District of Columbia, though not Washington, King always parenthetically tacked the phrase "of William" to his name in order to distinguish himself from others identically christened.

Politics was mixed in the problem without being referred to, for the merchants were for the most part Whigs. The courts, on the other hand, had been created by the Democrats, who had curvetted to power on the equestrian skill of John Coffee Hays.

Sam at first called his organization of dissatisfied citizens Regulators, but as that term had also been used by the malignant Hounds the name was changed to Committee of Vigilance. If it didn't control the judges, the group was able to dictate to the grand jury. Through this body it fired at the courts such indictments as "assault with intent to kill" in the instance of a man who had but fist-knocked another out while both were at a demi-reps' cotillion, where sobriety wasn't the key tone.

The feud between the Vigilantes and the courts grew in bitterness until Hays as sheriff was not the only dignitary who attended trials under arms. Bearing in mind that the governor referred to was the current chief executive of California and that Broderick was then the state's senate majority leader, the following quotation from McGowan is a telling word picture of a trial at which he presided, armed to the teeth himself:

"The mobites who had crowded the court house, jumped on the benches and commenced hissing and showing other marks of disapprobation . . . They offered no further violence; if they had, many of them would have bitten the dust that day. David C. Broderick, Governor McDougall . . . and the prisoner himself had on a pair of Colt's revolvers, and many others were armed, two or three with double barrel shotguns under their cloaks."

The fact of the prisoner being armed, so that he could have peace of mind while being tried, had a history. There had been efforts to take prisoners away from officers conducting them from the ship which served as a jail to the courthouse.

It seems probable that the Vigilantes might have remained frustrated had not William Coleman stepped upon the stage. A Forty-niner from Kentucky, Coleman had left Hangtown-turned-Placerville in 1850 and gone to New York City. There he had prospered so in trade that he returned to California early in 1851, to open a San Francisco office of his commission merchandising firm.

A Democrat, and in any case a man who had had little time to become involved in local affairs, William didn't take an interest in the operations of the Vigilantes until he passed their headquarters while returning from work. Like Brigham Young in being possessed of a genius for organization, Coleman was struck by the aimlessness of the wrangling he had heard. What was instantly clear to his talent was that the Committee of Vigilance needed a program which consisted of more positive action than heckling the courts. After he had taken off the starched collar he wore while at work, he returned to tell the Vigilantes how they should proceed.

In brief what he proposed was the formation of a tribunal which would be superior to the authorized courts and would tell them how to function. It would also try cases itself, whenever necessary. For sanction it would appeal to the general populace of the city by calling itself "the People's Court." It would avoid the onus of personal identity on the part of any participating individual by conferring numbers on all. After Coleman's proposals had been accepted, for example, the edicts of the Committee were not signed by a name but by "No. 67, Secretary."

In February 1851 a store was robbed after its proprietor had first been bludgeoned, and the Vigilantes pounced on two suspects. Of these one, who said his name was Burdue, was identified as James Stuart, a manslaying bandit long active in the mining camps. As the courts indignantly refused to cooperate with the Vigilantes, the latter decided to try Burdue, or Berdue, and his associate themselves.

Although nobody had been killed in the course of the robbery in question the lives of the accused pair were at stake, for the Committee had different views than the law respecting the nature of capital crimes. Fortunately for Burdue, who turned out not to be Stuart, or guilty of assault and robbery, Coleman couldn't get a conviction while acting as prosecutor in his kangaroo court. Two or three men who had heard Stuart described as several inches taller than Burdue held out against the rest of the jurors.

The discovery that establishing guilt isn't as simple as it seems might have made the Vigilantes less critical of professional jurists, but it failed to. Finding that they had been earnestly trying to hang a guiltless man, furthermore, might have expectedly had the effect of making them doubt their own infallibility. Neither transpired, however, so as Ned McGowan grimly watched, the minions of Sam Brannan and William Coleman finally hanged a man on June 11, 1851.

There is a tradition to the effect that San Francisco was blood-
ied at this period by murders whose number would have shocked
Nero. The Vigilantes didn't seem to know about them, though,
for the best candidate for the gallows they could turn up after
months of trying was a burglar of modest pretensions named
John Jenkins.

It is not certain that Jenkins was guilty of so much as grand
larceny, for the safe he walked off with was so small that he carried it unaided. But he was lynched while a supporting crowd
stood by, and in due course three others were hoisted aloft, while
some who thought they might be decamped.

Satisfied with efforts which included at least one case of
shanghaiing, the Committee ceased operations in September of
1851. But it was in a bitterly divided city that Ned continued to
work for the realization of Broderick's desire to be in the national senate. As for Coleman, at the outset of 1852 he left the
city where he had made mob violence respectable and was not
seen in it again for many months.

𝕭𝕺𝕾 53 𝕭𝕺𝕾

The Sacking of Fort Bridger

THE MEETING OF Prairie nations promoted by Fitzpatrick
did not take place until September 1851, the site being Fort
Laramie. It could not be the complete gathering which Broken
Hand had hoped for, because no location would have been satisfactory to all the tribes. In this case the Comanches, Kiowas and
Apaches didn't want to move north into a country where they
wouldn't know where to hunt for the horses they felt sure would
be stolen from them. But Arapahoes, Cheyennes and Sioux were
there, as well as Crows, Assiniboins, Arikaras and Minitaris. The
Pawnees were no longer a wandering tribe, as they had sold their
hunting range to the federal government and were raising crops

along the Loup River. But the Shoshones, Jim Bridger riding with them, unexpectedly came over the mountains to take part. Old Gabe had been able to bring the Snakes, because he was related by marriage to Washakie, their head sachem. For a while, though, the wisdom of inviting them wasn't apparent, as their advent nearly broke up the council before it got started. Although truce was supposed to have prevailed, it hadn't kept Cheyennes from lifting the scalps of a couple of Shoshones unwise enough to stray from the main body of their fellows. Then, right at the site of the peace conference, the Sioux remembered that they and the Snakes had been conducting transmontane wars.

Through Bridger's good offices the Shoshones were better armed than the other tribes, being equipped with rifles. But a Dakota whose father had been an unavenged victim of Snake prowess dashed with bow and arrows to take on the oncoming phalanx of his enemies singlehanded.

Luckily for the cause of peace, this brave's pony was not as fast as that of one of the interpreters on duty at the time. Catching up with the berserk Sioux, the white man ruined the former's moment of high drama by dumping him to the ground.

In consequence the two hundred dragoons at Fort Laramie did not have to attempt to keep the warriors of about all the northern Plains tribes from picking sides and trying for scalps and booty. As there were an estimated ten thousand Indians present, two or three thousand males of fighting age must have been among them. Nomads, they traveled with their families when not officially on the warpath. There were, accordingly, thousands of squaws and children gabbling and romping amidst the hundreds of tepees, not to mention hordes of dogs and all the horses owned by nations which reckoned wealth in terms of the equines owned by individuals.

As these were all still buckskin Indians, and were in full panoply of feathered headgear for the men and foofaraw for the squaws, it must have been the greatest Wild West show of all time. It took a hardy constitution to mingle with it, though, for that many savages and animals cohabiting under a hot sun for weeks could and did raise a stench from which the very welkin retreated.

It had weeks in which to ripen, because the government was late in sending the wagonloads of food and other gifts which Fitzpatrick had promised by way of persuading the Indians to foregather. At length the situation got so bad that the conference wasn't held at Fort Laramie after all. Shifting east to a new campsite and new grazing grounds along Horse Creek, the peace commissioners put up a conference pavilion there.

The delay was hard on the dog population, for as other stores became exhausted, into the pot went Fido. And as the inedible parts of dogs hastened the process of giving the new camp a fragrance that matched the old, Fitzpatrick, Bent and Bridger had to keep assuring the increasingly restive Indians that the Great White Father had not really forgotten the items promised.

The only happy man present was Father De Smet, who no longer specialized in Flatheads. He had, indeed, so widened his activities that he had started, along the Willamette, a bona fide mission for the Indians of western Oregon whom Jason Lee and his ilk had left to their heathen devices. On this occasion, though, Black Robe had come as missionary to the Minitaris.

Setting up his Christian medicine lodge, De Smet had a salvation field day. Among the Sioux, Cheyennes and Arapahoes alone he baptized upwards of eight hundred children. The count was swelled by half-breeds, as well as the pure strain children of other tribes, including Andrew Jackson Fitzpatrick.

Three weeks off schedule the government's caravan appeared, greatly to the relief of Andrew Jackson's father. When the gifts had been distributed and a final feasting held, the tribes began to go their separate ways, though all pledged alike to permanent peace.

The terms upon which this was to be kept called for keeping to agreed hunting ranges, where poaching had formerly been the practice. To make this treaty clause one that could be adhered to, government representatives promised supplemental food supplies as well as funds for equipment. A conference of chiefs with the Great White Father, in this case President Fillmore, had also been arranged, so that the tribes could present their respective ideas as to how they could continue to flourish amicably. The Indians on their part had conceded the right of way through their hunting grounds to whites bound for more westerly parts. They had, in addition, granted the Army sites for protecting forts.

As everybody went away satisfied, counting even Red Cloud and Sitting Bull, there actually was peace for a while among the Indians. But as the council hadn't disposed of paleface feuds, Jim Bridger returned home to find himself at open odds with the Saints of Salt Lake City.

When the Territory of Utah had been formed, it had been composed of all the acreage acquired from Mexico which was not comprehended by the boundaries of California, New Mexico and Texas. Exactly where one of these left off and another began had been no means defined in 1850; but Governor Young had as good a right as anybody to consider that parts of western Colorado and Wyoming were in his dukedom.

No harm for Old Gabe could reside in that fact alone, for theoretically a territory of the United States was occupiable by any citizen not at odds with the law; and where Jim dwelt there was none to offend. In spite of Brigham's failure to get authorization for the theocratic State of Deseret, however, his assumption was that Utah should be inhabited by Mormons only.

The Gentiles whose residence he most opposed did not visit his settlements or personally intrude upon his prerogatives in any way. Yet they controlled facilities by which he wished his own people to benefit. These were the trading station of Jim Bridger and a ferry service across the Green, maintained by some lesser mountain men.

Possessing absolutely unchecked power among the Saints, and not curbed to any noteworthy degree by distant Washington, Young inevitably grew in arrogance. By 1851 he had become so convinced of his ability to do as he wished that he sent word to

Bridger and the ferrymen that they should find employment elsewhere.

At first this ukase seems to have taken the form of an indirect word to the wise. When this didn't get results, an order from Young as territorial governor was sent—and also ignored. Old Gabe continued to offer supply, repair and blacksmithing service to the pilgrims of the Oregon-California Trail; and his friends and former fellow trappers, in spite of the fuming Prophet, kept on shuttling the wagons of pilgrims from one shore of the Green to the other.

In 1852 the Danites came to the mountains, but they found that it was one thing to intimidate captive settlers, nailed down by families to support, and another to try to bluff mountain men. With Old Gabe directing strategy, there was a showdown on the Green which the trigger-fingered Saints lost.

Competition was Brigham's next move. When the trail again became flush with traffic in the spring of 1853, the Mormons had charted a bypass of Fort Bridger which led to a ferry of their own. Featuring it, too, was a trading station, stocked with whiskey as well as other supplies. Though opposed to it for Saints, Young was not averse to trafficking in hard liquor.

It didn't work out well for the Mormons for several reasons, most of them hinging on the renown of Old Gabe. By then, stopping at his post was a tradition. His trail wisdom was a byword. As his personality and fame as a reconteur had become a part of national lore, he was revered in advance by those who had scanned reading matter for tips as to how best to negotiate the distance between where they were east of the Mississippi and where they wanted to be west of it. So the caravans continued to stop at Bridger's station, and to cross the Green where Jim advised them to.

Moving for the kill in his wrath at that development, Brigham announced his knowledge—Prophets not finding it necessary to palter with less than positive information—that Bridger had been responsible for Indian raids on the Mormon settlements. As that made Jim's life forfeit, Governor Young sent out a posse, deputized by a pair of sheriffs, to pick his enemy up. Of its 150 members, though, most were members of the Nauvoo Legion of home guards, while the real leader was the Danite sagamore, Bill Hickman.

By way of appetizer this war party of Saints first took care of the mountain men found on duty at the Green River ferry. These left dead, Hickman led the way to Fort Bridger, where they arrived on August 26, 1853.

Old Gabe, as it chanced, was in the act of leaving the post, in answer to an appeal for help from a party of immigrants, just as the posse neared it. Summoned to halt and be arrested, he stooped to no such folly; and when the Mormons tried to close in on a veteran of more narrow escapes than they had wives between them, they surrounded nothing but air.

At the time there was no one at the trading station but Jim's wife, the daughter of the Shoshone chief Washakie, and their two little children. Defying that garrison, the posse entered Fort Bridger and pounced on the supply of whiskey on hand. Not being able to drink where Brigham was paramount, these tough frontiersmen had worked up Gargantuan thirsts which didn't call quits until the last keg had been drained.

Taking advantage of Hickman's enthusiastic reunion with Barleycorn, Mrs. Bridger and the two youngsters slipped out of the fort, near which Old Gabe was hovering. The united family was off and away before the raiders remembered what they had come for, but it had no home to return to. Not content with looting Fort Bridger, the Saints set fire to it.

Although his wife wanted to have the Shoshones take the matter up with the Mormons, and although Washakie and his braves were eager to ride the warpath to Great Salt Lake, Old Gabe would be no party to spurring redskins against whites. So when he had put his family in safekeeping with his father-in-law, he crossed the mountains and at Fort Laramie sought redress from the United States Army.

Because of Brigham's carefully stacked deck, Jim got no help. The fort's commander explained that as troops sent out by Governor Young ranked as territorial militia, these were in turn part of the national defense organization, against which the War Department would not order troops to move. The officer added that the government would take the side of Utah's territorial militia if Jim and the battalion of mountain men he could easily have assembled should attack the Mormons.

The one thing Old Gabe could and did do was to file claim to the land surrounding Fort Bridger and have the papers forwarded to Washington. Gathering some friends along the way, he then returned to his post.

Brigham Young, in the meantime, had been chagrined to learn that what amounted to a prophecy of his hadn't been fulfilled. Having fulminated against Bridger, he had let it be known that the Saints could momentarily expect to see their archenemy brought to face the wrath of God in Salt Lake City. Upon learning from the unhappy Hickman that Bridger had escaped, Young decided to send a garrison to Fort Bridger, as insurance against Jim's return in an effort to rehabilitate his post.

Old Gabe and those in league with him were, indeed, trying to see what could be salvaged from the gutted fort when the new set of Mormon warriors showed up in November of 1853. Although the mountain men were able to drive the Saints back where they came from, Jim saw that his position would have been tenable only if he could have afforded to maintain a strong defending force. As this was not the case, he left Fort Bridger, pending government action on his complaint.

While he was waiting to see what would happen in Washington, Fitzpatrick went there in person. Although there were still seasons when the Indians lived high on the buffalo hump, there were periods now when they starved, because immigrant hordes had diverted the bison from their normal migration paths.

In bad health though he was, Broken Hand went East in hopes of securing relief for desperate people. He caught pneumonia in Washington, though, as Bill Sublette had in Pittsburgh; and by the Potomac the great dean of the mountain men died on February 7, 1854.

No longer a senator, having drawn the short term while William Gwin gripped the lot which gave him the long one, John Charles Frémont was again in the Rockies at the time. In the fall of the previous year he had stopped at the new version of Bent's Fort and secured from William the supplies and equipment for his fifth expedition. Its practical goal was a second effort to find a 38th-parallel railroad route, or one which would take rails over the mountains directly west of Missouri. Its moral goal was to reclaim the kudos lost during the disastrous try of 1848–1849.

But his wasn't either the sole or the first expedition so engaged in 1853, for a federal party led by Captain John Gunnison had crossed the Colorado Rockies during the summer. The Captain hadn't lived to turn in a report, though, for the Utes slew him and six of his following.

Adhering to his former plan of testing the practicability of a pass by traveling through it in winter, Frémont showed the hole in his theory by the very ease with which he got through the same mountain crossing which the Gunnison party had used. It was a much milder winter than the one which had made a shambles of his earlier expedition. Nevertheless his report helped to establish the feasibility of the desired regional rail crossing without at the same time leading to any immediate action. Others besides Tom Benton and his colleagues were pressing for a transcontinental railroad, but no two groups wanted it to span the West at the same latitude.

54

A Quintet of Hanged Cayuses

THE GOVERNOR OF Oregon Territory who fared west with Joe Meek in 1849 was General Joseph Lane, under whom Sam Walker had been killed at Huamantla two years before. The regiment of mounted riflemen which Sam had joined, after Hays's first Ranger outfit had been disbanded, had originally been formed for the purpose of guarding settlers, following the acquisition of Oregon in 1846. But plans for pressing the Mexican War had caused it to be shipped south instead of being sent west overland.

After Joe's appeal had finally led to the organization of Oregon, though, the regiment was reformed and ordered to take the long trail to the Pacific Northwest. Thus what Jed Smith had declared practicable two decades earlier was at last in the way of becoming a reality.

Having established a superb record in Mexico, the riflemen had a unit pride which did not survive the trip across the wilderness. For the year was that of the Gold Rush, and soldiers were no more immune to the fever than others. Singly or in groups, they sneaked off to join parties bound for California. As supply-train teamsters did likewise, riding away on mules whose supposed duty was drawing wagons, what was left of the regiment had a hard time in getting its quartermaster and ordnance sections as far as the Columbia estuary.

Yet what Governor Lane discovered, when he arrived later in the year, was that there were fewer settlers for the outfit to defend against Indians than the War Department had counted on when ordering it to post beyond the Cascades. Hopes of turning up gold, at the expense of much less effort than raising crops demanded, had caused such an exodus that there were hardly enough whites left to justify territorial organization.

On the other hand Oregon still had an abundance of Indians, still unpunished after the general rising which had followed the Whitman massacre. There was thus danger of another at a time when there were few frontiersmen to help ward off attack; for what the mountain men had long ago learned still held true. Unavenged Indian atrocities invited more.

Up to the time of Lane's arrival in December, the only retaliatory step taken had been made by Peter Skene Ogden. The factor at Fort Vancouver after the resignation of McLoughlin,

Peter had forced the Indians to relinquish some seventy captives.

As of 1849, however, Great Britain had at length agreed to have the Hudson's Bay Company give up its property holdings in United States territory, once a blanket price for the various posts and land improvements had been arrived at. Pending settlement of this matter, Ogden stayed on at Fort Vancouver; but his position was no longer administrative.

The problem of dealing with the Indians was Lane's to solve, bearing in mind that he couldn't afford to carry war to the tribes collectively. His decision was to treat a limited number of savages just as he would have an equivalent group of white culprits. Nobody west of the States had thought of doing that before. Customarily an accused and available redskin had been killed out of hand, if it hadn't been found expedient to let him off with a fine. Governor Lane now proposed to give indicted Indians a trial at which they would have the full benefit of defense counsel.

The next problem was which of the bloody-handed tribesmen to try. A great many had been gleefully involved in wholesale murder and rapine; but Lane did not wish to commit slaughter on a matching scale in the name of the law, even if he had had the guns to round up the guilty braves. What he planned to do was to force one tribe to make a sacrifice designed to impress all the savages at once with the fairness of American justice and the undesirability of massacring any more palefaces. For this purpose he decided to go back to the seed incident of the Indian rebellion and corral five of the Cayuses who had attacked the Whitman mission.

With the aid of the mounted riflemen he put the Cayuses in the mood to agree that atonement was in order, if guilt could be established. It remained for the Indians to decide which of a mob of savages should put their necks in jeopardy, but at length five were turned over to U.S. Marshal Meek in the fall of 1850. But the business of getting evidence against them which would hold up in court took so long that the case wasn't decided for months.

Of all those concerned with a serious effort to do the right thing only Joe Meek was well enough acquainted with Stone Age mentality to grasp the tragicomic side of the business. Curious to find out how the Cayuses were reacting to arguments based on abstruse points of law, as well as on precedents going back to Coke's expounding of Littleton, the mountain man talked things over with his prisoners. Without understanding why the white men were taking so long to get around to the point, they thought they knew perfectly well what was going on. The palefaces were going to use them to square accounts for the killing of Marcus Whitman and his wife, and there was nothing to be done about it.

They thought they also understood their relation to their own tribe and told it to Joe in terms that would have curdled the blood of the slain missionary. After their guilt had been at length painstakingly established, Meek asked one of the scapegoats how he felt about the business. "We're like Jesus," the Cayuse shrugged. "He gave his life to save the rest of his people, didn't he?"

On June 12, 1851, Joe supervised the hanging of five braves who probably took it for granted that they'd be scalped later. Yet the novel method of manslaying no doubt made the watching Indians blink, so the episode can be viewed as having had a quieting effect on the tribes along the lower Columbia. South along the Rogue and Umpqua rivers, though, were Indians who remained a menace to existing settlements as well as an obstacle to further pioneering.

Expansion of the settlements was made possible by the Land Donation Act of September 1850. A Congressional answer to an appeal from Lane stressing the need for an incentive for coming to Oregon, the bill granted generous freeholds, at no cost to all who immigrated between December 1, 1850, and the same date of 1853.

Of the thousands who eventually responded, many were men who had not found the gold pickings in California satisfactory. Of these some merely pushed into the southern portion of Oregon, giving the Rogue River Indians settlements to strike at there, as well as along the upper Willamette.

In June of 1851 one-armed Major Phil Kearny, the nephew of New Mexico's conqueror and Frémont's nemesis, attacked and defeated a band of these Indians. But the forests were thick, the savages wily and the men available to seek them out never numerous. The battles went intermittently on, and even when the tribesmen agreed to sell the Rogue River Valley, in September of 1853, nothing had been accomplished toward establishing peace. All that really happened was that the Indians had taken the $60,000 they had been offered and withdrew until they saw fit to return.

The white population of Oregon had by then diminished for a reason not connected with gold or Indian wars. In March Congress had detached the region north of the Columbia and created Washington Territory.

Fort Vancouver, once the capital of the Pacific Northwest, had for years been of no more political importance than any other United States military outpost. As for its last Hudson's Bay Company commandant, he had followed the example of John McLoughlin by staying with the land he had hoped to help win for the British Empire rather than with the corporation which had lost control of the region. Yet it was not on the north side of the Columbia that Peter Skene Ogden took his final stand. In September of 1854 the first explorer of the river which Frémont had renamed the Humboldt died in Oregon City.

༄ 55 ༄

Wild Cat's Confederacy

As a member of the United States Senate, Sam Houston had found himself confronted with two problems following the conclusion of America's war with Mexico. One sectional and one

303

social, both menaced the territory claimed by the former Republic of Texas in ways which couldn't be answered by a resort to arms.

The maps of Texas, as drawn by French cartographers and reproduced by Texian ones, had shown that the Republic's boundaries extended well north of the Mason and Dixon line as theoretically stretched westward by the Missouri Compromise. A slave-labor state, Texas thus had provinces in free-labor territory which had to be lopped off.

If that had perhaps been foreseen as inevitable, the other issue could hardly have been, inasmuch as it represented an irony of no mean proportions. What had brought on the Mexican War more than any other single point had been the federal administration's insistence that it would recognize the claims of Texas to Santa Fe and other Spanish-speaking towns east of the Rio Grande's dip south from Colorado's mountains. Texas accordingly had every right to think that what so many men had died for was a seriously intended pronouncement; and it may have been at the time. When the smoke of battle had cleared away, though, the United States government took a close enough look at the situation to observe that it had two sides.

The people of New Mexico did not want to have their province's identity lost by fusion with any other political subdivision; and least of all did its Mexican majority wish to be connected with Texas. In addition to remembering the Snively Expedition, these former natives of Mexico had been taught to regard all Texans as implacable enemies. Nor was it an attitude which the Treaty of Guadalupe-Hidalgo could expectedly have sufficed to erase from their minds.

Yet if standing fast on their prewar prejudice was understandable, where they were concerned, there was also an excuse for the government's shift of stance, even though Texans might not have been able to see it. Before the conflict the Mexicans of New Mexico had been enemies whose opinions carried no weight, but after it they were American citizens whose voices had to be listened to.

In the upshot, however, the non-ballot-holding Comanches had as much to do with the decision which was finally reached as any other consideration. Notwithstanding the existence of the wagon road running from San Antonio to El Paso, the hunting grounds of these Indians constituted a huge territorial wedge separating settled Texas from the valley of the upper Rio Grande.

So New Mexico's right to separate territorial status was recognized in 1850, but the arguing didn't stop there. It was not until November 25, 1852, that Texas formally relinquished title to eastern New Mexico by accepting a payment of $10,000,000.

Texas by then had long had other grounds for resenting the Washington spoon it found in its cup after joining the Union. In chief its citizens raged at the substitution of federal agencies for the Rangers when it came to dealing with the local tribesmen.

Although Houston had always been sympathetic toward Indians in general, his views were not shared by most of his white constituents. Either they themselves or their relatives or friends were frontier farmers who never knew what moonlight night would bring the next Comanche raid. To people in protected communities the Indian might stand for primitive nobility or be delighted in as a picturesque flaunter of war plumes. To pioneers possessed of harsh knowledge at first hand, the savages stood for all that was horrifying in the way of a threat to their wives, children, themselves and their hopes of prospering.

The Indian policy of the Rangers, which had consisted of killing all braves found on the warpath, had seemed natural and sensible to the citizens of the Republic. As citizens of the State of Texas, though, they were pained by the far different policy of the U.S. Army, acting on orders from Washington.

To the federal administration, of course, the tribesmen of Texas were in no different category than those in the rest of the country. They were wards of the government, who must be taught better ways in the fullness of time by the combined use of superior military power, patience and a willingness to arbitrate. The better to understand the problems of the Indians, the government had allotted the usual agents. Comprehending that the savages did, indeed, have problems, these officials submitted reports which would make it clear to political leaders in the East that forbearance was in order. Yet their counsel did not soothe the frustrated fury of people who continued to suffer Indian outrages and had been deprived of the services of their crack Indian fighters.

For the Rangers of the Republic had not been reorganized by the State of Texas, because the Army didn't want them in action. Unofficially, however, they began to take the field again under the leadership of such men as Big Foot Wallace, once of the Mier Expedition, Ben McCulloch's brother Henry, and Rip Ford.

Without challenging the Army's right to bring the Comanches to order, as well as to police the other tribes on the western frontier, the Rangers of the new dispensation began to try to meet another threat to peaceful settlement.

Cleared of Mexican bandits during the war, the lower Rio Grande Valley had become once more uninhabitable a year after its close. This time the predators who overran it were in chief not Mexicans but by-products of the old policy of shoving tribes west of the Mississippi Valley and trusting to luck that all would go well with them. Even swamp-bred Seminoles had been sent to take pot luck on the plains, and some of these were among the nations and fragments of tribes which had drifted into Texas by the late 1840's.

The most enterprising among these uprooted strays was a politically talented Seminole called Wild Cat. Some hundreds of his people had settled down to farming along the Red River. Not gaited for agriculture himself, Wild Cat had gone on to the Rio Grande and there found a stamping ground which suited him.

What the Seminole chief saw was that if Indians had no future to his taste in Texas, they would be welcome to do as they liked in Mexico, as long as they liked to attack Texans. Having a score to settle with white men, he talked with the dusky natives south of the boundary river and got permission to bring in such warriors as he could. As there weren't enough Seminoles available for his purpose, Wild Cat went recruiting among other tribes. He also enlisted runaway Negro slaves to the number of two or three hundred.

Although he operated from Mexican river towns such as Camargo—*hic jacet* Mustang Gray—his boast was that he would carve out a state for the members of his confederacy on the American side of the border. Not quite achieving that, Wild Cat made a good try, and in so doing brought the Rangers back into being.

So bold had the Indians ranging the international border country become by the spring of 1849 that on May 14 they struck north of the Nueces and raided Goliad. There were other attacks on settlements, and the Army wasn't able to cope with the situation, not for lack of ability but for lack of authority to go where it must to punish redskins who withdrew into Mexico when followed in force. But if United States soldiers could not cross the Rio Grande without orders from the War Department, Texans, acting on their own initiative, could carry the war to the Indians without fear of court-martial.

Semiofficial as to status, which is to say that they had the quiet approval of the state's administration and the hearty backing of the state's populace, the Rangers took the war to Mexico in 1849. In September of that year they burned the Seminole stronghold of Piedras Negras, without, however, smoking out and catching Wild Cat.

His confederacy continued to flourish, because the Rangers could only take the field briefly and at intervals. Sometimes they operated as unpaid volunteers; sometimes settlers got up a small purse for them; sometimes they rode forth with no better surety than promises of compensation in the undated future. Texas administrations wanted the Rangers, but there was always the federal government to buck.

In 1850 the governor of Texas privately asked Big Foot Wallace, Rip Ford, Henry McCulloch and two others to raise five companies of Rangers. They did what they could with no supporting funds and made occasional punitive raids against Mexican bandits as well as Indians; but in 1851 General Brooke, as commander of the Military Department of Texas, ordered the Rangers to disband.

Like Old Rough and Ready Taylor, the General had been shocked by the refusal of the Rangers to take prisoners. The Indian fighters for their part saw no sense in letting perpetrators of atrocities live to repeat them, as they were sure to do at the next opportunity.

The General could not look at an Indian with the eyes of a Ranger. Nor could even a mountain man do that; for the trappers had gone into the wilderness as bachelors, to take part in wars in which only their own scalps were at stake. But the Rangers had memories which ran back through years in which Indians had stood for the utternesses of sacked homes, scalped kinsmen, unspeakably brutalized women, and children swept back to the Stone Age.

The year 1851, or the twelvemonth in which Brooke ordered the Indian fighters to unsaddle, was the one in which a party of white hunters had seen Cynthia Ann Parker. The news shook the hearts of all Texas old-timers who knew her story, as well as some surviving relatives.

Her tale began with the Republic, for it was in the spring of 1836 that Comanches had raided Parker's Fort. Swarming into the inadequate stockade, they killed five men, of whom one was Silas Parker. They wounded two women and kidnaped two more, one of them pregnant. They spared Mrs. Silas Parker, apparently so that she could endure the agony of seeing the child they had torn away from her carried off by a mounted warrior. This was Cynthia Ann Parker, a blue-eyed, flaxen-haired girl of nine.

Of the abducted women—and there are firsthand accounts of what Indian captivity meant for white, female adults which might have led Rousseau to revise his views on the joys of a

308

primitive society—one was a Mrs. Plummer. In spite of what was then described as her delicate condition, she survived sadism which might have given pointers to the Marquis de Sade and was ransomed in New Mexico. Sold to the Keechis, Mrs. Kellogg was redeemed by a band of Delawares. Taking her to Nacogdoches, these turned her over to Sam Houston for a fee of $150. Some years later young James Plummer was also ransomed, this time by officers at Fort Gibson, where the First Dragoons had once trained. But Cynthia Ann and John Parker were reared to maturity as Comanches, albeit belonging to separate divisions of the tribe.

The girl grew up in the lodge of Kwahadi foster parents, which is to say that she lived with the clan least in contact with any white men and where ancient Indian customs were, in consequence, still unwatered by outside influence to any degree worth mentioning. Her homeland was the canyon-seamed Staked Plains region, where even other Indians seldom ventured.

Between her ninth and twenty-fourth years, she had been seen by white men but once. Having become a Comanchero, or a trader on friendly enough terms with the tribe to be allowed to bring his wares into Comanche hunting grounds and come out alive, a Colonel Williams had found Cynthia Ann while doing business with the Kwahadis in 1840. He had known who she must be—the children lost to savagery were on the minds of all Texas frontiersmen—but his efforts to ransom her were vain. No longer regarded as a captive but an adopted member of the tribe, she was not for sale.

When seen for the second time in 1851, there was no talk of ransoming her, for by that time she was the wife of Peta Nocona, a noted Comanche chief. She was also the mother of several children, one of them the seven-year-old who would be known as Quanah when he had earned a warrior's name.

Having entirely forgotten English, she was an Indian in all respects but physical ones. But that only added to the poignancy of the episode when an account of it was brought back to settled Texas. The picture of a squaw with blue eyes and yellow hair—

even though its gold had been tarnished by grease and lodge smoke—was a painful vision for people with other notions of what maturity should bring to womanhood of their kind. A religious viewpoint added to the sorrow which the tale caused, moreover. In the eyes of bedrock Christians the Comanches, in separating Cynthia Ann from her faith, had been guilty of wrecking her chances of redemption in the next world as well as dragging her down to barbarity in this one.

As more children were dragged off to share Cynthia Ann's fate in the 1850's, the Rangers returned to action, generals or no generals, and no matter who was President, either. The news that Zachary Taylor had been voted into the White House in 1848 doubtless cheered the Great Western, but it was glumly received in Texas. For although Walker and Hays had saved him from paying for his military blunders in 1846, while Ben McCulloch had performed the same service the following year, Old Rough and Ready had walked off the stage of battle grumbling that he didn't want any more Rangers in his command.

After Vice-President Millard Fillmore inherited in 1850, it was thought in Texas that he was extending Taylor's grudge against Rangers to cover all the settlers of the state from which they came. As Indian depredations continued without drawing the all-out counteraction from the Army which Texans wanted, it seemed to the latter that the President was more interested in preserving redskins than he was in protecting palefaces.

The outlawed Rangers stole back into the field from time to time but only against Wild Cat's confederacy of Rio Grande Valley Indians. The Army stood on its right to guard the Western frontier, which it did by building a string of small posts designed to contain the Comanches and their Kiowa allies. This might have worked had Texas pioneers been content to stay behind the line of forts, but by 1855 they were establishing a new frontier farther to the west.

310

56

Weightman Draws His Bowie Again

IN SPITE OF the fact that Texan claims to more than half of New Mexico had not been settled, the former Mexican province was made a United States territory on September 9, 1850, the same day on which California was recognized as a state. New Mexico had bid for that higher political standing, too. Earlier in the year it had adopted a constitution, chosen a governor and elected a Congressional delegation which included Richard Weightman as one of the senators. Unlike California, though, New Mexico had not yet drawn enough Americans to outnumber the natives. As a region in which Spanish rather than English was the common tongue, it was not yet thought ready for statehood.

In 1851 Weightman did return to his home town of Washington but in the capacity of the territory's first Congressional delegate. When not thus on duty he practiced law in Albuquerque. He also edited a paper there which reflected his views as to where a transcontinental railroad should run.

This was very much of a political question, as more entered into it than the natural desire of every state or territory to have the advantage of rapid transit service. Middle Western states were backing an effort to bridge the Mississippi at Davenport and run rails west from there. Thus the North would be best served. Another coalition wanted the long tracks to pass through the South, while a third group backed Benton's middle route.

Weightman was interested because of what Philip St. George Cooke had done and what the Treaty of Guadalupe-Hidalgo had failed to do. No matter what special interests might try to say in favor of other approaches to the Pacific Coast, Cooke's wagon road offered by far the easiest crossing of the Great Divide which

311

had been found, and it was one which would never offer Frémont a chance to plow through drifts in order to prove its passability in winter. Without detouring, additionally, it avoided the Sierras. The 32nd-parallel route was, in short, admirable at all points but one. Much of Cooke's wagon road cut through Sonora in Mexico, well to the south of the international boundary.

In common with other favorers of the southern railroad route, Weightman wanted the United States to acquire the needed portion of Sonora. As Mexicans felt that they had already forfeited too much territory, however, the prospects of the suggested purchase were for many months not bright.

That seemed to kill New Mexico's chances of being connected with both coasts by rail. Yet Felix Aubry (called François by some) had not come to the end of his hotspur travels.

In 1850 the hard rider of the Santa Fe Trail had taken a trade caravan from New Mexico to San Antonio. In accomplishing something long wished for by Texas, though, he threatened Missouri's monopoly of trade with the Southwest. He seems to have been bought off, for praises of his new commercial route abruptly changed to growls about it; and his subsequent wanderings must have been planned with Missouri's interests, as well as those of New Mexico, in mind.

In 1852 Felix astonished his contemporaries by taking the Santa Fe Trail in January. But that must have been done on the same theory which had prompted Frémont to plunge into the Rockies during the frost months. In this case Aubry wanted to see how high gales could pile snow in all the natural receptacles for it along the great wagon trace.

But having proved to his own satisfaction that rails could run from Missouri to the Rio Grande Valley more easily than they could get that far west by penetrating Colorado's mountains, Felix still had no answer to the question as to how trains could cross New Mexico's jagged spinal ridge.

From November of 1852 to the following summer, Aubry was constantly in the saddle, zigzagging through New Mexico west of the Rio Grande in the course of two trips to California. During the first three legs of these journeys he discovered nothing but hostile Indians, but on the return trip the second time he found what he was looking for. Crossing the Colorado just below Pyramid Canyon and cutting northeast around the framing mountain range, he reached the great level shelf which spans Arizona along the 35th parallel.

In September of 1853 Felix blew into Albuquerque at the end of that ride and proudly announced that he had found the answer to New Mexico's railroad problem. Weightman seems to have praised him editorially for his achievement; but Felix was not long able to claim that his discovery was the only way along which tracks could be stretched to California. For in 1853 the unsinkable Santa Anna came back into power as Mexico's dictator.

In need of cash to support his exalted estate and forever venal, he approached the United States with one proposition, involving the Tehuantepec Isthmus, in which America wasn't interested. As Santa Anna had opened the door for bargaining, though, Washington countered by offering to buy a strip of northern Mexico extending from the Rio Grande to the Colorado. When the dictator agreed that such a deal could be made, General James Gadsden, the United States minister at Mexico City, was authorized to begin haggling. Unknown to the general public, this back-room deal was still pending at the time of Aubry's gallop into Albuquerque with news of a pass across the Great Divide and a level shelf beyond it.

Drawn up in December of 1853, the Gadsden Treaty to buy Cooke's wagon road was not ratified until the ensuing spring. This was done over the bitter opposition of Tom Benton, for once trying to narrow the West as he fought for a Western railroad which would stem from Missouri. But the 45,535 square miles of what was generally known as the Gadsden Purchase were bought for $10,000,000 because all unprejudiced parties could see exactly what Benton feared they would. The railway route from the Mississippi to the Coast which offered the least in the way of natural obstacles and the most in the way of favorable weather conditions the year around ran from New Orleans to El Paso and thence west along the general line followed by Philip St. George and his Mormons.

Aubry could have known nothing about the Gadsden Purchase when he began driving sheep to California in October of 1853. But by the time he reached the coastal market in January 1854, adventurers were on their way to a zone which was not supposed to be open for American immigration until the following July.

Just what trails Herman Ehrenberg had traveled after the deactivation of Frémont's California Battalion are matters that await their investigator; but at some point in his restless journeying he had heard tales of rich silver mines south of the Gila, exploited in Spanish colonial days but long abandoned. In San Francisco when word of the Gadsden Treaty's signing reached that city, Herman proposed prompt investigation of the metal wealth of America's new addition.

The one he proposed it to was a man of partially cracked parts named Charles Poston. A Kentuckian who had gone west to avoid domesticity but had found nothing nearer gold than a position in San Francisco's customs house, he jumped at the chance to try his yet unused adventure wings.

Having made friends with Ehrenberg, he was flying before he knew it. In no time at all the partners, plus the platoon of riflemen they had recruited to take care of such Indians and bandits as they might encounter, were on a sailing vessel bound for Guaymas, on the Gulf of California. And before January of 1854 had run its course, they were wrecked on an island off the Mexican coast.

Some went down when the *Zoraida* broke up, but Herman and Charles weren't among them. Succeeding in reaching the mainland, they found replacements among American and other foreign drifters hovering in Hermosillo and made their way into the forbidden area many months before it could be legally prospected. For although the final extension of the continental United States was announced as a fact as of June 30, 1854, offi-

314

cial American occupation could not take place until a survey of the new boundary had been conducted by an international commission.

On deck before anybody else had given the mineral possibilities of the Gadsden Purchase a thought, the partners proved that there's an exception to even the rule that lost Spanish mines are never retrievable, or at least by anyone in a position to exploit them. Bowie had found one, to be sure, but died in the Alamo before he could profit by his discovery; and all the Spanish glory holes west of it have remained as ungraspable as the one Peg-leg Smith discovered without trying, and never could locate again when he wanted to.

But what Ehrenberg had somehow heard was true. The Spanish had discovered rich silver veins near the Santa Cruz River, nor had they exploited them to more than a small degree before abandoning them—no doubt for lack of equipment to do more than dig out surface veins. The original miners of the region had been wandering prospectors, no better skilled than the average Forty-niner with his crude implements for gathering placer gold.

Herman Ehrenberg, however, was a mining engineer. He knew that he had found realizable wealth, although he also knew that it would take capital to make the rock give up its treasure.

He and Poston had not yet returned to California for the purpose of raising funds, though, when Aubry arrived in New Mexico once more. His trip through Arizona was not the happy excursion enjoyed by the two silver finders, for Apaches dogged his party all the way, flinging arrows at men and mounts with indiscriminate enthusiasm. Reaching Albuquerque at the far end of this ordeal, he found a disappointment in store for him. Weightman's paper, once enthusiastic about the 35th-parallel route, had come out against it.

The editor's change of heart had, of course, been due to the Gadsden Purchase, about which all in New Mexico were in ignorance when Aubry had left there the previous fall. Now that the line of Cooke's wagon road was feasible, he wanted it used, not only for sound practical reasons but for emotional ones.

315

Weightman was, as he came to prove with finality, Southern in sympathies.

Richard had attacked the northern Arizona route, not its finder, but Aubry took it personally. Probably, too, adoption of the track line he had discovered would have meant something to him financially. In any case he was in bad humor when he rode on to Santa Fe, which he reached on August 18, 1854.

Even in a city that's over a mile and a quarter up in the air, summer in New Mexico is plenty of summer. As soon as he had stabled his horse, Felix took his thirst to a cantina. Had Aubry been able to get the refreshment he was panting for, it might well have mellowed him; but before he reached the bar he found himself confronted by the Albuquerque newspaperman whose musings had angered him.

Unaware of anything amiss, Weightman was cordial, though not for long. Felix demanded why the editor had ridiculed him; and when Richard denied having done so, Aubry gave him the lie in pure Mule-skinnerese.

There was whiskey in Weightman's glass which he threw with good aim. The sting of the spirits, in his eyes, primed the charge of an already hot man and blew his gun loose. Fortunately for his enemy, Felix fired before he could see well, and missed at point-blank range. Aubry was given no second chance, for Richard snicked out the bowie at his belt—the same one, it was claimed, whose wielding had caused his dismissal from West Point—and sliced an end to the greatest rider's riding.

🏵 57 🏵

The Great American Desert

THE UTES TOOK the warpath against white settlements in the spring of 1854, which was the year in which Kit Carson was made Indian agent at Taos. Nor did Old Bill's former tribe cease its raids until Kit guided the New Mexico militia, led by Colonel Ceran St. Vrain, to their mountain fastnesses.

There were clashes on the plains, too, for complaints leveled by immigrant parties pitted regulars against the Sioux and Cheyennes, who did not always lose. In the summer of 1854, for instance, a detachment rode out of Fort Laramie, complete with two cannon to use against the Dakotas, and not a man returned.

Yet the real war of that year involved white men who struck at other whites. And a conflict that was more savage than the battles between races did not take place in the Far West but at the very doorstep of the States.

At the bottom of the trouble lay an exploded myth, which was that of the Great American Desert. Quaintly enough, in the light of later knowledge, that term had been applied not to the genuinely barren regions to be found in sundry parts of the West but to the peerless soil of the prairies.

For many years people in search of good farming land had trekked past the site of the marvelous national granary-to-come in order to reach Oregon and California. More recently Mormons had been driving wagons over the Rockies, bent on tilling the irrigated acres of the Great Salt Lake area. At first nobody had looked for fertile soil nearer home than the far side of the mountains, because the great grassland had been posted as useless for agriculture, notwithstanding the tall herbage which fattened bison, by government experts. Then, when it was finally found that these had been massively in error, the prairie was off limits for white settlers. In addition to having declared all the region Indian territory, as of 1834, the government had established numerous reservations there, alike for native tribes and transplanted ones.

But having acquired a realm which bridged the continent, the people of the United States insisted on the right to live in all the parts of it where they could profitably do so. In May of 1854, accordingly, certain prairie tribes were moved to Oklahoma, and on the 30th of that month the federal government announced the existence of the new territories of Kansas and Nebraska.

317

The unprecedented thing about this was the formation of political entities in advance of settlement. And the firebrand tossed on the prairie by the same hasty hand was the announcement that the inhabitants-to-be could decide for themselves whether they would be free- or slave-labor communities. As that was a challenge to a race which the embattled North and South hurried to accept, the West became a cockpit of intersectional strife over an issue in which it historically had nothing to win.

Because of its latitude, Nebraska was conceded to the North and was therefore largely ignored by both factions. The contest was for the control of Kansas, which, though extending north of the free-labor line, lay in the same latitude as slave-owning Missouri.

In view of the fury with which the settlers rushed into fight for the bone of contention, it is worth noting that it was all but remarkable for its absence. For although they were valiant to fight about whether they should or should not be allowed to have slaves, the fact was that they were in general too poor to own any. The census taken in February 1855 turned up a total of 192 unpaid laborers in a population of 8501, or about one helot for every 44 freemen. Yet the theory was what counted, not the local reality. The people who raced to Kansas to become feudists were thinking of other parts of the country and not of the one in which they intended to live. They represented the cotton states of the South, which the climate of Kansas forbade it to resemble. Or they represented the industrial states of the North, where Kansas had not so much as a flour mill.

But kill and die for shadows cast by other parts of the country these shoestring frontier farmers did. Then there were some who were not farmers, though what part they took in the slayings, burnings, tar-and-featherings, as well as the heroic election frauds perpetrated by both sides, can only be guessed in many instances, for the story of the epoch adds up to turmoil viewed through a haze.

Richard Weightman settled at Atchison, a slave-labor town which had been founded before he had cause to leave New Mex-

318

ico. Although there can be little doubt that he found occasion to use pistol and bowie knife in the cause of helping "bleeding Kansas" to earn its slogan, that is all that can be said with confidence. Langford Peel could not have kept his pistol holstered while so many others were drawing theirs, either; but his residence at the town of Leavenworth is all that Clio admits. Extant, however, is an account of one of the Kansas exploits of Jack Swilling, even though it is not tagged with a date.

A South Carolinian reared in Georgia, Swilling was a man whose wide range of abilities included a genius for getting into trouble. Before coming to Kansas he had managed to be a "wanted" man in places as remote from one another as Yucatán and California. Indians had taken unfavorable notice of him, too, for a friend of his recalled that Jack wore his hair long to hide the fact that he had survived scalping.

As was to be expected, a man of his penchants did not abide quietly amidst the tumult which had turned the so-called settlement of an American region into a shambles. That he became a prominent partisan can be gathered from the fact that some delighted Southern editor dubbed him "the high cock of Georgia." He earned a war chief's name, too, for when an uncle of his was slain by a gang of Northerners, he hunted down and killed eleven of those implicated.

Yet most of those involved were not men who ordinarily lived by their guns. They were conscientious, even pious people—and egged on by crusaders from other parts of the nation who were convinced that Heaven would bless the slaughter of those opposed to their own respective views. The revered Henry Ward Beecher, for example, sent twenty-five Bibles and twenty-five rifles to Kansas in the same shipment.

Certainly nobody ever felt more God-sent than John Brown, born in Connecticut but latterly of New York State. Yet he performed what was perhaps the greatest atrocity in the history of a horrendous conflict. Upon learning that five free-labor men had been killed, he led a band which descended upon Pottawatomie on May 25, 1856, and rounded up five on the proslavery side.

319

The men he seized had had nothing to do with the killings he wished to avenge, but he had them hacked to death with sabers and then further multilated the corpses.

The Indians had some reason for hoping that the whites would kill each other off and open the door for the return of good hunting again. But better times were not in sight for the harried tribes of the plains in 1856, nor for Jim Bridger, either.

After the Mormons took over his fort, Old Gabe left the mountains for a while and stayed on a farm he had bought near Westport. That wasn't where he wanted to be, though. He longed for the station in the Rockies on which he had filed legal claim; and when the government did nothing about honoring his rights Jim began taking steps of his own.

🙠 58 🙠

A Pickled Head and a Stovepipe Cannon

THERE WAS SOME gold in southern California, because Jim Savage, the white king of the Tulare Indians, had a barrelful of it; at least he did until he was killed in a duel by Major Walter Harvey. But the region was primarily ranching country, and one in which Hispanic influences persisted. This was true of its unofficial capital, Los Angeles, which was half a Mexican town as compared with wholly Americanized San Francisco.

By 1852 the vicinity was the stamping ground of a bilingual mixture of native Californians, American settlers, Mexican bandits, whites who had been chased out of the gold camps for cause, and a corps of professional gamblers. Choice among their resorts was the Headquarters Saloon, Roy Bean its proprietor. Located in the precinct of San Gabriel, this establishment had been owned earlier in the year by Roy's brother, the murdered General Bean—slain by Murrieta, as some claimed.

Having come from Texas by way of Chihuahua, Roy affected

colorful Mexican attire with American trimmings which took the form of two strapped-on revolvers and a boot-sheathed bowie knife. If the clothes were for show, the weapons were practical equipment for a man in young Bean's business. He was, as he recalled, on duty at the Headquarters when he first met Joe Stokes.

Joe was a minister's son from Albany, New York, who had brought the gentle habits which had been instilled in him to California. Finding him easy to push around, rougher spirits among the Forty-niners had gleefully done so. The hazing had gone on for months—months during which, unknown to them, the frontier was slowly changing the spots on Joe's no longer church-conditioned skin. But at some point during 1851 Stokes had tired of turning the other cheek. To the astonishment of all acquainted with his past history he stood up to a hard character named Tom Collins, so enraging the latter that he began shooting. In spite of being wounded, Joe did not make for cover. Instead he took the gun offered him by a fellow saloon patron and killed Collins with one pull of the trigger.

Nobody bothered Stokes after that, or no one who knew him did, for from then on he carried a revolver he was always ready to use. But Roy Bean did not know that Stokes had come to Los Angeles to wait for the excitement caused by a scrape he'd got in to die down. He therefore undertook to warn Joe to be careful, when the latter laughed at a ruffian who had begun heckling him in December of 1852.

Knowing the big tough for a killer, Bean was gravely concerned by his threats to shoot Stokes, but Joe wasn't. Whisking out his own gun, he shoved the muzzle against the other's belly, backed him against the wall and called for a cigar. When he had lit it, Joe thrust the burning end up the ruffian's nose, telling his opponent meanwhile that any flinching before the cheroot lost fire would invite instant death.

Stokes was merely a transient who soon returned to northern California. Permanently in the spotlight of the state's southern segment was Jack Power, usually called Powers in local chronicles; but the military record which gives the former form would seem to be more reliable.

Born in Ireland and reared in New York, Power had come to California as a volunteer. Well mannered, educated and liked, he had by 1852 become the recognized prince of the region's gambling fraternity, said to have numbered four hundred, with chapters in Santa Barbara as well as Los Angeles. His was by no means a purely urban career, however. One of the West's great riders, he was an all-around hand at field sports, not to mention being the owner of a horse ranch.

It was in this last capacity that Power fell out with the law. An early settler, he had acquired his land before there was such an office—Jack Coffee Hays was the appointed incumbent in 1852— as a state surveyor-general. Previously property titles had been acquired in almost any old fashion, so the move to regularize real estate ownership uncovered many overlapping claims, not to mention cases where there was no legal ground at all for asserting possession.

For an unsung reason Jack Power was one of those adjudged to have come by his ranch improperly, so that in 1853 he received notice from the sheriff of Los Angeles County that he should vacate his land. To this order Power replied that he would stay where he was; and in order to be able to sustain his stand, he garrisoned his ranch with some of his many friends. He did more than that. Calling to mind next the lone cannon to be found in Los Angeles, he rode with a following to commandeer it.

When the defied sheriff showed up with his *posse comitatus*, though, he found that both the front and rear doors of Jack's hacienda were guarded by guns of formidable bore. Not getting near enough to discover that one had started out in life as a stovepipe, the officer hastily led his deputies away; and Power rejoiced in his horse barony for some while longer.

It has been asserted that another regional excitement of 1853 was as bogus as one of Jack's field pieces. Yet men living at the time certainly believed in the reality of Joaquin Murrieta.

322

Whether he came from Mexico, as some accounts assert, or whether he was a pre-Forty-niner native son, the reports which admit of his existence are alike in declaring his ferocious hatred of all Americans—a fervor in which he was seconded by his lieutenant. Although a Mexican by the name of Garcia himself, this fellow was commonly known as Three-fingered Jack.

Actually southern California was the hunting ground of numerous bandit gangs—local or operating out of Sonora—so the killings and robberies which came to be ascribed to one demoniac crew were probably the work of many. But Murrieta's mob got credit for such a host of crimes that a special corps of field police was organized to hunt them down. Granville Oury, brother of William of the Alamo, was one of the California Rangers. Bill, usually called Bunk, Bradshaw, of Frémont's volunteer legion, was another; and Major Harvey, who'd put the Tulares in mourning by plowing their white king under, was a third. Roy Bean joined, in order to avenge his brother. Yet none of these ever saw Joaquin, if anybody did.

In answer to popular clamor, the State of California had offered a reward for the bandit and his chief partner in villainy, payable to anybody who could produce them dead or alive. In 1853 it was collected by a Captain Love, who submitted as proof of his prowess two large glass jugs. In addition to perpetuating alcohol, these were occupied respectively by a Mexican's head and a dark-skinned hand which lacked two digits.

Placed on display, these were much admired. Whether the pickled heirlooms had ever belonged to Murrieta and Three-fingered Jack are questions which no Delphic oracle was there to answer. But as Californians of the day were satisfied that the Captain had earned his money, Murrieta was not again charged with any of the crimes which Mexican bandits continued to perpetrate in quantity.

At the time the head and the hand were exhibited to a gratified California public, Joe Stokes was once more living by the harbor mouth which Frémont had been the first to call the Golden Gate—even though he had done so in Greek and in ignorance of the fact that it would indeed become a portal to a land with a foundation of gold. Because Ned McGowan had eased him out of a predicament into which his trigger finger had twitched him, Joe had become the henchman of a man still known as "Judge," in spite of the fact that the Vigilantes had seen to it that he was not chosen to continue in office, when posts on the bench had been made elective rather than appointive, in 1852.

But Ned was flourishing on patronage secured through Broderick as well as the returns from his legal practice. He was also charmed with life as he was able to lead it in San Francisco, where good liquor, good food, good plays, good conversation and not always good women were present in abundance, along with political wars and dueling.

A recognized expert in affairs of honor, McGowan was much in demand as an official. He was for this reason able to report of William Walker that the latter had such remarkable self-control that nobody knew that he had been hit the first time, in the course of one encounter, until a second wound caused him to fall.

Some of the duels in which Ned took part were pleasantly remembered, because the authorities had to be outwitted before men could take their stands upon the outlawed field of honor. There was, for instance, an occasion when Joe Stokes had found that officers were on their way to the scene of proposed action, so he dashed up with warning notice, just in time to prevent arrest. Then there were less amusing times, when one of the principals didn't leave the field alive.

On the whole, though, it could be affirmed that dueling was no more dangerous than San Francisco politics. This was particularly true after the Whigs gave way to the militant Know-Nothing party in 1854. On election day of that year McGowan and the man he was still trying to make a United States senator arrived at a polling place to find the Know-Nothing candidate for city attorney with a gun aimed at a Democratic stalwart.

Himself unarmed, this was Billy Mulligan, once of the Texas Rangers.

Broderick wanted Colonel Peyton, a former U.S. Minister to Chile, to row to one of the uninhabited islands in San Francisco Bay to shoot it out with him. This was not done, as, after some of the war dancing to which they were addicted, the Know-Nothings withdrew. But there was another and wilder example of how Westerners exercised the privilege of ballot casting, this time with Democrats making the first move.

Made on that same day, it was no trifling one. In order to insure peace at the ballot station of a certain precinct, the incumbent mayor (who was a candidate for re-election, by the by) had a cannon wheeled into watchdog position. Standing by for instant action, in the event of a Know-Nothing attempt to rush the polling place, was Joe Stokes, lighted fuse in hand.

South of San Francisco, in the meantime, the affairs of Jack Power had taken a turn for the worse. Finally driven from his ranch, and more than ever at odds with the law in Los Angeles County, the man who had once been so popular there moved out as a drifter. While his fortunes didn't visibly improve in 1854 and 1855, it was noted of him that he both continued to be in funds and exercised signal influence over dubious elements of the Mexican population of Santa Barbara County.

Nobody seems to have caught him at anything malign up to this time, for he came and went unmolested by local officials. But rumors to the effect that he was a behind-the-scenes director of Mexican bandits began to circulate. By the summer of 1856, in fact, these had hardened into accusations which newspapers printed as established truths. Some lyrical journalist had even undertaken to refer to Power as "the Destroying Angel," and the phrase had caught on.

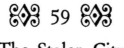

59

The Stolen City

ON THEIR RETURN journey from the Gadsden Purchase to California, Ehrenberg and Poston crossed the Colorado where John Glanton had once maintained dangerous ferry service. To prevent a duplicate from taking over, as well as to protect pilgrims against the Indians, the government had built Fort Yuma on the bluff above the river's western bank.

Due to a clause in the Treaty of Guadalupe-Hidalgo which defined California as beginning where the Gila met the Colorado, both sides of the latter stream were considered in the coastal state as of the fall of 1854. When the current ferryman, a man called Jaeger, asked more in the way of fare than the partners had, or felt they could afford, Poston bore this in mind and drew Ehrenberg aside.

The curiosity of the greedy boatman was next aroused by the sight of Herman gravely going about the business of surveying the area. Questioning drew from Charles the news that they were a townsite team engaged by the State of California to lay out Colorado City. Wishing to hold property in a municipality of which he and his assistants were at that time the sole residents, Jaeger traded ferry service for town lots.

Stopping at Fort Yuma, the partners enjoyed a meal cooked by the Great Western. As commander of the post, Major Samuel Heintzelman had remembered the culinary ability of Old Rough and Ready's admirer and had put her in charge of the officers' mess.

As the capitalists of California were embarrassed by bank failures in 1855, Charles Poston went to New York and, with the aid of the financially well-connected Heintzelman, got backers, who included William Tell Coleman. In the spring of 1856

326

Charles was thus able to lead a party of armed miners from San Antonio across Comanche and Apache country to where Ehrenberg was waiting by the Santa Cruz. Making their headquarters at the deserted Spanish garrison town of Tubac, they began to pry silver out of the earth in huge quantities.

Before Poston got as far as Texas, however, Coleman returned to San Francisco for the first time in four years. Still a fierce political arena, it had also become a socially divided city by the beginning of 1856.

In the ebullient days of '49 all had shared a boom-town social life which chiefly featured gambling and the dances given in an otherwise bachelor community by demimondaines. At that time, too, all had shared the perfect democracy of equal hopes. Seven years later, though, men who had once ridden the same cloud were as far apart as their respective good and bad fortunes. The big winners had not only tended to club together as men apart from the masses, they had been caught up with and captured by the moral outlooks they had left on the Atlantic Seaboard when heading west as unfettered prospectors. In a word, they had married and settled down to become the church pillars their wives wanted them to be, and they looked askance at those who still carried on publicly as they now did only in secret, if at all.

It so came about that when Ned McGowan got in a scrape over a French courtesan only a part of the town was amused. And she wasn't laughing at the end, although she had the first chuckle.

Early in 1856 Ned had had a cottage on Pike Street redecorated to suit the taste of Madame Fanny Perrier and deeded it over to her in gratitude for services rendered. To his chagrin, then, McGowan learned that the real owner of his forfeited property was a pimp named Alfred Godeffroy. Ned shot this fellow, who was fleeing at such speed that a pistol could do no better than give him a minor rump wound; but Fanny still occupied the cottage, so McGowan conferred with Joe Stokes.

As the upshot of their talk Joe decided to plant a small petard, as a contribution to the housewarming Ned had learned she was

327

planning to hold. It was designed merely to blow in the door; but a servant, standing by to let the guests in, smelled the burning fuse, or heard it cracking. Looking out to see what was going on, he picked the petard up at the crucial moment.

As the explosion did no more than loft, shock and burn him a bit, the matter was settled out of court, though McGowan first sent Stokes out of town, while Godeffroy found it expedient to send Madame Perrier back to Paris. In general a genial soul, Ned laughed at himself for having been taken in and rejoiced that he had paid some part of his debt to those who had cheated him. But San Francisco chose up sides. The incident, complete with Joe's robust practical joke, hit the funny bone of the unregenerate, while members of the new plutocracy shook their heads. Many of them former Vigilantes, too, they recalled quarrels with the ex-judge, when he had fought their attempted supervision of his court, and refurbished their old grudge.

A more constant town topic, though, was the editorial policy of James King (of William). Driven out of banking by some of the series of failures which had made it impossible for Poston to raise the money he had needed in San Francisco, King had founded the *Evening Bulletin* in October 1855. Taking a line of lofty scurrility, he had built up circulation by attacking a wide range of public figures. Remembering that he had once belonged to the Vigilantes, he also adopted their policy of accusing judges of malfeasance.

A rabble rouser without an observable principle to his name, James was yet of better stuff than his brother, Tom, who wrote for him as well as working in the customs house. Ned, who had known the younger King in Philadelphia, where McGowan had for some years acted as superintendent of police, charged him with having been a small-change yegg and confidence man. A bold wrecker of reputations, James repeatedly pointed out in print that he carried a gun which he would gladly use on anybody who didn't like what he wrote. Tom lacked that kind of cardboard, although this fact had not been demonstrated when he picked a quarrel with a politician called James Casey.

328

A Democrat, Casey was not a Broderick man; in fact he had achieved the position of being able to swing the balance of power between the main bloc of the Democratic party and the opposition. He had proved that he had this ability, furthermore, by teaming up with the Know-Nothings and beating the Democratic regulars.

Probably Ned, as Broderick's San Francisco strategist, had been courting Casey; it would have been strange under the circumstances if he had not. At all events he was glad to provide the other with a revolver when Casey consulted McGowan, as an old dueling blue, on how best to deal with quarrelsome Tom King.

Not believing the latter would back his bark with action, McGowan undertook to be present at the showdown, and when Tom slunk off, Ned happily launched the story on its round of the city's saloons. His position as a connected party had thus been established when James, galled at having his brother laughed at, took up the feud with Casey by publishing an editorial. Hitting the street on May 14, 1856, it cited the fact that Casey had done time in New York's Sing Sing penitentiary.

As he resented that excavation of his past, Casey went to see James and was told by a much bigger man that he would be kicked out in the street if he didn't use his own legs for leaving. He then went to get the gun he had borrowed from Ned for another purpose. There was nothing secret about his intention, for many gathered hopefully about the *Bulletin*'s door, in order to see what would happen when the editor emerged. Yet most, including McGowan, had walked disappointedly off before Casey showed up, just as King was starting home.

By frontier standards what Casey then did was perfectly in order. He approached an armed man who understood the serious nature of their quarrel and told the other to defend himself in advance of drawing his own gun. Firing then, he shot his antagonist.

High on the chest, the wound did not kill James King (of William); indeed, attending physicians at first expected him to recover. Without waiting to see whether this would happen, though, the Vigilantes sprang from their office cocoons and reorganized. Sam Brannan wanted to be their chief again, but the others remembered the man who had given them a course of procedure in 1851.

For this occasion Coleman worked out a scheme which duplicated the first, albeit with a significant addition. The weakness of the 1851 organization had been a failure to support the People's Court with military strength. As a result of that lack the Vigilantes had now and again been thwarted by the *posse comitatus* or militia groups. What William Tell proposed was to enlist sympathetic national guard officers, take over armories together with their contained weapons, and provide the San Francisco Committee of Vigilance of 1856 with a standing army.

Put into action forthwith, the plan was such a success that within forty-eight hours the City of San Francisco had been administratively separated from the State of California. By May 16 the sheriff's posse assembled to guard Casey was besieged inside the county jail. As for Governor Johnson, who had hurried in from Sacramento, he was at first treated politely and then ignored. On May 18 he and his militia general, William Tecumseh Sherman, watched helplessly while the Vigilante chieftains, backed by a regiment under arms, had a cannon rolled up to the door of the prison. They then took Casey and another to their stronghold, called, because of ramparts made of sand-filled sacks, Fort Gunnybags.

Their second prisoner was Charles Cora, who had killed U.S. Marshal Richardson over a personal matter. According to witnesses, the officer had been the aggressor and Cora had shot in self-defense; but the Vigilantes were not pleased with the fact that his first trial had misfired, because of a hung jury, and decided to try him for the manslaying themselves.

They planned to try Casey for first-degree murder, too, in spite of the fact that the man he had shot was still alive and that no such charge was warranted by the circumstances. Yet of the two trials for killing, scheduled by men who had murder in their hearts before they began, that of Cora was the more interesting, inasmuch as the Vigilante jury turned out to be a hung one, too. In the Committee's constitution, however, there was a loophole which allowed its chiefs to hide from the public the fact that their court had arrived at the same place as the criticized regular one. This was a clause which stipulated that any decision passed by a mere majority would be announced as unanimous.

Though the decision to kill Cora was based on policy—if the People's Court could not outshine those of the county it could hardly presume to stay in business—the sentencing of Casey was, like his own, a crime of passion. For on May 20 a bell boomed notice that James King, tagged as a martyr to civic virtue by mass hysteria, had finally done the right thing and died. Men who had been trying him for murder, in advance of the fact, then rapidly wound up a trial at which the jurors were as emotionally off balance as all others there.

By then the Committee had enrolled some 8000 members, of whom about 5700 belonged to San Francisco's army, while the rest were police or administrators of one sort or another. To the delight of a supporting mob, the troops paraded during a torchlight ceremony whose climax was the suspension of Casey and Cora from plank extensions of two Fort Gunnybags window sills. When that had been done in the small hours of May 21, the question arose as to who was next on the kangaroo court's list.

At the beginning there had been wild talk of purging the community of the host of unpunished murderers said to be at large in it. But if they existed, the Committee seemed as unable to discover their whereabouts as had been the 1851 group. Even before Casey had been taken from prison, though, the controlling executive committee of the Vigilantes had singled out one old enemy of many of its members. Neatly transferring McGowan's known association with Casey in opposition to Tom King and making it applicable to Casey's quarrel with James King (of William), the Committee's sagamores arranged for

Ned to be indicted as accessory to the murder of the late editor.

Luckily for McGowan, his foes had had this in mind almost from the moment of organization and had begun spreading word of his putative guilt. He had thus been warned that his life was in danger as early as May 17, and when the Vigilantes got around to reaching for him, he was not to be found.

Although trying to do so, he didn't leave town, because the man supposed to smuggle him out of the city in a wagon lost his nerve when mounted guards began patrolling all of central San Francisco's streets. Broderick's organization still included men who would risk supplying the fugitive with food, however. Nor would any of Ned's friends sell him out, in spite of the fact that several were picked up on the charge of concealing the whereabouts of one whom propaganda had refashioned as a monster. Ex-Ranger Billy Mulligan, for instance, was deported for failing to divulge what he was rightfully suspected of knowing.

For the Committee had torn up the Constitution of the United States and was shipping out native-born American citizens, who were promised the death penalty if they returned to California. The state and not merely its metropolis was specified, for as Governor Neely Johnson had proved powerless to control the rebellious city, its directors had come to see themselves as rulers of the West's one sovereign domain.

They became contemptuous of federal authority, too, after General John Wool and Commodore Farragut, mindful of instructions not to interfere in civil affairs, refused to cooperate with Governor Johnson in the absence of orders from Washington. If the Vigilantes were not yet openly challenging the national administration, their temper at the time can be read in the conduct of a San Francisco mob early in June. Beginning by heckling an open-air gathering of people who pled for the return of law and order, the Committee's minions tore down the American flag which had been raised by the speakers' stand and pelted with rotten oranges a chap who undertook to restore the national banner to its place.

Ned did not know of this until the next day. Ransacking the

city for him had at last taken the form of house-to-house searching which was bound to turn him up sooner or later, if he didn't
manage to get clear. Yet as the patrols guarding all avenues of
egress from San Francisco were searching vehicles, he could not
safely be borne away in one. Ahorseback, on the other hand, he'd
be undesirably conspicuous. McGowan accordingly decided that
his best chance of getting out of the closing trap was to depart
as a disguised pedestrian.

He did that on the night of June 3, 1856, got up as a Mexican
peon. The hard part of it was that he couldn't afford to draw
notice by hurrying past any of the numerous guards whom he
encountered but must rather walk more slowly than he normally
would have done, by way of keeping in character with the part
he was playing. But he kept his nerves in order and strolled beyond the city to where a wagon was waiting. In this conveyance
he was driven to the house on the Mission Dolores road which
was to be his next hideout.

ஃ 60 ஃ

The Needle in the Big Haystack

THE CHIEF JUSTICE of California's Supreme Court in
1856 was David Terry. As the highest symbol of constitutional
law in the state, he took his responsibility toward law and order
seriously; and as a man who had ridden with Jack Coffee Hays,
he was prepared to take action.

Up until late June he had nothing to work with, but at that
time a small issue of arms to the national guard by the federal
arsenal at Benicia was due. Learning that he could get these
weapons, the Governor of California applied to General Wool
and was told that the promised items would be available, if he
sent to get them. As there was one armory in San Francisco

which the state still theoretically controlled, Johnson did send for the rifles and ammunition promised. As a military gesture it was a forlorn hope, but there was a possible development which Terry saw as usable.

Next to killing men on the authority of unauthorized courts, the most heinous offenses committed by the Committee were arresting men without warrant and holding them incommunicado. It was Terry's idea, then, that sending for the rifles would work out well, whether they were secured or intercepted by the Vigilantes. In the first instance adherents of law and order would at last have a supply of arms, even if a pitifully small one. But if those sent for the weapons were seized and imprisoned, he would be in a position to challenge the Committee with a writ of habeas corpus. If that was ignored, he felt that the State of California would have a charge to prefer of which the federal government must take notice.

Counting McGowan but not Casey and Cora, all previous targets of Vigilante action seem to have been in political alliance with Broderick. One called Yankee Sullivan had died while being held incommunicado at the end of May: a suicide, according to official Vigilante reports; slain because the former prize fighter had attacked one of his jailers, according to a more probable version. It was perhaps designedly, therefore, that non-Broderick men were picked to go for the rifles. There would thus be a test case in which the usual pretext for arrests—participation in election frauds—did not figure.

On June 23 one J. Reuben Maloney and a companion sailed in charge of a sloop which was supposed to carry the rifles back across the bay to San Francisco. Actually it was stopped by Vigilantes doubling as pirates, who confiscated the government-issue weapons and arrested the pair responsible for seeing that they were turned over to officials of the State of California.

At the outset Judge Terry seemed to have been balked, for the Committee soon released their prisoners if not the stolen arms. But before reporting back to Ashe, the federal agent who had arranged for the transaction at Governor Johnson's request, the released men visited a saloon, where they talked of their captors in terms which were soon quoted to the tyrants of Fort Gunny-bags. Like other tyrants they wanted to abuse people without being criticized for it and sent a police patrol to round up their detractors. In command of it was a man called Sterling Hopkins, who had been Casey's hangman.

As Terry was staying with Ashe, and as Maloney had belatedly decided to report to the latter, it was in the presence of the Chief Justice of the Supreme Court of California that Hopkins finally found one of the men he had been told to arrest. Upon finding that he had no proper warrant, Terry ordered the Vigilante offi-cer to leave; and he had the guns to back up that ukase. As they suspected, the incident wasn't a closed one, nevertheless; Terry, Ashe and a dozen or so backers decided that they could better defend Maloney in the one armory which the Vigilantes hadn't bothered to confiscate. On their way to it, they met Hopkins with a much stronger detachment than he had earlier com-manded.

In the scuffle which followed, Hopkins succeeded in jerking the judge's rifle from his grasp. Enraged alike by that and by a bullet which had whizzed past him, the former Ranger drew his bowie and plunged it in the Vigilante. That won the engage-ment; but the armory to which the victors then hurried was in short order surrounded by thousands of the Committee's janis-saries, and in order to save his friends from sacrificing their lives to no purpose, Terry gave himself up.

Craftily delivered, the blow he had aimed at Hopkins had slid past the collarbone and sunk the point deep downward from the base of the neck. It should have been a permanent cure of contempt of court, and the Vigilantes thought it would prove so. Although Hopkins was still alive on June 27, they began, on that day, the trial of California's highest magistrate in a kangaroo court on a murder charge.

Up to that time Ned McGowan had nourished the hope that the Vigilantes would be overthrown by people who had grown weary of their usurpation. But when the arrogance implicit in

335

the arrest of Terry met with no counteraction, he decided to return to Pennsylvania.

On the night of the first day of Terry's trial he stole from hiding and met a pair of guides, one with an extra horse. Friends had arranged for these men to take Ned through the coastal mountains by little-used trails to the port of Santa Barbara. There he could, as all felt sure, catch a ship for Panama.

What neither McGowan nor his allies understood was the efficiency of Coleman's organization, or the reach of its expanding ambitions. One reason for the helplessness of Governor Johnson was the speed with which moves had been made to win sympathy for the Committee among the residents of California's other towns. Banning John Nugent's opposing *Herald*, the Vigilantes allowed only Tom King's *Bulletin* and other concurring papers to go from the metropolis to the provincial cities. Delegates had been sent to the latter, too, and in each of them had won the support of influential citizens.

When Ned unsuspectingly rode into Santa Barbara on July 6, he was on this account as much in the enemy's camp as he had been in San Francisco. Everybody knew him as California's public enemy number one; everybody knew there was a reward posted for him; and nearly everybody was eager to prove good citizenship by joining in the chase for him. As there were Santa Barbarans who knew McGowan, because of visits to or former residence in San Francisco, a posse was in the making before he had been long in town.

Caught for once off guard by this development, McGowan would surely have been lagged but for a timely arrival which the hounded man himself later described. "At this moment, when I was about giving up all for lost, a horseman came dashing toward us at full speed, mounted on a magnificent animal, beautifully caparisoned. He reined up in front of us and, springing to the ground, said to those who were with me, 'The party is made, and the hunt is up for *him*,' pointing to me. I recognized the speaker at once. It was Jack Power."

Taking the other outcast under his wing, Power led the way

to a house in which lay a bundle of carpeting. Rolling Ned up in this, he jumped out the window by which they had both entered and joined man hunters so implacable that they even tried to burn McGowan out of a sun-dried cattail patch, where it was thought he had taken refuge.

That night after dark, Jack led Ned out of town. Sticking to the role of Good Samaritan, the so-called Destroying Angel also found an isolated ranch as a haven for a man he had met only once before, and seven years in the past at that.

News that their man had been seen in Santa Barbara revived the hopes of the Vigilantes, who had begun to believe rumors that Ned had made his way out of the state. Two expeditions, one traveling in a ship which had been bought especially for the purpose, left San Francisco for Santa Barbara later in July. Although they finally forced McGowan to take to the woods, they didn't catch the man they so badly wanted to; for his continued evasion of the Committee's best efforts represented at once its sole defeat and the only balm for aghast members of the opposition.

The one other setback for men who had become utterly lawless in the name of reform was the failure of Sterling Hopkins to die. Making a dramatic business of their loyalty to him, because he'd been stabbed while in the Committee's service, its leaders had hired several of the city's best doctors to attend him. Unexpectedly they pulled him through, leaving the People's Court in the position of trying a citizen for murder while the man he was supposed to have slain was known to have stopped short of the point of no return.

The trial of David Terry ground to a halt on July 22, but it wasn't an apologetic one. He stayed on as a prisoner in Fort Gunnybags while his fate was debated by his captors, now deep in a game in which no man's life counted but his own.

Controlling San Francisco and then for a while most of California, the leaders of the Vigilantes had swelled with greed for more power. As long as they remained Americans, they could not have it; nor could they even keep what they had. If they con-

337

tinued in allegiance to the federal government, in a word, they could not continue to defy all articles of the United States Constitution and trample on all whom they wished to abuse, abetted by an unauthorized army. Yet as they desired to prolong their sway, they were planning not only to secede but to incorporate Oregon and Washington in an independent pan-Coastal state.

Why they thought they could do so with impunity is to be explained by San Francisco's position. It was so big and rich as compared with any city within two million square miles of it that it seemed to its isolated citizens more imperial than it was. Western frontiersmen, for all their status as urbanites, they had lost the feel of the collective power of the settled regions from which they were weeks away by the fastest mail. Knowing the difficulties of Western travel, too, they thought they could take care of any expedition which could be sent against them.

Before they undertook to found a new nation, though, they had to be sure that they had the support of California's lesser cities in this as in other matters. They had therefore sent emissaries to the provincial towns; and the response from these, not embarrassment over a misdirected trial, was what was on their minds as they withheld sentence from Terry. Assured of support, they doubtless would have hanged him on the other charge they had lodged against the Chief Justice, which was that of breaking the Committee's laws. But while they were waiting to see whether this would become feasible, they hoisted two others.

Although they had nothing against these men, the latter were sacrificed to policy. The mobs, organized and disorganized, through which they ruled, grew restive when Terry wasn't found at the end of a rope. As the plebs had to be given something else to think about, the pair in question were lynched as the band played, soldiers strutted and people cheered.

The one called Hetherington was no more guilty of first-degree murder than Cora or Casey. Swindled, he had shot it out with a sharper who was so far from being unprepared as to have shot first. The one called Philander Brace had been tried and freed by a court which had allotted far more time to considering his case than did the Vigilantes. According to the estimate of the next cell's occupant, only minutes separated Brace's departure from his cubicle and his return to it with the complaint that he had been doomed. So up he went the next day, which was July 30.

That kept the man in the street happy for a while. But good cheer began leaving the Executive Committee's members at this time, for bad news was brought in from one provincial city after another. The trial of the still imprisoned Chief Justice of California had been revealed as such a burlesque of judicial procedure that people outside the gun-ruled metropolis had begun to see that the men who placed themselves above constitutional law were as dangerous to follow as other desperadoes.

With San Francisco's leadership rejected, the lesser outlaws of the Executive Committee began to lose their nerve. Coleman and some with him wanted to carry on with a high hand; but those with weaker knees freed Terry early in the morning of August 8. They not only did this without the knowledge of their sleeping leader; they smuggled the prisoner out of town, so that their followers wouldn't find out about it and string the Judge up.

They learned something about mobs they hadn't known then, for they nearly got lynched themselves for robbing the public of its distinguished prey. After that they yearned to return to private life; so, seeing that his organization was breaking up, Coleman staged a martial festival in mid-August of 1856 at which he announced that all had done their work nobly and could now go peaceably about their business in their purified city.

That city still belonged to the Vigilantes, and the law of the land wasn't honored there. Realizing as much, Ned McGowan dared not go back to be tried on the trumped-up charge which had made him a man for whom reward seekers still looked. Having found a new haven, he survived, but as a woodchuck does, ducking out of sight whenever strangers approached.

🎕 61 🎕

Jim Bridger Returns a Call

ALTHOUGH UTAH had been declared a United States territory in 1850, the law of the land was as much in the discard
there two years later as it was in the San Francisco of 1856. Brigham Young was the law, and in 1852 he was so sure of his power
that he announced that God had approved what Brigham very
well knew was without legal sanction anywhere else in America.
On August 29, that is to say, he declared that Heaven favored
more than one mate for male Saints.

Theretofore only the Mormon hierarchy had been allowed to
indulge in blessed lechery, nor had they sought publicity on that
score. But now polygamy had become identified with the entire
sect. For most Americans, indeed, it became the one distinguish-
ing trait of the people of Utah, and a peculiarly shocking one.
For while those in other parts of the nation might not stick to
the letter of monogamy, they were devout in honoring the theory.

In taking the step he did, Brigham thus put not only a high
legal wall between his people and all others in America but a social one of even more formidable proportions. Monogamy was a
peculiarly Caucasian custom; plural marriage was associated
with the other subdivisions of humanity. In plumping for polygamy, Prophet Young had separated his people from their ancestral connections, or to all intents and purposes he had. In the
thinking of most others they joined the Moslems in adhering to
an alien faith, as well as belonging to a race apart.

But that was what Brigham wanted, for he wished at once to
keep his people from drifting off to mingle with Gentiles and to
discourage non-Mormon immigration. Then the doctrine had
another practical side. Many more women than men were
among the proselytes recruited in Europe. These had been prom-

340

ised husbands when they came to America, and the message Young received from Heaven in 1852 arranged for them to be in some measure satisfied. It became a community duty for men who could afford it to take on extra spouses; and the Danites were there to attend to any who might feel that one wife was all he could cope with.

By that time Brigham had for months been without a rival west of the Great Divide. What with business affairs and his activities as a Vigilante, Sam Brannan had lost interest in being a religious chieftain. His colony on the Sacramento disintegrated on that account, most of its members going to the Great Salt Lake region. Among those who had done so in 1851, for example, were veterans of Cooke's Mormon Battalion—united after five years of wandering with people they had last seen at the Council Bluffs community of Kane.

They were also again under the man who had sold them down the river in 1846. Yet that was what they wished, as did most other Latter-day Saints. In 1855 and the following year there developed some factions which the Danites were called on to eradicate; but the Prophet's leadership was not seriously challenged.

In the meantime his policy of limiting residence in a territory of the United States to the people of one faith had been successfully sustained. About the only exceptions were a few federal officials, and they weren't respected. In 1856 the decisions of a federal judge named Stiles were reproved by means of sacking both his residence and his office.

The judge complained; but the same factors which favored the San Francisco Vigilantes in the same year sided with the Mormons. When Governor Johnson of California finally got a message of appeal across the continent by way of Panama, the national administration told him he was in the wrong for not first asking the support of his legislature; and no steps to arrest or otherwise interfere with Coleman and his confreres were taken. In part this was due to the difficulty and expense of putting an adequate restraining force on the Pacific Coast, but mainly it represented indifference to what was going on in the West. The days of "Fifty-four forty or fight" were gone, and as national attention was now focused on the mounting bitterness between the two populous sections of the country, nobody in the East cared about feuds on isolated frontiers.

The discovery that they could abuse federal officials unchecked had the natural effect upon Mormons of increasing their conviction of separateness. In the beginning they had hoped to find a section of the West which did not belong to the United States. All along they had thought that their settlements in Utah properly constituted a new nation. Now they began to think that autonomy had been attained.

The belief that Mormons were citizens of a country upon which foreigners were trespassing is the only thing which can fully account for the worst crime in the history of the West. The victims were a group of California-bound whites known as the Arkansas Party. The perpetrators were Indians, egged on and in the end superseded by Saints.

Resenting Americans who had undertaken to cross an American territory, the Mormon hierarchy had passed the word that such birds of passage were not to be aided or comforted by so much as a crumb of food. In September of 1857, however, a Mormon called Laney flouted this order, albeit under palliating circumstances. While doing missionary work in Tennessee, he had been saved from an anti-Mormon mob by two men named Aden, one the son of the other. Somehow discovering that his benefactors were members of the Arkansas Party, he entertained them. For this act of gratitude Laney was murdered by one of the Avenging Angels at the instigation of a Bishop Dame. He and other Mormons then tracked down the pilgrims who had been guilty of making punitive action against a fellow Saint necessary. Their estimated motive was to administer an object lesson which would put an end to further intrusion on the part of Gentiles.

At this time the Danites seem to have been a hush-hush society incorporated in that openly paraded military arm, the Nauvoo Legion. Probably a member of the former, John Doyle

Lee was certainly an officer of the latter. His sectarian connections were of the highest, as he was the foster son of Brigham Young. Lee had, besides, the companionship of the Prophet's chief assistant, George Smith, as he took the trail of a party which included many women and children.

Their first plan was to let Indians perpetrate the intended slaughter. When they caught up with the Arkansas Party, in southwestern Utah, the Mormons pinned the caravan down with their rifles, fired from a distance, but let their Paiute allies try for scalps and plunder.

The Paiutes weren't equal to the occasion, though, for the backwoodsmen forted up near Mountain Meadows broke repeated charges, albeit at the expense of most of their ammunition. The Mormons then called the Indians off and appeared in the role of peacemakers. They could, they said, arrange for an end of hostilities but a concession had to be made to the Paiutes. The latter, it was declared, would not agree to discussing any truce unless the pilgrims first turned their weapons over to the Saints as a warrant of good will.

As their rifles were all but useless anyhow, the desperate immigrants did give up their arms. Driving on, as they were next told to do, they were ambushed by teamed Indians and Mormons. The men who had trusted the Saints died by the bullet, the knife or the tomahawk, and so did their women and children. Of the some 140 members of the Arkansas Party, only 17 infants lived to be brought up by the murderers of their kin.

Taking place on September 6, the Mountain Meadows Massacre brought Utah's patriotism to a head. Immunity from federal interference had reacted on Brigham Young as it had on Coleman and other leaders of the San Francisco Vigilantes. All-powerful wherever he strode, he began to think himself mightier than he was. Some have claimed that he planned the atrocity in which close associates of his were prime movers; certainly he capitalized on an act calculated to draw demands for vengeance from all sections of Gentile America. Far from apologizing for what had been wrought at Mountain Meadows, Brigham flaunted his contempt of the rest of the country by declaring war against the United States on September 15.

The attitude of the federal government, with Jim Bridger's aid, had meanwhile stiffened. Still not able to occupy a place to which he had been granted legal title four years earlier, Old Gabe finally went to Washington and talked to James Buchanan, the old Philadelphia associate of Ned McGowan then in the White House. Newly in office, Buchanan was impressed by Jim Bridger's recital of Mormon activities and sent Brigham orders to conform to the laws of their mutual country. Arriving during the summer of 1857, they only irritated the Prophet, who finally took the step described above.

That act of defiance at last caused action by the Army. Colonel Albert Sidney Johnston, who had been Secretary of War for the Republic of Texas under Mirabeau Lamar, was chosen to prosecute the Mormon War; and he in turn selected Jim Bridger as his guide through the Rockies. In Johnston's command, too, was Lieutenant-Colonel Philip St. George Cooke, glad to be in another part of the West than unforgiving Texas. Ordered there some years earlier, Cooke had been sniped at by survivors of the Snively Expedition, or those who remembered some who didn't survive because he had taken their weapons.

Organized in the fall, Johnston's force did not reach the mountains until the passes were deep in snow. Having a less knowledgeable guide, the vanguard suffered, losing so many horses that it was incompetent to deal with the Utah militia which guarded approaches to the Wasatch Range. With Old Gabe for cicerone, though, the main body reached Fort Bridger in good shape and there wintered.

Brigham Young, the while his enemy was enjoying being home again, was blowing hot and cold as his faith in the power of a prophet waxed or waned. At times he asserted that he would destroy Johnston's army, or any other force sent against Utah by the United States, but in realistic intervals he wasn't so confident. In the end, therefore, he decided that he must step down as Governor of the Territory of Utah, a post which had been awarded to a Gentile named Alfred Cumming.

Chosen in 1857, this gentleman didn't assume office until Johnston's snowbound army came down from the mountains late the following spring. It was not until June 13 that the trails were firm enough for the wagons of the supply train. Leaving Fort Bridger then, the troops reached undefended Salt Lake City thirteen days later.

It was on June 26, 1858, that Jim Bridger, riding in the lead at his post beside the commander, took the last trick in his feud with Brigham Young. Yet neither the Prophet nor any of his disciples was present to watch Old Gabe grin at the sight of the citadel he had done so much to help take. As a last gesture of defiance, Young had ordered the withdrawal from his capital of all its inhabitants. So neither were any present to watch the auld lang syne gesture of Colonel Cooke, who rode through Salt Lake City bareheaded as a tribute to the men with whom he had suffered and achieved in Arizona a dozen years earlier.

Soon afterward Brigham came into camp and accepted the administration of non-Mormon officials, together with the ruling that Gentile Americans had the right to come and go in Utah, or abide there, if it so pleased them. The end of the only theocracy in the history of the United States had thus been brought about, and Utah was at last in train to becoming an integral part of America.

To be sure, it was still a part of America where polygamy was legal—Brigham maintained a hen yard of wives with a muster roll of 36. And there was one more issue which had not been settled. Although claiming to decry the Mountain Meadows Massacre, the Saints threw up a rampart of silence about the identity of those guilty of it. Known to other Mormons, if not to the Gentiles who wished to bring them to book, these continued to flourish as honored churchmen.

⁸⁄⁂ 62 ⁸⁄⁂

The Martyrdom of Joe Stokes

S ANTIAGO K IRKER DIED on his California ranch in 1853.
According to some he died under mysterious circumstances; according to others the cause of his death was delirium tremens, which may amount to the same thing.

Andy Sublette, said to have been the best shot on the Pacific Coast, was slain the same year by a grizzly he had neglected to hit in a vital spot. With his bowie the brother of Bill and Milton killed his antagonist, but fangs and talons put an end to thirty years of Sublette wandering in the West.

Remaining aboveground, Peg-leg Smith devoted much of 1853 to searching for the heaps of great gold chunks he had once found without knowing what they were. The only bearing he had was that it was near Warner's Ranch—the home and holding, that is to say, of the man who had served as Jed Smith's clerk during the former's fatal journey down the Santa Fe Trail.

Jim Clyman, at last staked down by marriage, continued to develop the ranch he had acquired following his return to California. Stepping out of his role as a more or less peacefully engaged citizen, on the other hand, William Walker chose 1853 as the year in which he turned to filibustering.

A Tennessee lawyer and journalist, Walker was probably inspired to become a conqueror by membership in the Knights of the Golden Circle. Launched very early in the 1850's, this organization was a fantastic offshoot of the struggle between the not yet warring North and South. But if the initiating concept was mainly crazy, it had one rock of realism for a footing. The Knights grasped the fact that the growing industrial might of the North was making that section of the nation too powerful for their own South to cope with. They therefore planned to reach out for additions to their section's economic strength.

346

The Golden Circle of these chevaliers was a geographical one which swept southward from both east and west of the United States and was completed in Central America. Embraced were Cuba and other islands of the West Indies. The comprehended territory was to be acquired by filibustering and added to the South. Once achieved, the entire slave-labor empire was supposed to detach itself from the North, which it would then have the strength to defy.

It has been asserted both that Walker's exploits were a part of this scheme and that he was an independent adventurer. But as he was a Southerner and as all that he did fitted in with the schemes of a society which was operating very secretly, connection can reasonably be assumed.

In any case William Walker set sail from San Francisco in the *Caroline* in October of 1853 as president of the Republic of Lower California and Sonora. With him were other officers of the not-yet-formed nation and riflemen to see that their political claims were honored.

At first they were, for La Paz in Lower California was captured in November, and the Republic's army was victorious in another battle, fought with rebelling native sons. Eventually, though, too many of these assembled at La Gruella. Losing there, the filibusters tried their luck in Sonora, where it was no better. Forced out of Mexico, they returned to San Francisco in 1854. There Williams resumed the practice of journalism and was wounded in a second duel at which Ned McGowan officiated.

While Walker was recuperating, as Ned recorded, the latter visited the former on several occasions during which the chief topic was a planned second grab for Latin America. In May of 1855 William sailed for Nicaragua. With him were only sixty-six men, but with them Walker made himself master of a country about the size of the State of New York and set up a government which survived for a while, in spite of the opposition of Northern capital as represented by Cornelius Vanderbilt.

Walker was still in control of the nation through which Vanderbilt hoped to run a canal connecting the Atlantic with the Pacific when Joe Stokes blew a Frenchman up in San Francisco's air, and Ned McGowan found it expedient to get the mine layer out of town. Ned thought that the best thing to do with Joe was to send him to join Walker in Nicaragua. The ship he sailed on in March of 1856 was, however, captured by one acting in the interest of Vanderbilt, and the party of would-be filibusters to which Stokes belonged were dumped ashore at Panama.

Traffic across the isthmus was so heavy at this point that travelers to the number of about three thousand were waiting either for a ship which would take them to the next ports they respectively desired, or transportation overland to the Atlantic Coast. Most of the travelers were American and British men of affairs, not accustomed to carrying weapons when they put to sea. Not a few of them had their families with them.

That was the case when, on April 6, a drunk tourist ignited the always smoldering hatred of half-castes for whites by taking a melon from a native and refusing to pay for it. A riot broke out which local troops at first tried to quell; but after they were fired on by some armed foreigners who couldn't tell one Panamanian from another, the soldiers ran amok, too.

Many defenseless men, women and children were quite literally torn to pieces by the frenzied mob, while many others were shot, slashed, bayoneted or trampled to death. More would have met these and similar fates, had it not been for Joe Stokes.

The transient foreigners who hadn't been caught by the demoniac mob had taken refuge in an English hostelry, called the Aspinwall, and a depot for baggage awaiting transfer from marine to shore transportation and vice versa. The hotel was defended by a group of the filibusters who had been on their way to join Walker. Between the mob and those huddled in the baggage station stood only Joe. While others passed him guns which had been found among the luggage, he held the natives at bay until nightfall by picking off any who started to make for the door he was guarding.

After dark Stokes and an employee of the depot called Bob

Marks recommissioned an old swivel cannon which was part of the station's furnishings. Although powder was available, there was no shot; but searching turned up a box of boiler rivets, nails and similar useful stuffing for the gun's muzzle. Having learned about cannon while protecting the rights of Democratic voters in San Francisco, Joe manned this piece and was ready to tear the mob which rushed the depot's door at dawn with makeshift but none the less effective canister.

Leaving fifteen dead and many more who wished they were, the natives withdrew. Fury kept bringing them back, though, and there was only enough ammunition for a limited number of charges.

But by the time it was used up, so was the general destructive frenzy of the mob. Their hatred concentrated on the men who had been so long balking it, the natives were anxious only to get their hands on the cannoneer and his chief assistant, when they finally succeeded in storming the depot. Retreating upstairs to the station's telegraph room, the two men made their last stand there. Out of ammunition, Bob Marks was bayoneted. Dying with his teeth still bared, Joe was shot as he tried to reload his pistol.

But as grateful others survived to tell how and why Stokes met finality, word of him went back to San Francisco. Proud of him before Casey fired at James King (of William), the citizenry planned to erect a statue to Stokes in a public place. After the second coming of the city's Vigilantes, however, Joe was repudiated because of his association with Ned McGowan.

Ned himself had planned to bring his friend's body back for interment by the Golden Gate; but month after month found him unable to take even his own live body there. Yet if still the secret guest of a Santa Barbara rancher named Nicholas Den, McGowan had changed his mind about fleeing from California. As his enemies had not let him go when he wanted to leave, he was determined to remain and strike back at them.

The first word of cheer that came his way was the information that something he had long worked for had come to pass. Late in the fall of 1856, in brief, David Broderick had at last been voted into the U.S. Senate by California's legislature. As that had occurred, it could be taken for granted that the same legislative body would give favorable attention to the predicament of one of the new senator's political stand-bys. Ned was emboldened to send communications to figures in Sacramento through roundabout channels, and in due course a friend of McGowan's, Captain J. Martin Reese, rode out of the capital with a message for the fugitive.

Dated January 27, 1857, this missive was from the speaker of California's legislative house. Its tenor was to the effect that if Ned could manage to make his way to Sacramento, a bill would be introduced which would grant him a change of venue, on the murder charge, from San Francisco County to a neutral one in which he might reasonably expect a fair trial.

To the chagrin of the still vindictive Vigilantes, McGowan did reach the capital, where he arrived on February 28, following a rough trip through the mountains on winter trails. As the House's leader promptly made good, and as the presented bill was passed in spite of San Francisco opposition, the change of venue was in order. Chosen by the controlling court because it was a county in which Ned had never sojourned, Napa became the theater of a legal battle which people from all over the state flocked to attend.

Actually the legal sparring lasted only four days. Going all out for the kill, the Vigilantes had hired the nationally renowned Henry Foote as special prosecutor, but he could do nothing with the string he was given in place of a hangman's rope. As the Napa *Reporter* summed up the case against McGowan, "there was not evidence enough against him to hang a cat."

So Ned was a free citizen at the conclusion of his trial, on June 1—free to go anywhere but San Francisco, that is. Tom King of the *Bulletin* had given the Vigilante attitude toward the trial by describing it as "the farce at Napa."

As it turned out, the Committee's members were given many more reasons for wishing to hang McGowan after he left San

Francisco than before he had done so. Once he had first published a book which exposed their wrongheadedness as a group, he began, in August of 1857, to analyze them individually in a weekly mustang of journalism known as the Sacramento *Phoenix.*

In publishing their edicts the Vigilantes had naïvely exposed themselves to satire by referring to themselves as San Francisco's "purest and best citizens." But Ned, not pretending to purity himself, had known many of them in California's uninhibited "flush times" epoch, before they had established homes and otherwise come into the fold of respectability. As a lawyer and as a man active in politics, moreover, he knew how certain fast fortunes had been made, who had slipped dollars under the table to what public figures, and who had been engaged in both petty and grand larcenies. As a man, lastly, who associated with the madams of bawdyhouses openly when he felt like it, he not only knew who did it on the sly, but what churchgoers were supported in whole or in part by prostitution.

As Ned made his knowledge public in racy prose and verse, he obtained two results. One was a mounting hatred which did not stop short of an attempt to have him assassinated. The other was an embarrassment which finally drove the Executive Committee to abdicate. Although the Vigilantes as a whole had been inactive since August of 1856, their leaders had remained publicly dominant. But on November 12, 1857, when McGowan had been in the newspaper business but seventy-four days, the Executive Committee announced its dissolution.

As it also lifted the ban against the return of the men it had shanghaied into exile, San Francisco was once more an American city, after eighteen months of rule by a usurping oligarchy. The only one in a position to benefit by the return of constitutional law who could not was the one who had hastened its restoration. McGowan was so far from being welcomed back to San Francisco that he almost didn't make it, when he tried to catch a ship outward bound from there in 1858.

By June of that year Ned had realized that scourging the Committee could not be a lifelong occupation. As he could not return to his metropolitan law practice, he decided to join a gold rush to the Fraser River, in British Columbia, which was writing front-page headlines at the time.

His idea was to risk reaching, unobserved, the northward-bound ship on which he had booked passage. A misguided friend of his, however, tried to obtain open permission for McGowan to pass through San Francisco. When Ned arrived by water from Sacramento, in consequence, he was met by policemen, every one of them an ex-Vigilante into whose past he had lustily delved.

He had hoped to sail for the new gold field on June 26. Instead he was booked on a libel charge the day before. After he had raised bail, furthermore, Ned stepped into the corridor of the courthouse, there to find officers Chappell and Boyce waiting for him. The latter promptly shot at McGowan, the near miss piercing his coat.

After he had stormed back into the court on whose doorsill this had happened, Ned was forced to realize that the judge could offer him none but the escort of other hostile police. Included was their chief, concerning whose fondness for a dusky harlot McGowan had been newsy.

The police sachem was among those waiting when Ned stepped from the courthouse; but so were Captain J. Martin Reese and some other staunch friends. Although these last were outnumbered, they eventually caused a diversionary loophole through which McGowan, Reese and an additional ally slipped to the clear. Reaching the waterfront, at the conclusion of the chase that followed, Ned hid out, while the others located a dory for salt-water escape.

His first haven a U.S. marine revenue cutter, McGowan moved on to an isolated point on the bay, presided over by a hermit named Horsehoe Bill. When, on June 29, Bill rowed Ned out to the ship whose skipper had agreed to pick up the fugitive at sea, the latter's second close Vigilante call was at length a passed crisis.

352

Now at the same time that McGowan was sailing away from where he could no longer live, the man who had saved him on the first such occasion was riding south for an identical reason. A hero of the sporting world only seven weeks earlier, Jack Power was no longer in esteem.

On May 9, 1858, Ned had published the word that Power had bet $2500 against a like amount that he could ride 150 miles in under eight hours, the place being the Pioneers Race Course in San Francisco County. In a subsequent issue McGowan had had the satisfaction of announcing that his friend had pulled off this remarkable feat of endurance. The cheers had hardly died down, though, when there was other news of Jack.

On June 28 the *Bulletin* had carried the story that a gang supposedly controlled by him had killed a man in the course of committing highway robbery. On July 5 the *Alta California* noted, "Jack Power has not yet been caught, but a number of men are in pursuit of him. He has started for Sonora."

Jack Power outraced his pursuers, as they might have expected he would. Sonora, however, had not been a safe place for Americans since Walker's filibustering expedition had made all visiting gringos suspect on the score of like designs. On some unspecified day during the summer of 1858 the Destroying Angel was shot by Mexican officials, who threw, as was their wont on such occasions, the body of a once gay man to roving hogs.

63

A Beheaded Dead Man

IN THE SPRING of 1856 the Oury brothers, William and Granville, decided to leave California and return to Texas. Passing through the Gadsden Purchase, though, they were taken with the vicinity of Tucson. Settling there, they both ranched;

and Gran, who had practiced law in Missouri before going to Texas in 1848, indulged a flair for politics.

As the Mexican flag had flown over Tucson's walls until March of 1856, its English-speaking population was not large. There were more Americans in Tubac, after Poston's party arrived during the summer, pumping new blood into what had been a ghost town. But most of the miners there, having been picked up in New Braunfels, Texas, were more articulate in German than in the language in which government is conducted in the United States. If a few Americans, besides, lived at other points in the Santa Cruz Valley, no whites but the ferrymen of Colorado City lived elsewhere in western New Mexico.

With Gran Oury and Herman Ehrenberg participating, nevertheless, a convention was held in August at which it was agreed that the region was entitled to be considered a separate political entity. A constitution for the Territory of Arizona was therefore drawn up, and a delegate took it to Washington.

As Congress was not convinced by the less than three hundred signatures to the accompanying petition that enough citizens dwelt in the region, no action was taken, following its presentation in January of 1857. Before that news could have been carried back to isolated Tucson, though, the younger Oury had gone to Mexico for debatable reasons.

If Henry Crabb was not a Knight of the Golden Circle, he was a friend of his fellow Southerner, William Walker. It was believed by those who knew them both, besides, that Crabb entered Mexico as an associate of Walker, who was still holding on in Nicaragua at the time. Crabb himself, nonetheless, insisted that his intentions were peaceful, and chroniclers have gone to some lengths to uphold him.

In any case Henry Crabb of Tennessee had gone to California before the Forty-niners, prospered there and married a señorita called Philomena Ainsa. Not natives of the West Coast, her people had been ousted from Sonora because of being Spanish tories opposed to Mexican independence. Attempts to get considerable mining and other properties back had proved fruitless; but the Ainsas were connected with other prominent and still entrenched Sonora families. Through them Crabb entered into a dicker with one Ignacio Pesqueira, who aspired to take the governorship away from the incumbent Gandara but needed a war chest. Anxious for the funds which Crabb was able to provide, Pesqueira agreed to allow the American a strip of northern Sonora.

For publication, at least, Crabb maintained that he wished to colonize the region in question with farmers. He had, however, shipped rifles to Guaymas in addition to the ones carried by his followers.

In the light of the available evidence it seems clear that all concerned must have known that the stake of the Ainsas was to recover their property and that this could only have been done— other methods having failed—through a revolution. They must have known, too, that once Sonora had been detached from the rest of Mexico, other Americans would surge into it, making further conquests possible. Still Crabb went to the trouble of taking farming implements along, when his party sailed from San Francisco in December of 1856.

The journey across the desert from Los Angeles turned out to be such a laborious one that quite a few of Crabb's hundred and some men broke down under the strain of getting their caravan through encountered sand hills. Then the trip had taken so long that it was late in March of 1857 before the Mexican border was reached, and by that time Pesqueira had become governor without Crabb's aid.

In the saddle he had coveted, Pesqueira realized that he would not be popular in Sonora were it known that he had agreed to give Americans some of its territory. On the other hand he didn't want people to know about the money which had exchanged hands, either. He had therefore posted a man at Sonoita who warned Crabb, without saying where the message came from, that he would meet armed resistance if he entered Mexico.

Relying on Pesqueira, nonetheless, Crabb did cross the boundary on March 26. But he left his brother-in-law, Jesus Ainsa, in charge of a few invalids. To bring his party up to strength, in the meantime, he had already sent an appeal for recruits to Tucson.

If there was not a Golden Circle "castle" in that town, Crabb got the response to be expected of one. With a minimum of delay, twenty-six men, Gran Oury their captain, rode to meet the other Americans at Caborca.

A few miles short of that community Crabb *et al.* were ambushed April 1. Fighting their way into the town, though, the survivors made a fort out of a church, where they held out for six days against the fifteen hundred men thrown against them by Governor Pesqueira. At the end of that time they walked out from under a burning roof on the promise they would be treated as prisoners of war.

The leader of the Mexican troops, however, was Hilario Gabilondo, the go-between who had trapped Crabb on Pesqueira's behalf. Making a great show of patriotic rage, he had the Americans promptly shot, with the exception of their leader and a fifteen-year-old boy who was inexplicably present. To make sure that Crabb wouldn't talk, Gabilondo personally killed him with a sword. Not content with that private act, he next ordered public decapitation with an ax.

At about the same time a party of Mexicans attacked the sick men who had been left at Sonoita, murdering them all and capturing Ainsa. The Crabb expedition was thus completely destroyed with the exception of the detachment under Oury.

Nearing Caborca, they got word of the massacre in time to avoid being captured. Finding they were cut off, though, Oury divided his men into parties, the better to get through the closing Mexican net. At the expense of some blood and much hard riding this was achieved and the Arizona border crossed again by men glad to do so.

In the fall of 1857 Lieutenant Edward Beale, who had accompanied Kit Carson when the latter was sent to get help for General Kearny's cornered dragoons, took a string of camels along Aubry's 35th-parallel route through Arizona. It was hoped that the hump-backed beasts would prove as useful in the Southwest as they had been found in other parts of the world. Although that didn't turn out to be the case, southern Arizona was supplied with a more reliable form of transportation in the same year.

Previously better linked with Mexico than any other part of the United States, the settlements in the Santa Cruz Valley were at last tied to the rest of the nation by the establishment of stagecoach service. Running between San Antonio and San Diego, the comparatively luxurious vehicles took passengers and mail along the general routes which had been painfully pioneered by Jack Coffee Hays and Cooke.

Soon to be run as the Butterfield Overland Stage Line, this utility brought three figures of regional note into Arizona. As a guard or in some other roving capacity, Jack Swilling, once of Kansas and sundry other places, arrived in Tucson in 1857. Then, or during the following year, the Great Western moved from Fort Yuma to Colorado City, where she ran a restaurant in the first permanent structure of that town. From some direction, also, Jacob Snively emerged as the manager of a station east along the Gila from the ferry crossing.

Of all the well-known Westerners the case of Snively is the most mysterious. On the staff of two Texas presidents, he was in the local public eye for a number of years. As the head of the Snively Expedition, he became the bone of a contention involving three nations. In 1844 he was found smelting treasure ore at the old mission associated with the lost Bowie mine—and then he dropped from recorded notice for fourteen years.

He didn't stay a station manager long. During the spring of 1858 he found gold twenty miles east of what is now Yuma, and the boom town of Gila City came into being. Its months of glory were few, however, and Ned McGowan was not tempted to go there when he arrived in 1859.

After reaching British Columbia Ned had arranged to have a troublesome magistrate arrested and fined, he himself acting in the capacity of constable. But he had won his own case before the judge who came to Fort Yale, accompanied by several pla-

357

toons of British redcoats, in January of 1859. So he had come well out of what historians refer to as "McGowan's War."

But in addition to thus enjoying himself, Ned had been a successful prospector at Hill's Bar. Having picked up capital to the extent of $37,000, he had arranged by mail to join Captain Charles Stone and other members of a party from California in Mexico. The purpose of the Stone expedition was to survey the mineral resources of Sonora for an interested American corporation. But as Governor Pesquiera mistook the prospectors for filibusters, he issued a heeded warning. Remembering the massacre at Caborca, the ex-surveyors hastened north; and by early June of 1859 they were in the silver-mining town of Tubac.

Up to that time Tubac had been vying with Tucson in a pygmy race for metropolitan leadership. The fact that the Butterfield stages ran through the latter, though, gave it a communications advantage which put it ahead. McGowan soon moved to Tucson for that reason, although in so changing residence he went nearer to the frontier rather than the contrary.

If Colonel B. L. E. de Bonneville had brought the Apaches in the easterly parts of New Mexico more or less under control, the former beaver-seeker's jurisdiction had not covered the Santa Cruz Valley settlements, of which Tucson was the most exposed. To cope with Indians who were increasing the frequency of their swoops upon animal herds and ranch houses, an organization called the Gila Rangers was formed, with Jack Swilling as commander.

As its name implied, the mission of this police force was to keep the Apaches north of the river which formed the boundary between settled and unsettled Arizona. If the records of other moves to this end are missing, there is a preserved report which shows that in January of 1860, Jack tried to carry the war into the mountains of central Arizona, where the raiders principally hived up.

To pad the thin ranks of the Gila Rangers, Jack had invited a nearby group of Pimas—friendly to whites but rabidly anti-Apache—to join him in taking the trail of a strong band of raiding Tonto Indians. Not expecting to be followed, the Apaches had stopped short of the Gila for a feast of horse and mule meat. Their favorite viands, these were preferably prepared by cutting off steaks while the beasts were still alive.

Knowing that they would gorge and sleep heavily if allowed to do so, Swilling kept away from the gulch into which trackers had traced the Tontos until long after dark. As usual the Apaches, who differed from other Indians in being fearful of night activity, had not posted sentries. Swilling was therefore able to throw a circle of men around them who closed in and slew fifteen. The rest vanished as only Apaches could in a land offering little natural cover.

Wishing to follow these survivors across the Gila, Jack first lost an argument with the Pimas. Not averse to night fighting, like the Apaches, they had taken a dead horse, found at the point where they reached the river, as a warning to turn back. As they did that, only the Rangers went on into Apache country.

Of themselves not strong enough to do more than reconnoiter, the white men scouted the Gila as far as the Hassayampa, up which stream Swilling found gold. Not wanting his men to begin prospecting where it was so unsafe to do so, however, he said nothing about his discovery at that time.

With Gran Oury and Ned McGowan as prime movers, meanwhile, the move to separate Arizona from New Mexico had taken on new life. Approaching the business more systematically than had been done before, they divided the proposed new territory into four counties, made possible by collaborating with Mesilla and other inhabited Gadsden Purchase points in southern New Mexico. Having no historical kinship with Santa Fe, these former Sonora towns didn't like being governed by officers seated there.

On April 2 a convention was held in Tucson at which Gran and Ned were elected territorial judges. Somebody else was originally supposed to take the matter up with Washington, but in the upshot—and doubtless because of his standing with President Buchanan—McGowan was given that assignment likewise.

359

Yet as Congress would not again be in session for quite a few months Ned did not immediately go East. He was therefore able to join the stampede when Snively made another gold strike, this time in mountainous Pinos Altos, New Mexico.

Ned's only known activity there was to kill a man in a duel fought with Navy revolvers. His victim, whose name was reported only as Porter, seems to have been a former Vigilante, once employed in San Francisco's customs house.

But the prospectors of Pinos Altos, in that summer of 1860, were in time given something to shoot at besides each other. Mangas Colorado, with whom John Glanton had been convivial at Tucson, was the ablest chief in Apache history. Habitually the many subdivisions of the tribe didn't cooperate, but he had built up a confederacy which looked to him for orders. On that account he was able to assemble a formidable war party when he moved against the paleface gold hunters.

Fortunately for the besieged miners, Jack Swilling was no longer with the Gila Rangers. As Arizona was having its first immigration boom in 1860, the Arizona Scouts had been organized, their function being to escort caravans through the Indian-infested mountains west of the Rio Grande Valley. Before Mangas got thirsty for paleface blood, Jack had been second in command of this unit. But as Captain Thomas Martin had undertaken to get between the Apaches and the men at Pinos Altos, he and those with him had all been killed.

Jack was in Mimbres with what was left of the Arizona Scouts when a man who had managed to sneak through the Indian net arrived with a message from Snively. Rousing the town and those around it, as well as recruiting immigrants waiting to cross the mountains, Swilling sped north with enough men at his back to make Mangas willing to call the siege off.

On that account McGowan survived to make his scheduled trip to Washington, where a bill favoring the creation of Arizona Territory was introduced in December of 1860. As it turned out, though, having Buchanan at his back was of no use to Ned, for the former was a lame-duck President who had lost his influence with Congress. If McGowan had been in Jim Clyman's shoes and been friendly with Buchanan's elected successor, Lincoln, the delegate from Arizona might have accomplished what he wished to. Under the circumstances, though he could get no hearing. The angry politicians of the North and the South did not then think that the West might have a role in their vendetta.

✂ 64 ✂

Sam Houston's Great Scheme

SETTLED FAR MORE recently than Texas, Oregon and Washington west of the Cascades were free of Indian depredations much sooner. With California as a supply base and with ships to deliver men and materiel at convenient coastal points, the Army was able to finish what pioneers had begun. Even the Navy participated, for in January of 1856 a man-of-war shelled Indians who had invaded Seattle.

Later that same year General Wool broke the back of the Rogue River Indians. Going beyond the Cascades next, the troops subdued the Coeur d'Alenes and Spokanes in 1858, the Columbia making that inconsiderable feat of arms convenient. But after nearly thirty-five years of American settlement, and a dozen of occupation by the Army, attacks by Indians westward of San Antonio went on unabated.

The Army put good men there but not enough of them to cope with the flying squadrons of the Comanches and Kiowas. And then there were too many shackling rules. In its anxiety to settle tribes in the Indian territory, the government made that a haven where they were not supposed to be hunted. Discovering as much, blanket Indians used the region north of the Red as a base from which to raid frontiersmen living south of it.

In January of 1858 the governor of Texas did what had long been urged by a bitter citizenry and reorganized the Rangers as a state Indian-fighting force. Selecting Rip Ford as senior officer, His Excellency authorized him to form five fully equipped companies; and when doing so, he spoke for all Texans. For without mincing any words, he ordered Ford to ignore federal directives, whatever their source, and go where he must to punish warring Indian bands.

Ready for the field in April, Rip led his men across the Red on the 29th of that month in pursuit of raiders led by, among others, Cynthia Ann Parker's husband. The head chief, however, was a Comanche called Iron Jacket. Having somehow acquired an old Conquistador's shirt of metal plates, he was greatly admired for the invulnerability it supposedly gave him.

On May 12 the Rangers found the allied bands of Peta Nocona and Iron Jacket in the Antelope Hills along the South Canadian. In the fight that followed the Comanches learned that armor heavy enough to turn off arrows and lance thrusts was yet no talisman against bullets. Along with seventy-five who went naked into battle, in the old fashion of the tribe, Iron Jacket was slain. Peta Nocona escaped, however, taking the hovering Cynthia Ann with him.

After a campaign which lasted until September, the Comanches were quiet for a while, but the aroused Texans were not. Having taken the bit in their collective teeth, they wanted to get rid of reservation Indians as well as those on the loose. Perhaps there was justice in their complaints that the reserved redskins didn't stay within their allotted boundaries. Possibly there was truth behind the accusations of Indian agents that such charges were trumped up by greedy land grabbers. Probably there was some verity in both contentions, and certainly great cruelty was exercised even against groups which had helped fight the blanket Comanches. But the citizenry wanted all the Indians they could put their hands on underground or north of the Red River, and that's what happened in most instances.

But if the western frontier had become safe for whites who didn't venture too far from the settlements, the Rio Grande became a river which was crossed both ways by warring men again.

Wild Cat's confederacy had collapsed, and Wild Cat himself had died or gone elsewhere, but in 1859 a Mexican called Juan Cortinas stepped high and shot straight.

His first victim was a Texas sheriff, who was in the act of arresting a Mexican youth in the streets of Brownsville on July 13. Considering the officer unduly rough, Cortinas fired and killed him.

Although he retreated into Mexico at the time, Juan kept Brownsville on his mind, and toward the end of September he rode back into it at the head of a bandit gang. Not content with plundering the American town, he stayed there, attempts to oust him notwithstanding.

Even when Rangers went against him in the spring of 1860, they lost because the wrong officer was in command. Rare for a corps with a tradition of little talk and much action, Captain Tobin seems to have been a braggart with a white feather. After proclaiming that he would be the conqueror of Cortinas, he fell so far short of making good that he left two cannon in the bandits' hands when he hastened to retreat.

The Rangers didn't promptly schedule a return engagement, because Peta Nocona got tired of peace and had begun attacking the western frontier again. But Sam Houston had left the U.S. Senate to become Governor of Texas; and he was no longer the tolerator of Indians that he once had been.

Without confiding his plans to many, the Raven had returned to Texas with a plan of complex facets. Essentially it was the biggest filibustering scheme of them all. Yet it was to be carried out in the name of the general good, not for personal gain or at the behest of the Knights of the Golden Circle.

An intense nationalist at a time when talk of dissolving the Union was common, Sam seems to have begun by thinking that the only way to keep the North and the South together was to give them some common cause. With that as a starting point, the man who had taken Texas from Mexico had decided that the most feasible move would be for him to seize the rest of that country.

Knowing Americans, he knew that myriads would swarm into a sparsely developed region which was much more accessible to the populous Atlantic Seaboard than most parts of the West. And he hoped that the diversion of men and capital for the constructive purpose of exploiting a land known to be minerally rich would postpone civil hostility long enough to give reason a chance to take the lead away from bad temper.

But as he knew he could not get the federal government to undertake an arrant war of conquest, Houston was prepared to attempt the conquest of Mexico with a homespun army. In part it would consist of the Cherokees and other Indian nations with whom he was influential on the score of the friendliness he had always shown redskins. Its backbone would be the rifle-skilled settlers of Texas, supplemented by the volunteers from other states whom he was sure he could count upon. Its elite corps would be the Rangers, the one trained unit at his disposal.

As for the Comanches, they had to be now given the knife for two reasons. In the first place Sam was aware that he couldn't get the recruits he had to have, should frontiersmen still find their homes in need of defenders. Secondly, he wanted to enlarge the Rangers and to give the outfit as much combat experience as possible.

So under leaders such as Rip Ford, Sul Ross and John Baylor, the Rangers carried the war deeper into Comanche territory than ever before. And at the climax of that 1860 campaign, Captain Ross closed with Peta Nocona's band, along the Pease River, on December 18.

Cynthia Ann, a child in her arms, raced beside her husband, when the Indians at length broke and fled. Chased by Captain Ross, the chief lost out after a shot killed the half-grown girl riding behind him; for in trying to catch the falling body, he tumbled to the ground himself. The three arrows which the Comanche then swiftly slung all missed their mark, while Sul tore his opponent with as many pistol slugs. But whether Peta Nocona died that day is an argued point, some saying he did and others that he lived for several more years.

364

The fate of his wife was not a matter of dispute, however. Preloch, as the Comanches called Cynthia Ann, was captured at the time and brought back to a civilization for which she had neither fitness nor desire. On more than one occasion she tried to escape back to her tribe, but well-meaning people kept her where she was wretchedly out of her element.

The Army had, in the meantime, turned from Indian warfare to give attention to the still rampant Cortinas. The officer in command of the Department of Texas was Colonel Robert E. Lee. During the previous year, he had been given the task of corraling John Brown, the perpetrator of the Pottowatamie massacre, albeit said to have had a soul. As this was his second tour of duty in Texas, Lee was aware of both how much there was to be done and how little the Army had been given to do it with. Still he took Cortinas seriously enough to have assigned the task of rounding the brigand up to his most capable subordinate. That is to say that in March of 1860 the Colonel ordered Major Samuel Heintzelman to go after the troublesome Mexican.

Back in the service after having temporarily replaced Poston as supervisor of the mines at Tubac, Heintzelman had then gone to the Rio Grande Valley with 165 soldiers, as well as 120 Rangers under Tobin. But due to the latter's ineffectuality, as the Major charged in a report to Lee, the engagement fought near Matamoros had been indecisive.

Heintzelman had continued to watch for his man, however, and when he got a second chance at the bandit leader, the Major had a better hand working for him. In the vanguard with his Rangers, Rip Ford pinned Cortinas down at a scrub settlement called Rio Grande City. That happened on December 26, 1860, which was Juan's last day.

Twice at this period Sam Houston had felt called upon to shoo away from the Mexican border parties of Americans who were bent on causing more in the way of international disturbances than Cortinas had ever hoped to bring about. After finally losing out in Nicaragua, William Walker had attempted to take Honduras, where he had been executed by a firing squad on

September 12; but the Golden Circle knights hadn't given up their imperial design. Armed groups belonging to the order had moved into Texas, accordingly, only to be thwarted by a man who had a better-worked-out filibustering plan of his own.

The onrush of intersectional strife, though, kept Houston from ever putting into action a scheme aimed at preventing exactly that. As a Union man, next, Sam lost his influence with a citizenry which voted secession for Texas, following a convention held on February 1, 1861. Resigning as governor, the Raven began to sit out the two years of life that remained to him. And meanwhile the Rangers readied themselves to give the Comanches and Mexican banditti a respite by taking part in a conflict that was no part of the man of San Jacinto's plans.

 65

The Printed Word in the Rockies

NOT LIVING TO see the realization of his dream of a railroad through the West, Tom Benton died in Washington on April 10, 1858. Out beyond his cherished Missouri, Kansas was still the scene of slayings and bipartisan skulduggery with regard to whether the people of the territory should or should not have largely imaginary slaves. Free-labor men predominating, the territory did increase as to white men, though. Spreading ever westward, the settlements narrowed the range of the hunting tribes month by month.

Up until 1858 nobody had begrudged the Indians space in the Colorado mountains, which were a part of Kansas as originally constituted. During that year, though, prospectors began investigating stories such as William Bent told to those who stopped at his post. Although gold was of no interest to him while it was still in the ground, he had long known that Indians had found a soft, yellow metal in the Rockies. There was, for example, a tra-

366

dition that a battle had been fought in which golden bullets had replaced standard ammunition for the side which had run out of lead.

Although only traces of gold were found in Cherry Creek during the summer of 1858, that confirmation of rumors drew settlers to where the stream neared the South Platte. Promptly, indeed, there were two stream-bracketing hamlets. Manhattan and Brooklyn in miniature, one was called Auraria and the other Denver, after the governor of Kansas.

Before the first real strike was made, Denver was a mountain metropolis and the market center for prospectors combing mountains where none but Indians and beaver trappers had earlier thought it worth while to be. By February of 1859 one log cabin served as a combination hotel and gambling palace. Then on April 23 no less than two newspapers issued their first numbers.

Of these one was published by William Byers, an Ohioan who had been a surveyor in Nebraska Territory until he committed the error of trying to pacify two drunks who were trying to stage a duel with shotguns. Although it seems that neither of the antagonists had got hit, William had been so severely winged that he couldn't follow his trade. At this juncture a fellow citizen of Omaha who owed him money had given Byers a printing press instead of the cash he would have much preferred. Making the best of matters, though, he had gone to the mile-high wonder town and started the *Rocky Mountain News* in a building belonging to the once junior mountain man who had come to be known as Old Dick Wootton.

At the time it seemed possible that the wonder town would fizzle, for gold in the large had not been found by anybody. Disappointed, many had drifted away when, on May 10, the great strike made by John Gregory along the north fork of Clear Creek restored excitement to its former pitch.

The "Pike's Peak or Bust" gold rush of 1859 sprinkled towns among the Colorado Rockies, but Denver served as the gateway city to the new treasureland, just as San Francisco had done in the

367

case of the older one. So it was into Denver that the caravans all rolled—running the gantlet of roving Indian bands in many cases. Disturbed by the paleface invasion of the mountains, as well as eager for loot, the Arapahoes and others who hunted in the region were a constant menace.

Killing some whites and frightening others into turning back, the redskins had neither effect upon a hearty old harridan named Mother Maggard. When her caravan was pursued by a war party, she cautioned its male members to hold their fire while she dealt with the savages. Rising to view in one of the forted-up wagons then, she called attention to herself by shrieking and waving a frying pan at the oncoming braves.

Not used to such conduct, the Indians did watch her, as desired. But when they were near enough to shoot, they were also near enough to observe that the teeth of the white squaw were snarling at them from a position outside her mouth. When she sucked them back in and snapped them forth again, the horrified warriors wheeled about and fled. With her store teeth firmly in place again, Mother Maggard then continued in triumph to Cherry Creek.

Having absorbed Auraria in December of 1859, Denver became the unchallenged king city of the Rockies. Yet if the community had been united geographically, it was still socially divided. For having found himself as a newspaperman, William Byers had become a crusader, battling it out with a mile-high underworld.

The chief target of the *Rocky Mountain News* was Charlie Harrison, his antecedents vaguely the South and his leanings definitely so. It was said by one who knew him well that Charlie had been tutored in Indian fighting and the general lore of the mountains and the plains by Kit Carson. It was rumored that Harrison had learned the trade he followed in Denver aboard Mississippi River packets; but more probably he had acquired facility with cards in Santa Fe or the California gold camps. Be that as it may, he had come to Denver with the capital which enabled him to open the Criterion Saloon, and the capabilities which made it possible both to deal as he saw fit and to stay alive.

Popular as well as skillful and quick with weapons, Charlie became the rajah of the local gamblers. On this score alone he had been opposed by Byers, to whom saloons and all that went on in them were indiscriminately anathema, due to the reports of others. For like the Irishman who rejoiced that he didn't like olives, for otherwise he might have been tempted to eat them, William hadn't been in any saloons.

Possessed of something of a sense of humor, Charlie hadn't paid much attention to the thunderings of the people's palladium until he was accused of fracturing not the editor's moral code but his own, pertaining to the wielding of arms. This came about when a Negro called Stark tried to butt into a card game over which Harrison was presiding. Rebuffed, Stark drew a bowie, which he used with such near efficiency that Charlie had to ward off at least one stab with the butt of the gun he drew from under his coat, before he could whip the barrel into firing position.

A Northerner in addition to being anti-everything else that Harrison stood for, Byers jumped to the conclusion that the gambler had not only been the aggressor, because of prejudice against Stark's race, but had shot him out of hand without giving him a chance. If Charlie was probably unconcerned about the fact of the killing, the charge of not having fought fairly so bothered him that he took the trouble to visit the editor and diagram the circumstances.

A fair man himself, Byers admitted his mistake when Harrison showed him the fresh knife-nick on the butt of his gun, in proof of the fact that the bowie had gone into action before the pistol could. But though the gambler and the editor parted amicably, following a conference which took place in July of 1860, the episode wasn't over. Charlie had hardly left the office of the *Rocky Mountain News* when a colleague of his called Carl Wood barged into the sanctum, derringer in hand. Clapping the muzzle snug against William's back, he ordered Byers to proceed to the Criterion and apologize to Harrison.

Returning to his premises quite a bit later, Charlie found the editor in the custody of men busy celebrating his capture. Although the abduction was becoming town knowledge by then, Wood and the gang with him announced that they were prepared to hold the Criterion against a growing crowd of would-be rescuers.

Sober himself, Harrison explained that he and Byers were no longer at odds, but for once he couldn't call the turn among his own crowd. In their fuddled fury many present vowed that they would avenge him, whether he had the sense to wish to be avenged or not. And besides, they had scores of their own to settle with a man who had criticized some of them personally as well as inveighing against them as a group.

By that time blood retribution was in the wind rather than the hazing which was all that had at first been intended. Nor was it even safe for Harrison to try to cross them openly, after they had talked themselves into a lynch-mob frame of mind. But by diverting the attention of most of them to the business of barricading the front door, Harrison and his gun were able to ease Byers past guards at the rear.

That incident did more than convince William that all gamblers weren't the villains he had taken them to be. It cured him of pacifism, and so completely that the man who had once interfered when others wanted to fight now wasted no time in girding for war himself.

There had been no weapons in the office of the *Rocky Mountain News*, but Byers invested in rifles and shotguns enough to arm all the members of his staff as well as the composing-room crew. The editor's plan was to ambush Wood, if the gambler came after him; nor did he have long to wait.

Not being able to find their escaped prey elsewhere, Wood and others who had been at the Criterion approached the newspaper plant toward evening. As his office was on the second floor of Wootton's building, Byers watched, without being seen himself, his enemies take over a deserted log house across the street. From this position a gunman called George Steeles was at length sent as a cat's-paw.

As the men of the *News* were by then all stretched out on the floor, none of them was hit, after Steeles changed his mind about opening the door to the silent room at the head of the stairs and fired shots through it instead. He raced away then, but not very far. Missed at first, the foiled assassin was wounded when he turned to jeer from the far side of Cherry Creek. What's more, he was run down then and incontinently slain.

As for Wood, the log structure had proved more of a trap than an attacking point, and an aroused town had had enough of him. In the upshot he rode from the sight of a crowd of angry men, glad to be allowed to do so.

With guns ever ready, the *Rocky Mountain News* flourished on its own terms from that time forward, but Harrison was not one of its targets. He on his part did not remain a gambler, in point of fact. Before many months had passed, more than local strife was afoot. Charlie therefore put away his cards but kept his gun and hastened east—out of what had become Colorado Territory on February 28, 1861—to join the South.

৬৪৪ 66 ৬৪৪

Pistols for the Judge and the Senator

ONE OF THE reasons why Ned McGowan had left California in 1858 was that he had broken with Senator David Broderick, the man he had steadfastly served and who had faithfully stood by him in turn. To walk with Broderick it was necessary to agree with him; and Ned no longer could.

In his opinion his older friend, James Buchanan, was right in pursuing a course aimed at holding the nation together and the Senator was wrongheaded in joining a faction engaged in bucking the head of its own party, not to mention siding with political foes against members of Congress whom it should have regarded as colleagues. A Northerner himself, Ned had energetically fought the Southern Democrats of California, banded under the leadership of Senator Gwin; but nationally he foresaw that only the emerging Republican Party could benefit by a split between the Democrats of the agrarian South, who wanted slave labor, and the Democrats of the Northern cities, who drew their strength from slum labor, whether they wanted it or not.

Few besides McGowan were thinking in any but sectional terms, however, and minds were fixed on the problems of the older divisions of the country, never the new one. The savagery still current in Kansas was but the worst symptom of a national state of mind which need not have infected the removed coastal West. It did, though, for men of both camps forgot where they were, and remembered where they had been.

So there was a struggle to hold California for the North or the South, carried on by those who had nothing but a sentimental stake in the victory of either. They were willing to die, in a word, for regions where they had taken great pains not to live.

Inevitably the national friction separated local allies, such as Broderick and Terry had been in opposition to the Vigilantes in 1856. Three years later these Westerners belonged to factions which sneered at each other as "Yankees" or "the Chivalry"; and individual rancor sprang from group name-calling.

It could only have been because of irritation at Broderick's attacks on the South that David Terry undertook public criticism of a man with whom he had had no personal quarrel. Yet he did that in the spring of 1859.

His remarks struck at Broderick's political judgment rather than at his personal integrity, and ordinarily the Senator would probably have answered him in kind, if at all. As things stood, however, he publicly declared that he had changed his mind about considering Terry an honorable judge.

Still Chief Justice of California, the former Ranger did not call the other out. Instead he sent Broderick a note which in effect asked the other to reconsider what he had said. Firm but not sharp, it gave both the Senator and himself a chance to withdraw with dignity from the situation they had both created. Yet it was soon made clear to the Judge that Broderick did not want the episode to die a peaceful death.

Terry's term on the bench had three months to run when he received the Senator's uncompromising reply. He therefore pigeonholed it and went on with the duties he had been elected to perform.

As Broderick was a duelist who had been out a couple of times since reaching California, the quarrel between him and the man who had stabbed Hopkins had caused excitement which faded when Terry failed to take up the gauntlet. By then, though, there was another stirring topic of conversation, for in June of 1859 a man known as Old Virginny Comstock made a massive silver strike in the Washoe spur of the eastern Sierras.

Previously not many people had found any reason for wishing to stay in the western or Nevada half of Utah Territory. In addition to Genoa, where the *Territorial Enterprise* flourished, the only considerable settlement was Carson City. Named for Kit, it was important only as a repair, supply and refreshment depot for travelers who had either just finished crossing the Sierras or were on the brink of doing so.

Traffic increased enormously after silver was found in Six Mile Canyon, only fifteen miles to the north. Although the camp which sprang up had no name for many weeks, it grew by geometric progression, as more and more prospectors sent word back over the mountains that the pickings in the Washoe district were all a man could ask for and more.

But while stampeders from the Golden State were staking out claims in a realm veined with silver, Judge Terry was watching the days fall off the calendar and thinking of lead. When September finally arrived, he pointed out that he was not up for re-election and stepped down from the bench. No longer barred by his position from doing so, he next consulted dueling seconds with regard to what Broderick had said about him.

According to those who were called upon to represent the Senator, the affair could have ended with a handshake even then. But three months had only served to increase the heat of sectional partisanship, and Broderick wanted to chop Terry down. He said as much to concerned friends of his, though adding that he would give up dueling once he had dispatched the man in the offing.

As David Broderick was said to have been an excellent pistol shot, the outcome might have justified his confidence. He kept it, as a matter of fact, until he had met Judge Terry near Lake Merced, stepped off the agreed ten paces and whirled to shoot. But at that moment a factor which could have given him a decisive advantage kicked back at him. The hair trigger he'd geared for fast shooting this time fired his gun before he could bring it level. Pulling trigger with less speed but more accuracy, on the contrary, the Judge scored while the dust kicked up by the Senator's harmless bullet was still in the air.

Not promptly fatal, it was a mortal wound, as of September 16, 1859. It was likewise a wound which gaffed the inflicter.

For the partisans of the North, in especial the Vigilantes whom Terry had once defied, raised cries of "Martyrdom!" for the fallen man and "Murderer!" with respect to the one who had felled him. This was a sequel not prepared for by the original story. Although Broderick's popularity throughout the rest of California had prevented the San Francisco Committee of Vigilance from laying violent hands on him, destroying his power had been an announced and consistently pursued goal of the Fort Gunnybags usurpers. But the Senator had been killed by the one whose opposition had spilled the Committee's hopes, so the same men who had stopped at nothing they dared to, in order to break Broderick while he was alive, contrived to drip visible tears into his open coffin.

In the face of the hysterical wrath which was turned against him, Terry saw that it was useless to consider returning to the practice of law in California, at least for the time being. Accordingly he rode east across the Sierras toward the new land of opportunity, opened by the finding of silver in the mountains of Washoe.

Four months after making his treasure strike, Old Virginny

374

Comstock had not yet exercised his prerogative of naming the town which had leaped into being near where he had found what he sought. But on October 7, or about the time Terry was deciding that he and the laments for Broderick couldn't live in the same state, a rock slide knocked a whiskey bottle out of Comstock's hand and inspiration into his head. Finding that a shard of the flask still held a few drops of liquor, the prospector used them to christen Virginia City.

The fastest-growing community since San Francisco, Virginia City took the *Territorial Enterprise* away from Genoa and developed native urban features even more rapidly than had Denver. The Paiutes took a dim view of its rise to glory, nevertheless. The lakes and streams of that part of Nevada, together with the timbered Washoe mountains, made the area choice amidst barrens. Resenting the miners who pitted the grazing land and felled trees to shore up shafts, the Indians struck in the spring of 1860.

The Paiutes were then led by two able chiefs, a father and son alike named Winnemucca. Possessing something of Wild Cat's statesmanship, they had persuaded the Bannocks and Shoshones to throw in with them for the purpose of sweeping the palefaces from their hunting grounds. In launching what was called the Paiute War, the Winnemuccas were thus able to put better than a thousand warriors in the field.

Their first blow was no more than a raid on a trading station near Carson City. Still, five whites lay dead about the burning building as the Indians made off, on the night of May 7, to await developments.

Not knowing what they were up against, a hundred or so volunteers from Virginia City got on the track of the war party. With a Major Ormsby at their head, they galloped into an ambush which forty-six of them did not outlast. Indian casualties, as it was later learned, amounted to only three wounded braves.

The Winnemuccas, *père* and *fils*, went far toward accomplishing their purpose with that one victory. A quarter of Virginia City's population decided that free silver cost too much. And doubtless many more would have climbed back over the Sierras if business hadn't brought Jack Coffee Hays into the vicinity at that critical point.

The news that the famous Ranger leader was on hand was the needed morale booster for men who knew they must handle the situation but didn't know how to go about it. For there was only one military unit in the western half of Utah Territory, a detachment of 144 men commanded by a Captain Stewart.

On May 24 Hays agreed to lead volunteers against the Indians on the condition—for he knew the bent of frontiersmen to act independently—that he be given absolute military obedience. Of the two hundred who swore to jump at his command, one was Captain John Blackburn.

Believing that the Indians had grown overconfident, Jack Coffee ordered Blackburn to lead the vanguard to where scouts had told the Colonel that the Indians were camped. But at sight of any considerable body of them, the Captain and his men were to feign panic and scamper back to where the main body would be waiting at a point called Big Meadows.

On May 28, after Blackburn had successfully followed orders, the tables of the Ormsby massacre were turned. Hays and the Winnemuccas then jockeyed for position until the former saw the opportunity he wanted on June 4. Strengthened by 100 regulars by then, he attacked an estimated 800 to 1000 Indians near Pyramid Lake. When forty or fifty of the savages had fallen, the rest broke, and the Paiute War was over.

Yet if they had not succeeded in gaining their own ends, the Winnemuccas had conferred a boon on David Terry. At Virginia City the ex-Chief Justice had found a way to serve the South which was more practical than going on Golden Circle journeys into other lands. With talk of secession current below the Mason-Dixon line, not too many who voiced it worried about how an economically ill-balanced region could sustain itself—or meet the force with which those above the Line were threatening it, should speech be translated into action. But Terry not only gave thought to a question of such crucial importance, he thought he had found the answer in the great silver hoard at Washoe. Not a man of great wealth himself, though, he had been unable both to build forts at strategic points and to arm their garrisons adequately. Or he had been before Hays disbanded the volunteers on June 7.

In preparation for accepting command, Jack Coffee had sent to California for eighty first-class rifles with which he didn't wish to be burdened on his trip back to San Francisco Bay. He was for this reason glad to turn them over to his old subordinate in the Rangers, who then had the firepower he wanted.

On other Virginia City fronts Terry was opposed by a rugged Northern partisan from New York State named Bill Stewart. Formerly Attorney-General of California, Stewart fought a battle with his fellow lawyer for control of a rich property which had been discovered, as 1860 grew older, near a landmark known as the Devil's Gate.

As pawns they used no less than two federal judges, the one sent by Buchanan to replace the other. Terry then held the advantage until the pro-Northern administration of Utah Territory undertook to announce that the President's appointment was invalid. A stalemate now resulted until, while Terry was in San Francisco early in 1861, Stewart pistol-bullied an old man who knew no more of weapons than former ambassadors to Holland usually do and made him send out telegrams announcing his resignation from the judiciary.

So the legal battle for the Devil's Gate property was won by Bill. Terry still held the forts he had built on heights dominating the silver city, however; and he left men in them when he tired of lesser action and went from the West to stand fire in the real war which had broken out between the North and the South.

❦ 67 ❦

Slade of the Central Overland

AN ENGLISHMAN WHO may or may not have been the university graduate some claimed he was, Langford Peel had prospered at gambling in Leavenworth, Kansas, where he was said to have helped some down-and-outs in the bad winter of 1856. His next meeting with them took place in Salt Lake City, after the Mormon War of 1858 had made the place more cosmopolitan than it had been. The wheel of fortune having turned with classic completeness, Rucker and Conley were flush high-rollers, while Langford didn't have the money to sit in at monte or faro.

As the former refused to remember how the latter had befriended them, Peel used a chair to chase Conley from the game he was dealing in one saloon. Shortly waylaid by Rucker in another, Langford thoroughly cured him of ingratitude, albeit shot himself.

Not thankful for Gentile company at best, a crowd of lynch-minded Saints began gathering. At this crucial moment, though, friendly gamblers enlisted the aid of a Mormon bishop for forty-five dollars. A resourceful prelate, he got the wounded man out of the city garbed as a woman and took him to a haven in the suburbs.

California and sundry asserted but undescribed gunfights came next for Peel, but the early months of 1859 found him in Carson City. Only a stopping point for stages going to and from Salt Lake City at that time, it included a station of a transcontinental travel route by May.

The original San Diego–San Antonio stages had offered no more than passenger and message service between those points. In taking over the line, however, John Butterfield had seen the importance of establishing through connections between San Francisco and the great cities of the Atlantic Seaboard. Nor was more passenger traffic all that he gained. By shifting the line's eastern terminal to St. Louis, he had been able to obtain a mail-carrying contract from the government. At the end of a loop—through Arkansas to El Paso, and thence west and up the Coast—his stages brought mail from the Mississippi to the Golden Gate in twenty-four days.

But if it avoided wintriness, this route exposed travelers to harsh summer weather, nor was it as direct as the more northerly trails which had long been used by covered-wagon pilgrims. Looking where mountain men and pioneer farmers had first fared, government surveyors had, indeed, concluded that the 41st parallel offered a feasible way for the spanning of the country by fast transportation. For although the snow which seasonally piled up in high passes could and did block horse-drawn vehicles, engineers believed that steam-powered ones could negotiate paths through the Rockies and the Sierras in all weathers.

Cutting corners which the Oregon Trail had not, the trace staked out by the Topographical Engineers snipped days from former time schedules. When stages commenced wheeling and swaying along it in the spring of 1859, the extent of the service offered was described by the line's name: the Pike's Peak, California and Central Overland.

From St. Joseph, which had been founded on the Missouri by the old fur trader Joe Robidoux, the route ran northwest to Fort Kearny, then along the Platte and South Platte to Julesburg. From that northeastern Colorado station, the spur line to Denver branched off. Returning to Nebraska, as then constituted, the stages next rolled on to the new Fort Laramie, which stood near the site of the original one built by Cut Face Sublette. On they went over South Pass, haunted by Broken Hand Fitzpatrick, and so to Fort Bridger, where Old Gabe—who had leased his post to the Army—was only an occasional visitor now. They wheeled through Salt Lake City, where Brigham Young yet maintained sway in all but official government matters. They threw up dust on the way to Carson City and toiled over Donner Pass, of grisly associations. They creaked past the site of New Helvetia, for whose loss John Sutter was annually in the business of trying to get compensation from a deaf Congress. Finally, at the end of 1960 miles, they deposited passengers across the bay from the metropolis which owed its being to luckless James Marshall's find.

Now wherever the environing country wasn't so rugged as to shut out the possibility, every station on the line was automatically a settlement nucleus. Asking nothing but some sort of market center, pioneers were prompt to accept such invitations to try out new territory.

But many of these men were not of the same strain as the ones who had plodded to Oregon in search of good acreage. Some were deserters from Western military posts. Some had left California in preference to being hanged. Some were fugitives from the law elsewhere, or merely from any form of organized society. It followed that their ways of earning their sourdough bread were not always approved by others, including officials of the Central Overland. Finding itself preyed on by stock thieves and similar rogues, the line began hiring hard men to cope with them.

Of the copers, the most renowned was Captain Joseph Slade, of Illinois prior to killing a man with a rock there. Although he had served creditably in the Mexican War, nobody trailed him to see where he went or record what he did thereafter. Only one fight with Apaches, from which he was said to have emerged with a collection of eight redskin ears, gave any clue to his whereabouts between 1848 and 1859; but in the fall of the latter year he stepped back into history with the title of Superintendent of the Central Overland's Sweetwater Division.

Stretching from Julesburg westward to the Rockies, this was the line's toughest sector. In Joseph Slade, usually called Jack for reasons which have slipped from the record, it had quite literally found a trouble shooter, however.

On one occasion he rode alone up to a cabin occupied by four horse thieves, kicked the door open and shot them all. He was credited, too, if that is the correct word, with not only killing another outlaw in his shanty but burning it up, complete with a contained wife and three children.

Detective work on Slade's part, though, soon turned up the fact that one who was fattening on the line was none other than Jules Reni, the founding father of Julesburg and the Central Overland's station agent there. Although Reni left when ordered to by the line's manager, he swore to get Jack and meant it.

From ambush, somewhat later, he slung five bullets into Slade, following them up by firing a load of buckshot into his enemy's prostrate body. Yet when Jules cheerfully gave directions as to how Jack should be buried, Slade had news for him. "I shall live long enough," he announced, "to wear one of your ears on my watchguard."

Catching Reni, employees of the line hauled him up to the beam on an improvised scaffold three times, on each occasion lowering him an instant short of quietus. They let him go then, with a promise to sin no more, but that didn't satisfy Slade.

Repaired, though still carrying some of Reni's lead, he returned from St. Louis in 1860 to keep his promise to Jules. This was done after some of Slade's followers waylaid his enemy and chained the fellow to a tree in the rear of Jack's headquarters.

After leaving Reni there all night, the Sweetwater Division Superintendent strolled forth, gun in hand, and began shooting his captive in all but vital places. When Jules finally bled to death, Slade shaved off his ears with two purposes in mind. One ear he did carry for a while as a watch charm, but the other he used to amuse himself after a fashion all his own. In the presence of passengers whose clothes and bearing showed them not to have been frontiersmen he would toss the shriveled feature on the bar and demand, "Give me change for this."

Yet as he proved an effective policeman, the Central Overland winked at his idiosyncracies. And a lot of men liked him, moreover, for one of his oddities was that when not bent on viciousness, he went to the other extreme, being willing to go out of his way to help people far more than most. Because the ones he aided survived to cheer for him, while the ones he opposed died, the votes were still largely in his favor on April 12.

On that 1860 day the firm of Russell, Major and Waddell launched a subsidiary of the line known as the Pony Express. Although Butterfield still held the regular contract for mail bound to and from the Pacific Coast an arrangement was made with the government for special-delivery service, open to all who were willing to pay five dollars per letter.

On account of the loudening war talk, many were willing to pay that much to have their communications carried by hustling riders instead of lumbering stages. Then the Pony Express gallopers made for San Francisco over the short central route instead of cutting south of the Rockies and the Sierras.

Allowed only a revolver and a bowie knife for weapons, each messenger was limited to twenty pounds of mail. Thus lightly freighted, he sped for a minimum of thirty-three miles, in the course of which he used three mounts. Neither weather nor Indians were supposed to halt him, though as protection against warrior bands he had nothing to depend on but speed and a few pistol balls.

From St. Joseph the riders packed the mail to the West Coast in ten days. But as telegraph wires ran from Washoe to the Golden Gate, news could be flashed to there, at the end of eight days, from Virginia City. Only nine suns, therefore, separated the publication of a story in "Go West, young man" Greeley's New York *Tribune* and its reprinting in the San Francisco *Bulletin*, now no longer run by Tom King.

By tripling the stations along the Central Overland's route, the Pony Express multiplied the focal points for settlement, which were now only ten to fifteen miles apart. As for the main depots, they had all become towns of some sort by 1861. It followed, then, that pioneers were settled at and about Rock Creek, Nebraska Territory, the station at which James Hickok had been made agent.

Born in Illinois, Hickok was hostile, at the time, to the McCanles brothers, of North Carolina. The feud was probably sectional as to origin, although the only clear point in connection with it is that one of the brethren was responsible for having changed Hickok's nickname. That in the natural course of things had at first been "Jim." But if owning general good looks as well as yellow hair that he liked to wear long, the Overland Central and Pony Express agent had a somewhat protruding lower lip. Perceiving this flaw and observing that the otherwise handsome young man was sensitive about it, David McCanles undertook to begin calling him "Duck Bill."

The story that Hickok slew eleven of the clan to which his tormentor belonged is contradicted by the basic fact that there were but two of the name—James McCanles in addition to David; and James wasn't involved in the showdown which materialized. The tradition that Duck Bill's enemies were notorious killers is not supported by any produced evidence, either.

The only thing ascertainable is that Hickok quarreled with David McCanles and two friends of the latter (no doubt sufficiently tough characters all) in the Rock Creek station on July 12, 1861. Words led to shooting; and when the damages were assessed, it was found that McCanles, a chap called James Woods and a man remembered only as Gordon had all cashed in.

Hickok had been so little recognized before that exploit earned him grapevine headlines that many at other points along the line knew him only by the nickname McCanles had popularized. Not getting that straight, some referred to the famous new pistoleer as "Dutch Bill." But after eight stiffs had been added to the three of reality, and after heroic details had further embellished a story which has no like in the usually matter-of-fact accounts of manslaying in the West, Hickok wound up with a handsome *nom de guerre* fashioned on the framework of an insult.

For as "Bill" was accepted as his name, and "Dutch" was found too pale an epithet for the lone author of a massacre, he became known as "Wild Bill Hickok." And it was with this monicker that he went on to further feats of arms, after a new development put an end to the Pony Express in the autumn of 1861.

 68

The Baker from Nevada City

NO DOUBT THE possibly fictitious Murrieta was blamed for many acts committed by men from the other states, as well as those wrought by Mexicans and the immigrants from South America, whom Californians lumped under the name of Chilenos. Very probably, for example, the fellow who came to be represented by a head in a bottle was accused of doing things which in truth were done by one or both Tom Bells.

Of the twain in question, one was a thug who seems to have come by his appellation honestly, if nothing else. The other was a Dr. Thomas Hodges, who used the surname of his fellow rogue along with many other plundered items.

A physician from Tennessee who was credited with giving some of his victims medical care, after failing to shoot them fatally, this Tom Bell had not otherwise been criminally remarkable prior to his imprisonment in and escape from Angel's Island in 1855. But on August 12 of the following year he began a new and lengthy chapter in the history of the West by trying to hold up public transportation. Specifically, he did what no one had thought of before by setting a snare for the stage running from Camptonville to Marysville.

Because a feminine passenger was shot to death as the vehicle sped away, Tom (Bell) Hodges was hanged in October of 1856. Yet he left a legacy comprising more than state robbery and the railroad raiding which inevitably grew out of it. The front of respectability behind which he operated must have served as a model for a younger but aspiring California crook.

Once of Connecticut, Henry Plummer had opened the Empire Bakery at Nevada City three years before Tom was brought up

384

short at the end of a rope. Only nineteen in 1856, he was at once the town's marshall and the lover of Mrs. John Vedder. Caught in her boudoir by Mr. Vedder, he responded to the husband's indignation by executing him with a bullet.

Given only ten years in San Quentin by a friendly jury, Plummer reduced it to two by feigning galloping consumption. When he had been released, via a gubernatorial pardon to die outside, though, he hastened back to Nevada City and killed one Jim Ryder in a cathouse brawl, after first having nearly killed another fellow under similar circumstances. In between whiles, besides, Henry had taken time out to raid the Wells Fargo Express office which had been established in the newly booming Washoe district.

Although he had escaped indictment with respect to the Wells Fargo case, Plummer was jailed for his second murder in the fall of 1859. Behind bars, he made or renewed the acquaintance of another man who was awaiting trial in the person of Billy Mayfield.

Because they killed a jailer and escaped, neither appeared in court. Instead, they sped north to the newly admitted State of Oregon. Under other circumstances, they might have been in danger of extradition proceedings there, but Plummer quashed them in advance by arranging to have the news published in California that he and Mayfield had been lynched by Oregonians.

With his trail thus covered, Henry went to the so far unorganized section of the Pacific Northwest known as Idaho. Gold had been discovered on the therefore named Oro Fino Creek in 1858, starting a stampede which was still in progress.

After murdering and robbing the owner of a gaming establishment in the settlement of Oro Fino, Plummer continued with his travels and, as 1860 opened, was banking games with the proceeds himself. But though he had cut something of a felonious swath, he still hadn't found a place to use what Dr. Hodges, alias Tom Bell, had impressed on the mind of a criminal genius.

Billy Mayfield, in the meantime, seems to have parted from

385

Plummer before Henry went to Idaho. In any case he had turned up in Nevada by 1860, rating as one of Virginia City's considerable corps of dangerous men.

These were not necessarily crooks, or even professional gamblers. For a refinement of manslaying had evolved in the West which had nothing to do with the practicalities of self-preservation or the willingness to kill in order to acquire. Nor did it really spring from animal bad temper, as in the case of the anthropoid Joe Stokes had cooled off with a hot cigar. It was hatched out of pride in the craft of being able to shoot straight with the chips down, and only other gunmen were considered fair game by true practitioners of the sport.

If it doubtless had a California ancestry, the game of seeing who could get to be, and stay, "Chief" seems to have emerged as a formally recognized institution in Nevada. Charlie Harrison's leadership of the gamblers of Denver was not the same thing, for he was liked as well as followed. But the chief, in the Virginia City sense, was the cock of the saloons only because he had killed any challengers. Once atop, furthermore, he recognized every other gunny in town as an aspirant who might any day try to replace him in the only way possible.

Ritual wasn't honored as uniformly as in the case of the guardians of the Golden Bough, to be sure. At least one chief broke the rules by bullying men with no claims to gunfighting ability and died a repentant fourflusher.

But when Langford Peel decided to leave Carson City for the place which had dwarfed it, Old Virginny's town gained a chief who was a stickler for etiquette. Nothing of a swashbuckler, he was courteous to all except his challengers; nor did he ever seek any unfair advantage in a fight.

On described occasions, indeed, he didn't even draw until his opponent was gun-in-hand. Having laughed at one fellow's challenge, Peel strolled away, keeping his back turned while his excited opponent missed him several times. Casually Langford then turned and killed the other with one shot.

There was also the time, in 1861, when a man known only as

Eldorado Johnnie thought he had perfected his skill sufficiently to be able to take over. After donning his best clothes and getting well barbered for the occasion, Johnnie searched for the man who held the office he aspired to.

Although there are two versions as to just what happened when Peel was located, they both had the same ending, so one will suffice. The head gunman was playing cards when Johnnie thrust a pistol within inches of his rival's face and announced, "I'm Chief." "You're a liar," Langford answered, shooting him by way of proof.

Henry Plummer, as of 1861, had joined the stampede to Idaho's Clearwater district, where a man called Lewis had found gold. In addition to killing several men in Lewiston himself, Henry became a leader of other manslayers. Turning the example set by Tom Bell at last to account, moreover, he operated as a baker who was as shocked as any other citizen at the activities of his gang. And when a vigilance committee was formed to combat the criminals he was directing, Plummer promptly became a member.

At length fearing that he was suspected, though, Henry went to Nevada during the winter of 1861–1862. But as that region had been separated from Utah and organized as a separate territory during the previous February, his move was a mistake. For Virginia City was filled with former Californians, and he was spotted by some that knew of his activities west of the Sierras.

Turned over to U.S. Marshal John Blackburn, who had served in the Paiute War under Hays, Plummer was jailed in Carson City, the territorial capital. While Henry was sweating out extradition proceedings, however, Billy Mayfield undertook to see what he could do in the way of springing his old friend.

Wise in the ways of jailers, it can be gathered, Billy began kibitzing at the poker games with which the turnkeys and some associates whiled away the time. Fortune favored his loyalty, for the time arrived when all but Mayfield were breathlessly watching the respective holders of a king-high flush and a queen-high flush raising each other's bets. As Billy summed up the situation,

"I knew that if I couldn't do it then, I'd never get a better chance."

So Plummer was free to return to Idaho, where Mayfield didn't go until after he was called on by John Blackburn. Finding his prisoner gone and knowing that Henry and Billy had once been associates, the Marshal guessed what had happened. He should have been readier to shoot, however, when he prodded the outlaw with a revolver and demanded Plummer's whereabouts. Sidestepping the muzzle, Mayfield slashed the officer to death with his bowie.

Put where Plummer had been, on that account, Billy was freed in turn by a pair of Carson City citizens whom he'd hardly met. Although said to have been normally law-abiding, these Westerners held such strong views on the right of self-defense that they burrowed under the prison and gave Mayfield the means of speeding to Idaho himself.

In that region he followed Blackburn underground a year to fifteen months later. In the spring of 1863 Billy was dry-gulched at Placerville, Idaho, by a man called Evans, with whom Mayfield had quarreled over cards but spared the night before, because the other wasn't armed.

৪৩ 69 ৪৩

A Bluff at Pinos Altos

ONE EFFECT OF the war being waged by the North and the South was that it deprived parts of the West of badly needed garrisons. This was especially the case in the Santa Cruz Valley, where protection was needed against not only the Apaches but Sonoran bandits.

In combination they sacked Tubac in August of 1861. Except for a hardy friend of Poston's named Pete Kitchen, who had built and manned a fortlike hacienda near the old Spanish settlement of Calabasas, all the whites who had been ranching in the

388

area moved elsewhere. Or if they didn't get out of the region entirely, they withdrew behind the walls of Tucson, itself restored to isolation by ceased stage service.

Mining officials held on for a little longer, but when their Mexican hands joined the raiders, even diehards saw that they had to leave. In some instances the decision was made too late. Poston's younger brother was one who was slain; but Charles himself and the later famous, but then unknown, engineer Raphael Pumpelly kept their footing in chaos.

Cut off by Apaches from retreating by way of the Gila Valley, they described a horseback arc in northern Mexico. There they were trailed at first by Sonoran banditti and then by American ones, led by a refugee from California known as One-eyed Jack. Outmaneuvering these, though, they reached Colorado City and dined at the Great Western's inn before crossing the river.

But though he next went East to campaign in Virginia under his friend General Heintzelman, Charles still had the West in mind. At the end of the one year for which he had volunteered, he quit the service, having thought of a way to return to Arizona under conditions which would make mining there again possible. In brief, he went to Washington, at the end of 1862, with a plan for organizing Arizona Territory which he thought the federal administration would listen to.

As of August 1, 1861, in the meantime, Arizona had been given territorial status by the Confederacy, which had appointed John Baylor, a former Ranger leader, as governor. As in the case of all previous administrative schemes the map of this Arizona was not the one of later shape. Its capital Mesilla on the Rio Grande, the territory was modern New Mexico and Arizona south of the 34th parallel.

It was to this region that Gran Oury and Ned McGowan returned in the winter of 1861–1862. After listening to Abraham Lincoln's inaugural address in March, politically consistent Ned had gone south to stand with the wing of the Democratic party which he held guiltless of causing the split which had put the White House in Republican hands. Oury meanwhile was Confederate Arizona's territorial delegate. Meeting in Richmond, the two agreed to round up the Southern borderers west of the Rio Grande and enlist them in a unit called the Arizona Battalion.

The men they gathered to serve under the Stars and Bars were said to have constituted the largest band of ready knife-and-pistol killers ever assembled in the West. The dean of Arizona's borderers was not among them, however, for Lieutenant Jack Swilling was already serving in another Confederate unit.

On April 15, 1862, as a matter of fact, Jack captained such Confederate forces as participated in the only War-between-the-States engagement fought west of the Great Divide. A federal unit known as the California Column was pressing east from Fort Yuma at the time, and on the day in question Swilling intercepted a detachment of the vanguard, Lieutenant James Barrett commanding.

A dozen or so to the side, the skirmishing took place halfway between Tucson and the Gila River at a point along the Santa Cruz called Picacho Pass. There Barrett's men retreated, after their leader had been killed, but the capture of Tucson by the California Column was only briefly delayed.

For reasons which had to do with his past, Jack did not retreat into Texas with the rest of his outfit when General Sibley ordered the withdrawal of Confederate troops from the Southwest in June of 1862. Although it is not clear at exactly what moment he detached himself from the service, there are indications that he didn't think it wise to venture even as far east as Mesilla.

In any case he spent some of the ensuing months prospecting with Jacob Snively. He was also with Herman Ehrenberg, who that year gave Arizona the new boom-town of La Paz by striking a sizable gold field along the Colorado.

All this treasure chasing while Swilling had not been able to organize a strong enough expedition to make it feasible for him to return to the Hassayampa River for prospecting purposes. Running through mountains where Apaches abounded, it was a stream which couldn't be safely probed by small groups.

In 1862, though, the mountain man who had come to be

known as Uncle Joe Walker decided to plumb the truth of long-standing rumors that gold had been seen in still unexploited ranges in the Southwest. Because of his reputation, he was able to enlist a following large enough to stand off any mountain-Apache war party of normal strength. While the warriors of the plains might ride to battle a thousand strong, these hillmen—who in general would rather eat a horse than ride one—trotted through their rocky fastnesses in less numerous bands.

After the Walker Party had made one fruitless trip through the gallimaufry of ranges between the Colorado and the Rio Grande, Jack Swilling joined it in 1863. As it mustered thirty-four rifles, he found the firepower he had been looking for and led the way to the stream in which he'd seen gold as a Gila Ranger over three years earlier.

The gold was still waiting in the Hassayampa, but its seekers didn't stop to prospect at large then. Wishing to see the extent of the treasure field, Walker insisted on swinging east again, and in doing so led the way into the domain of Mangas Colorado.

Here was an Apache chief who had enough braves at his back to make trouble for Uncle Joe's frontiersmen. Because Mangas had already done so in the case of other whites, a strong detachment of the California Column was trying to corral him at the time. Disdaining soldiers who were too inexperienced in mountain warfare to be able to keep up with him, though, Mangas began dogging the Walker Party.

Fearsome as the reputation of Mangas Colorado was, however, it made no impression on Joe, who had been fighting Indians for forty years and more. As an old mountain man, besides, he was of the faith that all redskin hostilities must be met with counter-measures lest worse should follow. Not that any of his own men had yet been killed, but they found other white men whom the Apaches had dealt with. Three, for instance, had been suspended by their heels from tree branches over fires which had begun burning their heads away before they died.

Having appointed Swilling second in command, because of Jack's knowledge of the country, Walker now gave him a large order. Although the Apaches led by Mangas were too numerous to be dispersed, Joe told his lieutenant to round up the chief and hold him as hostage.

They were then near Pinos Altos, where Jack had pulled Snively, McGowan and others out of the fist of this same chief in 1860. Tracking the Apaches with fifteen men, Swilling discovered that a favorite rendezvous of the Indians was a spot in the vicinity of an abandoned prospector's cabin. As it commanded a view of one of the runways leading to and from this trysting place, Swilling moved into it one night.

The lone buried ace which Jack had to call upon was the fact that Mangas knew that troops in the command of General Joseph West were also seeking him during that spring of 1863. Aware himself that the chief would have found he was in the area and would go looking for him, Swilling felt pretty sure that Mangas would walk into the wholly imaginary trap he had set.

According to the written account left by one who was watching with Swilling, this happened at daybreak. Having spotted Apaches on the move and having easily picked out Mangas Colorado because he was a tower of a man among a commonly short people, Jack stopped the Indians with a ferocious war whoop. As coolly as though he were indeed guarded by all the guns he claimed to have been trained upon the Apaches, he now strode alone to meet them.

At six-foot-three, Jack had to look up at the six-foot-six chief, upon whose shoulder he placed a captor's hand. To the other Indians, at the same time, he curtly explained, in the bastard Spanish which was the lingua franca of the Southwest, that their chief would be safe as long as they behaved themselves.

Although Walker and Swilling meant to keep faith, after the latter had counted that poker coup, the ability to do so was taken out of their hands. Discovering that the Walker Party had the buck they had been vainly chasing, the troops took charge of him. Nor did he live long thereafter. After singeing him with hot cleaning rods as the chief dozed by a campfire, a couple of soldiers shot him for objecting.

By then the man who had captured him was on the way back to the Hassayampa. Along it and its branches he and those with him spent the rest of 1863 scooping up deposits of golden flakes or picking up nuggets like boys gathering nuts that have fallen to the ground. From the slopes of an eminence justly named Rich Hill, for example, Jack plucked $11,000 worth of little, twisted aureate chunks.

As other parties had followed Walker's out of California, the previously unsearched highlands of central Arizona were swarming with prospectors. One was Pauline Weaver, formerly a guide of Cooke's Mormon Battalion. Another was Bunk Bradshaw, once with Frémont under the Bear Flag. After making the strike, though, which gave his name to the Bradshaw Mountains, the man from North Carolina's Buncombe County proved unable to stand prosperity. Retiring to the ferry he had established in the general vicinity of Needles, he celebrated so enthusiastically that he got d.t.'s. In despair because of the visions which then haunted him, he cut his throat by the Colorado before the year was out.

Yet because of Charles Poston's activities in Washington, gold finders were not the only white men drawn to the region of their happy hunting during the winter of 1863–1864. Succeeding where others had failed, Poston had talked Lincoln's administration into creating Arizona as a territory of the United States.

He had been able to do this because California's gold supply had come to be recognized, by leaders of the North, as the quickest means of developing its industrial might to the point necessary for victory in a dingdong war. The gold had to keep flowing, and the Central Overland road was not dependable in winter for horse-powered vehicles. The best all-weather route available to the North ran through the Gadsden Purchase as far as the Rio Grande Valley, through which it could connect with the Santa Fe trail. Yet because of the many Confederate sympathizers and the few policing soldiers south of the Gila, the road was—Charles stressed—dubiously feasible.

What he pointed out, however, was that the vehicular route would be usable by Union transportation, were the territory federally administered. While granting that Mesilla and adjacent eastern points of the Purchase could be satisfactorily governed by an administration seated at Santa Fe, Poston insisted that most of the region was too remote from New Mexico's capital. He had therefore proposed a vertical division of the territory, of which the western half should be directed from a capital located north of the Gila.

His proposal having been voted into effect in February of 1863, territorial officers were in due course appointed. But as the first governor of Arizona Territory died without ever seeing his domain, it was not until August that an administration in search of a capital began moving west.

Aside from the fact that it was ordered to avoid Tucson in particular and all the other known settlements of Arizona as well, the peripatetic government had no locational preferences in a vast region. After reaching northeastern Arizona late in December, however, its territorial officers learned that gold had at last drawn white men to some part of it other than the Gadsden Purchase. So in January of 1864 the government began functioning in the lee of a temporary Army post called Fort Whipple.

A part of the wandering administration but not with it, Poston returned to Arizona, by way of the Isthmus of Panama and California, as the new territory's Indian agent. In this capacity he was, of course, given a guard of troops. He had thus arranged not only to have the region from which he had been driven made habitable for him once more, but he had had his fare back paid via a route which guaranteed him a magnificent mileage allowance.

৪০৪ 70 ৪০৪

The Grouse upon the Cadaver

ALTHOUGH JACK SLADE controlled his division of the Central Overland Stage Line to the satisfaction of all except the bandits he rejoiced to rub out, he could not control himself. A chronic heavy boozer, he was nasty in his cups, doing things for which he apologized when sober.

He had a way of shooting very close to people just to see them jump. Or in order to have a good time himself, he would spoil everybody else's fun by riding into a saloon and shooting it up.

Still the bachelor West had a robust sense of humor, and as Jack paid for the damages and made handsome verbal amends, men laughed at the close of an episode and were glad to see him again. When not on a tear, he had a winning personality. As acute an observer as Sam Clemens testified strongly to that effect. Going west with his brother Orion, who had been appointed lieutenant-governor, following the creation of Nevada Territory, young Mark Twain was at Julesburg in August of 1861.

The man Mark met and the man whose ferocity and wild antics he had heard about did not, as Sam noted, seem the same people. Inevitably, though, the two halves of his personality grew closer together. Unchecked and always pardoned, his savage sprees became more frequent, while his pleasant phase forever held the beast in him more thinly under control.

Because of his efficiency in protecting the line, the Central Overland took no notice of his social offenses. Slade was still a prized officer when, in 1862, the line changed its route.

The cause was similar to the situation which had unleashed havoc in the Gadsden Purchase a year earlier. The garrisons of the West and of the northern Mississippi Valley had been stripped of strength, if not pulled out in toto, in order to provide more troops for the war on the South. Deciding that the paleface was at last in retreat, the Yankton Sioux struck to hasten his going in the summer of 1862.

In Minnesota they raided settlement after settlement, burning, torturing and slaying, as well as kidnaping many women and children. They also destroyed Sioux Falls, the lone town in Dakota Territory, which had been organized only the year before.

Fearing that the Yanktons would swoop farther south, the Central Overland ran its main line through Denver. By cutting north to the 41st-parallel route from there, the stage road would, it was hoped, avoid the attention of the rampaging hostiles.

One effect of the change was to put Denver and its protecting military post in Slade's bailiwick. If the purpose of Fort Halleck was to overawe the Indians, its officers soon found an unexpected enemy. Riding into the military post with a band of soused cronies at his back, the Central Overland's division superintendent shot up the sutler's store in which the fort's troops were regaling themselves.

The commander of Fort Halleck wasn't interested in hearing what Jack had to say after he emerged from his bender. He notified the Central Overland that it would have to get rid of its troublesome trouble shooter, and that without delay. Inasmuch as the line depended upon the cooperation of the Army at sundry points, it had no choice but to comply. The man detailed to notify Slade that he was fired was not happy about the assignment; he later recalled figuring that his chances of not being shot were no better than fifty-fifty. But as Slade was having one of his mild days, the severance took place, in the fall of 1862, without bloodshed.

Henry Plummer, meanwhile, had left comparatively settled western Idaho Territory for the huge esatern extension of it beyond the Rockies. Upon returning to Oro Fino, following the jail escape in Nevada which Billy Mayfield had engineered, Henry had encountered several Californians who knew more about his past than he found desirable. To shake that handicap, he went where the odds against meeting old acquaintances were at first enormous.

Montana at the time contained only one settlement, that at Deer Lodge. Only weeks old when Plummer arrived, it was peopled by Minnesota refugees from the area overrun by the Yankton Sioux. But as gold was discovered at Grasshopper Creek not much later, the winter of 1862–1863 saw a stampede into what had been the most remote of frontiers.

Bannack City was the metropolis to which Grasshopper Diggings gave birth. Like all previous wonder towns of the West it drew a mixture of young hopefuls, not so young but also honest pioneers trying for the success they'd missed elsewhere, a few restless men of some previous achievement, some decent enough gamblers, a lot of chameleons, ready to take their character from the tone of any community they might be in, and a plethora of determined bad hands.

Perhaps the worst the West ever fostered, Plummer went to booming Bannack City early in 1863. By then, though, his past, in the form of another gunny named Jack Cleveland, had caught up with him. Under what circumstances they had met before has not been shown, but in eastern Idaho they were inseparable for less than sentimental reasons. Each fearing that the other would tell what he knew, and each confident that the other would kill to preserve silence, they lived together so that they could keep track of one another.

It was said of Plummer that he could draw and fire five well-aimed shot within three seconds. Considering the cumbersome revolver of that period, his trigger speed was phenomenal. It didn't impress Jack Cleveland, though; at least it failed to one day in the spring of 1863 that found him in his cups.

Locating Henry in a saloon, Cleveland made war talk which included the announcement that he was Chief. He wasn't, because Plummer wearied, as he declared, of listening to the other's palaver and shot him in the stomach. Felled, Jack cried, "Don't shoot me while I'm down!" To do Plummer justice, he didn't take that advantage, but when his opponent staggered to his feet, Henry drilled him twice more.

As there was ample testimony that Cleveland had threatened Plummer's life, the latter was acquitted when tried for that manslaying. Yet because of Cleveland he had another on his mind. Arriving at the scene of the shooting after Henry had left, Sheriff Hank Crawford had conversed with the expiring target. What they had talked about wasn't disclosed, but when Plummer learned of the interview, he decided that Crawford was the bearer of information about his past which he had hoped to bury with Cleveland.

397

Too wise to accept challenges, or to fall into any of several out-of-town ambushes which Henry had prepared, the Sheriff eventually fired at his would-be killer while Plummer was watching the wrong door. As the rifle bullet lodged in the outlaw's pistol hand, it caused a temporary respite for the officer, but he had had enough of Bannack City. Handing in his star, Crawford went back to Minnesota and the arms of a bride awaiting him there.

He had plenty of other reasons to consider himself lucky to have got safe away from Beaverhead County. Cutthroats, many of them former members of Henry's Oro Fino gang, converged on Bannack City in unparalled abundance percentagewise. In point of fact the appalling situation which the Vigilance Committee of 1856 only imagined to be existent by the Golden Gate was an actuality of the Grasshopper and Beaverhead diggings. Murder stalked, and decent citizens who knew of its forays found it well to keep their knowledge to themselves.

The great strike at Alder Gulch, from which a new Virginia City sprouted in May of 1863, did more than recruit additional killers for southwestern Montana. It rounded out a crime-ruled principality which boasted two capitals.

There were peace officers at Bannack City, to be sure. Following whispered words to the wise, Henry Plummer had been elected sheriff. Then at his request the sheriff of Madison County resigned during the summer, and after that Henry wore the star of Virginia City, too.

The gang which exacted tribute from the cited towns and the surrounding countryside had a leader, naturally, and that was likewise Plummer. Many people had at least some inkling of this. They knew, for instance, that he was a regular caller at Rattlesnake Ranch, which was the hangout for Bannack City toughs. Nobody asked the Sheriff why he frequented such company, though, for nobody wanted to be the repository of perilous knowledge.

For the region was one in which men were disappearing. It was one in which masked and blanket-swathed creatures held up stages or horseback travelers with sawed-off shotguns. Resisters were killed; and sometimes those who cooperated were at least wounded. A man known as Dutch Fred was shot in one arm by a faceless bandit who told him that if he was found with only five dollars in his kick again, he would be killed.

A massacre, too, became common knowledge. After he had left Bannack City to take his mule train through the mountains to eastern Idaho, Lloyd Magruder and four with him had been murdered. Still it was the men who newslessly vanished that daunted the rest—now afraid to ask questions for fear of being the next to drop from sight.

One silent inhabitant of the port of missing men did turn up, nevertheless. And helpless revenant though he was, he put the finger of accusation on Plummer and his entire tribe.

During December of 1863 a Nicholas Tbalt had accepted money for a team of mules he had agreed to sell. Promising to deliver them to purchasing partners, he then left for no one could say where. A couple of weeks later, though, one William Palmer was coursing along a trail in a wagon. Being a frontiersman, he both had a gun with him and was keeping an eye out for pot meat.

Flushing grouse, Palmer stopped to shoot, and killed one of the birds on the wing. Plummeting into a clump of brush, it landed on Tbalt's body, where the huntsman soon found it.

Had the murder and its subsequent discovery taken place at another time of the year, buzzards, maggots or what not would have rendered recognition improbable. But the cold seasonal weather of these uplands had preserved the man alike from decay and creatures which delight in it. It preserved the story of what had happened to him, too, from the blood-rimmed hole near one eye to the grooves in the frozen flesh which showed where a lariat had bitten in as he was dragged behind a horse to a place of concealment. Then knowing the man, the discoverer knew not only the cause of the crime but the road along which it had taken place. For the disappearance of Tbalt, complete with the sold mules and the money he had been paid in advance for them, had led local gossip to declare that he had absconded.

So now at last people knew what had happened to dozens who had mysteriously lost touch with ken. And the manner in which the truth had been pointed out to them seemed like a message from deity to men accustomed to think of Heaven as an aerial realm. As the grouse had dropped from the sky to tell the answer to a dread riddle, it appeared to Palmer and those with whom he had shared his news that they had a directive from God to do something about it.

Although there had been talk of vigilante action before, it had begot nothing, in part because of the feeling that the surrounding vicious circle was too big to cope with and in part because people had been able to detect no starting point in it. With the finding of Tbalt's body, though, inertia was a thing of the past. Having a course to pursue, the Vigilantes of Bannack City organized under the leadership of Colonel W. F. Sanders and got on the trail of murder.

Gravitating to the strong side, through the nature of their beings, the characterless drifters had teamed up with crime to make the odds against its opposers greater even than they would otherwise have been. But as the Vigilantes first suspected one of these barnacles—a wight known only as Long John—he swiftly changed sides and talked. If John didn't know the gang's entire anatomy, he knew who had done some things, the killing of Tbalt included.

While the Vigilantes caught the accused George Ives at a gang outpost, they nearly lost him on the way back to town. Honoring a custom of the country, someone proposed a horse race, when they had reached a suitable level stretch, and it developed that the man with the swiftest steed was the prisoner. In a fairly run contest George would have won the roses of freedom, but by picking up fresh mounts, the Vigilantes wore his down and recaptured him.

As Ives denied everything, he had to be given a people's-court trial, which was held in Nevada City, Idaho. In spite of that change of venue, there was a determined effort by the thugs of

Bannack City and their sympathizers to have proceedings called off. Yet as the firmness of Colonel Sanders prevailed, George Ives was found guilty of first-degree murder on December 21 and was forthwith strung up.

Acting next upon information supplied either by Long John or some similar informer, the Vigilantes made a night swoop on a ranch which resulted in the capture of a pair respectively named G. W. Brown and Red Yager. If the former turned out to be nothing more interesting than a villain who whined when handed his bill, the other was the salmon of knowledge for which the honest citizens of Bannack City had been fishing.

For in trapping a man who turned out to have been a gun and victim go-between, they found themselves in possession of a fellow who had gone so far along roads he hadn't meant to travel that he was relieved at having been caught. Showing no fear of what he knew to be in store for him and saying that he didn't want to live any longer anyhow, Red Yager described in detail the gang, of which he named Henry Plummer as the leader. Though unable to account for quite a few disappearances, furthermore, he cited 102 Plummer gang killings.

On January 4, 1864, Yager and Brown were hanged along a Styx-like stream called the Stinkingwater. As the man who had been their chief had, of course, no inkling of Red's confession, he was alone, unarmed and about to retire when called upon some days later by men who knew his history. Many times a murderer and the instigator of scores of waylayings and assassinations, Sheriff Plummer moaned, wept and pleaded, when he found what the Vigilantes had come to do, in the manner of an infant that's trying to avoid taking medicine.

He was, he wailed, too wicked to die. But as others thought that plea was really an admission against interest, it availed him nothing. He was dropped from aloft in Bannack City on January 10, and so were his two deputies for that town, Ned Ray and Buck Stinson.

In Virginia City, the reign of malignance was not challenged until after the news of Plummer's execution reached it. Organizing with the aid of friends from Bannack City, then, Vigilantes swung a seine that netted five of what had been the Sheriff's gang on January 14.

Of them all only the most depraved kept his chin up while on the brink of what they had cheerfully visited upon others. Boone Helm was a Kentuckian who had developed a zest for cannibalism after moving West to escape the consequences of having other bestial proclivities. As he had no manifested ethics, and as he had not troubled to put his gun at the service of the Confederacy, it is anybody's vote as to why his last phrases should have occurred to him. It was nonetheless recorded of Boone that he cried, "Every man for his principles! Hurrah for Jeff Davis! Let her rip!" And with that last word he jumped to stretch the rope before anybody could pull the platform out from under him.

Having arrived there the previous fall, Jack Slade was one of the Vigilantes of Virginia City. Outside of it he had established a horse ranch in an effort to settle down which ingrained habits defeated. Used to a following of men who took his cue, he couldn't abide the solitude of a rancher's life. He therefore sought companionship in a town where he had to frequent saloons to find it, and when in drink he couldn't keep his hand away from his gun.

Had he understood human nature better, the man from Julesburg would have known that what was true of pistol killers was also true of citizen hangmen. As with each new victim the act of taking a life was performed with less hesitation, the grounds which justified manslaying became more comprehensive. It thus came about that where Vigilantes once had had to brace themselves to exact retribution from a murderer, they came to be able to do away with people for lesser offenses.

Slade did not kill or rob anybody at Virginia City, but his gun-bullying and his disregard of other people's nerves and property became more and more irritating. Although warned by his fellow Vigilantes, Jack defied them, revolver in hand, and went on to heights of barbarous horseplay which ended with holding Judge Alexander Davis as a hostage against reprisal.

Sobering, Slade apologized to the Judge, but it was too late. The men of Virginia City could have banished him, as they had done in the case of lesser members of the destroyed Plummer gang. But they paid no attention to suggestions that this be done, or to Jack's own abject prayers and tears for the wife they insisted on making a widow. Never having had to answer for some brutal crimes of his, the man who had been the bane of countless bandit foes of the Central Overland was hanged on March 10, 1864, for being a public nuisance.

If the Vigilantes had pretty well scraped the bottom of the barrel with that execution, the noise of their necessary activities had been heard in Washington. Doubtless Henry Plummer would have been among the last to believe that he had ever accomplished a public service, yet in some measure he must be considered the sponsor of a huge division of the United States. From the civic point of view the lesson taught by his sheriff-gang leader activities was that counties across the Rockies from the rest of it could not be properly governed by Idaho. After doing the necessary planning, then, the national administration announced, as of May 1864, the creation of Montana Territory, Bannack City its capital.

৩৩ 71 ৩৩

The Message of the Ditches

THE NORTH'S CIVIL WAR and the South's War between the States took some toll of noted Western characters. Under the leadership of General Ben McCulloch, Richard Weightman died for the South in the Battle of Wilson's Creek, fought in Missouri in August of 1861. During the following March, McCulloch himself fell in the course of the Arkansas conflict known to his side as the Battle of Elkhorn but to the North as that of Pea Ridge.

In May of 1863 Charlie Harrison, by that time a Confederate colonel, took his last ride. Because of his former residence in the Southwest, Charlie had been detailed by General Holmes to recruit what men he could in New Mexico. Some there were known to have fled from Missouri in order to avoid federal conscription, and the General hoped they would rally for the purpose of regaining a state which Union forces had all but overrun.

From the Confederate foothold in southwestern Missouri, Harrison led a detachment of only seventeen men into Oklahoma. Because Kansas was a Northern state, the Santa Fe Trail could not be safely used, but Charlie planned to parallel it, keeping about fifteen miles south of the Jayhawk border.

While he and his men were in Osage country, however, they were attacked in strength by members of that tribe. Although Harrison led a charge which routed the Indians, more bands kept rushing to the scene. When they were present in overwhelming numbers a massacre took place of which there were only two survivors. Not one of them, Charlie remained at the site of the engagement; abbreviated, however. The Osages were redskins who collected the entire head instead of merely the scalp.

Harrison's mentor, Kit Carson, had better Indian-fighting luck than his pupil, albeit with the advantage of a sizable command. During the winter of 1861–1862 Kit had shared Union defeats while General Sibley's Confederates had been briefly triumphant in New Mexico. Following the expulsion of Sibley, though, the eastern Apaches had become so obstreperous that Carson had been ordered by General Carleton to kill all men of that tribe, "whenever and wherever found."

As the upshot of the campaigns that followed, New Mexico's Apaches accepted reservation life or left to join the still untrammeled bands in Arizona. But by then the Navajos had become a serious problem, and in June of 1863 Kit was ordered to proceed against that numerous and canyon-entrenched people.

Except for the treaty which Doniphan had extracted, through

the show of arms rather than by the use of them, the Navajos had never been challenged. Growing in boldness, they had supplanted the Apache as a general territorial peril when Colonel Carson rammed war down their throats in July. Attacking them in the great gashes in the earth where they had always been safe from harassment before, he killed and captured so many that numbers were voluntarily surrendering by September.

In another two months there was nothing left of Navajo resistance outside of the tribe's natural citadel, Canyon de Chelly. Snow slowed the cracking of that picturesque nut, but by March of 1864 Kit had winnowed 3500 Indians out of precipitous depths thirty winding miles long.

When these and the 4500 previously rounded up had been put on reservation, Indian warfare in the Southwest was largely conducted by the pioneers of Arizona, as well as the soldiers on duty there. Of the latter, none belonged to the Arizona Battalion.

After it had been organized by Gran Oury, Ned McGowan and another former resident of Tucson called Philemon Herbert, that unit appears to have conducted about the first grand-scale cattle drives in the history of Texas. Having the assignment of supplying Confederate forces in Mississippi and Louisiana with beef, the battalion probably raided the vast herds of northern Mexico in addition to rounding them up on the western Texas frontier. There, because ranches were ill tended or not at all, following the departure of so many men for the front, the longhorns throve and multiplied as mavericks for anyone's catching.

By the spring of 1863, however, the Arizona Battalion had been assigned to the command of General Dick Taylor, the son of Old Rough and Ready, who was campaigning against General Banks in western Louisiana. In an amphibious engagement fought at Bayou Teche the Confederates had but one vessel, a gunboat called the *Diana*, but as the stream was only one gunboat wide, it could and did hold off the federal flotilla for hours. Captured by Confederate troops after it had run aground, the *Diana* was largely manned, in this desperate action, by volunteers from the Arizona Battalion.

405

In command, after Captain Oliver Semmes, son of Raphael of the *Alabama,* was wounded, Ned McGowan was seized, after the *Diana* blew up, and penned up for a couple of months in New Orleans. But when, in June of 1863, an effort was made to convey him and fellow Confederate officers to confinement in the North, Ned and Semmes successfully plotted to take over the prison ship *Maple Leaf* and ran it ashore in Virginia.

From there McGowan and other officers of the Arizona Battalion were returned to their unit. If Ned did not return to the Southwest after the outfit was disbanded, Gran Oury did, but only after some hesitation.

At first he joined a group of Confederate officers, of whom General David Terry was one, who had decided not to live in a nation which had been put together again by force of arms. In caravan a group of them and their families entered Mexico with a determination to settle there. Yet it was a plan that did not survive further acquaintance with a country which neither offered them what they wanted nor had any reason to welcome them. After some desultory wandering, therefore, Terry returned to California, and Gran rejoined his brother William at Tucson.

Arrived there late in 1865, Oury resumed the practice of law and the pursuit of politics. An immediate goal, for example, was to win for Arizona's metropolis what the prejudice of the national administration had denied it. The unrooted government authorized by Lincoln had finally found a home in a mountain settlement named Prescott; but the citizens of Tucson were bound to have the capital located there.

Poston was no longer a resident, for he had gone East as the territory's first Congressional delegate. Jack Swilling lived there for a portion of 1865, but by the time of Gran Oury's return Jack had been lured back to the valley of the Hassayampa. West of that stream one Henry Wickenburg had made a fabulous gold find which he dubbed the Vulture Mine, and a town named for the miner had come into being which proffered the twin advantages of business opportunity and boom-town excitement.

Wickenburg offered Swilling Indian-fighting excitement, too, for the Yavapai Apaches were constantly on the warpath. On one occasion they slew two men within a stone's toss of the town limits, while unprepared residents helplessly watched. An organizer of the Arizona Volunteers, Jack led eye-for-eye attacks, as well as counterraids which were sometimes successful in rescuing kipnaped children.

His fighting wasn't limited to Apaches, to be sure. In October of 1867, which happened to be the year in which Tucson accomplished its aim of taking the capital away from Prescott, Swilling's life was threatened by a Chileno, who may or may not have come from Chile, called José Gonzalez. Said to have been a justice of the peace at the time, Jack not only blew José down with a load of buckshot but deftly scalped him withal.

Yet it was at the end of that same month that Swilling made a trip memorable in the West's economy. His destination was Fort McDowell, where he was due to deliver lumber tailored by a mill he owned in Wickenburg; but en route he camped with one John Y. T. Smith. Another Fort McDowell caterer, Smith was gathering wild hay at about the point along the Salt River where Michel Robidoux's party of trappers had been massacred by the Papagos thirty years earlier.

Covered by mesquite and other desert growths, where it was not sparsely fledged with coarse grass, the region was considered to be as utterly unpromising as it looked. In the normal course of events white men only visited the area because it was near the river crossing of the trace connecting Tucson and Prescott.

In loafing around Smith's camp, though, Swilling noticed what he had not during previous jaunts through the vicinity. It was seamed with shallow depressions, slanting toward the river, which was itself the spinal stem of a fish-skeleton pattern. Finding that from the main channels smaller ones in turn diverged, Jack concluded that what he had traced was an ancient Indian irrigation system.

So after he had dumped his lumber at Fort McDowell, he returned to the town where he had left the scalp of José Gonzalez to organize the Swilling Irrigation Canal Company. Duly incorporated at Prescott, it began operations by the Salt on December 10, 1867.

How this borderer knew what he did about irrigation, or why he thought the discarded waterworks of long-dead Indians could be made serviceable once more, are matters for guesswork only. The canals, as has since been scientifically shown, had not been used for half a millennium. But after personally directing the scooping-out operations, and the building of makeshift dams to turn the river into his ditches, Jack was so sure that he had started a basis for settlement which would stand pat that he wished to name the area Stonewall.

As not all with him were Southern in sympathy there was a demur at this reference to General Jackson, whose nickname was in any case forgotten after Darrel Duppa had spoken. Among the tales circulated about this remittance man was one to the effect that he had been dismissed from the British Army after having killed his superior officer in a duel. Be that as it may, before taking permanent seizin of the American frontier he had received a fine education, buttressed by extensive travel.

Now, which is to say on April 5, 1868, he reached into this past and produced the precisely right name for the community which Jack expected to materialize, as soon as the desert began greening with crops anew. Pointing out that the counted-on community would spring from the ashes of a dead culture, Darrel invoked the parallel of the mythical Arabian bird and christened the place Phoenix.

And while the first planted grain was justifying Jack Swilling's faith in the desert by growing with phenomenal speed, Duppa affixed another name to the map of the West. Climbing the butte where James Ohio Pattie had taken refuge after most of his comrades had been slain by the Papagos, Darrel looked south from the Salt at a scene which reminded him strongly of Tempe, that valley blessed of the Muses which he had visited while in Greece.

But if Swilling had created, and Duppa had named, new phases of the Southwest, men who had seen it while it was pristine had gone the way of the Hohokam Indians—once the builders of canals on both sides of the Gila's main tributary. Among them was the trained engineer who might expectedly have achieved what Jack mysteriously had had the inspiration to do.

For in 1866, after thirty years of borrowed time since his escape from the Fannin Massacre of Santa Anna's ordering, Herman Ehrenberg came to the end of wanderings in search of everything but the truce with restlessness he never found. Near the vicinity of Palm Springs, California, he was brought down by a band of Mojaves.

Later in the year, on October 15, Peg-leg Smith, who had been trapping the Gila with Ewing Young when Pattie and Michel Robidoux came out of the night with a tale of disaster along the Salt, died in San Francisco. Never having found his lost mine, he had nevertheless discovered a way of utilizing it. For in his final years he had become a Western version of the Ancient Mariner, who would collar passers-by and—in return for a liberal allowance of drinks—tell them just where those who located the right landmarks would be sure to find immense quantities of gold.

During the following year Pauline Weaver died in the tent he had erected near Fort Whipple, because he could not abide the air within sturdier walls. An old arrow wound was said to have hastened the demise of a man who had served with the Hudson's Bay Company before acquiring the desert lore which had enabled him to guide Cooke through the Southwest.

Then, only a few weeks after the naming of the Southwest's revitalized desert farming area, the region as a whole lost its most celebrated human link with its newer past. Done with such rides as the one he had taken up the Gila with dispatches about the deeds of Frémont and Commodore Stockton, Kit Carson died at Fort Lyon, Colorado, on May 23, 1868.

ৡ৯ঽ 72 ৡ৯ঽ

The Tethered Mustang

THE PONY EXPRESS was superseded, about eighteen months after its founding, by a means of communication which made dawdlers out of even its hotspur couriers. During 1860 an Ohioan named Edward Creighton had undertaken to plot the course of a proposed telegraph line across the plains and Rockies. Starting from Omaha, he had proceeded to Salt Lake City by way of Fort Kearny, Fort Laramie and South Pass, returning with a report which showed the feasibility of planting the needed poles all along that route.

Because of the outbreak of war and the resultant desire of the federal government for a wire hookup with the West Coast, the Pacific Telegraph Company was formed in 1861 and authorized to begin construction at several points simultaneously. Assuming the roughest assignment, Creighton took charge of operations between Slade's Julesburg and Salt Lake City. He accomplished this tremendous task in a trifle over three and a half months, having brought Morse code service to Brigham Young's capital by October 24. Twenty-two days later completion of the other sections jerked the Far West into almost the same time belt as the Atlantic Seaboard, where news was concerned.

Anxious for speedier passenger and mail service, the federal Congress voted for the construction of a transcontinental railroad, likewise to follow the 41st-parallel route, in 1862. As in the instance of the telegraph line, provision was made for work to begin at both ends of the proposed utility, but the first subsidy made available was turned over to a company which had been formed on the West Coast. Nothing was immediately attempted at the Missouri Valley end, because savage human obstacles had been added to the formidable natural ones which already stood in the way of spanning the Great Plains and the Rockies.

The uprising of the Yankton Sioux, following the reduction of garrison troops in their vicinity, was a development which was duplicated wherever the Indian tribes were yet strong, and white settlers were too few or scattered for mutual protection. Immigrants trekking along one trail or another were slain, these being luckier than the ones of both sexes taken alive. Exposed settlements on both sides of the Rockies were raided, especially along the Platte and its various forks.

If other tribes participated, the chief perpetrators were the dominant peoples of the area, these being certain divisions of the Sioux and Cheyennes. Not that the leading chiefs of the latter were at first for war, but they were as helpless to curb their young warriors as was the federal government in the matter of keeping pioneers from aggravating the Indians by settling in their respective domains.

As a venerated counselor of the Cheyennes, William Bent did all he could to hold the nation into which he had married on the track of peace. But by the onset of 1863 he had a more personal problem.

One of the Western injustices of logic was the fact that the most conscientious begetters of half-white children were the very ones who created the most misery for themselves and their young. The casual accepter of squaw hospitality sired beings who grew up as Indians and never gave their other heritage a thought. But the white men who married Indian women, and who tried to confer the benefits of civilization upon children born with one foot in the Stone Age, made these aware of having two pulses. If the savage one beat more strongly than the other, the hybrid not only left the world of his father but hated it and him for the duality which prevented satisfaction with Indian life, either.

Although there were numerous cases of half-caste bitterness at that period, the most notorious were those of George Bent and the son William had named after his slain brother, Charles. When they had come of school age, they had been taken from the care of their combination aunt and stepmother, Yellow

Woman, and sent to Missouri. Like the kinsmen with whom they were educated and given general polish, they had gone off to fight for the Confederacy in their late teens. But by 1863 they were back in the West with a fremd light in their eyes.

It had been their father's expectation that these young men would assist him at his very profitable business. Of his three sons, however, only Robert was gaited to live as a white man. The others slipped off to join their mother's people; and by summer George and Charles Bent were among the naked riders charging here and there across the plains in search of plunder, women and scalps.

Reprisal, when it raked the Cheyennes, was nearly, if not quite, as brutal as their own method of making war. As head of a force of Colorado volunteers, Colonel J. M. Chivington had veered the tide in favor of the North in New Mexico. In 1864, though, this minister-turned-soldier showed up on the plains with a roving commission to punish all Indians for depredations of which only some had been guilty.

With him at first as guide, and for once briefly in the spotlight of history, was a former trapper and putative chief of the Crows named James Beckwourth. But it had been forty-one years since this self-minted myth had fared up the Missouri with Ashley—if he did—and a man who must be awarded the palm for being the West's most accomplished liar was so chilled through, when the expedition reached Bent's post late in November, that he could hardly so much as wag his gifted tongue. His commander therefore gave Robert Bent a gun-point order to lead him to an encampment of Cheyennes along Sand Creek, presided over by a peaceably inclined chief called Black Kettle.

Arrived in sight of the lodges, Chivington ordered cannon to be unlimbered and loaded with grape. Without warning of any sort, he had his men open fire on a village in which squaws and children were far more numerous than braves, some of the latter being on the warpath.

Yet Charles and George Bent happened to be at the scene of that massacre. Both survived it, though the former was captured and the latter wounded, but their status was settled, once they were free for action again. Previously they had at times raided white immigrants and settlers because that was one of the occupations of an Indian warrior. Now they were vindictive enemies of their father's race.

The railroad plan to cross the plains had not been forgotten, meanwhile, and two months after Chivington's blood wallow, General Grenville Dodge was sent West. Already designated as technical counselor for the Union Pacific, the General had both an Indian-fighting and an investigatory mission.

For although the 41st-parallel route had been agreed upon, that had been about as much as had been definitely achieved in the direction of deciding where the tracks should run. Possible rail-traffic lanes had been mapped, to be sure, and by skilled men. None had been versed, however, in recognizing which gradients a wheeled steam engine could or could not swiftly negotiate. Long experienced in the field, Dodge was given the prerogative of deciding the path of the rails westward of Omaha.

Reaching the plains in January of 1865, Grenville began campaigning against the Sioux and the Crows along the Powder River. With Jim Bridger for guide, he handled his military assignment capably, whereupon his engineering one took him south into the knots of mountains which hump their backs in Wyoming east of where the Rockies stand taller yet.

In particular the problem of finding a way for a roadbed through the Black Buttes troubled him. It was a crux he did not solve, as a matter of fact, until he and a small scouting party were almost wiped out by Crows during '65's summer. Eventually troops summoned by signal fires drove the Indians off; but as in coming and going the raiders had used a nicely graded pass, earlier hidden from the General by natural formations, he sent his blessings after the warriors.

Because of a breadth which gave winds excessive play, Dodge had found historic South Pass too liable to be blocked with snow. At a lower latitude, however, he had plotted a less exposed route. Via a pass which Bridger had discovered, it ran by Old

Gabe's fort, thus cutting off the long north and south loop which had been followed by the stages of the Central Overland. From Jim's post, next, it extended toward Great Salt Lake, in whose vicinity the General expected that his line-to-be would make contact with the Central Pacific, or would if its engineers saw things his way.

In May of 1866, Grenville was at last freed by the Army for the purpose of operating as chief engineer of the Union Pacific. Until the rails reached west of Fort Kearny there were only the usual construction hazards. Beyond there, though, Dodge bumped into the first of two situations created by Colonel Chivington's atrocity.

When the truth of what had happened on Sand Creek was finally substituted for the Colonel's glozing report, the battles of the Civil War between the States were no longer pre-empting attention along the Atlantic Seaboard. And in the cities there, as Texas pioneers had already discovered, the Indians had long been objects of sympathy on the part of people who did not have to worry about being attacked by them.

The Indians, be it noted, had always waged war on women and children, red as well as white. But the news that white soldiers had paid them in kind drew wails of anguish from people who had had no tears to hold back when worse barbarities than even Chivington was guilty of were visited upon fellow palefaces. In penitence for the Colonel's crime, dwellers on faraway streets had demanded that the tribes should not again be subject to military policing of any sort.

Grasping the spirit of the times, politicians began making proposals, none of which included court-martialing Chivington and having him shot, as reason might well have considered the proper course. As though the West did not then house the citizens of four sovereign states, in addition to those living in the various territories, some proposed the withdrawal of all protecting garrisons. The alternative, as these declared, would be a general Indian war which it would be financially ruinous to prosecute.

414

As the skeleton Western garrisons were not restored to prewar strength, due to this clamor, Dodge had to fight his way across the plains as well as build a traversing roadbed. This was especially the case after Julesburg had ceased to be the construction depot town. Grenville named the next one Cheyenne in a vain effort to placate a vengeful nation bent on blocking his passage through the heart of their hunting range.

How the sons of William Bent now ranked as marauders can be ascertained from a letter which Dodge wrote in 1867. "If the Bent brothers are with the Cheyennes," he postulated in this missive, "they will play hell with the road."

They and other Cheyenne leaders did so. Two of Grenville's chief assistants were among the many slain. Construction was constantly interrupted by raids which forced men to lay aside tools and pick up guns. Ties were burned and supplies stolen. Pegs and other surveyors' markers were carried away. And after track-laying crews had moved ahead, Indians unseated the recently laid rails.

It was not until some government commissioners came West to inspect progress that conditions improved. For once cooperating in spite of themselves, the Cheyennes staged a raid which sent bullets whizzing near the startled gentry from Washington. Agreeing then that some protection for the line's builders was in order, the commissioners made recommendations which effected that.

Yet when the Sioux, the Cheyennes and the Crows had been left behind, there was Brigham Young to contend with. At first proffering generous cooperation, the Prophet had at that time taken it for granted that the Union Pacific's tracks would run through Salt Lake City. Grenville had discovered, however, that a better route ran north of Great Salt Lake.

As the name of Dodge's line was anathema—following that revelation of 1868,—Brigham held out the blessing of Heaven to the Central Pacific instead. After having managed the superb engineering feat of scaling the Sierras via Donner Pass, the eastward-reaching outfit had been able to plot an easier course than the Union Pacific, once the latter had got as far as the serried ranges of Wyoming. As for tribal opposition, the former had encountered none which was seriously impeding. To take advantage of the northerly-slanting valleys of Nevada, nonetheless, it had had to follow a more circuitous route than its rival, so the race for what was reckoned the midway point was a fair one.

The spike-driving contest which did indeed develop could not have done so had the Central Pacific agreed with Brigham Young that Heaven expected it to have a main-line station in Salt Lake City. But to Grenville's satisfaction, the delayed report of the C. P.'s engineers recommended the northward passage of the inland sea, too.

Never less than a sound businessman, Brigham consented to deal with both—after obtaining the promise of a spur line to his capital—upon finding that he could not profitably oppose either. By withholding supplies from one or the other, he could have appreciably altered the course of events. As it was, nothing but the skill and drive of paired veteran crews conditioned the 1869 race for the city named after Peter Skene Ogden.

After the Union Pacific had won that with leagues to spare, a meeting point of rails at Promontory Point, fifty-three miles west along the lake from Ogden, was agreed upon. This time the Central Pacific arrived first. Not by much, though, and before the end of May 10, 1869, symbolic gold and silver spikes were given gentle taps before they were replaced with the iron ones by which the once wild West was irrevocably bound to the Industrial Age.

৪৩ 73 ৪৩

Recessional Along the Colorado

THE YEAR BEFORE the confluence of rails at Promontory Point, the town named for the unappreciative Cheyennes became the capital of Wyoming Territory. In 1868, too, the man who had striven hardest to prevent the Union Pacific from keeping its Great Salt Lake tryst was foiled as to another enterprise.

Disgusting even the brother who had once been in alliance with him by his orgiastic delight in ravin, Charles Bent was disowned by his father. Upon learning of that act by the man who had given him one strain of blood too many, the renegade attempted to bushwack William.

The would-be parricide didn't get another chance, because of an intercepting incident of the same year. One reason for the ineffectiveness of Indian resistance to white invasion was that when not combating troops or frontiersmen, the tribesmen warred upon each other. As the Cheyennes were not exceptions, neither was young Bent. In a fight with Pawnees—some of whom had slain and scalped, two or three years earlier, the aunt his father had married—Charles was stricken with a wound from whose effects he perished.

The one whose siring of him he had tried to avenge did not long survive his son of two worlds and no hope. On May 19, 1869, William Bent died at his stockaded trading post in the shadow of Fort Lyon. Nine days earlier the epoch which had made possible the great self-sustaining caravanserais, such as was the original Bent's Fort, had virtually come to an end. Hitched by rail to the industrial North of post-Civil War days, the West was no longer a sphere for much in the way of empire building by resident adventurers. It was a province mainly exploited by outsiders who invested their money rather than their hearts and their lives.

Even the West's one capital city slid downhill into provinciality. In metropolitan isolation San Francisco had become a publishing center and in general the seat of an indigenous culture; but the railroad reduced it to the status of other backcountry cities of the second magnitude, from which top talent moved to the scene of louder plaudits and better pay along the Atlantic Seaboard.

Elsewhere, and with astounding completeness, the West became ancillary to railroads. Rails created and controlled the marketing, at distant points, of its not numerous raw materials: lumber, leather, wool and cotton. With the cream of placer gold skimmed, mining was carried on by outside concerns which hired men to work wherever tracks reached the vicinity of ore fields. The meat packers of other regions wanted beef, so Westerners drove them to the railroads, which split the profits with the corporate butchers.

But in 1869 the clock had not ticked all the way into a new division of the West's history. There were still some each of both buffalo and Indian fighting.

The war on the redskins, though, had become a mopping-up operation, where it wasn't conducted in the manner of people eradicating animals below the horizon of humanity. In requital for attacks on Kansas settlements, for instance, General George Custer imitated Chivington, in 1869, by turning the guns of his troops on a Cheyenne village standing by Oklahoma's Washita River.

Soldiers were not all who engaged in such massacres, however. Long embittered by the perpetrations of Apache bands, some of the pioneers of Arizona went berserk upon learning that certain of these Indians had sought to escape retribution by surrendering at Fort Grant. Led by former Ranger and Alamo messenger William Oury, these and a supporting force of Papagos stole upon the unsuspecting Apaches in April of 1871 and slew bisexually, albeit sparing the children the Papagos bore off as slaves. In response to protests from the Atlantic Seaboard most of the raiders were brought to trial; but Arizona jurors who knew people whom the Apaches had staked out on anthills to be eaten alive found the slaughter a venial sin.

If a great number of the tribe in question had been killed off or nailed down on reservations, Jacob Snively, for one, found that there were some still on the loose. Caught by Big Rump's Yavapais while prospecting in 1871, Houston's quondam lieutenant cashed his last chip.

In the meantime more tracks were on the march. The Atchison, Topeka and Santa Fe Railroad, to name but one outfit, added to the number of Kansas cattle-loading points by stretching from a town which Richard Weightman had helped found toward the route to the Pacific discovered by the victim of his bowie knife. By the end of 1872 the line's steel lane extended as far as Colorado, but financial considerations temporarily kept the rails from following Aubry's path over the Great Divide.

Yet if cattle were marching up the Chisholm Trail from Texas to Kansas, and on up to Idaho as in the instance of Seth Mabry's drive of 1873, the bison which the longhorns were rapidly replacing had not all been stripped of their skins. If the hide hunters had pretty well wiped out the herds of the northern plains, the animals grazed south of the Arkansas, thanks to a tough set of Indian game wardens. Following innumerable campaigns most of the Comanches had been more or less picketed in the Indian Territory, but as of 1874 the Kwahadi branch of the tribe continued to free-foot it in the Texas Panhandle.

Their chief at this time was Quanah, the son of Peta Nocona and the now also dead Cynthia Ann Parker. Aghast at the shrinking of the buffalo swarms upon which his people depended for survival, Quanah had vowed to exterminate at all costs any white hunters found active on the land of his people.

Not many had earlier risked trespassing on the range of the Kwahadis, but in June of 1874 Billy Dixon, Bat Masterson and 17 other hide collectors rode from Kansas down to the Canadian and made their headquarters at Adobe Walls. The ruins of the Bent and St. Vrain post which William had blown up when abandoning it, the structure also had a place in the annals of Kit Carson. In November of 1864 his command of four hundred, together with a pair of cannon, had fought a draw with an estimated three thousand Comanches and Kiowas there.

Confident in the protection offered by still sturdy ramparts, the hunters did not take the precaution of standing watch by night. Had not a makeshift roof fortuitously collapsed just before dawn one morning, the surprise attack which Quanah had carefully planned would have been executed with gory smoothness. But as it chanced, one of the frontiersmen arose to probe under the fallen shelter, which had been built for the protection of supplies. If these had totted no more than food, he wouldn't have stirred from his blankets. As whiskey was included, though, he was concerned for possible damage.

Although nothing turned out to be amiss, he felt the need of a drink to quiet his fear-racked nerves. Glancing about while he was having this tranquilizer, he noted mounted figures limned against the horizon. His nick-of-time shout brought men to their feet, rifles ready, and the siege of Adobe Walls was on.

Having enlisted some Kiowas, Arapahoes and Cheyennes, Quanah had about a thousand plumed lancers to hurl against the rifle bullets of the hunters. Then, as the warfare lasted a fortnight, the grapevine was given time to spread the news of the showdown along the Canadian. Getting the smoke-broadcast word, hundreds of other Indians skipped off their reservations and raced to bet on the outcome.

Quanah gave the spectators a fine time. Repeatedly he mounted assaults in the hope of being able to smash through the barrier of bullets. Yet always the far-shooting guns of the bison hunters broke the force of the charges short of their goal.

At the end the chief had to give up, but in his rage at defeat he made uncomplimentary gestures from a height supposedly out of range. It turned out not to be so, though. If missing the part pointedly turned toward those in Adobe Walls, the buffalo gun of Billy Dixon broke two of the Comanche's ribs from an estimated mile away.

During his recuperation Cynthia Ann's son came to the conclusion that as the hide collectors could not be stopped from killing off the bison, his people could no longer live as free nomads. Before the end of the year, then, he led the Kwahadis into the Indian Territory, where he strove for peaceful advancement under the name of Quanah Parker.

In July of 1874, meanwhile, General Custer entered the Black Hills of Dakota Territory as head of what was described as a mixed military and scientific expedition. Although gold had been found there seven years earlier, the discovery had been hushed up, in order to prevent prospectors from rushing into an area which had been granted by treaty to the Sioux. When dust and nuggets were discovered by some in Custer's party, though, the news got about. If the report wasn't sensational, it was yet exciting enough to draw pioneers into a region which was still as much of a wilderness as it had been when Jed Smith nearly lost his head to a grizzly bear. At first only a few were willing to risk their scalps for treasure not known to be present in quantity; but in 1875 a big find was made in Deadwood Gulch.

As the railroad town of Cheyenne was only a couple of hundred miles thence, the stampede which took place was promptly large as to scale. In an effort to avoid trouble, the government tried to persuade the Sioux to surrender title to the Black Hills. The Dakotas had been pushed as far as they were willing to be, however.

Sitting Bull and Red Cloud, who had been at the Fort Laramie council of the tribes which Tom Fitzpatrick had arranged in 1851, agreed to go to Washington to confer with Great White Father Grant. The President failed to shake their resolve to retain the Black Hills; but as pioneers continued to pour into them, the government's hand was forced. Seeing the necessity of surveying territory which American citizens were in the process of seizing, the Army was ordered to map the disputed region.

If Red Cloud did no more than protest, Sitting Bull sparked a revolt of the Oglala Sioux which was fought out the following year. As the Modocs of Captain Jack had made their stiff stand in the lava beds of northern California in 1873, this was the last of the Indian wars except for chases after fugitive, badly outnumbered bands. The Dakotas, moreover, took the aggressive in strength enough to snatch one victory from the ashes of Stone Age aspirations.

Not having been shot or cashiered for warring on noncombatants, Custer was allowed to lead 275 men into ambushment along the Little Big Horn River in June of 1876. Some Cheyennes who had cause to remember the General helped see to it that none of his command escaped; but they and the Sioux were up against a foregone conclusion. So little did the Custer massacre matter to an army which could race men and supplies to the West by rail that it did not delay the war's outcome by so much as another full season.

While the troops and the Indians were deciding the question of title to the Black Hills, the treasure hunters in possession carried on daily pursuits which included playing cards in saloons. Among those who did so was Wild Bill Hickok, once a guide of Custer's against less prepared tribesmen than those encountered on the lesser Big Horn. As of 1876, Bill's reputation as a pistoleer was so formidable that he ranked as had Langford Peel, before the latter had been shot, nine years earlier, as he unsuspectingly strode from a bar in Montana. As Langford was born in England, it is perhaps worth noting that the one who took advantage of him—and whom Peel had a while since refrained from shooting, upon finding that the other wasn't armed—bore the name of John Bull.

The chief of the local gunmen, without having that title applied to him, Hickock was assassinated because Jack McCall wished to take no risks when seeking acclaim as the slayer of a dangerous man. In Jack's favor, though, it can be adduced that he chose a moment in which his victim had a smile in his heart, if not on his face, as the deal had given him something worth betting on. But in any case, on August 2, while the U.S. Cavalry was hauling the curtain down on action which had begun at the Arikara siege, McCall pulled trigger. Shot in the back for a brag, Wild Bill then let fall, in Deadwood City of Deadwood Gulch, the pairs of aces and eights, with a queen standing by, ever since known as the Dead Man's Hand.

William Oury died in Tucson that year, which was one that found Jack Swilling back in the Bradshaw Mountains. For having founded a peaceful community with a stable economy, he had left it for the brief and hectic flowerings of mining camps which he better enjoyed.

Yet the free gold which had once been so plentiful in Central

Arizona had been used up—as had, two years later, Jack's luck, his hopes and his once enormous vitality. In order to ease the pain of one of his souvenirs of battle, he had taken to a combination of laudanum and liquor. Aware, too late, of the danger, he had tried to throw off the incubus; but it kept on coming back, staying longer every time.

A curious effect of this entrenched enemy was a heavy concern for the remains of Swilling's old friend Jacob Snively. Ever since that great prospector had been killed by the Yavapais in 1871, his bones had lain, far from hallowed ground, in the White Picacho Mountains. The recurrent haunt of Apaches, truant from reservations, this still was not a safe zone for white men seven years later.

In 1878, though, a pair of men agreed to help Swilling retrieve what was left of Snively, alike to enable their friend to win back peace of mind and to work free of his growing lethargy. With their aid Jacob's bones were duly brought back for interment in a Christian cemetery; but no good came of this piety. Accused of holding up the Wickenburg stage while he was absent from the Bradshaws, Jack ended up behind bars in Yuma.

Never brought to trial for a crime which was later properly assigned to somebody else, he did not leave the town which Poston and Ehrenberg had chartered in order to swindle a ferryman. While the Southern Pacific was preparing to span the Colorado —at last to justify the Gadsden Purchase of Cooke's 32nd-parallel route—Jack's health collapsed utterly in the foreign atmosphere of confinement.

On August 12, 1878, the captor of Mangas Colorado and the prophet of the Hohokam canals put an end to being a caged holdover from a gone era by giving up his rugged ghost. And before prison officials boxed him for burial, they found the scars of thirty-nine bullet, knife and arrow wounds as vouchers for the nature of the epoch in which he had lived, as well as the manner in which he had largely wrought in it.

The Face Above a Grave: An Epilogue

MOST OF THE buffalo hunters who had stood the Comanches off at Adobe Walls were old-time plainsmen. Only eighteen, however, Bat Masterson had been west of the Mississippi but two years.

After briefly having stepped into the buckskin West in 1874, he went on to figure largely in the cowhide one. The year before Jack Swilling's demise, as it happened, Masterson became sheriff of the Kansas county whose seat was Dodge City, named for the nearby fort, which in turn was christened in honor of the officer who had led the dragoons to the Rockies in 1834. Sometimes known as "the Cowboys' Capital," Henry Dodge's namesake was frequented by the railhead-town peace officers and gamblers, the cattle ranchers and cattle rustlers, the railroad and bank robbers, as well as the range feudists and range detectives who made up the new roster of adventurers on the Great Plains.

Many of these were also active in rail-served mining camps in the Rockies, and the railroad war through which the Santa Fe won the right to reach the West Coast. Some of them became, or fought with, the new type of Texas Rangers, detailed to subjugate erring white men, not Indians. Some thronged and fired in the Southwestern town which came into being after Ed Schieffelin found silver instead of a threatened tombstone—also in 1877—near where Cooke's Mormon Battalion had fought the Battle of the Bulls.

425

In all its linked ramifications the story of these bravos forms another great and thoroughly integrated Western tapestry. Yet it is of a different texture from this of the West's seizure and weaning from wilderness, to which a few threads must be added.

In 1877 John Doyle Lee was killed by a firing squad of soldiers on the site of the Mountain Meadows Massacre, of which he had been one of the engineers twenty years earlier. While confessing his part in the atrocity, Bishop Lee did not seem to be repentant, or have any feeling about the matter outside of his bitter insistence that the Mormon hierarchy had sold him out. What he meant, and what was doubtless true, was that he had been surrendered to quiet accusations that the church had been willfully shielding the Arkansas Party's murderers.

The top-ranking Saints of the day could afford to turn over Brigham's foster son to United States military authorities, because the Prophet was on his deathbed at the time. Leadership in the church had thus become available to men who were less determined than he to have Mormons separated from the rest of their countrymen by adhering to different legal and moral codes.

At the time of Young's death, his old enemy Jim Bridger had long left the mountains his failed eyes would have been unable to see and was living in a Missouri community called Little Santa Fe. There the blind anachronism passed away on July 17, 1881—the same year in which Jim Clyman went under.

As Old Gabe's illiteracy had prevented him from imitating Clyman in the matter of leaving memoirs, an admirer of Bridger's saw to it that he was incorporated in another type of personal record. During the months in which they had pursued Indians and sought a railroad route together, a warm friendship had developed between Grenville Dodge, the brisk industrialist from Massachusetts, and the aging mountain man from Virginia. When advanced in years himself, accordingly, the engineer who had created the new West erected a monument emblazoned with the face of the frontiersman who had come to be thought the most representative figure of the old.

Quite properly Jim Bridger's monument marks the taking-off

point for a now resurgent American subdivision which looks to its lore of frontier hardihood for that breath of the spirit which will continue to characterize it, no matter what changes industrial advancement may bring. Erected in Kansas City, that is to say, it stands at the gateway to an ancient sphere for neck-or-nothing individuals, once with the epic name of Westport.

Bibliography

(This partial list of consulted items is limited to books and other separately published works and does not include the numberless newspaper and magazine articles examined in the course of preparing to write *The Deaths of the Bravos*. J.M.M.)

Adams, J. C. *Life of J. C. Adams, Known as Old Grizzly Adams.* New York, 1861.

Ainsa, J. Y. *History of the Crabb Expedition into N. Sonora.* Phoenix, 1951.

Alter, J. Cecil. *James Bridger: Trapper, Frontiersman, Scout and Guide.* Columbus, Ohio, 1951.

Anonymous. *Biography of Joseph Lane, Late Governor of Oregon.* Washington, 1852.

Appleton's Cyclopaedia of American Biography. 6 vols. New York, 1899–1901.

Asbury, Herbert. *The Barbary Coast.* New York, 1933.

Atherton, Gertrude. *California: An Intimate History.* New York, 1914.

Atwood, Wallace W. *The Rocky Mountains.* New York, 1945.

Aubry, François (Felix) Xavier. *Diaries of François Xavier Aubry, 1853–1854.* Edited by Ralph P. Bieber. Glendale, California, 1938.

Bailey, Philip A. *Golden Mirages.* New York, 1949.

Baker, DeWitt C. *A Texas Scrapbook.* New York, 1875.

Baker, James, and Hafen, LeRoy. *History of Colorado.* 3 vols. Denver, 1927.

Bancroft, Hubert Howe. *California inter Pocula.* San Francisco, 1888.

————. *History of Arizona and New Mexico*. San Francisco, 1889.

————. *History of British Columbia*. San Francisco, 1888.

————. *History of California*. Vols. V, VI and VII. San Francisco, 1888.

————. *History of Nevada, Colorado and Wyoming*. San Francisco, 1890.

————. *History of North Mexican States and Texas*. 2 vols. San Francisco, 1889.

————. *History of Northwest Coast*. 2 vols. San Francisco, 1884.

————. *History of Oregon*. 2 vols. San Francisco, 1886.

————. *History of Utah*. San Francisco, 1889.

————. *History of Washington, Idaho and Montana*. San Francisco, 1890.

————. *Popular Tribunals*. 2 vols. San Francisco, 1887.

Barker, Eugene C. (Ed.). *The Austin Papers*. Annual Reports of the American Historical Association, 1919 (2 vols.) and 1922 (2 vols.) Washington, 1924-1928.

Bartlett, John Russell. *Personal Narrative of Explorations . . . during the Years 1850, '51, '52 and '53*. 2 vols. New York, 1854.

Beadle, J. H. *Western Wilds and the Men Who Redeem Them*. Cincinnati, 1878.

Beebe, Lucius, and Clegg, Charles. *The American West*. New York, 1955.

————. *The Saga of Wells Fargo*. New York, 1949.

Bell, Horace. *On the Old West Coast*. New York, 1930.

————. *Reminiscences of a Ranger*. Los Angeles, 1881.

Bell, William A. *New Tracks in North America*. New York, 1861.

Benton, Thomas, H. *Thirty Years' View*. New York, 1856.

Bieber, Ralph P. (Ed.). *Marching with the Army of the West: The Journals of Abraham Robinson Johnston, Marcellus Ball Edwards and Philip Gooch Ferguson*. Glendale, California, 1936.

————. *Southern Trails to California in 1849*. Glendale, California, 1937.

Bigelow, John. *Memoir of the Life and Public Services of John Charles Fremont*. New York, 1856.

Billington, Ray Allen. *The Far Western Frontier*. New York, 1956.

Blair, Walter, and Meine, Franklin J. *Half Horse and Half Alligator: The Growth of the Mike Fink Legend*. Chicago, 1956.

Bloss, Roy S. *Pony Express: The Great Gamble*. Berkeley, California, 1959.

Boatright, Mody C. (Ed.). *From Hell to Breakfast*. Dallas, 1944.

Bonner, T. D. *Life and Adventures of James P. Beckwourth.* New York, 1856.

Bonsal, Stephen. *Edward Fitzgerald Beale, A Pioneer in the Path of Empire.* New York, 1912.

Botkin, B. A. *A Treasury of Western Folk Lore.* New York, 1951.

Bourke, John G. *On the Border with Crook.* New York, 1891.

Bowles, Samuel. *Across the Continent: A Summer's Journey to the Rocky Mountains . . . and the Pacific States.* Springfield, Massachusetts, 1865.

Brewerton, George Douglas. *Overland with Kit Carson.* New York, 1930.

Brook, Juanita. *Mountain Meadow Massacre.* Palo Alto, California, 1950.

Brown, Jennie Broughton. *Fort Hall on the Oregon Trail.* Caldwell, Idaho, 1932.

Brown, John Henry. *History of Texas from 1685 to 1892.* 2 vols. St. Louis, 1893.

———. *Indian Wars and Pioneers of Texas.* Austin, Texas, 1904.

———. *Life and Times of Henry Smith.* Dallas, 1887.

Brown, Mark H. *Before Barbed Wire.* New York, 1956.

———. *The Plainsmen of the Yellowstone.* New York, 1961.

Browne, John Ross. *Adventures in Apache Country.* New York, 1868.

Bruce, John Roberts. *Gaudy Century: The Story of San Francisco's Hundred Years of Robust Journalism.* New York, 1948.

Bruff, J. Goldsborough. *Gold Rush.* New York, 1949.

Bryant, Edwin. *What I Saw in California.* New York, 1848.

Buckbee, Edna Bryant. *The Saga of Old Tuolumne.* New York, 1935.

Burdett, Charles. *Life of Kit Carson.* New York, 1860.

Burt, Struthers. *Powder River.* New York, 1938.

Butterfield, Jack C. *Men of the Alamo, Goliad and San Jacinto.* San Antonio, 1936.

Caesar, Gene. *King of the Mountain Men: The Life of Jim Bridger.* New York, 1961.

California Historical Society. *Gold Discovery: Centennial Papers.* San Francisco, 1947.

Callcott, Wilfrid Hardy. *Santa Anna: The Story of the Enigma Who Once Was Mexico.* Norman, Oklahoma, 1936.

Calvin, Ross. *River of the Sun.* Albuquerque, New Mexico, 1946.

Camp, Charles L. (Ed.). *James Clyman, Frontiersman.* Portland, Oregon, 1960.

Camp, William Martin. *San Francisco, Port of Gold*. Garden City, New York, 1943.

Campbell, Walter S. *Jim Bridger, Mountain Man*. New York, 1946.

———. *Kit Carson, The Happy Warrior*. Boston, 1928.

———. *Mountain Men*. Boston, 1937.

———. *Warpath and Council Fire*. New York, 1948.

———. *Warpath, Story of the Fighting Sioux*. Boston, 1933.

Carleton, James Henry. *Report on the Subject of the Massacre at the Mountain Meadows*. Little Rock, Arkansas, 1860.

Carr, Harry. *Los Angeles, City of 1200 Dreams*. New York, 1938.

Carvalho, S. N. *Incidents of Travel and Adventure in the Far West*. New York, 1856.

Case, Robert Ormond. *The Empire Builders*. Garden City, New York, 1947.

Catlin, George. *North American Indians, Being Letters and Notes on Their Manners, Customs and Conditions*. 2 vols. Edinburgh, 1926.

Cattermole, E. G. *Famous Frontiersmen, Pioneers and Scouts*. Chicago, 1883.

Caughey, John W. *California*. New York, 1940.

———. *Gold Is the Cornerstone*. Berkeley, California, 1948.

———. *History of the Pacific Coast*. Los Angeles, 1933.

Chabot, Frederick Charles. *The Alamo As Mission, Fortress and Shrine*. San Antonio, 1941.

Chalfant, W. A. *Gold, Guns and Ghost Towns*. Palo Alto, California, 1947.

Chamberlain, Samuel E. *My Confession*. New York, 1956.

Chambers, William Nisbet. *Old Bullion Benton, Senator from the New West*. Boston, 1956.

Chapman, Arthur. *The Pony Express: The Record of a Romantic Adventure in Business*. Chicago, 1932.

Child, Andrew. *Overland Route to California*. Los Angeles, 1946.

Chittenden, Hiram M. *The American Fur Trade of the Far West*. 2 vols. Palo Alto, California, 1954.

Clarke, Mathew St. Clair (Putative author). *Life and Adventures of Colonel David Crockett of Tennessee*. Cincinnati, 1833. Same work published as *Sketches and Eccentricities of Colonel David Crocket of West Tennessee*. New York, 1833.

Cleland, Robert Glass. *From Wilderness to Empire*. New York, 1944.

————. *A History of California: The American Period.* New York, 1922.

————. *This Reckless Breed of Men.* New York, 1950.

Clemens, Samuel. *Roughing It.* Hartford, Connecticut, 1872.

Coblentz, Stanton A. *Villains and Vigilantes.* New York, 1957.

Conard, Howard Louis. *Uncle Dick Wootton.* Chicago, 1890.

Conner, David Ellis. *Joseph Reddeford Walker and the Arizona Adventure.* Norman, Oklahoma, 1956.

Conway, Cornelius. *The Utah Expedition, Containing a General Account of the Mormon Campaign.* Cincinnati, 1858.

Cooke, Philip St. George. *The Conquest of New Mexico and California.* New York, 1878.

————. *Cooke's Journal of the March of the Mormon Battalion.* Edited by Ralph P. Bieber. Glendale, California, 1938.

————. *Scenes and Adventures in the Army.* Philadelphia, 1857.

Corle, Edwin. *The Gila.* New York, 1951.

Couts, Cave J. *From San Diego to the Colorado.* Los Angeles, 1932.

Coyner, David H. *The Lost Trappers: A Collection of Interesting Scenes and Events in the Rocky Mountains.* Cincinnati, 1847.

Cozzens, Samuel W. *The Marvelous Country.* Boston, 1873.

Creel, George. *Sam Houston, Colossus in Buckskin.* New York, 1928.

Cremony, John C. *Life Among the Apaches.* San Francisco, 1868.

Crockett, David, *A Narrative of the Life of David Crockett, Written by Himself.* Philadelphia, 1834.

Croy, Homer. *Wheels West.* New York, 1955.

Custer, Elizabeth B. *Boots and Saddles.* New York, 1900.

Cutts, James M. *The Conquest of California and New Mexico.* Philadelphia, 1847.

Dale, H. C. *The Ashley-Smith Explorations.* Cleveland, 1918.

Dana, Julian. *Sutter of California.* New York, 1936.

Dana, Richard Henry, Jr. *Two Years before the Mast.* Boston, 1840.

David, Robert Beebe. *Finn Burnett, Frontiersman.* Glendale, California, 1837.

Davis, Clyde Brion. *The Arkansas.* New York, 1940.

Davis, Richard Harding. *Real Soldiers of Fortune.* New York, 1912.

Dawson, Glen (Ed.). *Don Santiago Kirker, The Indian Fighter.* Los Angeles, 1948.

De Ford, Miriam Allen. *They Were San Franciscans.* Caldwell, Idaho, 1941.

De Groot, Henry. *Sketches of the Washoe Silver Mines.* San Francisco, 1860.

Delano, Alonzo. *Life on the Plains and among the Diggings.* Auburn, New York, 1857.

———. *Old Block's Sketch Book.* Santa Ana, Calif., 1947.

Dellenbaugh, Frederick S. *Breaking the Wilderness.* New York, 1905.

———. *Frémont and '49.* New York, 1914.

DeQuille, Dan. *The Big Bonanza.* New York, 1947.

DeShields, James T. *Tall Men with Long Rifles.* San Antonio, 1935.

DeSmet, Father P. J. *Oregon Missions and Travels over the Rocky Mountains.* New York, 1847.

DeVoto, Bernard. *Across the Wide Missouri.* Boston, 1947.

———. *The Year of Decision: 1846.* Boston, 1943.

Dick, Everett. *Vanguards of the Frontier.* New York, 1941.

Dictionary of American Biography. 20 vols. New York, 1928–1936.

Dillon, Richard H. *Embarcadero.* New York, 1959.

Dimsdale, Thomas J. *The Vigilantes of Montana.* Norman, Oklahoma, 1953.

Dixon, Olive. *Life of Billy Dixon.* Dallas, 1914.

Dixon, Samuel Houston. *Romance and Tragedy of Texas History.* Houston, 1924.

Dobie, J. Frank. *Apache Gold and Yaqui Silver.* Boston, 1939.

———. *Coronado's Children.* New York, 1931.

Donaldson, Thomas. *Idaho of Yesterday.* Caldwell, Idaho, 1941.

Douglas, Claude LeRoy. *James Bowie: The Life of a Bravo.* Dallas, 1944.

Drannan, William F. *Thirty-one Years on the Plains and in the Mountains.* Chicago, 1903.

Driggs, Howard. *The Old West Speaks.* New York, 1956.

Duffus, Robert L. *The Santa Fe Trail.* New York, 1930.

Dunn, J. P. *Massacres of the Mountains.* New York, 1958.

Edwards, Frank S. *A Campaign in New Mexico with Colonel Doniphan.* London, 1848.

Edwards, Richard, and Hopewell, M. *Edwards' Great West.* St. Louis, 1860.

Eisele, Wilbert Edwin. *The Real Wild Bill Hickok.* Denver, 1931.

Eldredge, Zoeth Skinner. *History of California.* 5 vols. New York, 1915.

Elliott, N. W. and Company. *History of Arizona.* San Francisco, 1884.

Ellis, Edward S. *Life and Adventures of David Crocket.* New York, 1862.

434

Ellison, William H. *A Self Governing Dominion, California from 1849 to 1860.* Berkeley, California, 1950.
——— (Ed.). *The Life and Adventures of George Nidever.* Berkeley, California, 1932.
Emory, William H. *Notes of a Military Reconnaissance, 1846–47.* Washington, 1848.
Farish, Thomas E. *The Gold Seekers of California.* San Francisco, 1904.
———. *History of Arizona.* 8 vols. Phoenix, Arizona, 1915-1918.
Farnham, Thomas J. *Travels in the Great Western Prairies.* London, 1843.
Favour, Alpheus, E. *Old Bill Williams, Mountain Man.* Chapel Hill, North Carolina, 1936.
Fergusson, Erna. *New Mexico.* New York, 1951.
Fergusson, Harvey. *The Rio Grande.* New York, 1937.
Ferris, W. A. *Life in the Rocky Mountains.* Denver, 1946.
Field, Joseph E. *Three Years in Texas.* Boston, 1836.
Fisk, James Liberty. *Idaho, Her Gold Fields and the Routes to Them.* New York, 1863.
Fitzgerald, O. P. *California Sketches.* Nashville, Tennessee, 1879.
Foote, Henry Stuart. *Texas and the Texans.* 2 vols. Philadelphia, 1841.
Forbes, Robert H. *Crabb's Filibustering Expedition into Sonora.* Tucson, 1952.
Ford, John S. *Origin and Fall of the Alamo.* San Antonio, 1890.
Foreman, Grant (Ed.). *Adventures on Red River: Report on the Exploration of the Headwaters of the Red River by Captain Randolph B. Marcy and Captain G. B. McClellan.* Norman, Oklahoma, 1937.
Frémont, Jessie Benton. *Far Western Sketches.* New York, 1898.
Frémont, John Charles. *Narratives of Exploration and Adventure.* Edited by Allan Nevins. New York, 1956.
———. *Report of the Exploring Expedition to the Rocky Mountains . . . and to Oregon and Northern California.* Printed by Order of the Senate of the United States. Washington, 1845.
French, Parker H. *Journals of the Suffering and Hardship of Captain Parker H. French's Overland Expedition to California.* Chambersburg, Pennsylvania, 1851.
Friend, Llerena. *Sam Houston, The Great Designer.* Austin, Texas, 1954.
Fuller, George W. *A History of the Pacific Northwest.* New York, 1947.

Fulton, Maurice, and Horgan, Paul (Eds.). *New Mexico's Own Chronicle*. Dallas, 1937.

Gambrell, Herbert. *Anson Jones*. Garden City, New York, 1948.

Garnett, Porter (Ed.). *Papers of the San Francisco Committee of Vigilance of 1851*. Berkeley, California, 1910-1919.

Garrard, Lewis H. *Wah-To-Yah and the Taos Trail*. Edited by Ralph P. Bieber. Glendale, California, 1938.

Ghent, W. J. *The Early Far West: A Narrative Outline*. New York, 1936.

———. *The Road to Oregon, A Chronicle of the Great Immigrant Trail*. New York, 1934.

Ghent, W. J., and Hafen, LeRoy. *Broken Hand: The Life Story of Thomas Fitzpatrick*. Denver, 1931.

Gibson, George R. *Journal of a Soldier under Kearny and Doniphan*. Glendale, California, 1935.

Goodwin, Cardinal Leonidas. *John Charles Fremont: An Explanation of His Career*. Palo Alto, California, 1930.

Graham, W. A. *The Custer Myth*. Harrisburg, Pa., 1953.

Grant, Blanche. *When Old Trails Were New: The Story of Taos*. New York, 1934.

Gray, William. *From Virginia to Texas*. Houston, 1909.

Greeley, Horace. *An Overland Journey from New York to San Francisco*. New York, 1860.

Greenow, Robert. *The History of Oregon and California and the other territories of the Northwest Coast of North America*. Boston, 1845.

Greer, James Kimmins. *Colonel Jack Hays*. New York, 1952.

Greer, Leland Hargrave. *The Founding of an Empire*. Salt Lake City, 1947.

———. *Utah and the Nation*. Seattle, 1929.

Gregg, Josiah. *Commerce of the Prairies*. 2 vols. New York, 1944.

Gresinger, A. W. *Charles D. Poston, Sunland Seer*. Globe, Arizona, 1961.

Griffin, John S. *Diary of John S. Griffin*. Edited by George W. Ames, Jr. San Francisco, 1943.

Grinnell, George B. *The Fighting Cheyennes*. New York, 1915.

Gudde, Elizabeth (Trans. and Ed.). *Exploring with Fremont: The Private Diaries of Charles Preuss*. Norman, Oklahoma, 1958.

Gunnison, John Williams. *The Mormons or Latter Day Saints . . . A History of Their Rise and Progress*. Philadelphia, 1852.

Gunnison, John Williams, and Gilpin, William. *Guide to the Kansas Gold Mines at Pike's Peak*. Cincinnati, 1859.

436

Hafen, LeRoy. *Colorado and its People.* New York, 1948.

———— *The Overland Mail,* 1849–1861. Cleveland, 1926.

———— (Ed.). *The Utah Expedition,* 1857–1858. Glendale, California, 1958.

Hafen, LeRoy, and Hafen, Ann W. *The Old Spanish Trail, Santa Fe to Los Angeles.* Glendale, California, 1954.

Hafen, LeRoy, and Rister, Carl Coke. *Western America.* New York, 1941.

Hafen, LeRoy, and Young, Francis M. *Fort Laramie and the Pageant of the West.* Glendale, California, 1935.

Haines, Aubry L. (Ed.). *Osborne Russell's Journey of a Trapper.* Portland, Oregon, 1955.

Haley, J. Evetts. *Fort Concho and the Texas Frontier.* San Angelo, Texas, 1952.

Hall, Edward Hepple. *Emigrant Settlers' and Travellers' Guide and Handbook to the States of California and Oregon.* New York, 1864.

Hall, Frank. *History of Colorado.* Chicago, 1889.

Hall, Sharlot M. *Pauline Weaver: Trapper and Mountain Man.* Prescott, Arizona, 1929.

Hamilton, James McLellan. *From Wilderness to Statehood.* Portland, Oregon, 1957.

Hamilton, William. *My Sixty Years on the Plains.* New York, 1905.

Hammond, George (Ed.). *The Larkin Papers.* 5 vols. Berkeley, California, 1951.

Hardy, Robert W. H. *Travels in the Interior of Mexico.* London, 1829.

Harper's Encyclopaedia of United States History. 10 vols. New York, 1901–1905.

Harris, Benjamin Butler. *The Gila Trail.* Norman, Oklahoma, 1960.

Harrison, Burton. *John Colter.* New York, 1952.

Hastings, Lansford Warren. *The Emigrants' Guide to Oregon and California.* Cincinnati, 1845.

Heap, Gwinn Harris. *Central Route to the Pacific from the Valley of the Mississippi to California.* Glendale, California, 1957.

Heiskell, S. G. *Andrew Jackson and Early Tennessee History.* Nashville, Tennessee, 1918.

Hill, Alice Polk. *Tales of the Colorado Pioneers.* Denver, 1884.

Hill, Joseph J. *Ewing Young.* Eugene, Oregon, 1923.

Hittell, John S. *History of San Francisco.* San Francisco, 1878.

Hobbs, James. *Wild Life in the Far West.* Hartford, Connecticut, 1872.

Hodge, Frederick W. *Handbook of American Indians*. 2 vols. Washington, 1907–1910.

Hoig, Stan. *The Sand Creek Massacre*. Norman, Oklahoma, 1961.

Holbrook, Stewart. *The Columbia*. New York, 1956.

———. *The Story of American Railroads*. New York, 1947.

Holley, Mary Austin. *Letters of an Early American Traveler*. Dallas, 1933.

Hollon, Eugene W. *The Southwest Old and New*. New York, 1961.

Hollon, Eugene W., and Butler, Ruth Lapham (Eds.). *William Bolaert's Texas*. Norman, Oklahoma, 1956.

Horan, James D. *The Great American West*. New York, 1959.

Horgan, Paul. *Great River, . . . The Rio Grande*. 2 vols. New York, 1954.

———. *The Centuries of Santa Fe*. New York, 1956.

Hough, Emerson. *The Passing of the Frontier*. New Haven, Connecticut, 1918.

———. *The Story of the Outlaw*. New York, 1907.

Houston, Andrew Jackson. *Texas Independence*. Houston, 1938.

Hudson's Bay Record Society. *The Letters of John McLoughlin*. 3 vols. London, 1941–1944.

Hughes, John T. *Doniphan's Expedition*. Cincinnati, 1850.

Hulbert, Archibald Butler. *Forty-Niners*. Boston, 1946.

Hunt, Aurora. *James Henry Carleton, Western Frontier Dragoon*. Glendale, California, 1958.

Inman, Henry. *The Old Santa Fe Trail*. New York, 1899.

Irving, Washington. *The Adventures of Captain Bonneville, U.S.A.* Philadelphia, 1837.

———. *Astoria or Anecdotes of an Enterprise beyond the Rockies*. Philadelphia, 1836.

———. *A Tour of the Prairies*. Norman, Oklahoma, 1956.

Jackson, Joseph Henry. *Bad Company: The Story of California's Legendary and Actual . . . Outlaws*. New York, 1949.

——— (Ed.). *The Western Gate: A San Francisco Reader*. New York, 1952.

Jackson, W. Turrentine. *Wagon Roads West*. Berkeley, California, 1952.

James, Edwin. *Account of an Expedition from Pittsburgh to the Rocky Mountains . . . under the Command of Major Stephen H. Long*. Philadelphia, 1823.

———. *A Narrative of the Captivity and Adventures of John Tanner*. New York, 1830.

James, Marquis. *The Raven: A Biography of Sam Houston*. Indianapolis, 1924.

⸻. *They Had Their Hour*. Indianapolis, 1934.

Jefferson, Thomas, and Dunbar, William. *Documents Relating to the Purchase and Exploration of Louisiana*. Boston, 1904.

Johansen, Dorothy O., and Gates, Charles M. *Empire of the Columbia: A History of the Pacific Northwest*. New York, 1957.

Johnson, Francis White. *A History of Texas and Texans*. 2 vols. Chicago, 1914.

Johnson, Gerald W. *Andrew Jackson, An Epic in Homespun*. New York, 1927.

Johnson, Robert Cummings. *John McLoughlin, A Patriarch of the Northwest*. Portland, Oregon, 1935.

Jones, Nard. *The Great Command*. Boston, 1959.

Kearny, Stephen W. *Report of a Summer Campaign . . . 1845*. Sen. Exec. Doc. 1, 29th Cong., 1st Sess. Washington, 1845.

Keleher, William H. *Turmoil in New Mexico, 1846–68*. Santa Fe, 1952.

Kendall, George Wilkins. *Narrative of the Texan Santa Fe Expedition*. 2 vols. Austin, Texas, 1935.

Kennedy, William. *Texas, Its Rise, Progress and Prospects*. London, 1840.

Kneiss, Gilbert A. *Bonanza Railroads*. Palo Alto, California, 1947.

Kuhlman, Charles. *Legend into History*. Harrisburg, Pennsylvania, 1951.

LaFarge, Oliver. *As Long as the Grass Shall Grow*. New York, 1940.

Lamar, Mirabeau Buonaparte. *The Papers of Mirabeau Buonaparte Lamar*. 6 vols. Austin, Texas, 1927.

Langford, Nathaniel Pitt. *Vigilante Days and Ways: The Pioneers of the Rockies*. Chicago, 1912.

Laut, Agnes C. *The Overland Trail*. New York, 1929.

⸻. *Pathfinders of the West*. New York, 1904.

Lavender, David. *Bent's Fort*. Garden City, New York, 1954.

⸻. *The Big Divide*. Garden City, New York, 1948.

Layne, J. Gregg. *Western Wayfaring Routes of Exploration and Trade in the American Southwest*. Los Angeles, 1954.

Leonard, Zenas. *Narrative of Adventures*. Cleveland, 1904.

Lesley, Lewis B. (Ed.). *Uncle Sam's Camels*. Cambridge, Massachusetts, 1929.

Lewis, Meriwether. *History of the Expedition under the Command of Captains Lewis and Clark to the Sources of the Missouri;*

Thence across the Rocky Mountains and down the River Columbia to the Pacific Ocean. Philadelphia, 1814.

Loomis, Noel M. *The Texan Santa Fe Pioneers.* Norman, Oklahoma, 1958.

Lyman, George D. *The Saga of the Comstock Lode: Boom Days in Virginia City.* New York, 1937.

Lynch, Jeremiah. *A Senator of the Fifties: David Broderick of California.* New York, 1911.

McClintock, James H. *Arizona: The Youngest State.* 3 vols. Chicago, 1916.

McElroy, Robert McNutt. *The Winning of the Far West.* New York, 1914.

McGlashan, C. F. *History of the Donner Party.* Edited by George H. and Bliss McGlashan Hinkle. Palo Alto, California, 1947.

McGowan, Edward. *The Narrative of Edward McGowan, Including a Full Account of the Author's Adventures and Perils while Persecuted by the San Francisco Vigilance Committee of 1856.* San Francisco, 1857.

McGroarty, John S. *California: Its History and Romance.* Los Angeles, 1911.

McNeal, T. A. *When Kansas Was Young.* New York, 1922.

McWilliams, Carey. *Southern California Country, An Island on the Land.* New York, 1946.

Mack, Effie Mona. *Nevada: A History of the State from the Earliest Times through to the Civil War.* Glendale, California, 1936.

Magoffin, Susan Shelby. *Down the Santa Fe Trail and into Mexico.* New Haven, Connecticut, 1926.

Maillard, N. Doran. *The History of the Republic of Texas.* Austin, Texas, 1842.

Majors, Alexander. *Seventy Years on the Frontier.* New York, 1893.

Marcy, Randolph A. *Border Reminiscences.* New York, 1872.

———. *The Prairie Traveler: A Hand Book for Overland Expeditions.* New York, 1855.

Martin, Douglas D. *Yuma Crossing.* Albuquerque, New Mexico, 1954.

Mayne, R. C. *Four Years in British Columbia and Vancouver Island.* London, 1862.

Merrington, Marguerite. *The Custer Story.* New York, 1950.

Mitchell, Annie R. *Jim Savage and the Tulareno Indians.* Los Angeles, 1957.

Monaghan, Jay. *The Great Rascal: The Life and Adventures of Ned Buntline.* Boston, 1952.

440

Morgan, Dale. *The Great Salt Lake*. Indianapolis, 1947.
———. *Jedediah Smith and the Opening of the West*. Indianapolis, 1953.
Morphis, J. M. *History of Texas*. New York, 1875.
Morris, Maurice O'Connor. *Rambles in the Rocky Mountains*. London, 1864.
Mowry, Sylvester. *Arizona and Sonora*. New York, 1864.
Muir, Andrew Forest (Ed.). *Texas in 1837: An Anonymous Contemporary Narrative*. Austin, Texas, 1958.
Mumey, Nolie. *History of the Early Settlements of Denver*. Glendale, California, 1942.
———. *The Life of Jim Baker*. Glendale, California, 1931.
———. *Old Forts and Trading Posts of the West*. Denver, 1956.
Myers, John Myers. *The Alamo*. New York, 1948.
———. *I, Jack Swilling*. New York, 1961.
Nebraska State Historical Society. *Transactions and Reports*. Vol. 5. Lincoln, Nebraska, 1893.
Neider, Charles (Ed.). *The Great West*. New York, 1958.
Neihardt, John G. *The Splendid Wayfaring*. New York, 1920.
Nelson, Bruce. *Land of the Dacotahs*. Minneapolis, 1946.
Nevins, Allan. *Frémont, Pathfinder of the West*. New York, 1939.
———. *Frémont, The West's Greatest Adventurer*. New York, 1928.
Newell, Chester. *History of the Revolution in Texas*. New York, 1838.
Nichols, Alice. *Bleeding Kansas*. New York, 1954.
O'Brien, Robert. *California Called Them: A Saga of Golden Days and Roaring Camps*. New York, 1951.
O'Connor, Richard. *Wild Bill Hickok*. Garden City, New York, 1959.
Ogden, Peter Skene (putative author). *Traits of American Indian Life and Character*. London, 1853.
Olson, James C. *History of Nebraska*. Lincoln, Nebraska, 1955.
O'Meara, James. *The Vigilance Committee of 1856*. San Francisco, 1887.
Ormsby, Waterman Lilly. *The Butterfield Overland Mail*. Edited by Lyle H. Wright and Josephine M. Bynum. 3 vols. San Marino, California, 1954.
Parker, James W. *Narrative of the Perilous Adventures, Miraculous Escapes and Sufferings of Rev. James W. Parker during a Frontier Residence in Texas*. Louisville, Kentucky, 1844.
Parkman, Francis. *The Oregon Trail*. Boston, 1849.

Pattie, James Ohio. *The Personal Narrative of James O. Pattie of Kentucky . . . through the Vast Regions between That Place and the Pacific Ocean.* Edited by Timothy Flint. Cincinnati, 1831.

Perkin, Robert L. *The First Hundred Years.* Garden City, New York, 1959.

Perkins, Jacob Randolph. *Trails, Rails and War: The Life of General G. M. Dodge.* Indianapolis, 1929.

Peters, DeWitt C. *The Life and Adventures of Kit Carson.* New York, 1858.

Pike, Albert. *Prose Sketches and Poems Written in the West Country.* Boston, 1834.

Pike, Zebulon Montgomery. *An Account of Expeditions to the Sources of the Mississippi . . . The Arkansas, Kans, La Platte and Pierre Jaune Rivers . . . and a Tour through the Interior Parts of New Spain.* Philadelphia, 1810.

Plummer, Clarissa. *Narrative of the Captivity and Sufferings of Mrs. Clarissa Plummer.* New York, 1838.

Poston, Charles D. *Apache Land.* San Francisco, 1878.

———. *Report of the Sonora Exploring and Mining Co.* Cincinnati, 1856.

Potter, Reuben Marmaduke. *The Fall of the Alamo.* San Antonio, 1860.

Powell, Fred Wilbur (Ed.). *Hall J. Kelley on Oregon.* Princeton, New Jersey, 1932.

Prince, L. B. *A Concise History of New Mexico.* New York, 1883.

Proctor, Gil. *Tucson, Tubac, Tumacacori, to Hell.* Tucson, 1956.

Pumpelly, Raphael. *Across America and Asia.* New York, 1870.

Quiett, Glen Chesney. *They Built the West: An Epic of Railroads and Cities.* New York, 1934.

Railroads. *Reports of Explorations and Surveys to Ascertain the Most Practicable . . . Route for a Railway . . . To the Pacific Ocean.* 12 vols., one in two parts. Washington, 1855–60.

Reid, John C. *Reid's Tramp.* Selma, Alabama, 1858.

Richardson, Albert. *Beyond the Mississippi.* Hartford, Connecticut, 1867.

Richardson, Rupert N. *The Comanche Barrier to Plains Settlement.* Glendale, California, 1933.

Richardson, Rupert N., and Rister, Carl Coke. *The Great Southwest.* Glendale, California, 1934.

Riesenberg, Felix, Jr., *Golden Gate.* New York, 1940.

Rister, Carl Coke. *No Man's Land.* Norman, Oklahoma, 1948.

————. *Robert E. Lee in Texas.* Norman, Oklahoma, 1946.

————. The Southwestern Frontier. Cleveland, 1928.

Ritchie, Robert Welles. *The Hell-Roarin' Forty-Niners.* New York, 1928.

Roche, James Jeffrey. *Byways of War: The Story of the Filibusters.* Boston, 1901.

Roosevelt, Theodore. *Thomas Hart Benton.* Boston, 1891.

Rourke, Constance M. *Davy Crockett.* New York, 1934.

Royce, Josiah. *California, A Study of American Character.* Boston, 1886.

Ruxton, George F. *Adventures in Mexico and the Rocky Mountains.* London, 1847.

————. *Life in the Far West.* New York, 1849.

Sabin, Edwin L. *Kit Carson Days.* 2 vols. New York, 1935.

Sage, Rufus. *Scenes in the Rocky Mountains.* Philadelphia, 1846.

Salisbury, Albert and Jane. *Here Rolled the Covered Wagons.* Seattle, 1948.

Sanders, Helen Fitzgerald, and Bertsch, William H., Jr. (Eds.). *X. Beidler, Vigilante.* Norman, Oklahoma, 1957.

Saxon, Lyle. *Lafitte the Pirate.* New York, 1930.

Schell, Herbert S. *Dakota Territory during the Sixties.* Vermillion, South Dakota, 1954.

Schmitt, Jo Ann. *Fighting Editors.* San Antonio, 1958.

Seeley, Charles L. *Pioneer Days in the Arkansas Valley.* Denver, 1932.

Settle, Raymond W. *Saddle and Spurs: The Pony Express Saga.* Harrisburg, Pennsylvania, 1955.

Shackford, John R. *David Crockett: The Man and the Legend.* Chapel Hill, North Carolina, 1956.

Sherman, William Tecumseh. *Memoirs of Gen. William T. Sherman, Written by Himself.* 2 vols. New York, 1890.

Shinn, Charles Howard. *Graphic Description of Pacific Coast Outlaws.* Los Angeles, 1958.

————. *Mining Camps: A Study in Frontier Government.* New York, 1948.

Shirley, Glenn. *Buckskin and Spurs.* New York, 1958.

Sitgreaves, Charles L. *Report of an Expedition down the Zuni and Colorado Rivers.* Washington, 1853.

Smiley, Jerome C. *History of Denver.* Denver, 1901.

Smith, Justin H. *The Annexation of Texas.* New York, 1941.

Smith, Richard Penn (putative author). *Col. Crockett's Exploits and Adventures in Texas.* Philadelphia, 1836.

Soule, Frank (putative author). *Annals of San Francisco.* San Francisco, 1853.

Sowell, Andrew Jackson. *Early Settlers and Indian Fighters of Southwest Texas.* Austin, Texas, 1900.

———. *Rangers and Pioneers of Texas.* San Antonio, 1884.

Stanley, F. *The Civil War in New Mexico.* Denver, 1960.

Stiff, Edward. *A New History of Texas.* Cincinnati, 1847.

Stone, Irving. *Men to Match My Mountains.* Garden City, New York, 1956.

Stong, Phil. *Gold in Them Hills.* Garden City, New York, 1957.

Stratton, Royal B. *Captivity of the Oatman Girls.* San Francisco, 1857.

Streeter, Floyd Benjamin. *The Kaw.* New York, 1941.

Stuart, Granville. *Forty Years on the Frontier.* 2 vols. Glendale, California, 1925.

———. *Montana as It Is.* New York, 1865.

Sullivan, Maurice. *The Travels of Jedediah Smith.* Santa Ana, California, 1934.

Sunder, John E. *Bill Sublette, Mountain Man.* Norman, Oklahoma, 1959.

Sutherland, John. *The Fall of the Alamo.* San Antonio, 1936.

Swisher, John M. *Journal of John Milton Swisher.* Austin, Texas, 1937.

Taylor, Bayard. *Eldorado.* 2 vols. New York, 1950.

Tevis, James Henry. *Arizona in the '50s.* Albuquerque, New Mexico, 1954.

Thornton, Jesse Quinn. *Oregon and California in 1848.* New York, 1849.

Thwaite, Reuben Gold (Ed.). *James' Account of S. H. Long Expedition.* 4 vols. Cleveland, 1905.

Tinkle, Lon. *13 Days to Glory.* New York, 1958.

Tobie, Harvey E. *No Man Like Joe: The Life and Times of Joseph Meek.* Portland, Oregon, 1949.

Toole, K. Ross. *Montana, An Uncommon Land.* Norman, Oklahoma, 1959.

Triplett, Frank. *Conquering the Wilderness.* New York, 1883.

Turner, Frederick Jackson. *The Frontier in American History.* New York, 1920.

Twain, Mark (see Clemens, Samuel).

Twitchell, Ralph E. *Leading Facts of New Mexico History.* 5 vols. Cedar Rapids, Idaho, 1912.

Tyler, Daniel. *Concise History of Mormon Battalion.* Salt Lake City, 1881.

United States Navy Department. *Official Records of the Union and Confederate Navies in the War of the Rebellion.* Series I, vol. 29. Washington, 1905.

Upham, Charles Wentworth. *Life, Explorations and Public Services of John Charles Frémont.* Boston, 1856.

Van de Water, Frederic F. *Glory Hunter: A Life of General Custer.* Indianapolis, 1934.

Van Tramp, John C. *Prairie and Rocky Mountain Adventures or Life in the West.* Columbus, Ohio, 1867.

Vestal, Stanley (see Campbell, Walter S.).

Victor, Frances F. *The River of the West.* Hartford, Connecticut, 1870.

Villard, Henry. *The Past and Present of the Pike's Peak Gold Region.* Cincinnati, 1860.

Wagstaff, A. E. *Life of David S. Terry.* San Francisco, 1911.

Wallace, Edward S. *The Great Reconnaissance.* Boston, 1956.

Wallace, Ernest, and Hoebel, F. Adamson. *The Comanches.* Norman, Oklahoma, 1952.

Walter, George. *History of Kanzas* [sic] . . . For Sale at the Office of the Kanzas League, New York, 1854.

Ward, Harriet Sherrill. *Prairie Schooner Lady: The Journal of Harriet Sherrill Ward.* Los Angeles, 1959.

Warren, Harris Gaylord. *The Sword Was Their Passport.* Baton Rouge, Louisiana, 1943.

Waterhouse, Benjamin. *Oregon or A Short History of a Long Journey.* Cambridge, Mass., 1833.

Webb, James J. *Adventures in the Santa Fe Trade, 1844–47.* Edited by Ralph P. Bieber. Glendale, California, 1931.

Webb, Thomas Hopkins. *Organization, Objects and Plan of Operations of the Immigrant Aid Company.* Boston, 1854.

Webb, Walter Prescott. *The Great Plains.* New York, 1931.

——. *The Texas Rangers.* Boston, 1935.

Well, Evelyn, and Peterson, Harry C. *The '49ers.* Garden City, New York, 1949.

Welles, Edmund W. *Argonaut Tales.* New York, 1927.

Wellman, Paul E. *Death on Horseback.* Philadelphia, 1947.

Wheat, Carl I. (Ed.). *The Shirley Letters from the California Mines.* New York, 1949.

Whipple, A. W. *Journal of an Expedition from San Diego, Cali-*

fornia to the Colorado. Edited by G. I. Edwards. Los Angeles, 1961.

White, Owen P. *Lead and Likker.* New York, 1932.

———. *Texas: An Informal Biography.* New York, 1945.

———. *Trigger Fingers.* New York, 1926.

Wilbur, Marguerite Eyer. *John Sutter, Rascal and Adventurer.* New York, 1949.

Wilkes, George. *The History of Oregon, Geographical and Political.* New York, 1845.

Williams, Amelia, and Barker, Eugene C. (Eds.). *The Writings of Sam Houston.* 8 vols. Austin, Texas, 1938–1943.

Williams, Chauncy P. *Lone Elk: The Life Story of Old Bill Williams.* Denver, 1935.

Wilson, Rufus Rockwell. *Out of the West: The Beyond the Mississippi States in the Making.* New York, 1930.

Winther, Oscar Osburn. *The Old Oregon Country.* Palo Alto, California, 1950.

———. *Via Western Express and Stage Coach.* Palo Alto, California, 1945.

Wislizenus, Frederick Adolph. *A Journey to the Rocky Mountains.* St. Louis, 1912.

Wissler, Clark. *The American Indian.* New York, 1931.

Woodward, Arthur. *Feud on the Colorado.* Los Angeles, 1955.

Wooten, Dudley G. *A Comprehensive History of Texas.* Dallas, 1898.

Wortham, Louis J. *A History of Texas.* 5 vols. Ft. Worth, Texas, 1924.

Wyllys, Rufus Kay. *Arizona: The History of a Frontier State.* Phoenix, Arizona, 1950.

Yoakum, Henderson. *History of Texas from Its First Settlement in 1865 to Its Annexation to the United States in 1846.* 2 vols. New York, 1856.

Young, Levi Edgar. *The Founding of Utah.* New York, 1924.

Young, Otis E. (Ed.). *The First Military Escort on the Santa Fe Trail . . . from the Journal and Reports of Major Bennet Riley and Lieutenant Philip St. George Cooke.* Glendale, California, 1952.

Zollinger, William Frank. *Kansas.* Norman, Oklahoma, 1957.

Zorner, James P. *Sutter: The Man and His Empire.* New York, 1939.

Leading Characters and Events

MAIN CHARACTERS	PRINCIPAL EVENTS
	Prologue
Andrew Jackson	Feud between Jackson and Benton climaxed
Thomas Hart Benton	by melee in Nashville, 1813.
John Charles Frémont	Houston wounded in war with Creeks, 1814.
Jean Lafitte	Jackson defeats British at Battle of New Or-
Sam Houston	leans, 1815.
Davy Crockett	
Mike Fink	
Ben Milam	
James Long	
	Chapter 1
Jean Lafitte	Founding of Campeachy on Galveston Is-
James Bowie	land by Lafitte c. 1817.
Hugh Glass	Capture of Glass c. 1817; escape from Cam-
	peachy c. 1818; Glass adopted by Pawnees c.
	1819.
	Chapter 2
James Long	Texas relinquished to Spain by U.S. in ex-
Jane Long	change for Florida; Natchez declares war on
David Long	Spain; James Long founds Republic of Texas;
Jean Lafitte	David Long killed near Trinity River as Spain
Jim Bowie	strikes back; James Long retreats to U.S. — all
Colonel Pérez	in 1819.

Chapter 3

Jim Bowie
Rezin Bowie
James Long
Jane Long
Jean Lafitte
John Austin
General Ripley
Trespalacios
Colonel Pérez
Iturbide

Rezin Bowie designs knife and gives it to Jim, c. 1819.

Long returns to Texas and reorganizes republic; Campeachy destroyed and Lafitte's departure ordered by U. S. Navy, 1820.

Mexicans revolt against Spanish rule; Long takes La Bahia and is captured himself, 1821.

Long assassinated in Mexico City and all Americans leave Texas, 1822.

Chapter 4

Thomas Benton
William Ashley
William Becknell
Joe Walker
Ewing Young
George Yount

Benton elected U. S. Senator from Missouri, 1820.

Mexican Revolution opens up possibility of trade between Missouri and New Mexico; Becknell takes mule train to Santa Fe, 1821.

Using another route, Becknell initiates Santa Fe Trail, 1822.

Chapter 5

William Ashley
Thomas Benton
Andrew Henry
Jed Smith
Tom Smith
Jim Kirker
Talbott
Carpenter
Mike Fink

Benton arranges for liberal licensing of Missouri River fur traders; Ashley and Henry take 100 white trappers to mouth of Yellowstone, 1822.

Fink and Carpenter quarrel while wintering at Ft. Henry, Carpenter killed by Fink in shooting match, Fink slain by Talbott, Talbott drowned, 1823.

Blackfeet harry trappers and Jed Smith sent for aid, 1823.

Chapter 6

Hugh Glass
William Ashley
Jed Smith
Tom Fitzpatrick
Bill Sublette
Jim Clyman
Jim Bridger

Ashley forms second expedition, his men attacked while visiting Arikaras, Glass wounded and Clyman swims and runs for life.

Missouri River traders send for U.S. Army and besiege Arikara villages; Vanderburgh takes head off chief with cannon ball.

Arikaras escape without making good on

William Vanderburgh	Leavenworth's easy surrender terms. All in
Colonel Leavenworth	1823.
Bennet Riley	

Chapter 7

| Andrew Henry | On way to Ft. Henry overland, Glass criti-
| Hugh Glass | cally mauled by grizzly; Henry leaves Fitzgerald
| Jim Bridger | and youthful Bridger with supposed dying
| John Fitzgerald | man; deserted and left destitute, Glass begins
| Bennet Riley | crawl to Missouri, 1823.

After escaping the Arikaras twice more, Glass recovers rifle at Ft. Atkinson, 1824.

Chapter 8

| William Ashley | Ashley details Jed Smith to lead party in
| Jed Smith | search of Rocky Mountain pass not blocked
| Tom Fitzpatrick | by Blackfeet; Jed attacked by grizzly and
| Bill Sublette | patched by Clyman, 1823.
| Jim Clyman | Eastern approach to South Pass discovered
| Ed Rose | and Green River trapped; in spite of separately

encountered disasters, Clyman and Fitzpatrick bring word of new beaver pelt source to Missouri River traders, 1824.

Chapter 9

| Jean Lafitte | Lafitte dies in one of several reported fash-
| Hugh Glass | ions several years after leaving Campeachy,
| Tom Benton | 1824–1826.
| Andrew Jackson | Reunited, Senators Benton and Jackson col-
| Milton Sublette | laborate to get appropriation for Santa Fe
| Tom Smith | Trail; Hugh Glass becomes Santa Fe trader;
| Sylvester Pattie | the Patties, father and son, strike for Santa Fe
| James Ohio Pattie | from Council Bluffs, 1824.
| Jacova Melagres | Comanches raid outskirts of Santa Fe and
| Etienne Provost | are intercepted by trappers from the U.S.;

James Pattie rescues captured Mexican girl, 1824.

Taos becomes headquarters for American trappers; Glass gives up trading for trapping, 1825.

449

Chapter 10

Jed Smith
Bill Sublette
Chief Pierre
Alexander Ross
Peter Skene Ogden

Smith and Sublette remain west of Rockies and move north toward country once claimed by the U.S. but exploited by the Hudson's Bay Company since War of 1812; Smith helps luckless H.B.C. trappers but commandeers their furs, 1824.

Wintering at Flat Head Post, Americans observe methods by which Canadians are quietly taking over Oregon, 1824–1825.

Rival parties under Smith and Ogden move south through the Great Basin, 1825.

Chapter 11

Jim Bridger
Johnson Gardner
Peter Skene Ogden
Chief Pierre
William Ashley
Jim Clyman
Tom Fitzpatrick
Jed Smith
Bill Sublette

Mountain men under Johnson Gardner cause a revolt of H.B.C. Indian trappers and force Ogden to withdraw to form another brigade.

Ashley's third expedition cashes in hugely west of the Rockies; the first rendezvous held along the Green.

Jim Bridger discovers Great Salt Lake, beating out the returning Ogden. All in 1825.

Chapter 12

Tom Fitzpatrick
Hugh Glass
Jim Bridger
James Ohio Pattie
Ewing Young
Milton Sublette
George Yount
Tom Smith

Fitzpatrick and Bridger lead counter raid against Bannocks, 1825.

Hugh Glass wounded in brush with Indians and rides 700 miles to have arrowhead cut out of his back, 1826.

James Pattie survives massacre of trappers by Papagos; Ewing Young leads punitive attack, also strikes aggressive Mojaves, 1827.

Chapter 13

Jim Clyman
Henry Fraeb
Bill Sublette
Major or Black Harris
Jed Smith
David Jackson
Governor Echeandia

Clyman and Fraeb sail around Great Salt Lake in bullboats; Ashley sells fur interests to firm of Smith, Jackson and Sublette; Jed leads party to California, where he is suspected of being a spy, 1826.

To escape capture, Jed makes first crossing of Sierras, 1827.

450

Chapter 14

Bill Sublette
John Colter
Jed Smith
Governor Echeandia

Sublette visits Yellowstone Park region (first glimpsed by unbelieved Colter); going back for furs left in California, Jed is attacked by Mojaves, 1827.

Going to Oregon after detention in California, Jed's party massacred by Kelawatsets; escaping himself, Jed makes way to H.B.C. post Ft. Vancouver, 1828.

Chapter 15

Old Bill Williams
Ceran St. Vrain
Milton Sublette
Tom Smith

Old Bill scalps three Blackfeet (not clearly dated).

Prowling Indians shoot leg from under Tom Smith; he and Milton Sublette amputate it with knife, 1828.

Carving substitute, Tom becomes Peg-leg Smith; going to California, he discovers and loses fabulous mine, 1829.

Chapter 16

Charles Bent
William Vanderburgh
Kenneth McKenzie
Hugh Glass
Jed Smith
John McLoughlin
Jim Bridger
Milton Sublette
Tom Fitzpatrick
Henry Fraeb

Hugh Glass sent to sound out American Fur Company on behalf of free trappers; with H.B.C. aid, Jed Smith regains property from Indians, 1828.

Wintering at Ft. Vancouver, Jed observes military and civil preparations for holding Oregon, 1828–1829; after rendezvous, Jed sends report of H.B.C. activities to Washington; Jed's firm sells to Rocky Mountain Fur Company, 1829.

Chapter 17

Bennet Riley
Philip St. George Cooke
Charles Bent
William Bent
Ewing Young
Kit Carson
Sylvester Pattie
James Ohio Pattie

Riley commands first military escort of Santa Fe Trail traders; troops beat off Indian attacks but infantry powerless to pursue raiders; Young rescues caravan from Indians at New Mexico end of the line; Patties go to California and are arrested, 1829.

Sylvester Pattie dies in Mexican prison; James survives and returns east, 1830.

451

Chapter 18

Jim Bowie
John Lafitte
Stephen Austin
Ben Milam
Ursula Bowie
Rezin Bowie
William Travis

Stephen Austin develops supposedly peaceful scheme for American exploitation of Texas, middle and late 1820s.

Jim Bowie kills Jean Lafitte's son in the course of becoming a living legend; settled in Bexar by 1828; discovering lost San Saba mine, he organizes expedition and stands off Caddos, 1831.

Chapter 19

William Bent
Charles Bent
Jed Smith
Bill Sublette
Tom Fitzpatrick
Kit Carson

William Bent's party fights way out of Apache country, 1830.

Desperate for water on Santa Fe Trail, Smith and Fitzpatrick search and separate; Tom survives but Smith is slain by Comanches, 1831.

Chapter 20

Andrew Jackson
Sam Houston
John Austin
Ben Milam
Deaf Smith
William Travis
Juan Bradburn
Jim Bowie

Fredonia flare-up; dissatisfaction of American colonists with Mexican rule crescent, 1829–1831.

Blowoff at Anahuac led by Travis; Travis imprisoned; John Austin takes Ft. Velasco in countermove; Bowie races in from Bexar and cuts off retreating Mexican troops; Travis sprung in exchange of prisoners; Houston sent to Texas by Jackson, 1832.

Chapter 21

Peg-leg Smith
Bill Sublette
Tom Fitzpatrick
Nathaniel Wyeth
Captain Bonneville
William Vanderburgh
Milton Sublette
Joe Meek
Mountain Lamb
Jim Bridger

Peg-leg Smith wins three Ute wives in combat, 1830.

Milton Sublette knifed in fight over Bannock girl, 1831.

Meek and Milton Sublette aided by Mountain Lamb; Fitzpatrick chased by Gros Ventres and earns name of White Hair; Bill Sublette leads trappers in Pierre's Hole fight, 1832.

Chapter 22

Milton Sublette
Henry Fraeb

Trailed by rivals Vanderburgh and Drips, Fitzpatrick and Bridger lead them into Black-

Tom Fitzpatrick
Jim Bridger
William Vanderburgh
Andy Drips
Hugh Glass
Johnson Gardner
Kit Carson
Nathaniel Wyeth
Kenneth McKenzie

foot country along the high Missouri; Vanderburgh slain there; Bridger shot in back and two arrowheads lodge there, 1832.

Glass slain by Arikaras on frozen Yellowstone, winter of 1832–1833. Johnson Gardner evens score with Arikaras, 1833.

Kit Carson wounded in fight with Blackfeet; Milton Sublette helps Wyeth take Indian freaks east, 1833.

Chapter 23

Captain Bonneville
Joe Walker
Joe Meek
Old Bill Williams
Nathaniel Wyeth
Jason Lee
Milton Sublette

Bonneville sends party under Joe Walker to California, 1833. After discovering Yosemite Park region, Walker winters in California, 1833–1834.

Wyeth's Flathead and Nez Percé inspire Easterners to send Jason Lee as missionary; Lee decides to go to Oregon instead, 1834.

Chapter 24

Jim Clyman
Philip St. George Cooke
Davy Crockett
Henry Leavenworth
Charles Bent
Ceran St. Vrain
William Bent
Old Bill Williams
Bill Sublette
Tom Fitzpatrick
Jim Bridger
Jason Lee
John McLoughlin
Marcus Whitman

Cooke recruits for mounted regiment formed so Army can police Indians, 1832–1833. Dragoons take the field, 1834.

Bent's Fort built; Bill Sublette begins Ft. Laramie, 1834.

Rocky Mountain Fur Company resolved into firm of Fitzpatrick, Milton Sublette and Bridger; Milton Sublette loses leg and Tom Fitzpatrick becomes known as Broken Hand; Marcus Whitman removes Blackfeet arrowheads from Bridger, 1835.

Chapter 25

Jim Bowie
John Austin
Stephen Austin
Ben Milam
Sam Houston
William Travis

Colonists request separate statehood for Texas; John Austin killed by cholera, 1833.

Growing tension between Peace and War parties in colonial Texas, 1833–1834.

Travis ambushes Mexican garrison and men of Gonzales refuse to surrender cannon; Bowie

453

General Cos
James Fannin
Deaf Smith

defeats Mexicans at Concepción Mission; Bowie and Deaf Smith lead volunteers at Grass Fight; Sam Houston elected commander of regular Texas army, 1835.

Chapter 26

Ben Milam
Sam Houston
James Fannin
Jim Bowie
William Travis
Davy Crockett
James Bonham
William Oury
Santa Anna

Milam leads assault that captures Bexar but is slain there, 1835.

Houston's efforts to build army blocked by insubordination, 1835–1836; Houston sends Bowie to Alamo; Travis and Crockett arrive; Santa Anna leads Mexican army to Bexar; surrender demand rejected, 1836.

Chapter 27

Jim Bowie
William Travis
James Fannin
Santa Anna
John Smith
George Kimball
James Bonham
William Oury
Herman Ehrenberg

Illness of Bowie passes full command of Alamo to Travis, who sends messages for aid; Houston powerless to help and Fannin refuses to; Kimball leads the men of Gonzales to the Alamo; Bonham returns; Santa Anna has the "Degüello" sounded; the deaths of Travis, Crockett, Bowie and all others at the Alamo; the Goliad garrison massacred; Ehrenberg escapes, 1836.

Chapter 28

Kit Carson
Andy Drips
Shunar
Singing Wind
Nathaniel Wyeth
Tom Fitzpatrick
Milton Sublette
Marcus Whitman
Narcissa Whitman
Jim Bridger
Black Harris
Joe Meek
Mountain Lamb
Charles Bent

Carson wins Singing Wind as outcome of duel with Shunar, 1835.

Wyeth fails in bid to buck H.B.C., which occupies Ft. Hall; Narcissa Whitman one of first two white women in Rockies; records show buffalo hides more profitable than beaver pelts; Milton Sublette dies at Ft. Laramie and Joe Meek marries the widowed Mountain Lamb; Wyeth visits Bent's Fort and leaves the West, 1836.

Jim Hobbs
Hall Kelley

Chapter 29

Sam Houston
Jacob Snively
Deaf Smith
Santa Anna
Herman Ehrenberg
Willaim Oury
Andrew Jackson
Ben McCulloch
Mirabeau Lamar

Houston rebuilds shattered Texian army; finding terrain to his liking along the San Jacinto, he attacks, destroys Mexican force and captures Santa Anna; Santa Anna ransoms himself by ordering all Mexican troops out of Texas; Houston becomes president of the Republic of Texas, 1836.

Chapter 30

Ewing Young
Hall Kelley
Governor Figueroa
George Yount
John McLoughlin
Jason Lee
Andrew Jackson
William Slocum

Kelley meets Young in California and persuades him to head Oregon expedition, 1834. McLoughlin and Jason Lee's missionaries try to freeze Young out, 1834–1835.

Kelley complains to Washington and Jackson sends Slocum to Oregon to investigate, 1836. Young goes to California with Slocum and heads cattle drive to Oregon, 1838.

Chapter 31

John Sutter
Captain Saunders
Andy Drips
Joe Walker
Jim Bridger
Andy Sublette

John Sutter swindles traders, who disappear near Bent's Fort, 1837. Sutter takes Oregon Trail, 1838. Going by way of Sandwich Islands, he reaches California, 1839.

Chapter 32

Jack Coffee Hays
Sam Houston
Deaf Smith
Kit Carson
Joe Meek
Henry Karnes
Sam Walker
Samuel Colt
Ben McCulloch
Mustang Gray

Texas Rangers become national unit after formation of republic; Hays transfers from army to Rangers, serving under Deaf Smith, 1836.

Expanding east, Comanches become chief foe of Rangers; the Arroyo Seco fight, 1837.

Death of Deaf Smith at Richmond, Texas, 1838.

Sam Walker confers with Samuel Colt, 1839.

455

Jim Hobbs

Bad Comanche joke leads to Council House fight, 1840.

Chapter 33

Jason Lee
Elijah White
Joe Meek
Mountain Lamb
Doc Newell
Joel Walker
Herman Ehrenberg
Tom Fitzpatrick
Henry Fraeb
Jim Bridger
John Sutter
John Bidwell

Elijah White returns to Oregon with commission as Indian sub-agent; Joe Meek and Doc Newell extend Oregon wagon road from Ft. Hall to the Dalles, 1840.

Henry Fraeb killed in fight with Indians at Battle Creek; Ewing Young dies in Oregon; Herman Ehrenberg leaves Oregon for Polynesia; Bidwell's party first to use California cut-off from Oregon Trail; Sutter builds fort at New Helvetia, 1841.

Chapter 34

Governor Armijo
Charles Bent
Jim Kirker
Jim Hobbs
Shawnee Spiebuck
Kit Carson
Peg-leg Smith
William Bent
Making Out Road
Josefa Jaramillo
John Charles Frémont

Armijo heavily taxes American traders; Jim Hobbs asks Carson to free him from Comanches, 1839. Hobbs ransomed from Comanches, 1840.

With Singing Wind dead, Carson marries Making Out Road and regrets it, 1841.

Hobbs joins Kirker's scalp hunters; Peg-leg Smith establishes Bear River horse camp; Carson meets Frémont, 1842.

Chapter 35

Ben McCulloch
Matthew Caldwell
Mirabeau Lamar
Jacob Snively
Governor Armijo
Charles Bent
Jack Coffee Hays
Ewen Cameron
General Canales
Santa Anna
Sam Walker

Plum Creek fight with Comanches, 1840.

Santa Fe Expedition launched by Texians; march of Texian prisoners to Mexico City, 1841.

Bexar taken twice by Mexicans; invaders repulsed at Salado; Laredo finally taken by Texians and Mier Expedition begun, 1842.

Tom Benton
Jessie Benton
John Charles Frémont
Etienne Provost
Kit Carson
Colonel Abert
Tom Fitzpatrick
Charles Preuss
John McLoughlin
John Sutter
Joe Walker

Chapter 36

Frémont participates in Benton's Western mapping project and marries Jessie Benton, 1841. Heads expedition to Rockies, 1842.

Jessie Frémont foils plan to halt husband's second expedition, 1843.

Frémont goes to Oregon and California, 1843–1844. Crosses Sierras and reaches Sutter's Fort, 1844.

Jason Lee
John McLoughlin
Old Bill Williams
Elijah White
Joe Meek
Marcus Whitman
John Gantt
Jim Bridger
Jim Clyman
Bill Sublette
Black Harris

Chapter 37

Oregon missionaries plot against McLoughlin, 1841–1842.

Oregon City founded, 1842.

Provisional government formed with assist from Joe Meek; Ft. Bridger built by Jim, 1843.

"Fifty-four forty or fight" slogan brings Oregon boundary dispute to head, 1844.

Bill Sublette dies in Pittsburgh, 1845.

Sam Walker
Ewen Cameron
Big Foot Wallace
General Canales
Santa Anna
Jacob Snively
Philip St. George Cooke
Charles Warner
Governor Armijo
Charles Bent
Sam Houston
Andrew Jackson

Chapter 38

Mier Expedition is captured, escapes and is recaptured; one out of every ten shot, the rest marched to Mexico City; murder of Ewen Cameron there; Snively Expedition formed; expedition defeats Mexicans but surrenders to Cooke, 1843. Americans clamor for annexation of Texas, 1844.

Texas becomes a U.S. state, 1845.

Alexander Doniphan
Joseph Smith

Chapter 39

Joseph Smith killed by Illinois mob; Brigham Young returns from England and

Brigham Young	seizes leadership of Nauvoo Mormons, 1844.
Sam Brannan	Sam Brannan recommends emigration to
John Charles Frémont	California by New York Mormons, 1845.
	Young leads Mormons from Illinois and founds Kane, 1846.

Chapter 40

Stephen Kearny	Kearny's dragoon regiment crosses Rockies;
Philip St. George Cooke	Old Bill Williams arrested by Cooke, 1845.
Tom Fitzpatrick	Cooke assigned to Kearny's Army of the
Old Bill Williams	West; Cooke and Magoffin take Santa Fe;
James Magoffin	Charles Bent appointed governor of New Mex-
Tom Benton	ico, 1846.
Governor Armijo	
Alexander Doniphan	
Richard Weightman	
Charles Bent	

Chapter 41

James Marshall	Frémont in California on third expedition;
Jim Clyman	Clyman warns Donner Party against Hastings
George Yount	cut-off; Frémont inspires Bear Flag uprising;
John Charles Frémont	news of Mexican war leads to raising of Amer-
Kit Carson	ican flag at Monterey and Yerba Buena; Stock-
Joe Walker	ton and Frémont take Los Angeles and Carson
Old Bill Williams	sent east with news, 1846.
Lansford Hastings	
James Reed	
John Sutter	

Chapter 42

Sam Walker	While a prisoner in Mexico, Sam Walker
Jack Coffee Hays	buries dime and promises to return for it,
Zachary Taylor	1843–1844.
David Terry	Zachary Taylor ordered to Texas, 1845.
William Oury	Paint Rock fight with Comanches; Rangers
John Glanton	mobilized for U.S. Army; Sam Walker orients
	Taylor; Battle of Palo Alto and declaration of war; Monterey captured, 1846.

Chapter 43

Commodore Stockton	Revolt of Mexicans in southern California;
Stephen Kearny	Kearny marches west but leaves Cooke with

Tom Fitzpatrick	Mormon Battalion; Cooke begins laying out
Philip St. George Cooke	wagon road to coast; Kearny's force badly
Pauline Weaver	mauled by Mexicans; 1846.
Kit Carson	Frémont accepts surrender of Mexicans and
John Charles Frémont	is appointed governor by Stockton; Kearny an-
	nounces he is rightful governor, 1847.

Chapter 44

Jim Kirker	Doniphan Expedition goes to Navajo coun-
Alexander Doniphan	try, then heads for Chihuahua; Mexicans de-
William Bent	feated at Bracito; Kirker volunteers services as
Ceran St. Vrain	scout, 1846.
Sterling Price	Revolt rocks New Mexico, Charles Bent
Big Nigger	murdered at Taos; troops and mountain men
Dick Wootton	defeat rebels at La Canada and El Embudo;
Richard Weightman	Taos pueblo stormed and revolt quelled; Doni-
James Collins	phan Expedition wins Battle of Sacramento
General Heredia	and takes Chihuahua City, 1847.

Chapter 45

Black Harris	Cayuses and Walla Wallas slay Whitmans
Jason Lee	and inmates of their mission, 1847.
Marcus Whitman	Meek and Squire Ebberts cross mountains
Narcissa Whitman	in midwinter to urge necessity of organizing
Elijah White	Oregon as a territory; help given Meek by
Joe Meek	Peg-leg Smith and Bridger, 1848.
Squire Ebbert	
Peg-leg Smith	
Jim Bridger	
Knox Walker	

Chapter 46

Ben McCulloch	Ben McCulloch and the Great Western
Santa Anna	help Taylor win the Battle of Buena Vista;
Zachary Taylor	Sam Walker recovers dime but is slain at Hua-
Sarah Bowman	mantla, 1847.
Sam Walker	Pursuit, surrender and deportation of Santa
Winfield Scott	Anna; Rangers return to Texas, 1848.
Joseph Lane	
Mustang Gray	
Jack Coffee Hays	

459

Chapter 47

Sam Brannan
Brigham Young
Black Harris
Jim Bridger
John Sutter
James Marshall

Sam Brannan leads Mormons to California, 1846.
Brigham Young leads Nauvoo Mormons to Great Salt Lake; Young rejects Brannan's invitation to go to California, 1847.
Marshall finds gold at Sutter's Fort, 1848.

Chapter 48

Philip St. George Cooke
George Donner
George Yount
Stephen Kearny
Commodore Stockton
John Charles Frémont

Mormon Battalion fights Battle of Bulls and captures Tucson, 1846.
The Donner Party disaster, 1846–1847.
Kearny's insistence on being governor leads to arrest and court martial of Frémont, 1847.

Chapter 49

John Charles Frémont
Jack Power
Felix Aubry
Jack Coffee Hays
Tom Benton
Tom Fitzpatrick
Old Bill Williams
Jim Kirker
Charles Preuss

Aubry's record ride of the Santa Fe Trail; Jack Hays seeks wagon road west from San Antonio, 1848.
Frémont launches fourth expedition, with Old Bill Williams for guide, 1848–1849; Old Bill killed by Utes in Colorado, 1849.

Chapter 50

James Marshall
John Sutter
Jack Coffee Hays
Black Harris
Peg-leg Smith
William Walker
Edward McGowan
William Tell Coleman
John Glanton
Mangas Colorado
James Ohio Pattie

Sutter ruined by the discovery of gold on his premises; Harris dies in Missouri; Glanton rescues Tucson from Apaches and turns scalp hunter, 1849. Pattie vanishes in California during winter of 1849–1850.
Glanton slain by Yumas along Colorado, 1850.

Chapter 51

Brigham Young
William Bent

Mormons try to form the theocratic state of Deseret, 1849.

Bill Hickman Sam Brannan Ceran St. Vrain	Young asks Brannan for tithes and starts a feud; firm of Bent and St. Vrain dissolved and William Bent blows up Bent's Fort, 1849. Government substitutes Utah Territory for Deseret, 1850.

Chapter 52

Ned McGowan Bennet Riley David Broderick Jack Coffee Hays John Charles Frémont James King (of William) William Coleman Sam Brannan	McGowan makes political alliance with Broderick; Hays elected Sheriff of San Francisco County, 1850. San Francisco's first vigilance committee formed, 1851.

Chapter 53

Tom Fitzpatrick Jim Bridger Red Cloud Sitting Bull Father DeSmet Bill Hickman Brigham Young John Gunnison John Charles Frémont Tom Benton	Prairie nations confer at Ft. Laramie, 1851. Mormons fight mountain men for ferry, 1852–1853. Ft. Bridger sacked, 1853. Frémont makes fifth expedition, 1853–1854. Fitzpatrick dies in Washington, 1854.

Chapter 54

Joseph Lane Joe Meek Phil Kearny Peter Skene Ogden John McLoughlin	Hudson's Bay Company prepares to give up U.S. territorial holdings, 1849. Following war against Cayuses, five of tribe tried for part in Whitman mission massacre, 1850–1851. Meek supervises quintuple hanging, 1851.

Chapter 55

Sam Houston Big Foot Wallace Rip Ford Henry McCulloch Wild Cat	Texas gives up claim to eastern New Mexico; Seminole Wild Cat organizes Rio Grande Valley Indians, 1849. Rangers encouraged by state administration, though outlawed by Army, 1850–1851.

Cynthia Ann Parker
Peta Nocona

Cynthia Ann Parker seen with Comanches, 1851.
Rangers become more and more official, 1852–1855.

Chapter 56

Richard Weightman
Felix Aubry
Herman Ehrenberg
Charles Poston

Aubry discovers 35th parallel railroad route, 1853.
Gadsden Purchase arranged, 1853–1854.
Ehrenberg and Poston enter Gadsden Purchase; Weightman slays Aubry at Santa Fe, 1854.

Chapter 57

Kit Carson
Ceran St. Vrain
Jack Swilling
John Brown
Jim Bridger

St. Vrain and Carson move against Utes; prairie tribes shifted in order to create territories of Kansas and Nebraska, 1854.
Bloody struggle between free and slave labor parties typified by activities of Swilling and John Brown, 1855–1856.

Chapter 58

Jim Savage
Walter Harvey
Roy Bean
Joe Stokes
Jack Power
Joaquin Murrieta
Three-fingered Jack
Granville Oury
Bill Bradshaw
Ned McGowan
William Walker
Colonel Peyton
David Broderick
Billy Mulligan

Stokes calms a killer down in Roy Bean's shebang, 1852.
Power defies Los Angeles County sheriff and his posse; rangers formed to run down Murrieta; somebody's head exhibited as Murrieta's, 1853.
Stokes holds off San Francisco Know-Nothings with cannon, 1854.
Power suspected of turning outlaw, 1855–1856.

Chapter 59

Herman Ehrenberg
Charles Poston
Samuel Heintzelman
William Coleman

Poston and Ehrenberg found Colorado City (Yuma) to pay ferry fare, 1854.
James King (of William) founds San Francisco hatchet sheet, 1855.

Ned McGowan
Fanny Perrier
Alfred Godeffroy
Joe Stokes
James King (of William)
Tom King
James Casey
Sam Brannan
Governor Johnson
William Tecumseh
 Sherman
Charles Cora
Marshal Richardson
David Broderick
Billy Mulligan
General Wool
Commodore Farragut

Joe Stokes plants petard as a favor to Mc-
Gowan; James Casey shoots James King (of
William); San Francisco vigilance committee
reorganizes; committee takes over city, commandeers state armories and forms private
army; Casey and Charles Cora hanged jointly;
vigilantes have McGowan indicted for murder
but fail to locate him; McGowan walks out of
patrolled city in disguise, 1856.

Chapter 60

David Terry
Governor Johnson
Yankee Sullivan
J. Reuben Maloney
Sterling Hopkins
Ned McGowan
William Coleman
Jack Power
Joseph Hetherington
Philander Brace

Yankee Sullivan dies while in vigilante custody; vigilantes commandeer shipment of Federal weapons; roughed by vigilante police,
Terry stabs Hopkins and is prematurely tried
for murder; McGowan secretly leaves San
Francisco, only to be set upon in Santa Barbara; Power saves McGowan from mob; vigilantes hang Hetherington and Brace; Terry
freed by nervous vigilante faction—all in 1856.

Chapter 61

Brigham Young
Jim Bridger
Sam Brannan
Bishop Dame
John Doyle Lee
Albert Sidney Johnston
Philip St. George Cooke

Mormons sack office and residence of fed-
eral judge in Salt Lake City, 1856.
 Bridger takes his case against Mormons to
Washington; Mormons perpetrate Mountain
Meadows Massacre; Brigham Young declares
war on the United States, 1857.
 Military expedition of 1857–1858 ends with
peaceful subjugation of Utah, 1858.

Chapter 62

Andy Sublette
Peg-leg Smith

Jim Kirker dies in California; Andy Sublette
killed by grizzly there, 1853.

Jim Clyman
William Walker
Joe Stokes
Ned McGowan
Bob Marks
Nicholas Den
David Broderick
J. Martin Reese
Henry Stuart Foote
Horsehoe Bill
Jack Power

William Walker raids Mexico, 1853–1854; Walker takes over Nicaragua, 1855.

Joe Stokes slain while defending travelers in Panama, 1856.

McGowan comes out of hiding and is cleared in court without being able to return to San Francisco, 1857.

McGowan publishes anti-vigilante newspapers in Sacramento, 1857–1858; trying to ship out of San Francisco, he is arrested but escapes and takes ship for Canada; also fleeing California, Jack Power is killed by Mexicans, 1858.

Chapter 63

William Oury
Granville Oury
Charles Poston
Herman Ehrenberg
Henry Crabb
Governor Pesqueira
Jesus Ainsa
William Walker
Hilario Gabilondo
Edward Beale
Sarah Bowman
Jacob Snively
Ned McGowan
Jack Swilling
Mangas Colorado

Henry Crabb's expedition enters Sonora; ambushed, Crabb's men fight way into Caborca; following general massacre, Crabb is beheaded; Gran Oury leads belated attempt at rescue, 1857.

San Antonio–San Diego stage taken over by Butterfield; Snively's gold strikes starts Gila City, 1858.

Ned starts and finishes McGowan's War, 1859.

Swilling leads Gila Rangers against Apaches; rescues besieged miners at Pinos Altos, 1860.

Chapter 64

Rip Ford
Iron Jacket
Cynthia Ann Parker
Peta Nocona
Juan Cortinas
Captain Tobin
Sam Houston
Sul Ross
Robert E. Lee
John Brown
Samuel Heintzelman
William Walker

Rangers attack Comanches in Antelope Hills, 1858.

Cortinas takes over Brownsville, Texas, 1859.

Cynthia Ann recaptured; William Walker executed in Honduras; Rip Ford gets Cortinas, 1860.

Houston's plan to conquer Mexico wrecked by onset of War between the States, 1861.

Chapter 65

Tom Benton
William Bent
William Byers
Mother Maggard
Charlie Harrison
Carl Wood
George Steeles

Benton dies in Washington, 1858.
Gold find in Colorado launches "Pike's Peak or bust" rush, 1859.
Byers is kidnapped in Denver and saved by Harrison; Byers and fellow newspapermen establish freedom of press at gunpoint, 1860.
Harrison goes off to war, 1861.

Chapter 66

Ned McGowan
David Broderick
David Terry
Old Virginny Comstock
Winnemucca *père*
Winnemucca *fils*
Jack Coffee Hays
John Blackburn
Bill Stewart

Quarrel between Terry and Broderick brings about duel in which latter is killed; Comstock strike starts Virginia City, Nevada, 1859.
Paiutes start war, in which whites are led by Jack Coffee Hays, 1860.
Terry fortifies Virginia City points, 1861–1862.

Chapter 67

Langford Peel
John Sutter
Joseph (Jack) Slade
Jules Reni
James (Bill) Hickok
David McCanles

Peel kills man in Salt Lake City and is smuggled out in feminine garb, 1858.
Central Overland stage line begins operating; feud between Slade and Reni ends in latter's death in Colorado, 1859.
Pony Express service launched, 1860.
Hickok slays three at Rock Creek, Nebraska, 1861.

Chapter 68

Tom (Bell) Hodges
Henry Plummer
Billy Mayfield
Langford Peel
Eldorado Johnnie
John Blackburn

Self-styled Tom Bell initiates vehicular robbery and is hanged, 1856.
Plummer sprung from San Quentin, 1858. Held for murder, Plummer and Mayfield escape, 1859.
Langford Peel kills Eldorado Johnnie, 1861.
Plummer jailed in Carson City but sprung by Mayfield; Mayfield dug out of prison after killing Blackburn in Carson City, 1862. Mayfield dry-gulched in Idaho, 1863.

465

Chapter 69

Charles Poston
Pete Kitchen
Raphael Pumpelly
Samuel Heintzelman
Sarah Bowman
John Baylor
Granville Oury
Ned McGowan
Jack Swilling
Jacob Snively
Herman Ehrenberg
Joe Walker
Mangas Colorado
Pauline Weaver

Poston and Pumpelly escape from pursuing bandits, 1861.

Gran Oury and Ned McGowan form Arizona Battalion; Jack Swilling leads Confederates at Battle of Picacho Pass, 1862.

Swilling leads Walker Expedition to gold along the Hassayampa River; Swilling captures Mangas Colorado; Poston talks Lincoln's administration into forming Arizona Territory, 1863.

Chapter 70

Jack Slade
Mark Twain
Henry Plummer
Jack Cleveland
Hank Crawford
Nicholas Tbalt
William Palmer
Colonel Sanders
Long John
George Ives
Red Yeager
Boone Helm

Slade fired by Central Overland for shooting up army post, 1862.

Plummer joins Grasshopper gold rush and kills Jack Cleveland; Plummer forms gang which terrorizes two counties of which he has become sheriff; body of murdered man found, causes forming of vigilantes, 1863.

Plummer gang broken up and Plummer hanged at Bannack City; Boone Helm and Slade hanged in Virginia City, Idaho; Montana Territory formed out of western Idaho, 1864.

Chapter 71

Richard Weightman
Ben McCulloch
Charlie Harrison
Kit Carson
Granville Oury
Ned McGowan
Philemon Herbert
Oliver Semmes
David Terry
Charles Poston

Weightman killed at Battle of Wilson's Creek, 1861.

McCulloch killed at Battle of Elkhorn, 1862.

Charlie Harrison slain by Osages; Ned McGowan steals Union prison ship, 1863. Kit Carson conquers Navajos, 1863–1864.

Ehrenberg killed by Indians near Palm Springs, California; Peg-leg Smith dies in San Francisco, 1866.

Jack Swilling	Jack Swilling rehabilitates ancient Indian
José Gonzalez	irrigation system and founds Phoenix; Pauline
Darrel Duppa	Weaver dies at Ft. Whipple, Arizona, 1867.
Herman Ehrenberg	Kit Carson dies at Ft. Lyon, Colorado, 1868.
Peg-leg Smith	
Pauline Weaver	

Chapter 72

Edward Creighton	Central Railroad route approved by Con-
William Bent	gress, 1862.
George Bent	William Bent's sons go native, 1863.
Charles Bent (the younger)	Sand Creek massacre of Cheyennes, 1864.
Colonel Chivington	With Bridger as guide, Dodge determines
James Beckwourth	where rails will run, 1865–1866; Dodge fights
Robert Bent	Indians, argues with Mormons and lays rails,
Grenville Dodge	1866–1868. Union Pacific joins Central Pa-
Jim Bridger	cific, 1869.
Brigham Young	

Chapter 73

Charles Bent (the younger)	Charles Bent dies following fight with Paw-
William Bent	nees; 1868.
General Custer	William Bent dies near Ft. Lyon, Colorado;
William Oury	Custer massacres Indians on Washita River,
Jacob Snively	1869.
Quanah	William Oury leader at Camp Grant mas-
Billy Dixon	sacre of Apaches; Snively killed by Indians in
Red Cloud	Arizona, 1871.
Sitting Bull	Quanah leads Comanches at Adobe Walls
Wild Bill Hickok	siege, 1874.
Jack Swilling	Discovery of gold in Black Hills causes stam-
	pede which arouses Sioux, 1875–1876; Battle
	of the Little Big Horn; Hickok assassinated in
	Deadwood; William Oury dies, 1876.
	Jack Swilling dies while imprisoned in Yuma,
	1878.

Epilogue

John Doyle Lee	John Doyle Lee executed for Mountain
Brigham Young	Meadows massacre at scene of the crime; Brig-
Jim Bridger	ham Young dies in Salt Lake City, 1877.
Jim Clyman	Jim Clyman dies in California; Jim Bridger
Grenville Dodge	dies in Missouri, 1881.

467

Printed in the United States
134007LV00002B/7/A

9 780803 282223